HARBRACE COLLEGE HANDBOOK
for Canadian Writers

HARBRACE COLLEGE HANDBOOK for Canadian Writers

Third Edition

John C. Hodges
Late of the University of Tennessee

Mary E. Whitten
North Texas State University

Judy Brown
Jane Flick
University of British Columbia

Harcourt Brace Jovanovich, Canada
Toronto   Orlando   San Diego   London   Sydney

Canadian Cataloguing in Publication Data

Hodges, John C., 1892-1967
    Harbrace college handbook for Canadian writers

3rd ed.
First ed. published under title: Harbrace college handbook. Canadian ed.
Includes index.
ISBN 0-7747-3136-2

1. English language — Grammar — 1950–
2. English language — Rhetoric.   I. Whitten, Mary E.   II. Title.

PE1112.H62 1990   808'.042   C89-093865-2

Publisher: David Dimmell
Acquisitions Editor: Heather McWhinney
Developmental Editor: Sandra Peltier
Publishing Services Manager: Karen Eakin
Managing Editor: Liz Radojkovic
Copy Editor: Darlene Zeleney
Typesetting and Assembly: Q Composition Inc.
Printing and Binding: John Deyell Company

Printed in Canada
    2 3 4 5   94 93 92 91

Preface

The third edition of the *Harbrace College Handbook for Canadian Writers* is based on the 1986 printing of the American tenth edition of the *Harbrace College Handbook* by John C. Hodges and Mary E. Whitten. Our aim in revising the American edition has been to adapt the text to reflect the Canadian context while preserving the organization and methods of the original. Throughout the book, we have drawn examples from the Canadian milieu and from the work of Canadian writers. The section on the research paper follows the practices of the *MLA Handbook* (third edition, 1988) and the reference works cited have been updated and revised to reflect Canadian as well as British and American resources. The student research paper on George Orwell cites editions of Orwell's works that are most commonly available in Canada. Readers will find that spelling conventions in the text follow those of the *Gage Canadian Dictionary*, with only two significant exceptions, represented by our preference for *-our* over *-or* and *-yze* over *-yse* spellings (for example, *labour* and *analyze*). We have edited the glossary to remove references to regional American usage and have converted units of measurement to metric throughout the book. (You will notice, however, that we have respected original spellings, punctuation, regionalisms, and units of measurement in all quoted excerpts.)

The *Harbrace College Handbook for Canadian Writers* is both a reference guide for the individual writer and a textbook for use in the classroom. A comprehensive yet concise summary of the principles of effective writing, the *Harbrace Handbook* promotes an efficient, effective, and easily-mastered system for the correction of student papers. The endpapers provide a useful overview and handy guide for quick reference. In addition, the directness and economy of the book's rules and examples make it a lasting resource for the writer. The text begins with a review of the essentials of grammar, to be used as needed to introduce subsequent sections of the book, and ends with a glossary of frequently used grammatical terms—a valuable reference for students throughout the course. Depending on the requirements of the particular instructor, sections of the book may be taught in any chosen order. For example, some instructors may want to begin with Section **33**, The Whole Composition, or Section **32**, The Paragraph; others may prefer to start with Sections **19–30**, which deal with diction and sentences. In every section, the large number and wide variety of exercises make it possible for instructors to select activities appropriate to the needs of their class. Supplementary exercises designed to give students additional practice are available, for Sections **1–32**, in the ancillary to this book—the *Harbrace College Workbook for Canadian Writers*.

The third Canadian edition of the *Harbrace College Handbook* reflects extensive revisions of material in the second edition. The two most heavily revised sections are The Paragraph (Section **32**) and The Whole Composition (Section **33**). In Section **32**, the discussions of unity and coherence have been rewritten, and the treatment of methods of development has been clarified and expanded. Section **33** has been entirely rewritten. It stresses the importance of purpose and audience as it fully describes the recursive process of planning, writing, and revising. Three new compositions illustrate the flexible guidelines. Additions to this section include discussions of writing essay examinations and in-class papers.

Some sections have been tightened (for example, Sentence Sense and Verb Forms). Some of the materials have been rearranged. A few of these changes are minor; for example, non-restrictive appositives are now covered along with non-restrictive clauses and phrases. Other changes in arrangement are major. No longer a part of Sentence Unity, Logical Thinking has a section of its own (Section **31**). Similarly, working plans and outlines are no longer part of The Research Paper, but appear in Section **33**, The Whole Composition.

A number of sections—for example, Adjectives and Adverbs (Section **4**) and The Research Paper (Section **34**)—have been expanded and rules added or changed. A clear description of the endnote or footnote style is now included in Section **34**, following a detailed treatment of the 1988 MLA style of documentation and preceding the discussion of the American Psychological Association style.

Although extensive, the changes are not radical. The character of the *Harbrace College Handbook for Canadian Writers*, familiar to users of the second edition, is intact. The third edition retains the best features of earlier editions as it blends in new materials, all of which have been thoroughly tested in the classroom.

Judy Brown and Jane Flick
University of British Columbia

To the Student

Numbers or Symbols / A number or a symbol written in the margin of your paper indicates a need for correction or improvement and calls for revision. If a number is used, turn directly to the corresponding number at the top of the page in the handbook. If a symbol is used, first consult the alphabetical list of symbols inside the back cover to find the number of the section to which you should turn. An appropriate letter after a number or symbol (such as **2b** or **frag/b** will refer you to a specific part of a section.

References / Your instructor will ordinarily refer you to the number or symbol (**2** or **frag, 9** or **cap, 18** or **sp, 28** or **ref**) appearing at the head of one of the thirty-four sections of the handbook. The rule given in colour at the beginning of each section covers the whole section. One of the more specific rules given within the section will usually be needed to guide you in revision. Study the section to which you have been referred—the whole of the section if necessary—and master the specific part of the section that applies to your writing.

Correction and Revision / After you have studied the rules called to your attention, revise your paper carefully, as directed by your instructor. One method of revision is explained and illustrated in Section **8**, page 96–97.

Contents

Contents

MECHANICS

8 Manuscript Form 90

9 Capitals 101

10 Italics 109

Contents

PUNCTUATION

Contents

SPELLING AND DICTION

18 Spelling and Hyphenation 177

19 Good Usage and Glossary 198

EFFECTIVE SENTENCES

Contents

LARGER ELEMENTS

Contents

Contents

34   The Research Paper   411

Contents

GRAMMAR

Sentence Sense

1

Master the essentials of the sentence as an aid to clear thinking and effective writing.

A key to good writing is to possess or develop sentence sense. Sentence sense is the awareness of what makes a sentence—the ability to recognize its grammatical essentials and to understand the relationships among its parts. A close study of this section will help you not only to develop or sharpen your sentence sense but also to make intelligent use of other sections of this handbook. (For explanations of any unfamiliar grammatical terms, see **Grammatical Terms**, beginning on page 532.)

In each of the following sentences, the plus sign connects the two basic grammatical parts of the sentence: the subject and the predicate. The first part functions as the complete subject (the simple subject and all the words associated with it), and the second part functions as the complete predicate (the verb and all the words associated with it). The grammatical subject (or simple subject) and the verb (or simple predicate) are in boldface.

> The hijacked **plane** + **has landed** safely.
> **Sandra** + thoughtfully **gave** us three houseplants.

These **trees + should have been planted** in March.
The **tomato + is** a fruit. **It + tastes** good in salads.

The pattern of these sentences is **Subject + Predicate**.

1a

Learn to recognize verbs.

A verb functions as the predicate of a sentence or as an essential part of the predicate.

Subject + PREDICATE.

Colleen **drives.**
Colleen usually **drives** her car to work.

Predicates may be compound:

Colleen usually **drives** her car to work and nearly always **arrives** on time. [compound predicate]

You can learn to recognize a verb by observing its *meaning* and its *form*. Often defined as a word expressing action, occurrence, or existence (a state of being), a verb is used to make a statement, to ask a question, to give a command or direction.

They **moved** to Toronto. **Is** this true?
The rain **stopped.** **Consider** the options.

In the present tense, all verbs change form to indicate a singular subject in the third person: *I ask—she asks; we eat—she eats.* When converted from the present to the past tense, nearly all verbs change form: *ask—asked; eat—ate.* (See also Section **7**.)

PRESENT TENSE PAST TENSE
I **ski.** Kay **skis.** I **skied.**
You **win.** She **wins.** You **won.**
We **quit.** He **quits.** BUT He **quit.**

When used with *have, has,* or *had,* most verbs end in *-d* or *-ed* (*have moved, had played*), but some have a special ending (*has eaten*). Used with a form of *be,* all progressive verbs end in *-ing,* as in *was eating.*

> Tom **has moved**.   They **have taken** the tests.
> He **is moving**.   We **had been taking** lessons.

As these examples show, a verb may consist of two or more words, a unit often referred to as a verb phrase or an expanded verb.

Auxiliaries   A phrase like *have eaten, was helped,* or *did eat* follows this pattern: **auxiliary + verb**. Since auxiliaries, or helping verbs, precede the verb, they are often called verb markers.

> The fight **had started**.   He **will be studying** late.
> Amy **ought to decide** now.   [Compare "Amy *should decide* now."]

The following words are commonly used as auxiliaries:

> have, has, had   do, does, did
> be, am, are, is, was, were, been
> will, shall, can   would, should, could
> may, might, must   ought to, has to, have to, had to, used to

Other words may intervene between the auxiliary and the verb:

> **Have** the members **paid** their dues? I **have** not **paid** mine.
> Television **will** never completely **replace** the radio.

Although not a verb, the contraction for *not* may be added to many auxiliaries: *haven't, doesn't, aren't, can't*. The full word *not* following an auxiliary is written separately; an exception is *cannot.*

Phrasal verbs A phrasal verb (sometimes called a merged verb) is an idiom that consists of a verb used with a particle like *across, away, down, for, in, off, out, up,* and *with.* Phrasal verbs function grammatically in exactly the same ways that single-word verbs do.

> He **ran across** an old diary. [Compare "He *found* an old diary."]
>
> I **put up with** the noise. [Compare "I *tolerated* the noise."]

Other words may intervene between the verb and the particle:

> We **looked** Yvon **up**. Bonnie **handed** her report **in**.

■ **Exercise 1** Underline the verbs (including any auxiliaries and particles) in the following sentences.

1. The wandering tourists abandoned their guide.
2. Housing costs escalated.
3. The collector bought up some of the most valuable paintings at the auction.
4. Demand for such products may never be satisfied.
5. Anna's idealism lent her writing the power of sincerity.
6. Is the Senate necessary in the Canadian political system?
7. There are still some hungry and homeless children in this city.
8. To his dismay, the bank denied him the right to close his account immediately.
9. Joggers and cyclists circled the park and entered the city.
10. They entered the studio, attended a script conference, and rehearsed the scene.

1b

Learn to recognize subjects and objects of verbs.

SUBJECTS OF VERBS

All grammatically complete sentences, except for imperatives (commands or requests), contain stated subjects of verbs. In the following sentences, the subjects are in bold-face, and the verbs are in italics.

> **Ontario** *produces* delicious corn.
> *Does*n't **Iowa** also *grow* corn?
> *Take*, for example, Ontario and Iowa.   [imperative]

Subjects of verbs may be compound:

> **Ontario** and **Iowa** grow corn.   [compound subject]

To identify the grammatical subject of a sentence, first find the verb; then use the verb in a question beginning with *who* or *what*, as shown in the following examples:

The two dogs in the cage ate.
Verb: **ate**
WHO or WHAT ate? **The dogs** (not the cage) **ate.**
Subject: **dogs**

The shack was built by Al.
Verb: **was built**
WHAT was built? **The shack** (not Al) **was built**.
Subject: **shack**

Subjects of verbs are nouns or pronouns (or word groups serving as nouns). See **1c**.

Subjects usually precede verbs in sentences. Common exceptions to the *subject + verb* pattern occur when subjects are used in questions and after the expletive *there* (which is never the subject).

> **Was** the **statement** true?   [verb + subject]
> **Did** these **refugees survive**?   [auxiliary + subject + verb]
> There **were** no **objections**.   [expletive + verb + subject]

OBJECTS OF VERBS

Verbs denoting action often require objects to complete the meaning of the predicate. When they do so they are called *transitive* verbs. In the following sentences, the objects are in boldface.

The clerk sold **him** the expensive **briefcase**. [direct object: *briefcase*—indirect object: *him*]

Kay met the **mayor** and his **wife**. [compound direct object]

I mailed **Ruth** and **him** four tickets. [compound indirect object]

Like the subjects of verbs, direct and indirect objects of verbs are generally nouns or pronouns.

To identify a direct object, find the subject and the verb; then use them in a question ending with *whom* or *what* as shown in the following example:

Karen completely ignored the reporters.
Subject and verb: **Karen ignored**
Karen ignored WHOM or WHAT? **reporters**
Direct object: **reporters**

Notice that direct objects in sentences like the following are directly affected by the action of the verb.

A tornado levelled a city in West Texas. [*tornado*, the subject, acts; *city*, the object, receives the action.]

Knowing how to change an active verb to the passive voice can also help you to identify an object, since the object of an active verb can usually be made the subject of a passive verb.

ACTIVE   The Expos finally **defeated** the **Mets**.
[*Mets* is the direct object of *defeated*.]
PASSIVE   The **Mets were** finally **defeated** by the Expos.
[*Mets* is the subject of *were defeated*.]

Notice that a form of *be* (such as *is*, *are*, *was*) is added when an active verb is changed to a passive. A passive verb form indicates that the grammatical subject is not the doer or the agent but the object, receiver, or effect of the action.

Some verbs (such as *give*, *offer*, *bring*, *take*, *lend*, *send*, *buy*, and *sell*) may have both a direct object and an indirect object. An indirect object generally states *to whom* or *for whom* (or *to what* or *for what*) something is done.

> Richard sent Sajida an invitation.
> Subject + verb + direct object: **Richard sent invitation**
> Richard sent an invitation TO WHOM? **Sajida**
> Indirect object: **Sajida**

Word order   Becoming thoroughly aware of the meaningfulness of English word order—normally **Subject + Verb + Object**—will help you to recognize subjects and objects. Study carefully three of the most commonly used sentence patterns, observing the importance of word order—especially in Pattern 2—in determining meaning. (For patterns with subject and object complements, see **4b**.)

PATTERN 1

> **SUBJECT + VERB.**

The **children did** not **listen**.
The **lights** on the patrol car **flashed** ominously.

PATTERN 2

> **SUBJECT + VERB + OBJECT.**

Mice frighten elephants.
Elephants frighten mice.
Our **team won** the gold **medal**.

PATTERN 3

> **SUBJECT + VERB + INDIRECT OBJECT + DIRECT OBJECT.**

Mark baked Fred a **cake**.
The **company will** probably **send me** a small **refund**.

In some sentences—especially questions—the direct object does not always take the position indicated by these basic patterns.

What **medal** did our team win?
[direct object + auxiliary + subject + verb]

■ **Exercise 2**   Circle the subjects of the verbs in Exercise 1 on page 5. Then put a wavy line under all nine direct objects and the two indirect objects.

■ **Exercise 3**   Label all subjects and all objects of verbs in the quotations below. Prepare for a class discussion of the use of the three basic sentence patterns on page 8.

1. Canada has earned the right to be heard, in peacetime and in war. —PIERRE TRUDEAU
2. Art and games need rules, conventions, and spectators.
   —MARSHALL McLUHAN
3. In the *Odyssey*, Homer gives us detailed information of wind and stars. —MAURICIO OBREGÓN
4. There are no lobbyists for children. —MARY VAN STOLK
5. We must put down our old industrial tasks and pick up the tasks of the future. —JOHN NAISBITT

1c

Learn to recognize all the parts of speech.

Two methods of classifying words in a sentence are illustrated in the chart on the following page. The first method classifies words according to their function in a sentence; the second, according to their part of speech. Notice here that one part of speech—the noun (a naming word with a typical form)—is used as a subject, a direct object, a modifier, and an object of a preposition.

Waiters usually offer us free coffee at Joe's cafe.

	FUNCTION	PART OF SPEECH
Waiters	subject	noun
usually	modifier	adverb
offer	verb of predicate	verb
us	indirect object	pronoun
free	modifier	adjective
coffee	direct object	noun
at	preposition	preposition
Joe's	modifier	noun
cafe	object of preposition	noun

Words are traditionally grouped into eight classes or parts of speech: *verbs, nouns, pronouns, adjectives, adverbs, prepositions, conjunctions*, and *interjections*. Verbs, nouns, adjectives, and adverbs (called vocabulary or lexical words) make up more than 99 percent of all words listed in the dictionary. But pronouns, prepositions, and conjunctions—although small in number—are important because they are used over and over in our speaking and writing. Prepositions and conjunctions (called function or structure words) connect and relate other parts of speech.

Of the eight word classes, only three—prepositions, conjunctions, and interjections—do not change their form. For a summary of the form changes of the other parts of speech, see **inflection**, page 544.

Carefully study the forms, meanings, and functions of each of the eight parts of speech listed on the following pages. For additional examples or more detailed information, see the corresponding entries in **Grammatical Terms**, beginning on page 532.

VERBS   *notify, notifies, is notifying, notified*
         write, writes, is writing, wrote, has written

A verb functions as the predicate of a sentence or as an essential part of the predicate: see **1a**.

> Herman **writes**.
> He **has written** five poems.
> He **is** no longer **writing** those dull stories.

Two frequently used verb-forming suffixes are *-ize* and *-ify*:

> *terror* (noun)—*terrorize, terrify* (verbs)

Note: Verbals (infinitives, participles, and gerunds) cannot function as the predicate of a sentence: see **1d**, pages 16–17.

NOUNS   *woman, women; kindness, kindnesses*
         nation, nations; nation's, nations'
         Carthage, Singapore, William, NDP
         the *money*, an *understanding*, a *breakthrough*

Nouns function as subjects, objects, complements, appositives, and modifiers, as well as in direct address and in absolute constructions. See **noun**, pages 547–48. Nouns name persons, places, things, ideas, animals, and so on. The articles *a, an,* and *the* signal that a noun is to follow (a *chair*, an *activity*, the last *race*).

> **McKinney** drives a **truck** for the **Salvation Army**.

Endings such as *-ance*, *-ation*, *-ence*, *-ism*, *-ity*, *-ment*, *-ness*, and *-ship* are called noun-forming suffixes:

> *relax, depend* (verbs)—*relaxation, dependence* (nouns)
> *kind, rigid* (adjectives)—*kindness, rigidity* (nouns)

Note: Words like *father-in-law, Labour Day, swimming pool,* and *breakthrough* are generally classified as *compound nouns*.

PRONOUNS *I, me, my, mine, myself; they, you, him, it*
this, these; who, whose, whom; which, that
one, ones, one's; everybody, anyone

Pronouns serve the function of nouns in sentences:

They bought **it** for **her**.   **Everyone** knows **this**.

ADJECTIVES *shy, sleepy, attractive, famous, historic*
three men, this class, another one
young, younger, youngest
good, better, best

The articles *a, an*, and *the* are variously classified as adjectives, determiners, or function words. Adjectives modify or qualify nouns and pronouns (and sometimes gerunds). Adjectives are generally placed near the words they modify.

These difficult decisions, whether **right** or **wrong**, affect all of us.
Wild flowers are most **beautiful** in April.

In the second of these two examples, *beautiful* is a predicate adjective (subject complement), a word that modifies the subject and helps to complete the meaning of a linking verb (*be, am, is, are, was, were, been, seem, become, feel, look, smell, sound, taste*, and so on): see **4b**.

Suffixes such as *-al, -able, -ant, -ative, -ic, -ish, -less, -ous*, and *-y* may be added to certain verbs or nouns to form adjectives:

accept, repent (verbs)—*acceptable, repentant* (adjectives)
angel, effort (nouns)—*angelic, effortless* (adjectives)

ADVERBS *rarely* saw, call *daily*, *soon* left, left *sooner*
very short, *too* angry, *never* shy, *not* fearful
practically never loses, *nearly always* cold

As the examples show, adverbs modify verbs, adjectives, and other adverbs. In addition, an adverb may modify a verbal, a phrase, a clause, or even the rest of the sentence in which it appears:

> I noticed a plane **slowly** circling overhead.
> **Honestly**, Ben did catch a big shark.

The -ly ending nearly always converts adjectives to adverbs:

> *rare, honest* (adjectives)—*rarely, honestly* (adverbs)

PREPOSITIONS *on* a shelf, *between* us, *because of* rain
to the door, *by* them, *before* class

A preposition always has an object, which is usually a noun or a pronoun. The preposition links and relates its object to some other word in the sentence. The preposition with its object (and any modifiers) is called a *prepositional phrase*.

> Byron expressed **with great force** his love **of liberty**.

The preposition may follow rather than precede its object, and it may be placed at the end of the sentence:

> What was he complaining **about**? [*What* is the object of the preposition.]

Words commonly used as prepositions:

about	behind	despite	like
above	below	down	near
across	beneath	during	of
after	beside	except	off
against	besides	excepting	on
along	between	for	onto
among	beyond	from	out
around	but	in	outside
at	by	inside	over
before	concerning	into	past

regarding	throughout	under	upon
round	till	underneath	with
since	to	until	within
through	toward	up	without

Phrasal prepositions (two or more words):

according to	by way of	in spite of
along with	due to	instead of
apart from	except for	on account of
as for	in addition to	out of
as regards	in case of	up to
as to	in front of	with regard to
because of	in lieu of	with respect to
by means of	in place of	with reference to
by reason of	in regard to	with the exception of

CONJUNCTIONS

cars *and* trucks, in the boat *or* on the pier
will try *but* may lose, *neither* Amy *nor* Bill
I worked, *for* Dad needed money.
The river rises *when* the snow melts.

Conjunctions serve as connectors. The co-ordinating conjunctions (*and, but, or, nor, for, so,* and *yet*), as well as the correlatives (*both—and, either—or, neither—nor, not only—but also, whether—or*), connect sentence elements (words, phrases, or clauses) of equal grammatical rank. See also Section **26**. The subordinating conjunctions (such as *because, if, since, till, when, where, while*) connect subordinate clauses with main clauses: see **1d**, pages 20–22.

Note: Words like *consequently, however, nevertheless, then,* and *therefore* (see the list on page 37) are used as conjunctive adverbs (or adverbial conjunctions):

Don seemed bored in class; **however**, he did listen and learn.

INTERJECTIONS   *Wow! Oh*, that's a surprise.

Interjections are exclamations. They may be followed by an exclamation point or by a comma.

A dictionary labels words according to their part of speech. Some words have only one classification—for example, *notify* (verb), *sleepy* (adjective), *practically* (adverb). Other words have more than one label because they can function as two or more parts of speech. Each classification depends upon the use of a word in a given sentence. The word *living*, for instance, is first treated as a form of the verb *live* (as in *are living*) and is then listed separately and defined as an adjective (*a living example*) and as a noun (*makes a living*). Another example is the word *up*:

> They dragged the sled **up** the hill.   [preposition]
> She follows the **ups** and downs of the market.   [noun]
> "They **have upped** the rent again," he complained.   [verb]
> Kelly **ran up** the bill.   [part of phrasal verb]
> The **up** escalator is jerking again.   [adjective]
> Hopkins says to look **up**, to "look **up** at the skies!"   [adverb]

■ **Exercise 4**   Using your dictionary as an aid if you wish, classify each word in the following sentences according to its part of speech.

1. He struts with the gravity of a frozen penguin. —TIME
2. Neither intelligence nor integrity can be imposed by law.
   —CARL BECKER
3. Speak up, gentlemen; I am not opposed to male participation in government. —CHARLOTTE WHITTON
4. Of all persons, adolescents are the most intensely personal; their intensity is often uncomfortable to adults.
   —EDGAR Z. FRIEDENBERG
5. We can remember minutely and precisely only the things which never really happened to us. —ERIC HOFFER

1d

Learn to recognize phrases and subordinate clauses.

Observe how a short simple sentence may be expanded by adding modifiers—not only single words but also word groups that function as adjectives or adverbs.

> The hijacked plane has landed.
> [subject (noun phrase) + predicate (verb phrase)]

Expansion:

> The **first** hijacked plane has landed **safely**.   [single-word modifiers added]
>
> The first hijacked plane **to arrive at this airport** has landed safely **on the south runway**.   [phrases added]
>
> The first hijacked plane **that we have ever seen** at this airport has landed safely on the south runway, **which has been closed to traffic for a year**.   [subordinate clauses added]

A word group used as a single part of speech (noun, verb, adjective, or adverb) is either a phrase or a subordinate clause.

PHRASES

A phrase is a sequence of grammatically related words without a subject and a predicate.

> the hijacked plane   [noun phrase—no predicate]
> has landed   [verb phrase—no subject]
> at this airport; on the south runway; to traffic; for a year
>   [prepositional phrases—neither subject nor predicate]

For a list of types of phrases with examples, see **phrase**, page 551.

   As you learn to recognize phrases, give special attention to verb forms in word groups used as a noun, an adjective, or an adverb. Such verb forms (called *verbals* and classified as participles, gerunds, and infinitives) are much like verbs in that they have different tenses, can take subjects and objects, and can be modified by adverbs. However, they cannot function as the predicate of a sentence.

VERBAL PHRASES IN SENTENCES

Shoppers **milling around** did not buy much.   [participial phrase (see page 550) modifying the noun *shoppers*]

Some people win arguments by **just remaining silent**.   [gerund phrase (page 543), object of the preposition *by*]

The group arrived in a van **loaded with heavy equipment**.   [participial phrase modifying the noun *van*]

Vernon went to Ottawa **to visit relatives**.   [infinitive phrase (see page 544) modifying the verb *went*]

As the examples illustrate, participial, gerund, and infinitive phrases function as single parts of speech and are therefore only parts of sentences.

(1)   Phrases used as nouns

Gerund phrases are always used as nouns. Infinitive phrases are often used as nouns (although they may also function as modifiers). Occasionally a prepositional phrase functions as a noun (as in "*After supper* is too late!").

NOUNS	PHRASES USED AS NOUNS
The **decision** is important.	**Choosing a major** is important. [gerund phrase—subject]
She likes the **job**.	She likes **to do the work**. [infinitive phrase—direct object]
He uses my room for **storage**.	He uses my room for **storing all his auto parts**. [gerund phrase—object of a preposition]

| He wants two things: **money** and **power**. | He wants two things: **to make money** and **to gain power**. [infinitive phrases in a compound appositive—see page 53] |

■ **Exercise 5**   Underline the gerund phrases and the infinitive phrases (including any modifiers) used as nouns in the following sentences.

1. Receiving mail from advertisers is irritating but inevitable.
2. Cold and damp, the campers decided to set up camp.
3. The government has been reducing the deficit by cutting important social programs.
4. To write solely for the purpose of attacking others is cynical.
5. All laboratory procedures—especially the mixing of chemicals after measuring or heating them—require care.

(2) Phrases used as modifiers

Prepositional phrases nearly always function as adjectives or adverbs. Infinitive phrases are also used as adjectives or adverbs. Participial phrases are used as adjectives. Absolute phrases are used as adverbs.

ADJECTIVES	PHRASES USED AS ADJECTIVES
It was a **sorrowful** day.	It was a day **of sorrow**. [prepositional phrase]
Appropriate language is best.	Language **to suit the occasion** is best. [infinitive phrase]
Destructive storms lashed the Prairies.	**Destroying many crops of corn and oats**, storms lashed the Prairies. [participial phrase containing a prepositional phrase]

| The **icy** bridge was narrow. | The bridge **covered with ice** was narrow. [participial phrase containing a prepositional phrase] |

ADVERBS	PHRASES USED AS ADVERBS
Drive **carefully**.	Drive **with care on wet streets**. [prepositional phrases]
I nodded **respectfully**.	I nodded **to show respect**. [infinitive phrase]
Consequently, we could hardly see the road.	**The rain coming down in torrents**, we could hardly see the road. [absolute phrase—see page 532]

These examples illustrate how phrases function in the same way as single-word modifiers. But phrases are not merely substitutes for single words: they can express far more than can be conveyed in one word:

The gas gauge fluttered **from empty to full**.
He telephoned his wife **to tell her of his arrival**.
The firefighters **hosing down the adjacent buildings** had very little standing room.

■ **Exercise 6** Underline each phrase used as a modifier in the following sentences. Then state whether the phrase functions as an adjective or as an adverb.

1. A moment like that one should last forever.
2. The fans blinded by the sun missed the best plays.
3. Crawling through the thicket, I suddenly remembered the box of equipment left on top of the truck.
4. The people to watch closely are the ones ruling behind the political scene.
5. They worked fast, one man sawing logs and the other loading the truck.

SUBORDINATE CLAUSES

A clause is a sequence of related words containing both a subject and a predicate. Unlike a main clause (an independent unit—see **1e**), a subordinate clause is grammatically dependent; it is used as a single part of speech. A subordinate clause functions within sentences as an adverb, an adjective, or a noun.

> Gary was my first and only blind date **because I married him**. [adverb clause]
>
> Simple illustrations, **which the instructor drew on the board**, explained the process. [adjective clause]
>
> Geologists know **why earthquakes occur**. [noun clause—direct object]

The following conjunctions are commonly used to introduce, connect, and relate subordinate clauses to other words in the sentence.

Words commonly used as subordinating conjunctions:

after	inasmuch as	supposing [that]
although	in case [that]	than
as	in order that	that
as [far/soon] as	insofar as	though
as if	in that	till
as though	lest	unless
because	no matter how	until
before	now that	when, whenever
even if	once	where, wherever
even though	provided [that]	whether
how	since	while
if	so that	why

The relative pronouns also serve as markers of subordinate clauses:

> that, what, which; who, whoever;
> whom, whomever; whose

(3) Subordinate clauses used as nouns

NOUNS	NOUN CLAUSES
The **news** may be false.	**What the newspapers say** may be false. [subject]
I do not know his **address**.	I do not know **where he lives**. [direct object]
Give the tools to **Amir**.	Give the tools to **whoever can use them best**. [object of a preposition]

The conjunction *that* before a noun clause may be omitted in some sentences:

> I know **she is right**. [Compare "I know *that she is right*."]

(4) Subordinate clauses used as modifiers

Two types of subordinate clauses, the adjective clause and the adverb clause, are used as modifiers.

Adjective clauses Any clause that modifies a noun or a pronoun is an adjective clause. Adjective clauses, which nearly always follow the words modified, usually begin with relative pronouns but may begin with such words as *when*, *where*, or *why*.

ADJECTIVES	ADJECTIVE CLAUSES
Everyone needs **loyal** friends.	Everyone needs friends **who are loyal**.
The **golden** window reflects the sun.	The window, **which shines like gold**, reflects the sun.
Peaceful countrysides no longer exist.	Countrysides **where one can find peace of mind** no longer exist.

If it is not used as a subject, the relative pronoun in an adjective clause may sometimes be omitted:

> He is a man **I admire**. [Compare "He is a man *whom I admire*."]

Adverb clauses   An adverb clause usually modifies a verb but may modify an adjective, an adverb, or even the rest of the sentence in which it appears. Adverb clauses are ordinarily introduced by subordinating conjunctions.

ADVERBS	ADVERB CLAUSES
Soon the lights went out.	**When the windstorm hit**, the lights went out.
No alcoholic beverages are sold **locally**.	No alcoholic beverages are sold **where I live**.
The price is **too** high for me.	The price is higher **than I can afford**.
Speak **very** distinctly.	Speak as distinctly **as you can**.

Some adverb clauses may be elliptical. See also **25b**.

> If I can save enough money, I'll go to France next summer. **If not**, I'll take a trip to Montreal. [Omitted words are clearly implied.]

■ **Exercise 7**   Find each subordinate clause in the following sentences and label it as a noun clause, an adjective clause, or an adverb clause.

1. Environmentalists argue that deforestation is contributing to the deterioration of the planet's ozone layer.
2. If a mountain climber who lacks experience and stamina becomes part of a major expedition, the rest of the team may well be endangered.
3. What the film suggested or tried to suggest was lost in the unnecessary violence in virtually every important scene.
4. Because public opinion surveys so frequently influence pol-

iticians and their advisers, pollsters have become powerful figures even though they are unelected.

5. As I investigated the topic, I learned that my original thesis relied on assumptions that now proved invalid.

1e

Learn to recognize main clauses and the various types of sentences.

Since both are independent units of expression, a main clause and a simple sentence have the same grammatical structure: **subject + predicate**. Generally, however, the term *main clause* refers to an independent part of a sentence containing other clauses.

SIMPLE SENTENCES

I had lost my passport.
I did not look for it.

MAIN CLAUSES IN SENTENCES

I had lost my passport, but **I did not look for it**.   [A co-ordinating conjunction links the two main clauses.]

Although I had lost my passport, **I did not look for it**.   [A subordinate clause precedes the main clause.]

Sentences may be classified according to their structure as *simple, compound, complex*, or *compound-complex*.

1. A simple sentence has only one subject and one predicate (either or both of which may be compound):

   Dick started a coin collection.   [SUBJECT–VERB–OBJECT.]

2. A compound sentence consists of at least two main clauses:

   Dick started a coin collection, and his friend bought an album of rare stamps.   [MAIN CLAUSE, and MAIN CLAUSE. See **12a**.]

3. A complex sentence has one main clause and at least one subordinate clause:

> As soon as Dick started a coin collection, his friend bought an album of rare stamps.   [ADVERB CLAUSE, MAIN CLAUSE. See **12b**.]

4. A compound-complex sentence consists of at least two main clauses and at least one subordinate clause:

> As soon as Dick started a coin collection, his friend bought an album of rare stamps; on Christmas morning they exchanged coins and stamps.   [ADVERB CLAUSE, MAIN CLAUSE; MAIN CLAUSE. See **14a**.]

Sentences may also be classified according to their purpose and are punctuated accordingly:

DECLARATIVE	He refused the offer. [statement]
IMPERATIVE	Refuse the offer. [request or command]
INTERROGATIVE	Did he refuse the offer? He refused, didn't he? He refused it? [questions]
EXCLAMATORY	What an offer! He refused it! Refuse it! [exclamations]

■ **Exercise 8**   Underline the main clauses in the following sentences. Put subordinate clauses in brackets: see **1d**. (Noun clauses may be an integral part of the basic pattern of a main clause, as in the second sentence.)

1. Canada has often participated in the United Nations' peace-keeping operations, and its efforts have generally been successful.
2. Acid rain poses a threat to the environment, and some scientists say it is destroying the maple sugar industry in Quebec.
3. The planet Mars has two satellites, which were discovered by Asaph Hall in 1877.
4. The film reached its climax as the hero, acting more decisively than she had ever done before, confronted her accusers.

5. Mount Logan is the highest peak in Canada; it reaches an altitude of almost six thousand metres.

6. Because it entrenches and increases the power of Canada's provinces, the agreement redefines the nature of Confederation.

7. In 1988, researchers made several attempts to isolate the causes of Alzheimer's disease, but when they tested their hypotheses, the results were inconclusive.

8. An argument may be supported or refuted by appeals to logic or emotion, as rhetoricians indicate.

9. Visitors to the Gaspé Peninsula frequently stop at Percé Rock, a landmark that draws many amateur photographers every year.

10. We know that recessions mean unemployment; unfortunately, those laid off first are often rehired last.

■ **Exercise 9**   Classify the sentences in Exercise 8 as *compound* (there are two), *complex* (five), or *compound-complex* (three).

■ **Exercise 10**   First identify the main and subordinate clauses in the sentences in the following paragraph; then classify each sentence according to structure.

[1]Jim angrily called himself a fool, as he had been doing all the way to the swamp. [2]Why had he listened to Fred's mad idea? [3]What did ghosts and family legends mean to him, in this age of computers and solar-energy converters? [4]He had enough mysteries of his own, of a highly complex sort, which involved an intricate search for values. [5]But now he was chasing down ghosts, and this chase in the middle of the night was absurd. [6]It was lunacy! [7]The legends that surrounded the ghosts had horrified him as a child, and they were a horror still. [8]As he approached the dark trail that would lead him to the old mansion, he felt almost sick. [9]The safe, sure things of every day had become distant fantasies. [10]Only this grotesque night—and whatever ghosts might be lurking in the shadows—seemed hideously real.

Sentence Fragments

2

As a rule, do not write sentence fragments.

The term *fragment* refers to a non-sentence beginning with a capital letter and ending with a period. Although written as if it were a sentence, a fragment is only a part of a sentence—such as a phrase or a subordinate clause.

FRAGMENTS	SENTENCES
My father always planting a spring garden.	My father always plants a spring garden.
Because he likes to eat vegetables.	He likes to eat vegetables.
Which help the body to combat infection. For example, yellow and green ones.	He likes to eat vegetables which help the body to combat infection—for example, yellow and green ones.

As you study the preceding examples, notice that the first fragment is converted to a sentence by substituting *plants* (a verb) for *planting* (a participle) and the second by omitting *because* (a subordinating conjunction). The last two fragments (a subordinate clause and a phrase) are made parts of a sentence.

Similarly, you can eliminate any fragment in your own papers (1) by making it into a sentence or (2) by making it a part of a sentence. If you cannot easily distinguish structural differences between sentences and non-sentences, study Section **1**, especially **1d**.

Test for a sentence   Before handing in a composition, proofread each word group written as a sentence. First, be sure that it has at least one subject and one predicate.

> FRAGMENTS WITHOUT A SUBJECT, A PREDICATE, OR BOTH
>
> And for days tried to change my mind.   [no subject]
> Water sparkling in the moonlight.   [no predicate]
> Without the slightest hesitation.   [no subject, no predicate]

Next, be sure that the word group is not a dependent clause beginning with a subordinating conjunction or a relative pronoun (see page 20).

> FRAGMENTS WITH SUBJECT AND PREDICATE
>
> When he tried for days to change my mind.   [subject and
>   verb: *he tried*; subordinating conjunction: *when*]
> Which sparkles in the moonlight.   [subject and verb: *which
>   sparkles*; relative pronoun: *which*]

Not all fragments are to be avoided. Written dialogue that mirrors speech habits often contains grammatically incomplete sentences or elliptical expressions within the quotation marks: see **9e**. Answers to questions are often single words, phrases, or subordinate clauses written as sentences.

> Where does Peg begin a mystery story? **On the last page**.

Occasionally, writers deliberately use fragments for effect.

> The job calls for extensive travel, for numerous trips to developing countries. **Better to examine the problems of the Third World in person than to observe them from continents away. Better to meet the people themselves than**

to study official reports about them. [Note the effective repetition and the parallel structure in the two fragments.]

Despite their suitability for some purposes, sentence fragments are comparatively rare in formal expository writing. In formal papers, sentence fragments are to be used—if at all—sparingly and with care.

2a

Do not capitalize and punctuate a phrase as you would a sentence.

Phrases containing verbals:

FRAGMENT	He will have a chance to go home next weekend. **And to meet his new stepfather.** [infinitive phrase]
REVISED	He will have a chance to go home next weekend and to meet his new stepfather. [fragment included in the preceding sentence]
FRAGMENT	Astronauts venturing deep into space may not come back to earth for fifty years. **Returning only to discover an uninhabitable planet.** [participial phrase]
REVISED	Astronauts venturing deep into space may not come back to earth for fifty years. They may return only to discover an uninhabitable planet. [fragment made into a sentence]
FRAGMENT	The children finally arrived at camp. **Many dancing for joy, and some crying for their parents.** [absolute phrases]
REVISED	The children finally arrived at camp. Many were dancing for joy, and some were crying for their parents. [fragment made into a sentence]

Prepositional phrase:

FRAGMENT	Soon I began to work for the company. **First in the rock pit and later on the highway.**

REVISED   Soon I began to work for the company, first in the rock pit and later on the highway.

Part of a compound predicate:

FRAGMENT   Sarah was elected president of her class. **And was made a member of Canada World Youth.**

REVISED   Sarah was elected president of her class and was made a member of Canada World Youth.

Appositive:

FRAGMENT   The new lawyer needed a secretary. **Preferably someone with intelligence and experience.**

REVISED   The new lawyer needed a secretary, preferably someone with intelligence and experience.

■ **Exercise 1**   Eliminate each fragment below by including it in the adjacent sentence or by making it into a sentence.

1. Simone finally left home. Earnestly seeking to become an individual in her own right.
2. The panel discussed the proposed amendment to the Constitution. A single issue dividing voters.
3. She did not recognize Walter. His beard gone and hair cut.
4. These commercials have a hypnotic effect. Not only on children but on adults too.
5. He killed six flies with one swat. Against the law of averages but possible.

2b

Do not capitalize and punctuate a subordinate clause as you would a sentence.

FRAGMENT   Thousands of young people became active workers in the community. **After these appeals had changed their apathy to concern.**   [detached adverb clause]

REVISED   Thousands of young people became active workers in the community after these appeals had changed their apathy to concern. [fragment included in the preceding sentence]

FRAGMENT   No one knew where he came from. **Or who he was.** [detached noun clause, part of a compound object]

REVISED   No one knew where he came from or who he was. [fragment included in the preceding sentence]

FRAGMENT   We were trying to follow the directions. **Which were confusing and absurd.** [detached adjective clause]

REVISED   We were trying to follow the directions, which were confusing and absurd. [fragment included in the preceding sentence]

OR

We tried to follow the directions. They were confusing and absurd. [fragment made into a sentence]

OR

We tried to follow the confusing, absurd directions. [fragment reduced to adjectivals that are included in the preceding sentence]

■ **Exercise 2**   Eliminate each fragment below by including it in the preceding sentence or by making it into a sentence.

1. I decided to give skiing a try. After I had grown tired of watching other people fall.
2. Pat believes that everyone should go to university. And that all tests for admission should be abolished.
3. Many students were obviously victims of spring fever. Which affected class attendance.
4. Paul faints whenever he sees blood. And whenever he climbs into a dentist's chair.
5. I am making a study of cigarette advertisements. That use such slogans as "less tar, more taste" and "the lowest in tar and nicotine."

■ **Exercise 3**   Find the nine fragments in the following paragraph. Revise each fragment by attaching it logically to an adjacent sentence or by rewriting the fragment so that it stands by itself as a sentence.

¹The little paperback almanac I found at the newsstand has given me some fascinating information.   ²Not just about the weather and changes in the moon.   ³There are also intriguing statistics.   ⁴A tub bath, for example, requires more water than a shower.   ⁵In all probability, forty or forty-five litres more, depending on how dirty the bather is.   ⁶And one of the Montezumas downed fifty jars of cocoa every day.   ⁷Which seems a bit exaggerated to me.   ⁸To say the least.   ⁹I also learned that an average beard has thirteen thousand whiskers.   ¹⁰That, in the course of a lifetime, a man could shave off more than eight metres of whiskers, over eight hundred centimetres.   ¹¹If my math is correct.   ¹²Some other interesting facts in the almanac.   ¹³Suppose a person was born on Sunday, February 29, 1976.   ¹⁴Another birthday not celebrated on Sunday until the year 2004.   ¹⁵Because February 29 falls on weekdays till then— twenty-eight birthdays later.   ¹⁶As I laid the almanac aside, I remembered that line in *Slaughterhouse-Five*: "So it goes."

Comma Splice
and Fused Sentence

3

Do not link two main clauses with only a comma (comma splice) or run two main clauses together without any punctuation (fused sentence).

The terms *comma splice* and *fused sentence* (also called comma fault and run-on sentence) refer to errors in punctuation that occur only in compound (or compound-complex) sentences.

COMMA SPLICE

The current was swift, he could not swim to shore.
[only a comma between main clauses]

FUSED SENTENCE

The current was swift he could not swim to shore.
[no punctuation between the main clauses]

You can correct either a comma splice or a fused sentence without changing your meaning by (1) placing a period after the first main clause and writing the second main clause as a sentence, (2) using a semicolon to separate the main clauses, or (3) using a comma before you insert an appropriate co-ordinating conjunction (*and, but, or, nor, for, so, yet*) to link and relate the main clauses.

REVISIONS

The current was swift. He could not swim to shore.
The current was swift; he could not swim to shore.
The current was swift, **so** he could not swim to shore.

When you use the second method of revision, keep in mind that the semicolon separates two grammatically equal units of thought: **Subject + predicate; subject + predicate**. As you proofread your papers to check for comma splices and as you make revisions, do not overuse the semicolon or use it between parts of unequal grammatical rank: see **14c**.

Often a more effective way to revise a comma splice or fused sentence is to make one clause subordinate to the other: see **24b**.

REVISIONS

The current was so swift that he could not swim to shore.
Because the current was swift, he could not swim to shore.

A subordinate clause may be reduced to a phrase and used as a part of a simple sentence: "*Because of the swift current* he could not swim to shore."

If you cannot always recognize a main clause and distinguish it from a phrase or a subordinate clause, study Section **1**, especially **1d** and **1e**.

3a

Use a comma between main clauses *only* when they are linked by the co-ordinating conjunctions *and, but, or, for, nor, so,* or *yet*. See also **12a**.

COMMA SPLICE   Canada observed its centennial in 1967, the United States celebrated its bicentennial in 1976.

REVISED   Canada observed its centennial in 1967 **and** the United States celebrated its bicentennial in 1976.   [the co-ordinating conjunction *and* added after the comma]
OR
Canada observed its centennial in 1967 ; the United States celebrated its bicentennial in 1976.   [A semicolon separates the main clauses: see **14a**.]

COMMA SPLICE   Her first novel was not a bestseller, it was not a complete failure either.

REVISED   Her first novel was not a bestseller **nor** was it a complete failure.   [Note the shift in the word order of subject and verb after the co-ordinating conjunction *nor*.]
OR
Her first novel was **neither** a bestseller **nor** a complete failure.   [a simple sentence with a compound complement]

COMMA SPLICE   The old tree stumps grated against the bottom of our boat, they did not damage the propeller.

REVISED   The old tree stumps grated against the bottom of our boat **but** they did not damage the propeller.   [the co-ordinating conjunction *but* added after the comma]
OR
Although the old tree stumps grated against the bottom of our boat they did not damage the propeller.   [Addition of *although* makes the first clause subordinate: see **12b**.]

Caution: Do not omit punctuation between main clauses not linked by *and, but, or, for, nor, so,* and *yet.*

FUSED SENTENCE   She bought him a novel he read it in a single afternoon.

REVISED   She bought him a novel He read it in a single afternoon.   [each main clause written as a sentence]
OR
She bought him a novel ; he read it in a single afternoon. [main clauses separated by a semicolon: see **14a**]

Note 1: Either a comma or a semicolon may be used between short main clauses not linked by *and, but, or, for, nor, so,* or *yet* when the clauses are parallel in form and unified in thought:

> School bores them, preaching bores them, even television bores them. —ARTHUR MILLER
>
> One is the reality; the other is the symbol. —NANCY HALE

Note 2: The comma is used to separate a statement from a tag question:

> He votes, doesn't he? You can't change it, can you?

■ **Exercise 1**   Connect each pair of sentences below in two ways, first with a semicolon and then with one of these co-ordinating conjunctions: *and, but, for, or, nor, so,* or *yet.*

EXAMPLE

I could have walked up the steep trail. I preferred to rent a horse.

a. *I could have walked up the steep trail; I preferred to rent a horse.*

b. *I could have walked up the steep trail, **but** I preferred to rent a horse.*

1. Dexter goes hunting. He carries a camera instead of a rifle.
2. The stakes were high in the political game. She played to win.
3. The belt was too small for him. She had to exchange it.
4. At the cineplex, they watched the musical comedy in one theatre. We enjoyed the horror movie in another.

■ **Exercise 2**   Use a subordinating conjunction (see the list on page 20) to combine each of the four pairs of sentences in Exercise 1. For the use of the comma, refer to **12b**.

EXAMPLE

***Although** I could have walked up the steep trail, I preferred to rent a horse.*

■ **Exercise 3**   Proofread the following sentences. Place a check mark after a sentence with a comma splice and an X after a fused sentence. Do not mark correctly punctuated sentences.

1. Belize is a newly independent country, its principal export is sugar.
2. Canada needs new markets for its exports those markets may lie in the Pacific Rim.
3. Alfred Nobel established the Nobel Prizes, which are awarded each year in the categories of physics, chemistry, medicine, economics, and peace.
4. Canada's fishermen face an uncertain future some may be forced out of the fishing industry in the next decade.
5. Smoking in public is becoming taboo, public pressure has brought about the change.
6. When a virus enters a computer system, it attacks and destroys memory.
7. The rains fell for three days straight, by the fourth day the road was blocked by several mudslides.
8. The Chinese New Year begins with the first moon in Aquarius, and so it may fall between January 21 and February 19 in any given year.
9. The history that we studied in school was inadequate in one respect, it failed to focus on the culture and heritage of native peoples.
10. I once thought that poetry was incomprehensible, a puzzle to be solved only by experts, but now I can read it with pleasure and without puzzlement.

■ **Exercise 4**   Use various methods of revision (see pages 32–33) as you correct the comma splices or fused sentences in Exercise 3.

3b

Be sure to use a semicolon before a conjunctive adverb or transitional phrase placed between main clauses. See also **14a**.

COMMA SPLICE   TV weather maps have various symbols, for
   example, a big apostrophe means drizzle.

REVISED   TV weather maps have various symbols; for example, a big apostrophe means drizzle.   [MAIN CLAUSE;
   transitional expression, MAIN CLAUSE.]

FUSED SENTENCE   The tiny storms cannot be identified as hurricanes therefore they are called neutercanes.

REVISED   The tiny storms cannot be identified as hurricanes;
   therefore they are called neutercanes.   [MAIN CLAUSE;
   conjunctive adverb MAIN CLAUSE.]

Below is a list of frequently used conjunctive adverbs and
transitional phrases.

CONJUNCTIVE ADVERBS

also	incidentally	nonetheless
anyway	indeed	otherwise
besides	instead	still
consequently	likewise	then
finally	meanwhile	therefore
furthermore	moreover	thus
hence	nevertheless	
however	next	

TRANSITIONAL PHRASES

after all	even so	in the second place
as a result	for example	on the contrary
at any rate	in addition	on the other hand
at the same time	in fact	
by the way	in other words	

Unlike a co-ordinating conjunction, which has a fixed position between the main clauses it links, many conjunctive
adverbs and transitional phrases may either begin the second
main clause or take another position in it.

> She doubted the value of daily meditation; **however**, she decided to try it.   [The conjunctive adverb begins the second main clause. See also **14a**, pages 145–46.]
>
> She doubted the value of daily meditation; she decided, **however**, to try it.   [The conjunctive adverb (set off by commas) appears later in the clause.]
>
> COMPARE   She doubted the value of daily meditation, **but** she decided to try it.   [The co-ordinating conjunction has a fixed position.]

■ **Exercise 5**   Write five correctly punctuated compound sentences using various conjunctive adverbs and transitional phrases to connect and relate main clauses.

3c

Do not let a divided quotation trick you into making a comma splice. See also **16a**.

> COMMA SPLICE   "Who won the lottery?" he asked, "how much money was in the jackpot?"
>
> REVISED   "Who won the lottery?" he asked. "How much money was in the jackpot?"
>
> COMMA SPLICE   "Injustice is relatively easy to bear," says Mencken, "it is justice that hurts."
>
> REVISED   "Injustice is relatively easy to bear," says Mencken; "it is justice that hurts."

■ **Exercise 6**   Divide the following quotations without creating a comma splice, as shown in the example below.

> EXAMPLE
> Oscar Wilde once wrote, "Anyone can make history. Only a great man can write it."
>
> *"Anyone can make history,"* Oscar Wilde once wrote. *"Only a great man can write it."*

1. "I never saw her again. In fact, no one ever saw her again," wrote Kenneth Bernard.
2. Bernard Shaw once said, "I must have been an insufferable child; all children are."
3. "I am saddest when I sing. So are those who hear me," Artemus Ward commented.
4. Gil Stern wrote, "Man is complex: he makes deserts bloom—and lakes die."
5. Auguste Rodin said, "I invent nothing. I rediscover."

■ **Exercise 7** Correct the comma splices and fused sentences in the following paragraph. Do not revise a correctly punctuated sentence.

¹"Age is just a frame of mind," Annie often says, "you're as old or as young as you think you are." ²Does she really believe this, or is she just making conversation? ³Well, when she was seventeen, her father said, "Annie, you're not old enough to marry Johnny, besides he's a city boy." ⁴So Annie ran away from her Melville, Saskatchewan, home in Toronto she found another city boy, Frank, and married him. ⁵When Annie was thirty-nine, Frank died. ⁶A year later she shocked everyone by marrying William, he was a seventy-seven-year-old veteran of the Boer War. ⁷"Billy thinks young," Annie explained, "and he's just as young as he thinks he is." ⁸Maybe she was right that happy marriage lasted eighteen years. ⁹Annie celebrated her seventieth birthday by going to Australia, there she married Tom, who in her opinion was a youngster in his late sixties. ¹⁰But her third marriage didn't last long because Tom soon fell ill and died, still Annie went on with her life. ¹¹In 1980, when Annie was eighty-three, she found and finally married her childhood sweetheart, then eighty-seven-year-old Johnny whisked her away to his home in Montreal. ¹²Annie's fourth wedding made front-page news in Melville, and then the whole town echoed Annie's words: "Life doesn't begin at sixteen or at forty. It begins when you want it to, age is just a frame of mind."

■ **Exercise 8** First review Section **2** and study Section **3**. Then proofread the following for sentence fragments, comma splices, and fused sentences. Make appropriate revisions. Put a check mark after each sentence that needs no revision.

1. Lily first visited the museum, then she strolled through the park.
2. The plaza was originally designed to attract office workers tourists use it now. Not to mention vendors and street musicians.
3. They wish to help the homeless, however, they are not prepared to pay higher taxes for the purpose.
4. The Canadian Club hosts political figures, it is not, however, a partisan political organization.
5. Pierre Trudeau attended the London School of Economics, where he studied modern economic theory.
6. In 1988, some Canadians expressed concern about the Canada–U.S. Free Trade Agreement. The reason being that social programs might be threatened by the pact.
7. Our choir will go to Holland in May, when the tulip gardens are especially beautiful.
8. A long article in the magazine describes botulism, this is just another name for food poisoning.
9. That is absurd. It's nonsense. An argument that is riddled with stupid assumptions.
10. After class, I often drop by the college bookstore. Usually buying bestselling paperbacks, then never getting around to reading any of them.

Adjectives and Adverbs

4

Distinguish between adjectives and adverbs and use the appropriate forms.

Adjectives and adverbs are modifiers. Modifiers qualify or limit the meaning of other words. As you study the following examples, observe that (1) the adjectives modify nouns or pronouns and (2) the adverbs modify verbs, adjectives, or other adverbs.

ADJECTIVES	ADVERBS
the **sudden** change	changed **suddenly**
a **brief, dramatic** one	a **briefly** dramatic one
armed squads	**very heavily** armed squads
She looked **angry**.	She looked **angrily** at me.
He made the cheque **good**.	He made the speech **well**.

Adverbs may also modify verbals (gerunds, infinitives, participles) or even whole clauses. See **1c**, pages 12–13.

The *-ly* ending can be an adjective-forming suffix as well as an adverb-forming one.

NOUNS TO ADJECTIVES	earth—earthly, ghost—ghostly
ADJECTIVES TO ADVERBS	rapid—rapidly, lucky—luckily

A number of words ending in *-ly* (such as *deadly, cowardly*), as well as many not ending in *-ly* (such as *far, fast, little, well*), may function either as adjectives or as adverbs. Some adverbs have two forms (such as *quick, quickly; slow, slowly; loud* and *clear, loudly* and *clearly*).

When in doubt about the correct use of a given modifier, consult your dictionary. Look for the labels *adj.* and *adv.*, for comparative and superlative forms, for examples of usage, and for any usage notes.

4a

Use adverbs to modify verbs, adjectives, and other adverbs.

> NOT   Meryl Streep played Isak Dinesen just perfect.
> BUT   Meryl Streep played Isak Dinesen just **perfectly**. [The adverb modifies the verb *played*.]
>
> NOT   The plane departs at a reasonable early hour.
> BUT   The plane departs at a **reasonably** early hour. [The adverb modifies the adjective *early*.]

Most dictionaries still label the following as informal usage: *sure* for *surely*, *real* for *really*, and *good* for the adverb *well*.

> INFORMAL   The Flames played **real good** during the first period.
> GENERAL   The Flames played **extremely well** during the first period. [appropriate in both formal and informal usage—see also **19b**]

■ **Exercise 1**   In each phrase, convert the adjective into an adverb, following the pattern of the examples.

> EXAMPLE   abrupt reply—*replied abruptly* [OR *abruptly replied*]

1. vague answer
2. safe travel
3. careless remark
4. sincere belief
5. regular visit
6. special appeal

EXAMPLE   complete happiness—*completely happy*

7. near possibility   9. sudden popularity
8. unusual anger   10. strange sadness

■ **Exercise 2**   In the following sentences, convert any non-standard or informal modifier into an adverb form. Put a check mark after each sentence that needs no revision.

1. Almost everyone took the joke serious.
2. When balancing a chequebook grows tedious, the pocket calculator certainly does help.
3. Our national known team played well but did not win.
4. We were lucky to escape as easy as we did.
5. I do not practise as regular as I should.
6. It all happened very sudden.
7. My notes are hard to read when I have to write that rapid.
8. Last night the stars seemed exceptional bright.
9. He talks very loudly when he is not sure of himself.
10. They act as though they are special privileged.

4b

Distinguish between adverbs used to modify the verb and adjectives used as a subject complement or an object complement.

NOT   The honeysuckle smells sweetly in the morning.
BUT   The honeysuckle smells **sweet** in the morning.   [The adjective *sweet* is a subject complement.]

NOT   We painted the sign careful.   [The adjective *careful* does not modify the noun *sign*.]
BUT   We painted the sign **carefully**.   [The adverb *carefully* modifies the verb *painted*.]

Subject complements (usually adjectives, nouns, or pronouns) refer to the subject, but they are part of the predicate and help to complete the meaning of linking verbs—such as *feel, look, smell, sound, taste,* and forms of the verb *be.* When used as subject complements, adjectives always modify the subject.

> SUBJECT + LINKING VERB + SUBJECT COMPLEMENT.

The speech sounded **bold**.
The soup tastes **different** with these herbs in it.

Object complements (usually adjectives or nouns) refer to, identify, or qualify the direct object as they help to complete the meaning of such verbs as *make, name, elect, call, find, consider.* When used as object complements, adjectives always modify the object.

> SUBJECT + VERB + DIRECT OBJECT + OBJECT COMPLEMENT.

These herbs make the soup **different**.
He considered the speech **bold**.

Either an adverb or an adjective may follow a direct object; the choice depends on meaning, on the word modified:

> He considered Jane **happily**.   [The adverb *happily* modifies the verb *considered*.]
> He considered Jane **happy**.   [An object complement, *happy* modifies the noun *Jane*.]

Caution: Do not omit the *-d* or *-ed* of a past participle used as an adjective. (See also **7a**, page 77.)

> NOT   The typist was experience.
> BUT   The typist was experienced.   [Compare "an experienced typist."]

■ **Exercise 3**   Using adjectives as complements, write two sentences that illustrate each of the following patterns.

Subject + linking verb + subject complement.
Subject + verb + direct object + object complement.

■ **Exercise 4**   Look up each pair of modifiers in your dictionary. Give special attention to specific examples of usage and to any usage notes. Then write sentences of your own to illustrate the formal use of each modifier.

> EXAMPLE   bad, badly—*I felt bad. I played badly.*

1. slow, slowly   3. awful, awfully   5. most, almost
2. real, really   4. good, well   6. quick, quickly

4c

Use the appropriate forms of adjectives and adverbs for the comparative and the superlative. See also **22c**.

Many adjectives and adverbs change form to indicate degree. As you study the following examples, notice that the term *positive* refers to the simple, uncompared form of the adjective or adverb.

POSITIVE	COMPARATIVE	SUPERLATIVE
cold	colder	coldest
warmly	more warmly	most warmly
sturdy	sturdier	sturdiest
helpful	more helpful	most helpful
fortunate	less fortunate	least fortunate
good, well	better	best
bad, badly	worse	worst
far	farther, further	farthest, furthest
little	less OR littler	least OR littlest

In general, many of the shorter adjectives (and a few adverbs) form the comparative degree by the addition of *-er* and the superlative by the addition of *-est*. Some two-syllable adjectives, especially those ending in a vowel sound (like *dirty, shallow*), regularly take the *-er* and *-est* endings. The longer adjectives and most adverbs form the comparative by the use of *more* (or *less*) and the superlative by the use of *most* (or *least*). A few modifiers have irregular comparatives and superlatives.

(1) Use the comparative to denote a greater degree or to refer to two in a comparison.

> The metropolitan area is much **bigger** now than it once was.
> Bert can run **faster** than his father.
> Dried apples are **more** nutritious per pound than fresh apples.
>   [a comparison of two groups]

With the use of *other*, the comparative form may refer to more than two.

> Bert can run **faster** than the *other* players.

(2) Use the superlative to denote the greatest degree or to refer to three or more in a comparison.

> The interests of the family are **best** served by open communication.
> Kate is the **fastest** of the three runners.
> OR   Kate is the **fastest** runner of all.

The superlative occasionally refers to two, as in "Put your *best* foot forward!" and "Both of us had a cold, but mine was the *worst*."

Note: Current usage, however illogical it may seem, accepts comparisons of many adjectives or adverbs with absolute meanings, such as "a *more perfect* society," "the *deadest* campus," and "*less completely* exhausted." But many writers make an exception of *unique*—using "*more nearly* unique" rather than "more unique." They consider *unique* an absolute adjective—one without degrees of comparison.

(3) Do not use a double comparison.

> NOT Out swimming hole is much more shallower than Lake
> Louise. [double comparative: *-er* and *more*]
>
> BUT Our swimming hole is much **shallower** than Lake
> Louise. [deletion of the comparative *more*]
>
> NOT That was the most funniest situation. [double superla-
> tive: *-est* and *most*]
>
> BUT That was the **funniest** situation. [deletion of the super-
> lative *most*]

■ **Exercise 5** Give the comparative and superlative of each adjective or adverb.

1. quick
2. quickly
3. thirsty
4. hollow
5. modest
6. ill
7. realistically
8. frightened
9. scared
10. inactive

■ **Exercise 6** Fill in each blank by using the appropriate comparative or superlative form of the modifier given at the beginning of each sentence.

1. *bad* That is absolutely the _____ grade I have ever received.
2. *useful* The _____ tool of all is the screwdriver.
3. *lively* A _____ music video has never before been produced.
4. *mellow* As one grows older, one usually grows _____ .
5. *little* Some smokers are _____ considerate than others.
6. *strong* Who in that quartet has the _____ voice?
7. *tiny* Even the _____ flaw lessens the value of the gem.
8. *thin* His chili is _____ than mine.
9. *good* Of the two applicants Jamie seems _____ qualified.
10. *mature* Naturally, a person's outlook on life is _____ at eighteen than at sixteen.

4d

Avoid awkward or ambiguous use of a noun form as an adjective.

Many noun forms are used effectively to modify other nouns (as in *reference* manual, *capital gains* tax, *Food and Agriculture* Organization), especially when appropriate adjectives are not available. But such forms should be avoided when they are either awkward or confusing.

AWKWARD	Many candidates entered the mayor race.
BETTER	Many candidates entered the mayoral race.
CONFUSING	The Brian Mulroney free trade policy was implemented after the 1988 Canadian election.
BETTER	Brian Mulroney's policy on free trade was implemented after the 1988 Canadian election.

4e

Do not use the double negative.

The term *double negative* refers to the use of two negatives to express a single negation. Like the double comparison, the double negative is grammatically redundant.

NON-STANDARD	He did not keep no records. [double negative: *not* and *no*]
STANDARD	He did not keep any records. [one negative: *not*]
	OR
	He kept no records. [one negative: *no*]

If used with an unnecessary negative like *not, nothing*, or *without*, the modifiers *hardly, barely*, and *scarcely* are still considered non-standard.

NON-STANDARD	I couldn't hardly quit in the middle of the job.

STANDARD	I **could hardly** quit in the middle of the job.
NON-STANDARD	Hardly nothing was in its right place.
STANDARD	**Hardly anything** was in its right place.
NON-STANDARD	The motion passed without scarcely a protest.
STANDARD	The motion passed **with scarcely** a protest.

The use of two negatives to express a positive is acceptable and can be effective.

> We can**not** afford to stand by and do **nothing** about child abuse. [a positive meaning: We have to do something about it.]

■ **Exercise 7**   Eliminate double negatives in the following sentences.

1. They don't have no home.
2. It was so noisy I couldn't hardly hear myself think.
3. We never do nothing but talk about the weather.
4. We needed gas but couldn't buy none.
5. The club didn't scarcely have any money left.

■ **Exercise 8**   After you have reread rules **4a** through **4e** and have studied the examples, correct all errors in the use of adjectives or adverbs in the following sentences. Also eliminate any awkward use of nouns as adjectives. Put a check mark after any sentence that needs no revision.

1. The magazine has been published continuous since 1951, but it does not sell good now.
2. Adding chopped onions and jalapeños to the chili makes it taste real well.
3. According to Environment Canada, December is supposed to be our most wettest month, but we've barely received a drop of rain.
4. It was easily the largest deficit in history.

5. Although yesterday's news commentary was relatively unbias, it was more duller than usual.
6. The repair estimates mechanic was out to lunch.
7. Our class enjoyed writing autobiography compositions.
8. My sister seems much more happier now that she has returned to college.
9. It was a really interesting hockey game between a well-coached team and a group of naturally good athletes.
10. A favourite device of detective novels authors is to cast suspicion on seeming innocent characters.

Case

5

Choose the case form that shows the function of nouns and pronouns in sentences.

Case refers to the form of a noun or pronoun that shows its relation to other words in a sentence. For example, the different case forms of the boldfaced pronouns below, all referring to the same person, show their different uses.

I [the subject] believe that **my** [adjectival] uncle will help **me** [direct object].

I is in the subjective (or nominative) case; *my*, in the possessive (or genitive); *me*, in the objective.

Nouns and some indefinite pronouns have a distinctive form only in the possessive case: a student's opinion, the students' opinions, everyone's vote. See **15a**.

As you study the following tables, observe that the pronouns *I, we, he, she, they,* and *who* have distinctive forms for all three cases.

PERSONAL PRONOUNS

Notice that some of the personal pronouns listed in the following table—*my, our, your, him, her, it,* and *them*—

are also used as parts of *-self* pronouns. (Formal English does not, however, accept *myself* as a substitute for *I* or *me*. See **intensive/reflexive pronoun**, page 544.)

	SUBJECTIVE	POSSESSIVE	OBJECTIVE
Singular			
1st person	I	my, mine	me
2nd person	you	your, yours	you
3rd person	he, she, it	his, her, hers, its	him, her, it
Plural			
1st person	we	our, ours	us
2nd person	you	your, yours	you
3rd person	they	their, theirs	them

THE RELATIVE PRONOUNS *WHO* AND *WHICH*

	SUBJECTIVE	POSSESSIVE	OBJECTIVE
Singular OR	who	whose	whom
Plural	which	whose	which

Although *who, whose*, and *whom* ordinarily refer to people, the possessive pronoun *whose* (in lieu of an awkward *of which*) sometimes refers to things: "The poem, *whose* author is unknown, has recently been set to music."

The subject of a verb and a subject complement are in the subjective case.

SUBJECTIVE **We** left early. **Who** noticed? [subjects of verbs]
That was **he** at the door. [subject complement]

The possessive case indicates ownership or a comparable relationship: see **15a**. Nouns and pronouns in the possessive case ordinarily serve as adjectivals, but a few pronouns (such as *mine* and *theirs*) take the position of nouns and function as subjects, objects, and so on. The possessive is used before a gerund (an *-ing* verbal serving as a noun).

POSSESSIVE   **Their** cat likes **its** new leash.   [adjectivals]
I resent **his** confusing one example with proof.
[before gerund]

The object of a verb, verbal, or a preposition and the subject
of an infinitive are in the objective case.

OBJECTIVE   Hans blamed **me**.   [direct object]
Feeding **them** is a nuisance.   [object of verbal]
I fried **her** two eggs.   [indirect object]
To **whom** was it addressed? [object of preposition]
I didn't want **him** to fail.   [subject of infinitive]

APPOSITIVES

Appositives are nouns or pronouns placed next to or very
near other nouns or pronouns to identify, explain, or supplement their meaning. An appositive has the same case as the
word that it refers to.

SUBJECTIVE   Some people—for example, **he** and **I**—did not
agree.   [*He* and *I* refer to *people*, the subject.]
OBJECTIVE   The officer ticketed both drivers, **Rita** and
him.   [*Rita* and *him* identify *drivers*, the object.]

5a

**Do not let a compound construction trick you into
choosing inappropriate forms of pronouns.**

Subjects, subject complements:

She and her brother play golf on Saturday mornings.
I thought **he or Dad** would come to my rescue.
It was **Maria and I** who solved the problem.   [See **5f**.]

Objects of prepositions:

between **you and me**   to **the chef and her**
except **David and him**   with **Carla and me**

Objects of verb or verbal, subjects of infinitive:

> Rajiv may appoint **you or me**. [direct object]
> They lent **Tom and her** ten dollars. [indirect object]
> He gets nowhere by scolding **Rae or him**. [object of gerund]
> Dad wanted **Sue and me** to keep the old car. [subject of infinitive]

Appositives:

> Two members of the cast, **he and I**, assisted the director.
> [Compare *"He and I*, two members of the cast, assisted the director."]
>
> The director often calls on her two assistants: **him and me**.
> [Compare "The director often calls on *him and me*, her two assistants."]
>
> "Let us, just **you and me**," he drawled, "sit down and reason together."
> [Informal English accepts the expression *Let's you and I.*]

Note 1: Do not let an appositive following *we* or *us* cause you to choose the wrong form.

> NOT Us students need this. Don told we students about it.
> BUT **We** students need this. Don told **us** students about it.

Note 2: As a rule, speakers and writers place first-person pronouns last in a compound construction—usually as a matter of courtesy (rather than for emphasis).

■ **Exercise 1**   Choose the correct pronoun within the parentheses in each of the following sentences.

1. When choosing a career, young women like Lucille and (I, me) have more options today than ever before.
2. (He, Him) and (I, me) wrote and directed a one-act play.
3. It was Awneet and (she, her) who volunteered to emcee.
4. Are Mitch and (they, them) still looking for a job?
5. Between Charlotte and (she, her) there is a friendly rivalry.
6. Mr. Allemeier will hire a new engineer, either Williams or (he, him).

7. Leaving James and (he, him) at home, they went to the airport to meet the actor and (she, her).
8. My family and (I, me, myself) expected Claude and (she, her) to declare bankruptcy any day.
9. Two players on our team, Chuck and (he, him), talked with the coach after the game.
10. After the game the coach talked with two players on our team, Chuck and (he, him).

5b

Determine the case of each pronoun by its use in its own clause.

(1) *Who* or *whoever* as the subject of a clause

The subject of a verb in a subordinate clause takes the subjective case, even when the whole clause is used as an object:

> I forgot **who** won the World Cup in 1980.   [In its own clause, *who* is the subject of the verb *won*. The complete clause *who won the World Cup in 1980* is the object of the verb *forgot*.]
> He has respect for **whoever** is in power.   [*Whoever* is the subject of *is*. The complete clause *whoever is in power* is the object of the preposition *for*.]

(2) *Who* or *whom* before *I think, he says,* and so on

Such expressions as *I think*, *he says*, *she believes*, and *we know* may follow either *who* or *whom*. The choice depends on the use of *who* or *whom* in its own clause:

> Gene is a man **whom** we know well.   [*Whom* is the direct object of *know*. Compare "We know him well."]
> Gene is a man **who** we know is honest.   [*Who* is the subject of the second *is*. Compare "We know that Gene is a man *who* is honest."]

(3) Pronoun after *than* or *as*

In sentences such as the following, which have implied (rather than stated) elements, the choice of the pronoun form is important to meaning:

> She admires Kurt more than **I**.   [meaning "more than I do"]
> She admires Kurt more than **me**.   [meaning "more than she admires me"]
> He talks about food as much as **she**.   [meaning "as much as she does"]
> He talks about food as much as **her**.   [meaning "as much as he talks about her"]

Formal usage still requires the use of the subjective case of pronouns in sentences such as the following:

> Mr. Chow is older than **I**.   [Compare "older than I am."]
> Aristotle is not so often quoted as **they**.   [Compare "as they are."]

■ **Exercise 2**   Using the case form in parentheses, convert each pair of sentences below into a single sentence.

> EXAMPLES
> I admire the woman. She cycled from Prince Edward Island to British Columbia. (*who*)
> *I admire the woman who cycled from Prince Edward Island to British Columbia.*
>
> Evelyn consulted an astrologer. She had met him in San Francisco. (*whom*)
> *Evelyn consulted an astrologer whom she had met in San Francisco.*

1. Hercule Poirot is a famous detective. Agatha Christie finally kills him off in *Curtain*. (*whom*)
2. Some parents make an introvert out of an only child. They think they are protecting their offspring. (*who*)
3. Does anyone remember the name of the Frenchman? He built a helicopter in 1784. (*who*)

4. One of the officials called for a severe penalty. The players had quarrelled with the officials earlier. (*whom*)

■ **Exercise 3**   In sentences 1, 2, and 3 below, insert *I think* after each *who*; then read each sentence aloud. Notice that *who*, not *whom*, is still the correct case form. In sentences 4 and 5, complete each comparison by using first *they* and then *them*. Prepare to explain the differences in meaning.

1. George Eliot, who was a woman, wrote *Adam Bede*.
2. It was Margaret Laurence who served for three years as chancellor of Trent University.
3. Maugham, who was an Englishman, died in 1965.
4. My roommate likes you as much as _____ .
5. The director praised her more than _____ .

5c

In formal writing use *whom* for all objects. See also **5b**.

In sentences:

> **Whom** do they recommend?   [object of the verb *do recommend*]
>
> For **whom** did the board of directors vote?   [object of the preposition *for*]
>
> Danny told Beth **whom** to call. Danny told Beth to call **whom**?   [object of the infinitive *to call*—see also **5e**]

In subordinate clauses:

> The artist **whom** she loved has gone away.   [object of the verb *loved* in the adjective clause]
>
> This is a friend **whom** I write to once a year.   [object of the preposition *to* in the adjective clause]

Formal and informal English accept the omission of *whom* in sentences such as the following:

> The artist she loved has gone away.
> This is a friend I write to once a year.

Note: Informal English accepts *who* rather than *whom*, except after a preposition:

> Who do they recommend?   She told me who to call.

■ **Exercise 4**   Formalize usage by changing *who* to *whom* when the pronoun functions as an object. Put a check mark after sentences containing *who* correctly used as the subject of a verb or as a subject complement.

1. Who do they suspect?
2. Who could doubt that?
3. He knows who they will promote.
4. He knows who will be promoted.
5. The witness who the lawyer questioned next could remember nothing.
6. Guess who I ran into at the airport.
7. No one cares who they are or what they stand for.
8. In a crowded emergency room she knows exactly who to help first.
9. To find out who deceived who, be sure to tune in for the next episode.
10. During registration whoever I asked for directions gave me a map of the campus.

5d

As a rule, use the possessive case immediately before a gerund.

> I resented **his** criticizing our every move.   [Compare "I resented his criticism, not him."]
> **Harry's** refusing the offer was a surprise.   [Compare "Harry's refusal was a surprise."]

The *-ing* form of a verb can be used as a noun (gerund) or as an adjective (participle). The possessive case is not used before participles:

Caroline's radioing the Ski Patrol solved our problem.
[*Radioing* is a gerund. Compare *"Her action* solved our
problem."]
The **man** sitting at the desk solved our problem. [*Sitting* is
a participle. Compare *"He* solved our problem."]

Note: Do not use an awkward possessive before a gerund.

AWKWARD   The board approved of something's being sent to
the poor overseas.

BETTER   The board approved of sending something to the
poor overseas.

5e

**Use the objective case for the subject or the object of
an infinitive.**

They expected Nancy and **me** to do the scriptwriting. [subject
of the infinitive *to do*]
I did not want to challenge Pierre or **him**. [object of the
infinitive *to challenge*]

5f

**Especially in your formal writing, use the subjective
case for the subject complement.**

That certainly could be **she** sitting near the front.
It was **I** who first noticed the difference. [Compare "I was
the one who first noticed the difference."]

Informal English accepts *It's me* (*him, her, us,* and *them*).

■ **Exercise 5**   Find and revise all case forms that would be inappropriate in formal writing. Put a check mark after each sentence
that needs no revision.

1. As for I and my wife, we prefer the mountains to the sea-shore, but she likes to camp out more than I.
2. There was no one who would listen to us, no one whom we could turn to for help.
3. It was Al and he who I blamed for me not making that sale.
4. Jack's racing the motor did not hurry Terry or me.
5. It is true that the Americans produce more goods than us, but we usually export more than them.
6. Do Tracy and she want you and me to help them paint the car?
7. Let's you and me tell Harvey who to put in charge of the organization.
8. Just between you and me, I think that her family and she could do these things for themselves.
9. We students wanted higher standards in high school, but most of us graduating seniors did not speak up much.
10. The clerk wanted us—Pierre-Marc and I—to choose one of the newer classical recordings.

Agreement

6

Make a verb agree in number with its subject; make a pronoun agree in number with its antecedent.

A verb and its subject or a pronoun and its antecedent agree when their forms indicate the same number or person. Notice below that the singular subject takes a singular verb and that the plural subject takes a plural verb. (If you cannot easily recognize verbs and their subjects, study **1a** and **1b**.)

SINGULAR   The **car** in the lot **looks** shabby.   [*car looks*]
PLURAL   The **cars** in the lot **look** shabby.   [*cars look*]

Lack of subject-verb agreement occurs chiefly in the use of the present tense. Except for forms of *be* and *have* (*you were*, *he has eaten*), verbs in other tenses do not change form to indicate the number or person of their subjects. For a list of various forms of *be* and the subjects they take, see page 74.

When a pronoun has an antecedent (the word the pronoun refers to), the two words usually agree in number. (See also Section **28**.)

SINGULAR   A **wolf** has **its** own language.   [*wolf—its*]
PLURAL   **Wolves** have **their** own language.   [*wolves—their*]

Note: A pronoun also agrees with its antecedent in gender. Agreement in gender is usually easy and natural:

the **boy** and **his** mother   [masculine]
the **girl** and **her** mother   [feminine]
the **garden** and **its** weeds   [neuter]

Subject and Verb

6a

Make a verb agree in number with its subject.

As you study the following rules and examples, remember that -*s* (or -*es*) marks plural nouns but singular verbs (those present-tense verbs with third-person singular subjects).

subject + *s*	OR	verb + *s*
Whistles blow at noon.		A whistle blows at noon.
The egotists like attention.		The egotist likes attention.

(1) Do not be misled by nouns or pronouns intervening between the subject and the verb or by subjects and verbs with endings not clearly sounded.

The **repetition** of the drumbeats **helps** to stir emotions.
Every **one** of you **is invited** to the panel discussion.
Scientists sift the facts.
The **scientist asks** several pertinent questions.

As a rule, the grammatical number of the subject is not changed by the addition of expressions beginning with such words as *accompanied by, along with, as well as, in addition to, including, no less than, not to mention, together with.*

Unemployment as well as taxes **influences** votes.
Taxes, not to mention unemployment, **influence** votes.

(2) Subjects joined by *and* are usually plural.

My **parents** and my **uncle do** not **understand** this.
The **band** and the **team were leading** the parade.
Skiing in the Rockies and **windsurfing at Maui** are similar
in several ways. [gerund phrases—compare "Two activities are similar."]

Exceptions: Occasionally, such a compound subject takes a
singular verb because the subject denotes one person or a
single unit.

The **inventor** and chief **producer** of the snowmobile was a
native of Quebec, Henri Bombardier.
Hooting and **jeering** at public rallies is characteristic of political life in many democracies.

Every or *each* preceding singular subjects joined by *and*
calls for a singular verb:

Every silver knife, fork, and spoon **has** to be counted.
Each cat and each dog **has** its own toy.

Placed after a plural subject, *each* does not affect the verb
form. Some writers use a singular verb when *each* follows
a compound subject:

The cat and the dog each **have** their own toys. [Or, sometimes, "The cat and the dog each *has* its own toy."]

**(3) Singular subjects joined by *or, either . . . or*, or
neither . . . nor usually take a singular verb.**

Paula or her secretary **answers** the phone on Saturday.
Either the mayor or the premier **is** the keynote speaker.
Neither praise nor blame **affects** her.

If one subject is singular and one is plural, the verb usually
agrees with the nearer subject:

Neither the quality nor the prices **have** changed.
Neither the prices nor the quality **has** changed.
[Compare "The prices *and* the quality *have* not changed."]

The verb also agrees with the nearer subject in person in sentences like the following.

Either Pat or **you were** ready for any emergency call.
Either you or **Pat was** ready for any emergency call.

(4) Do not let inverted word order (VERB + SUBJECT) or the structure *there* + VERB + SUBJECT cause you to make a mistake in agreement.

VERB + SUBJECT

Hardest hit by the budget cuts **were** Canadian **fishermen**.
Among our grandest and longest-lived illusions **is** the **notion** of the noble savage.   —JOHN PFEIFFER
Neither **do drugstores** sell only drugs.   [Here *neither* is a conjunction meaning *nor yet*.]

THERE + VERB + SUBJECT

There **is** a **photograph** on the desk.
There **are** several **photographs** on the desk.

There **are light** and **shadow** in the photograph.   [Singular subjects joined by *and* usually take a plural verb.]

There **is a child** and **an old man** in the photograph.   [If the noun immediately following the verb is preceded by *a* or *an*, the verb often appears in the singular. This usage is considered to be informal.]

(5) A relative pronoun (*who, which, that*) used as subject has the same number as its antecedent.

It is the **pharmacist who** often **suggests** a new brand.
Tonsilitis is among those **diseases that are** curable.

This is one of the **local papers that print** a daily horoscope.
[The antecedent of *that* is *local papers*, NOT *one*; several papers print horoscopes.]
BUT
This is the only **one** of the local papers **that prints** a daily horoscope. [*That* refers to *one*: only one paper prints a daily horoscope; the other papers do not. Compare "This is the only local paper that prints...."]

It is not better things but better **people that make** better living. —CARLL TUCKER
[Compare "Better people (not better things) make better living."]

(6) When used as subjects, such words as *each, either, neither, one, everybody*, and *anyone* regularly take singular verbs.

Neither likes the friends of the other.
Each of them **does have** political ambitions.
Everybody in the office **has** tickets.

Subjects such as *all, any, half, most, none*, and *some* may take a singular or a plural verb; the context generally determines the choice of the verb form.

Evelyn collects stamps; **some are** worth a lot. [Compare "Some of them are worth a lot."]
The honey was marked down because **some was** sugary. [Compare "Some of it was sugary."]

(7) Collective nouns (and phrases denoting a fixed quantity) take a singular verb when they refer to the group as a unit and take a plural verb when they refer to individuals or parts of the group.

Singular (regarded as a unit):

My **family has** its traditions.
The number of books **is** very small.

A **billion dollars is** a lot of money.
The **majority** of food **was** wasted.
Two-thirds of this road **has** been finished.

Plural (regarded as individuals or parts):

A **number** of students **were** absent.
The **majority** of us **are** for it.
Two-thirds of these roads **have** been finished.
The **media have** shaped public opinion.   [The use of *media* as a singular subject is questionable.]

The use of *data* as a singular noun has gained currency in recent years; many writers, however, prefer to use *data* only as a plural noun.

PREFERRED   The **data were** accurate.

(8) A linking verb agrees with its subject, not with its complement (predicate noun).

His **problem is** frequent headaches.
Frequent **headaches are** his problem.

Note: Because the number of the pronoun *what* depends on the number of the word (or word group) referred to, the verb does agree with its complement in sentences like these:

What I do, at these times, **is** to change the way the system works.   —LEWIS THOMAS
[Compare "That is what I do."]

Of course, what you see in the final commercial **are** pretty pictures—the bear in a canoe, the bear in a Jeep, the bear padding behind the man.   —JONATHAN PRICE
[Compare "Pretty pictures are what you see."]

(9) Nouns plural in form but singular in meaning usually take singular verbs. In all doubtful cases, consult a good dictionary.

Nouns that are regularly treated as singular include *economics*, *electronics*, *measles*, *mumps*, *news*, and *physics*.

> News **is** travelling faster than ever before.
> Physics **has** fascinated my roommate for months.

Some nouns ending in *-ics* (such as *athletics*, *politics*, *statistics*, and *tactics*) can be either singular or plural:

> Statistics **is** an interesting subject.
> Statistics **are** often misleading.

(10) **The title of a single work or a word spoken of as a word, even when plural in form, takes a singular verb.**

> *Harry and Tonto* **sticks** in the memory. [The movie, not the characters, sticks in the memory.]
> ''Autumn Leaves'' **is** a beautiful song.
> *Kids* **is** informal for *children*.

■ **Exercise 1**   The following sentences are all correct. Read them aloud, stressing the italicized words. If any sentence sounds wrong to you, read it aloud two or three more times so that you will gain practice in saying and hearing the correct forms.

1. The *timing* of these strikes *was* poorly planned.
2. There *are* a few *cookies* and *pickles* left.
3. A *wrench* and a *hubcap were* missing.
4. Every *one* of my cousins, including Larry, *has* brown eyes.
5. Sandy was the *only one* of the singers *who* was off-key.
6. *Does*n't *it* make sense?
7. *Each* of the episodes *is* exciting.
8. Every *one* of you *is* invited.
9. *A number* of citizens in this group *are* affected.
10. There *were* several *reasons* for this crisis.

■ **Exercise 2**   Choose the correct form of the verb within parentheses in each of the following sentences. Make sure that the verb agrees with its subject according to the rules of formal English.

1. Neither Anita nor Leon (feels, feel) that the evidence is circumstantial.
2. Tastes in reading, of course, (differs, differ).
3. Every one of the figures (was, were) checked at least twice.
4. A fountain and a hanging basket (adorns, adorn) the entrance.
5. Neither of them ever (asks, ask) for a second helping.
6. There (comes, come) to my mind now the names of the two or three people who were most influential in my life.
7. The booby prize (was, were) green apples.
8. A rustic lodge, as well as a game refuge and fishing waters, (is, are) close by.
9. Such computers, which (stores, store) personal data, (jeopardizes, jeopardize) the privacy of millions.
10. The study of words (is, are) facilitated by breaking them down into prefixes, suffixes, and roots.

Pronoun and Antecedent

6b

Make a pronoun agree in number with its antecedent.

A singular antecedent (one that would take a singular verb) is referred to by a singular pronoun. A plural antecedent (one that would take a plural verb) is referred to by a plural pronoun.

SINGULAR   The **leading man** often **forgets his** lines.
PLURAL   The other **actors** never **forget their** lines.

(1) Such singular antecedents as *man, woman, person, everybody, one, anyone, each, either, neither, sort*, and *kind* are usually (but not always) referred to by a singular pronoun.

Each of these companies had **its** books audited.   [NOT their]
One has to live with **oneself**.   [NOT themselves]

A **man** or a **woman** has a duty to follow **his** or **her** conscience.   [a pair of antecedents]

Note: Though avoided in formal writing, the use of a plural pronoun to refer to a singular antecedent is natural or sensible when the sex is unknown or when a singular pronoun would not fit the meaning. Wherever possible, however, recast the sentence to avoid this agreement problem.

INFORMAL   If **anyone** calls while I'm gone, ask **them** to leave a message.

RECAST   While I'm gone, ask anyone who calls to leave a message.

INFORMAL   **Everyone** was invited to lunch, but **they** had already eaten.

RECAST   **All** of them were invited to lunch, but **they** had already eaten.

Until recently the rule for formal English required the use of *he, his,* or *him* to refer to such singular antecedents as *everyone* or *a person*—as in "to *each his* own" or "As a *child* grows up *he* must assume responsibilities." This use of the masculine pronoun to include both sexes or either sex (common gender) is still widespread.

Everyone does as **he** pleases.
A **person** needs to see **his** dentist twice a year.

But this rule is less rigid now. During the seventies and eighties, such forms as *he or she* and *he/she* have gained currency.

In this class **anyone** is free to say whatever **he or she** thinks.
Every man and woman shows **his/her** essence by reaction to the soil.   —ROBERT S. De ROPP

Wishing to avoid sexism in language but disliking the substitutes for *he, his,* and *him* that are currently in vogue, many writers today avoid the problem by eliminating the singular pronoun or by making it and its antecedent plural.

A person needs to see **the** dentist twice a year.
People need to see **their** dentists twice a year.

Increasingly, however, writers are using plural pronouns to refer to singular antecedents that denote both sexes or either sex.

In fact, the fear of growing old is so great that every aged **person** is an insult and a threat to the society. **They** remind us of our own death.   —SHARON CURTIN

As you make choices about pronouns referring to singular antecedents such as *everyone* and *a person*, consider not only your own preferences but those of your audience.

(2) Two or more antecedents joined by *and* are referred to by a plural pronoun; two or more singular antecedents joined by *or* or *nor* are referred to by a singular pronoun.

Andrew and Mikis lost **their** self-confidence.
Did **Andrew or Mikis** lose **his** self-confidence?

If one of two antecedents joined by *or* or *nor* is singular and one is plural, the pronoun usually agrees with the nearer antecedent:

Neither the **package nor** the **letters** had reached **their** destination. [*Their* is closer to the plural antecedent *letters*.]
Stray **kittens or** even an abandoned grown **cat** has **its** problems finding enough food to survive long. [*Its* is closer to the singular antecedent *cat*.]

(3) Collective nouns are referred to by singular or plural pronouns, depending on whether the collective noun has a singular or plural sense. See also **6a(7)**.

Special care should be taken to avoid treating a collective noun as both singular and plural within the same sentence.

INCONSISTENT	The choir **is** writing **their** own music. [singular verb, plural pronoun]
CONSISTENT	The choir **is** writing **its** own music. [both singular]
CONSISTENT	The group of students **do** not agree on methods, but **they** unite on basic aims. [both plural]

■ **Exercise 3** Following the rules of formal usage, choose the correct pronoun or verb form in parentheses in each sentence.

1. A number of writers (has, have) expressed (his, her and his, his/her, their) concern about sexist usage.
2. If any one of the sisters (needs, need) a ride to school, (she, they) can call Trudy.
3. Neither the pilot nor the flight attendants mentioned the incident when (he, they) talked to reporters.
4. The basketball team (was, were) opportunistic; (it, they) took advantage of every break.
5. If the board of directors (controls, control) the company, (it, they) may vote (itself, themselves) bonuses.

■ **Exercise 4** All of the following sentences are correct. Change them as directed in parentheses, revising other parts of the sentence to secure agreement of subject and verb, pronoun and antecedent.

1. A sign in the lab reads: "This computer does only what you tell it to, not what you want it to." (Change *this computer* to *these computers*.)
2. Perhaps this sign was put up by some frustrated students who were having trouble with their computer manuals. (Change *some frustrated students* to *a frustrated student*.)
3. The sign in the lab reminds me of similar problems. A chef, for example, whose vegetables or casserole is ruined in a microwave might think: "This oven reads buttons, not minds." (Change *vegetables or casserole* to *casserole or vegetables*. Change *This oven* to *These ovens*.)
4. All too often what comes out of our mouths is the very opposite of what we intend to say but exposes what we

really think. (Change *what* to *the words that*. Change *our* to *one's*.)

5. Two of my instructors, together with a few of my class-mates, were talking about such Freudian slips the other day. (Change *Two* to *One*.)

6. Who knows what kind of label is attached to one's computer errors! (Change *kind* to *kinds*.)

7. Then there is the mirror. (Change *the mirror* to *mirrors*.) There are times when people don't like to face mirrors. (Change *people* to *a person*.)

8. At such times a person has to face how he or she actually looks, not how he or she wants to look. (Change *a person* to *people*.)

9. There is another thought that comes to mind. (Change *another thought* to *other thoughts*.)

10. Mirrors reflect images in reverse, so not even in a mirror do we ever see ourselves as we really are. (Change *we* to *one*.)

Verb Forms

7

Use the appropriate form of the verb.

The forms of verbs and auxiliaries may indicate not only the number and person of their subjects (see **6a**) but also tense, voice, and mood. A change in the form of a verb shows a specific meaning or a grammatical relationship to some other word or group of words in a sentence.

Regular and irregular verbs   The way a verb changes form determines its classification as regular or irregular. A regular verb takes the *-d* or *-ed* ending to denote the past tense.

REGULAR   *believe (believes), believed, believing*
         attack (attacks), attacked, attacking

Irregular verbs do not take the *-d* or *-ed* ending. They are inflected in various other ways to indicate past tense: see **irregular verb**, page 545.

IRREGULAR   *run (runs), ran, running*
         eat (eats), ate, eaten, eating

A few irregular verbs (like *cut* or *hurt*) have the same form in the present and the past tense.

Forms of the verb *be*   The most irregular verb in the English langauge is *be*. It has eight forms: *am, are, is, was, were, be, been, being*.

That may **be** true.   He **was being** difficult.

Below is a list of forms of *be* used with various subjects in the present and the past tense.

PRESENT	I am	you are	he/she/it is	[singular]
	we are	you are	they are	[plural]
PAST	I was	you were	he/she/it was	[singular]
	we were	you were	they were	[plural]

A form of *be* is used with the present participle to form the progressive: **is** *attacking, will* **be** *eating*. A form of *be* is used with a past participle to form the passive: **was** *attacked, had* **been** *eaten*.

Tense   *Tense* refers to the form of the verb that indicates time. There are different ways of classifying the number of tenses in English. If you consider only the form changes of single-word verbs, there are only two tenses (present and past); if you consider progressive forms and certain auxiliaries, there are twelve. The usual practice, however, is to distinguish six tenses. Of these six, one refers to the present time, three to the past, and two to the future.

Time	Tense	Verb
Present:	PRESENT	try, give
Past:	PAST	tried, gave
	PRESENT PERFECT	have tried, have given
	PAST PERFECT	had tried, had given
Future:	FUTURE	will (OR shall) try
		will (OR shall) give
	FUTURE PERFECT	will (OR shall) have tried
		will (OR shall) have given

The forms of the verb used in the following synopsis are *see (sees), saw, seen, seeing* (called the principal parts: see **7a**).

	Active	*Passive*
PRESENT	see/sees	am/is/are seen
Progressive	am/is/are seeing	am/is/are being seen
PAST	saw	was/were seen
Progressive	was/were seeing	was/were being seen
FUTURE	will see	will be seen
Progressive	will be seeing	will be being seen
PRESENT PERFECT	have/has seen	have/has been seen
Progressive	have/has been seeing	have/has been being seen
PAST PERFECT	had seen	had been seen
Progressive	had been seeing	had been being seen
FUTURE PERFECT	will have seen	will have been seen
Progressive	will have been seeing	will have been being seen

The preceding verb forms—the most frequently used for making assertions or asking questions—are in the indicative mood. In the imperative mood (used for commands or requests), verbs have only present tense (*see, be seen*). For verb forms in the subjunctive mood, see **7c**. See also **conjugation**, pages 538–39.

Note: Verbals (including their progressive forms) have voice and tense.

	Infinitives
PRESENT	to see, to be seen, to be seeing
PRESENT PERFECT	to have seen, to have been seen, to have been seeing

	Participles
PRESENT	seeing, being seen
PAST	seen
PRESENT PERFECT	having seen, having been seen

Gerunds

PRESENT   seeing, being seen
PRESENT PERFECT   having seen, having been seen

7a

Avoid misusing the principal parts of verbs and confusing similar verbs.

NOT   Has the prime minister spoke to the press about this?
      [misuse of a principal part of the verb *speak*]
BUT   **Has** the prime minister **spoken** to the press about this?

NOT   The hand-carved birds laid on the shelf for years.
      [confusion of past forms of the similar verbs *lie* and *lay*]
BUT   The hand-carved birds **lay** on the shelf for years.

(1) Avoid misusing the principal parts of verbs.

The principal parts of a verb include the present form (*see*), which is also the stem of the infinitive (*to see*); the past form (*saw*); and the past participle (*seen*). (See ''Principal Parts of Verbs'' on page 77.) The present participle (*seeing*) is often considered a fourth principal part.

The *present* form may function as a single-word verb or may be preceded by words such as *do, will, may, could, have to,* or *used to.*

I **ask**, he **does ask**, we **will begin**, it **used to begin**

The *past* form functions as a single-word verb.

He **asked** a few questions.
The show **began** at eight.

When used as part of a simple predicate, the *past participle* as well as the *present participle* always has at least one auxiliary.

He **has asked** them. I **was asked**. I **will be asking** questions.
They **have begun**. **Had** he **begun**? It **is beginning** to snow.

Both the past and the present participle serve not only as parts of a simple predicate but also as adjectivals: "pastries *baked* last week," "heat waves *rising* from the road." Nouns modified by participles are not sentences: see **2a**.

Caution: Do not omit a needed *-d* or *-ed* because of the pronunciation. For example, although it is easy to remember a clearly pronounced *-d* or *-ed* (*added, repeated*), it is sometimes difficult to remember to add a needed *-d* or *-ed* in such expressions as *had priced them* or *opened it*. Observe the use of the *-d* or *-ed* in these sentences:

> Yesterday I ask**ed** myself: "Is the judge prejudice**d**?"
> He use**d** to smoke. I am not suppose**d** to be the boss.

The following list of principal parts includes both regular and irregular verbs that are sometimes misused.

Principal Parts of Verbs

PRESENT	PAST	PAST PARTICIPLE
arise	arose	arisen
ask	asked	asked
attack	attacked	attacked
awaken	awakened	awakened
become	became	become
begin	began	begun
blow	blew	blown
break	broke	broken
bring	brought	brought
burst	burst	burst
choose	chose	chosen
cling	clung	clung
come	came	come
creep	crept	crept
dive	dived OR dove	dived
do	did	done
drag	dragged	dragged
draw	drew	drawn

PRESENT	PAST	PAST PARTICIPLE
drink	drank	drunk OR drank
drive	drove	driven
drown	drowned	drowned
eat	ate	eaten
fall	fell	fallen
fly	flew	flown
forgive	forgave	forgiven
freeze	froze	frozen
give	gave	given
go	went	gone
grow	grew	grown
happen	happened	happened
know	knew	known
ride	rode	ridden
ring	rang	rung
rise	rose	risen
run	ran	run
see	saw	seen
shake	shook	shaken
shrink	shrank OR shrunk	shrunk OR shrunken
sing	sang	sung
sink	sank OR sunk	sunk
speak	spoke	spoken
spin	spun	spun
spring	sprang	sprung
steal	stole	stolen
sting	stung	stung
stink	stank OR stunk	stunk
swear	swore	sworn
swim	swam	swum
swing	swung	swung
take	took	taken
tear	tore	torn
throw	threw	thrown
wake	woke OR waked	waked OR woken
wear	wore	worn
wring	wrung	wrung
write	wrote	written

Note: Mistakes with verbs sometimes involve spelling errors. Use care when you write troublesome verb forms such as the following:

PRESENT	PAST	PAST PARTICIPLE	PRESENT PARTICIPLE
lead	led	led	leading
loosen	loosened	loosened	loosening
lose	lost	lost	losing
pay	paid	paid	paying
study	studied	studied	studying

■ **Exercise 1**   Respond to the questions in the past tense with a past tense verb; respond to the questions in the future tense with a present perfect verb (*have* or *has* + a past participle). Follow the pattern of the examples.

> EXAMPLES   Did she criticize Don?   *Yes, she criticized Don.*
> Will they take it?   *They have already taken it.*

1. Did he give it away?
2. Will you run a mile?
3. Did the man drown?
4. Will they begin that?
5. Did the wind blow?
6. Will she choose it?
7. Did it really happen?
8. Will the river rise?
9. Did you do that?
10. Will they bring it?
11. Did you spin your wheels?
12. Will they freeze it?
13. Did he cling to that belief?
14. Will they go to the police?
15. Did she know them?
16. Will the fire alarm ring?
17. Did the sack burst?
18. Will he eat it?
19. Did you grow these?
20. Will Bert speak out?

(2) Do not confuse *set* with *sit* or *lay* with *lie*.

Sit means "be seated," and *lie down* means "rest in or get into a horizontal position." To *set* or *lay* something down is to place it or put it somewhere.

Learn the distinctions between the forms of *sit* and *set* and those of *lie* and *lay*.

PRESENT (INFINITIVE)	PAST	PAST PARTICIPLE	PRESENT PARTICIPLE
(to) sit	sat	sat	sitting
(to) set	set	set	setting
(to) lie	lay	lain	lying
(to) lay	laid	laid	laying

As a rule, the verbs (or verbals) *sit* and *lie* are intransitive; they do not take objects. *Set* and *lay* are usually transitive and therefore take objects. Transitive verbs may be passive as well as active. (If you cannot easily recognize objects of verbs, see **1b**.)

> **Sit** down. **Sitting** down, I thought it over. He **sat** up.
> **Lie** down. I **lay** down. It **was lying** here. **Has** it **lain** here long?
> Somebody **had set** the pup in the cart. It **had been set** there.
> We **ought to lay** these aside. These **should be laid** aside.

■ **Exercise 2**   Substitute the correct forms of *sit* and *lie* for the italicized word in each sentence. Follow the pattern of the example. Do not change the tense of the verb.

> EXAMPLE   I *remained* in that position for twenty minutes.
>
> > *I **sat** in that position for twenty minutes.*
> > *I **lay** in that position for twenty minutes.*

1. Jack doesn't ever want to *get* down.
2. The dog *stayed* near the luggage.
3. The toy soldier has been *rusting* in the yard.
4. He often *sleeps* on a park bench.
5. Has it *been* there all along?

■ **Exercise 3**   Without changing the tense of the italicized verb, substitute the correct form of one of the verbs in parentheses at the end of each sentence.

1. Last week we *put* down the new tiles in the hall. (lie/lay)
2. I often *stand* there and watch the tide come in. (sit/set)

3. After lunch Hanna decided to *plop* down for a nap. (lie/lay)
4. Dan was *sprawling* on the picnic table. (sit/set)
5. Dan was *putting* up the picnic table. (sit/set)

7b

Learn the meaning of tense forms. Use logical tense forms in sequence.

(1) Learn the meaning of tense forms.

Although tense refers to time (see page 74), the tense forms do not always agree with divisions of actual time. The present tense, for example, is by no means limited to the present time. As you study the following examples, observe that auxiliaries as well as single-word verbs indicate time.

PRESENT TENSE

I **see** what you meant by that remark. [now, present time]
Maureen **uses** common sense. [habitual action]
Mistakes **are** often **made**. [passive verb, habitual action]
Blind innocence **sees** no evil. [universal or timeless truth]
In 1939 Hitler **attacks** Poland. [historical present]
Conrad **writes** about what he **sees** in the human heart. [literary present]
Officially winter **begins** next week. [present form, used with the adverbial *next week* to denote future time]
I **am learning** from my mistakes. [a progressive form denoting past, present, and (probably) future]

PAST TENSE—past time, not extending to the present

I **saw** the accident. [at a definite time before now]
They **used** makeshift tools. [action completed in the past]
We **were enjoying** our reunion. [a progressive form denoting continuing action in the past]
The accident **was seen** by two people. [passive]
Westerns **used to be** more popular. [Compare "*were* more popular then."]

FUTURE TENSE—at a future time, sometime after now

He **will see** his lawyer.
Shall we **use** a different strategy?
He **will be seeing** his lawyer.   [progressive]
A different strategy **will be used**.   [passive]

PRESENT PERFECT TENSE—sometime before now, up to now

I **have seen** the movie.   [sometime before now]
She **has used** her savings wisely.   [up to now]
Has Kevin **been using** his talents?
Deer **have been seen** in those woods.

PAST PERFECT TENSE—before a specific time in the past

Carla **had talked** to me before the game started.
After he **had used** his savings, he applied for a loan.
Had they **been sailing** along the coast before the storm?
At his death their home **had been** on the market for ten years.

FUTURE PERFECT TENSE—before a specific time in the future

The top executive **will have seen** the report by next week.
By the year 2000 I **will have been seeing** my dreams in
    action.   [a rarely used passive, progressive, future-perfect
    verb]

Note: Sometimes the simple past is used for the past perfect:

Carla **talked** to me before the game started.

Far more frequently the simple future replaces the future
perfect:

The top executive **will see** the report by next week.
By the year 2000 I **will be seeing** my dreams in action.

■ **Exercise 4**   Prepare to discuss differences in the meaning of
the tense forms separated by slashes.

1. It *has rained* / *had rained* for days.
2. Mary *waxed* / *did wax* / *was waxing* the car.

3. Min Hua *teaches / is teaching* Chinese.
4. I *spoke / have spoken* to him about this.
5. The Singers *had sold / will have sold* their house by then.
6. Time *passes / does pass / has passed / had been passing* rapidly.
7. In 1840 Thomas Carlyle *calls / called* time a great mystery, a miracle.

(2) Use logical tense forms in sequence.

Verbs

Notice in the following examples the relationship of each verb form to actual time:

> When the speaker **entered**, the audience **rose**. [Both actions took place at the same definite time in the past.]
> I **have ceased** worrying because I **have heard** no more rumours. [Both verb forms indicate action at some time before now.]
> When I **had been** at camp four weeks, I **received** word that my application **had been accepted**. [The *had* before *been* indicates a time prior to that of *received*.]

Infinitives

Use the present infinitive to express action occurring at the same time as, or later than, that of the main verb; use the present perfect infinitive for action prior to that of the main verb:

> I am pleased **to meet** you. [present infinitive—for the same time as that of the main verb]
> He wanted **to meet** you. He wants **to meet** you. [present infinitives—for time later than *wanted* or *wants*]
> He seems **to have met** her before. [present perfect infinitive—for time prior to that of the main verb.]

Participles

Use the present form of participles to express action occurring at the same time as that of the main verb; use the present perfect form for action prior to that of the main verb:

Walking along the streets, he met many old friends. [The walking and the meeting were simultaneous.]

Having climbed that mountain, they felt a real sense of achievement. [The climbing took place first; then came their sense of achievement.]

■ **Exercise 5**   Choose the verb form inside parentheses that is the logical tense form in sequence.

1. When the fire sale (ended, had ended), the store closed.
2. Fans cheered as the goal (had been scored, was scored).
3. The team plans (to celebrate, to have celebrated) tomorrow.
4. We should have planned (to have gone, to go) by bus.
5. (Having finished, Finishing) the test, Leslie left the room.
6. (Having bought, Buying) the tickets, Mr. Leung took the children to the circus.
7. The president had left the meeting before it (had adjourned, adjourned).
8. It is customary for ranchers (to brand, to have branded) their cattle.
9. Marilyn had not expected (to see, to have seen) her cousin at the rally.
10. The pond has begun freezing because the temperature (dropped, has dropped).

7c

Use the appropriate form of the verb for the subjunctive mood.

Although the subjunctive mood is alive in such fixed expressions as *far be it from me, be that as it may, as it were,* and *God bless you,* it has been largely displaced by the indicative. But a few distinctive forms for the subjunctive still occur.

Forms for the Subjunctive

For the verb *be*:

Present, singular or plural: **be**
Past, singular or plural: **were**

(Contrast the indicative forms of *be* with various subjects on page 74.)

For all other verbs with third-person singular subjects:

Present, singular only: **see**   [The *-s* ending is dropped.]

EXAMPLES

It is necessary that I **be** on time.
Suppose he **were** to die before she does.
One debater insisted that the other not **avoid** the question.

ALTERNATIVES

I **have to be** on time.
Suppose he **dies** before she does.
One debater urged the other not **to avoid** the question.

Should and *would* (past forms of *shall* and *will*) are also used for the subjunctive.

(1) Use the subjunctive in *that* clauses after such verbs as *demand, recommend, urge, insist, request, suggest, move.*

I move that the report **be** approved.
The counsellor suggested that he **discover** the library.
OR
The counsellor told him *to discover* the library.

(2) Especially in formal English, use the subjunctive to express wishes or (in *if* or *as if* clauses) a hypothetical, highly improbable, or contrary-to-fact condition.

I wish I **were** in London. **Would I were** there now!

If I **were** you, I would accept the offer.

Act as if every other person on the stage **were** a member of your family.

Especially in formal English, *should* is still used in conditional clauses:

If she **should** resign, we **would** have grave difficulty locating a competent replacement.

OR

If she *resigns*, we *will* have grave difficulty locating a competent replacement.

The indicative is displacing this use of the subjunctive, just as *will* is displacing *shall*—except in questions such as "*Shall we tell?*"

(3) Do not use *would have* for *had* in an *if* clause that expresses an imagined condition.

NOT   If he would have arrived earlier, he wouldn't have lost the sale.

BUT   If he **had** arrived earlier, he wouldn't have lost the sale.

OR

Had he arrived earlier, he wouldn't have lost the sale.

■ **Exercise 6**   Prepare to explain the use of the subjunctive in the following sentences.

1. Had Linda been here, she would have explained everything.
2. We insist that he be punished.
3. I wish that peace were possible.
4. If there should be a change in policy, we would have to make major adjustments.
5. Some North Americans visit China as though it were just like any other vacation spot.
6. Present-day problems demand that we be ready for any emergency.

7. One reporter insisted that the candidate answer her directly.
8. If I were you, I would apply tomorrow.
9. The man acts as if he were the owner.
10. It is necessary that we be prepared in case of an earthquake.

■ **Exercise 7**   Compose five sentences illustrating various uses of the subjunctive.

7d

Avoid needless shifts in tense or mood. See also **27a.**

INCORRECT   She **stood** up to her opponents in the debate and **tries** to score a victory.   [shift in tense from past to present]

CORRECT   She **stood** up to her opponents in the debate and **tried** to score a victory.

INCORRECT   It is necessary to restrain an occasional foolhardy park visitor. If a female bear **were** to mistake his friendly intentions and **supposes** him a menace to her cubs, he would be in trouble.   [shift in mood from subjunctive to indicative]   But females with cubs **were** only one of the dangers.   [a correct sentence if standing alone, but here inconsistent with present tense of preceding sentence and therefore misleading]   All bears are wild animals and not domesticated pets. It **is** therefore an important part of the park ranger's duty to watch the tourists and above all **don't** let anyone try to feed the bears.   [shift in mood from indicative to imperative]

CORRECT   It is necessary to restrain an occasional foolhardy park visitor. If a female bear **were** to mistake his friendly intentions and **suppose** him a menace to her cubs, he would be in trouble. But females with cubs **are** only one of the dangers. All bears are wild animals and not domesticated pets. It **is** therefore an important part of the park ranger's duty to watch the tourists and above all not to let anyone try to feed the bears.

7d v

■ **Exercise 8**   In the following passage correct all errors and inconsistencies in tense and mood as well as any other errors in verb usage. Put a check mark after any sentence that is satisfactory as it stands.

¹Charles Dickens creates many memorable characters in *David Copperfield*.   ²He give many of his characters names that suggest their personalities.   ³Mr. Murdstone is unfeeling, Little Emily is shy, and Dr. Strong is virtuous.   ⁴Dickens also tags his characters with recurring peculiarities of speech; these may even be call their trademarks.   ⁵For example, Barkis continues to have proposed marriage with these words: "Barkis is willin'."   ⁶The proud Uriah Heep, a hypocrite, keeps calling himself a humble man.   ⁷Over and over Mr. Micawber rambled on and then concludes, "In short—"   ⁸When he owed debts this character shrugs off what he terms his "pecuniary difficulties."   ⁹With cheerful certainty, he repeats his favourite prophecy: "Something is bound to turn up."   ¹⁰Set down and read *David Copperfield* through to become acquainted with these interesting people.

MECHANICS

Manuscript Form

8

Put your manuscript in acceptable form. Revise and proofread with care.

8a
Use the proper materials.

Unless you are given other instructions, follow these general practices:

(1) **Handwritten papers**   Use regular looseleaf paper, size 21.6 cm × 27.9 cm (8½ × 11 inches), with widely spaced lines. (Narrow spaces between lines do not allow sufficient room for corrections.) Use black or blue ink. Write on only one side of the paper.

(2) **Typewritten or word-processed papers**   Use regular white typing paper (not sheets torn from a spiral notebook), size 21.6 cm × 27.9 cm (8½ × 11 inches). Or use a good grade of bond paper (not onionskin). Use a black ribbon. Double-space between lines. Type on only one side of the paper.

8b

Arrange your writing in clear and orderly fashion on the page.

(1) Margins   Leave sufficient margins—about 2.5 cm (1 inch) on all sides—to prevent a crowded appearance. The ruled vertical line on looseleaf paper marks the left margin.

(2) Indention   Indent the first lines of paragraphs uniformly, about 2.5 cm (1 inch) in handwritten copy and five spaces in typewritten copy.

(3) Paging   Use Arabic numerals—without parentheses or periods—in the upper right-hand corner to mark all pages.

(4) Title   Do not put quotation marks around the title or underline it (unless it is a quotation or the title of a book), and use no period after the title. Capitalize the first and last words of the title and all other words except articles, co-ordinating conjunctions, prepositions, and the *to* in infinitives. See also **9c**.

When you do not use a title page, centre the title on the page about 3.8 cm (1¹/₂ inches) from the top or on the first ruled line. Leave one blank line between the title and the first paragraph. When you do use a separate title page, include the following information attractively spaced: the title of your paper, your name, the course title and number, the instructor's name, and the date. See the example on page 501.

(5) Quoted lines   When you quote over four lines of another's writing to explain or support your ideas, set

the quotation off by indention: see **16a(3)**. Acknowledge
the source of quotations: see Section **34**, pages 434–57.

(6) Punctuation   Never begin a line with a comma, a
colon, a semicolon, a hyphen, a dash, or a terminal
mark of punctuation; never end a line with the first of a
set of brackets, parentheses, or quotation marks.

(7) Identification   Usually papers carry the name of the
student, the course title and number, the instructor's
name, and the date. Often the number of the assignment
is given.

8c

**Write or type your manuscript so that it can be read
easily and accurately.**

(1) Legible handwriting   Form each letter clearly; distinguish between *o* and *a*, *t* and *l*, *b* and *f*, and between
capital and lower-case letters. Use firm dots, not circles,
for periods. Make each word a distinct unit. Avoid
flourishes.

(2) Legible typing/clean printout   Before typing or printing out your final draft, check the quality of the ribbon
or tape and the cleanness of the type. Double-space
between lines. If you are using a typewriter, do not
strike over an incorrect letter; make neat corrections.
Leave one space after a comma or semicolon; one or
two after a colon; two after a period, a question mark,
or an exclamation point. To indicate a dash, use two
hyphens without spacing before, between, or after. Use
a pen to insert marks or symbols that are not on your
typewriter or in your word-processing system, such as

accent marks, mathematical symbols, or brackets. If you are using a word processor connected to a laser printer and have a choice of typefaces and sizes, check whether your instructor has any preferences or special requirements with regard to these elements.

8d

Whenever possible, avoid dividing a word at the end of a line. Make such divisions only between syllables and according to standard practice.

You will seldom need to divide words if you do not leave too wide a right margin. Remember that the reader expects a somewhat uneven right margin but may be distracted or slowed down by a series of word divisions at the ends of consecutive lines. (If you are using a word-processing system, avoid right-margin justification or alignment.)

When you do need to divide a word at the end of a line, use a hyphen to mark the separation of syllables. In college dictionaries, dots usually divide the syllables of words:

**re • al • ly   pre • fer   pref • er • ence
sell • ing   set • ting**.

But not every division between syllables is an appropriate place for dividing a word at the end of a line. The following principles are useful guidelines:

(1) One-letter syllables   Do not put the first or last letter of a word at the end or beginning of a line. Do not divide *o • mit, a • ble, spunk • y, bo • a.*

(2) Two-letter endings   Do not put the last two letters of a word at the beginning of a line. Do not divide *dat • ed, does • n't, safe • ly, grav • el, tax • is.*

(3) **Misleading divisions**   Do not make divisions that may cause a misreading: *sour • ces, on • ions, an • gel, colo • nel, re • ally.*

The vertical lines in the following examples mark appropriate end-of-line divisions.

(4) **Hyphenated words**   Divide hyphenated words only at the hyphen.

mass-| produced

father-| in-law OR **father-in-| law**

(5) ***-ing* words**   Divide words ending in *-ing* between those consonants that you double when adding *-ing*.

set-| ting   jam-| ming   plan-| ning

[Compare sell-| ing.]

(6) **Consonants between vowels**   Divide words between two consonants that come between vowels—except when the division does not reflect pronunciation.

pic-| nic   dis-| cuss   thun-| der BUT **co-| bra**

(7) **Abbreviations and acronyms**   Do not divide abbreviations, initials, or capitalized acronyms.

B.A. [degree]   **O.E.C.D.   CBC   UPEI   UNESCO**

(8) **Caution:**   Do not divide one-syllable words, such as *twelfth, through,* or *grabbed.*

■ **Exercise 1**   First put a check mark after the words that should not be divided at the end of a line; then, with the aid of your dictionary, write out the other words by syllables and insert hyphens followed by a vertical line to indicate appropriate end-of-line divisions.

1. cross-reference
2. economic
3. fifteenth
4. GATT
5. gripped
6. gripping
7. guessing
8. against
9. present (*now*)
10. present (*give*)
11. seacoast
12. eventual
13. recline
14. C.P.A.
15. magical
16. CHUM-FM
17. matches
18. dissolve
19. cobwebs
20. patron

8e
Revise and proofread your manuscript with care.

(1) Revise and proofread your paper before submitting it to the instructor.

When doing out-of-class papers, write a first draft, put the paper aside for a few hours or a day, and then revise it. As you revise, focus your attention on content and style. Use the Reviser's Checklist in Section **33**.

If only a few changes are needed, the paper may be handed in—after clear, legible corrections have been made—without rewriting. If extensive changes are necessary on any page, make a full, clean copy of it to submit to the instructor.

When doing in-class papers, use the last few minutes for proofreading and making corrections. As you proofread, focus your attention on manuscript form—on mechanics, punctuation, spelling. Watch for the items noted in the Proofreader's Checklist on page 99. For examples of how to make corrections, see page 97.

(2) Revise your paper after the instructor has marked it.

Become familiar with the numbers or abbreviations used by your instructor to indicate specific errors or suggested changes.

Unless directed otherwise, follow this procedure as you revise a marked paper:

A Paragraph Marked by an Instructor

Those who damn advertising stress its

3 disadvantages, however, it saves consumers time,

labour, and money. Billboards can save travellers

12 time for many billboards tell where to find a meal

18 or a bed. TV commercials announce new labour–

2 saveing products. Such as a spray or a cleaner. In

addition, some advertisers give away free samples

19 of shampoo, toothpaste, soap flakes, and etc. These

24 samples often last for weeks. They save the

consumer money. Consumers should appreciate

advertising, not condemn it.

(a) Find in this handbook the exact principle that deals with each error or recommended change.

(b) After the instructor's mark in the margin, write the letter designating the appropriate principle, such as **a** or **c**.

(c) Rather than rewrite the composition, make the corrections on the marked paper. To make the corrections stand out distinctly from the original, use ink of a different colour or a no. 2 pencil.

The purpose of this method of revision is to help you not only to understand why a change is desirable but to avoid repetition of the same mistakes.

The Same Paragraph Corrected by a Student

Those who damn advertising stress its

3b disadvantages/; however, it saves consumers time,

labour, and money. Billboards can save travellers

12a time, for many billboards tell where to find a meal

18d or a bed. TV commercials announce new labour—

2c ~~saveing~~ Saving products/, ~~Such~~ such as a spray or a cleaner. In

addition, some advertisers give away free samples

19i of shampoo, toothpaste, soap flakes, ~~and~~ etc. These

24a samples, often last for weeks/, ~~They~~ which save the

consumer money. Consumers should appreciate

advertising, not condemn it.

Examples of a paragraph marked by an instructor and the same paragraph corrected by a student are given above. Examine the corrected paragraph to see how deletions of words, corrections of misspellings, substitutions of words, and changes in capitalization and punctuation are made. Notice also the use of a caret (∧) at the point in the line where an addition is made.

This method of revision works equally well if your instructor uses abbreviations or other symbols instead of numbers. In the former case, instead of putting **d** after **18**, for example, you would put **d** or **18d** after **sp**.

8f

Keep a record of your revisions to help you improve your writing.

A clear record of the symbols marked on your papers by your instructor will show your progress at a glance. As you revise each new paper, refer to your record to avoid mistakes that have already been pointed out and corrected.

You can record your revisions in each paper by grouping them in columns according to the seven major divisions of the handbook, as the following Record of Revisions illustrates. In the spaces for paper no. 1 are the numbers and letters from the margin of the revised paragraph. In the spelling column is the correctly spelled word rather than **18d**. You may wish to add on your record sheet other columns for date, grade, and instructor's comments.

RECORD OF REVISIONS

Paper No.	Grammar 1–7	Mechanics 8–11	Punctuation 12–17	Words Misspelled 18	Diction 19–22	Effective- ness 23–30	Larger Elements 31–34
1	*3b* *2c*		*12 a*	*saving*	*19i*	*24a*	

Proofreader's Checklist

1. **Title**   Is there any unnecessary punctuation in the title? Is it centred on the line? Are key words capitalized? See **8b(4)**.

2. **Indention**   Is the first line of each paragraph indented? Is any lengthy quoted passage set off from the text? See **8b(2)** and **16a(3)**.

3. **Sentences**   Does each sentence begin with a capital and end with the appropriate end mark? Are there any fragments, comma splices, or fused sentences? See **9e, 17a–c**, and Sections **2–3**.

4. **Spelling, mechanics**   Are there any misspellings or mistakes in typing or handwriting? Are capitals and underlining (italics) used correctly? Should any abbreviations or numbers be spelled out? See **8c** and Sections **9–11** and **18**.

5. **Punctuation**   Have any end marks been omitted? Are apostrophes correctly placed? Are there any superfluous commas? See Sections **12–17**.

■ **Exercise 2**   Proofread the following composition. Circle the mistakes that you find and prepare to discuss in class the changes you would make to correct the text.

Programmed People.

A lot of people in the workaday-world is a machine—an insensitive, unhearing, unseeing, unthinking, unfeeling mechanism. They act like they are programmed, all their movements or responses triggered by clocks.. Take, for example my brother.

At 7:30 A.M. he automatically shuts off the alarm, then for the next hour he grumbles and sputter around like the cold, sluggish motor that he is.

On the way to work he did not see the glorious sky or notice ambulance at his neighbour's house. At 8:20 he unlocks his store and starts selling auto parts; however, all mourning long he never once really sees a customers' face. While eating lunch at Joe's cafe, the same music he spent a half dollar for yesterday is playing again. he does not hear it. At one o'clock my brother is back working with invoices and punching at a calculator; The clock and him ticks on and on.

When the hour hand hits five, it pushes the "move" button of my brother: lock store, take bus, pet dog at front door, kiss wife and baby, eat supper, read paper, watch TV, and during the 10-o'clock news he starts his nodding. His wife interrupts his light snoring to say that thier neighbour had a mild heart attach while mowing the lawn. My brother jerks and snorts. Then he mumbles, "Tell me tomorrow. I'm to tired now."

Capitals

9

Capitalize words according to standard conventions. Avoid unnecessary capitals.

A study of the principles in this section should help you use capitals correctly. When special problems arise, consult a good recent college dictionary. Dictionaries list not only words and abbreviations that begin with capitals but also acronyms that adopt full capitals:

> Halloween, World War II, Hon., Ph.D., ICAO, FORTRAN

If usage is divided, dictionaries also give options:

> Old Guard OR old guard, Nos. OR nos., Mountie OR mountie

A recent dictionary is an especially useful guide when the capitalization of a word depends upon a given meaning: "*mosaic* pictures" but "*Mosaic* laws," "on *earth*" but "the planet *Earth*," "a *prairie* dog" but "the *Prairies*."

9a
Capitalize proper names and, usually, their derivatives and their shortened forms (abbreviations and acronyms).

9a cap

PROPER NAMES

As you study the following examples, observe that common nouns like *college, company, memorial, park*, and *street* are capitalized when they are essential parts of proper names.

(1) Names and nicknames of persons or things, trademarks

> Vui Nguyen, T.S. Eliot, the Grey Fox, Gandhi, Henry V
> Skydome, the Peace Tower, Flight 41D, Gemini Award
> Noah's Ark, Banff, Olympics, Bay Street, Jeep Cherokee
> Dentyne, Apple II

(2) Geographical names

> America, Middle East, Peru, New Brunswick, the Yukon
> Quebec City, Great Divide, Arctic Circle, Lake District
> Pacific Northwest, Peace River, Fundy Park, Ocean Falls
> Baffin Island, Cape Breton

(3) Peoples and languages

> American, Aztec, Inuit, Indians, Filipinos, Poles
> Scottish, English, Polish, Spanish, French, Russian
> Swedish, Latin

(4) Organizations, government agencies, institutions, companies

> the Red Cross, Canada Post, Canadian Press, the Senate
> the Commons Justice Committee, B.C. Lions, Via Rail
> Acadia University, Ryerson Institute, CP Express

Option: *the Liberal party* or *the Liberal Party*

(5) Days of the week, months, holidays

> Tuesday, October, Thanksgiving, Groundhog Day
> Remembrance Day

(6) Historical documents, periods, events

the Free Trade Agreement, the Charter of Rights and Freedoms
the Child Care Act, the Stone Age, the Vietnam War
the Romantic Movement, Commonwealth Conference

(7) Religions and their adherents, holy books, holy days, words denoting the god or gods of a religion

Christianity, Hinduism, Islam, Buddhism, Judaism
Protestant, Catholic, Christian, Hindu, Moslem, Jew
Baptists, Mennonites, Anglicans

the Bible, the Veda, the Koran, Revelations, the Talmud
Easter, Yom Kippur, Buddha, Brahma, Allah, God, Messiah
Yahweh, the Supreme Being, the Deity

Option: Some writers always capitalize pronouns (except *who, whom, whose*) referring to God. Other writers capitalize such pronouns only when the capital is needed to prevent ambiguity, as in "The Lord commanded the prophet to warn *His* people."

(8) Personifications. See also **20a(4)**.

I could feel Old Man Time breathing down the back of my neck. —PATRICK McMANUS

Note: Occasionally, a common noun is capitalized for emphasis or clarity, as in "The motivation for many politicians is Power."

DERIVATIVES

(9) Words derived from proper names

Americanize [verb], Israelite, Christmas, Marxism [nouns]
Germanic, Orwellian [adjectives]

9c cap

When proper names and their derivatives become names of a general class, they are no longer capitalized.

> zipper   [originally a capitalized trademark]
> chauvinistic   [derived from *Nicholas Chauvin*]

ABBREVIATIONS AND ACRONYMS

(10) Shortened forms of capitalized words. See also 17a(2).

> B.C.   L.A. OR LA   D.O.T.   NFB   CBC   DST
> CRTC   OPEC   UNESCO   NATO   RCMP   MADD
> [words derived from the initial letters of capitalized word groups]

Common exceptions: B.C., A.D., A.M. OR a.m., P.M. OR p.m.

9b
Capitalize titles of persons that precede the name but not those that follow it.

> Premier Joe Ghiz, Captain Holt, Aunt Mae
> Joe Ghiz, our premier; Holt, the captain; Mae, my aunt

Note: Usage is divided regarding the capitalization of titles of high rank or distinction when not followed by a proper name: the Prime Minister (OR prime minister) of Canada.

Words denoting family relationship are usually capitalized when serving as substitutes for proper names: ''Tell Mother I'll write soon.''

9c
In titles and subtitles of books, plays, student papers, and so on, capitalize the first and last words and all

other words except articles, co-ordinating conjunctions, prepositions, and the *to* in infinitives.

The articles are *a, an, the*; the co-ordinating conjunctions are *and, but, or, nor, for, so, yet*. (Formerly, longer prepositions like *before, between*, or *through* in titles were capitalized; the style today, however, favours lower-cased prepositions, whatever the length.)

> *All Creatures Great and Small*
> "What It Takes to Be a Leader"
> "Why Women Are Paid Less Than Men" [The subordinating conjunction *than* is capitalized.]
> "Aerobics before Breakfast"
> *Looking Back: A Chronicle of Growing Up Old in the Sixties*
> [Not a preposition, *up* is part of a phrasal verb.]

Note: In a title capitalize the first word of a hyphenated compound. As a rule, capitalize the word following the hyphen if it is a noun or a proper adjective or if it is equal in importance to the first word.

> *A Substitute for the H-Bomb* [noun]
> *The Arab-Israeli Dilemma* [proper adjective]
> "Hit-and-Run Accidents" [parallel words]

Usage varies with respect to the capitalization of words following such prefixes as *anti-, ex-, re-*, and *self-*:

> *The Anti-Apartheid Movement*
> OR
> *The Anti-apartheid Movement*

9d

Capitalize the pronoun *I* and the interjection *O* (but not *oh*, except when it begins a sentence).

David sings, "Out of the depths I cry to thee, O Lord."

9e

Capitalize the first word of every sentence (or of any other unit written as a sentence) and of directly quoted speech.

Humorists often describe their zany relatives.

Oh, really! Do such jokes have a point? Not at all.

Most first drafts, in fact, can be cut by fifty percent without losing anything organic. (Try it; it's a good exercise.)
—WILLIAM ZINSSER   [a parenthetical sentence]
COMPARE: You do this by moving the cursor under the symbol for "carriage return" (it looks like an arrow) and then pressing DELETE.   —WILLIAM ZINSSER   [a parenthetical main clause]

One thing is certain: We are still free.   [an optional capital after the colon—see also **17d**]

She often replies, "Maybe tomorrow, but not today."
OR   "Maybe tomorrow," she often replies, "but not today."
OR   "Maybe tomorrow," she often replies. "But not today."   [See also **3c**.]

The difference between "Well!" and "Well?" is a difference of tune, hence of meaning.   —J. MITCHELL MORSE

Note: For the treatment of directly quoted written material, see **16a(3)**.

9f

Avoid unnecessary capitals.

If you have a tendency to overuse capitals, review **9a** through **9e**. Also keep in mind this rule: common nouns may be preceded by the indefinite articles (*a, an*) and by such limiting modifiers as *every* or *several*.

a speech course in radio and television writing
COMPARE   Speech 245: Radio and Television Writing

every university, **several** schools of medicine
COMPARE   the University of Manitoba School of Medicine

When preceded by *a, an*, or modifiers like *every* or *several*, capitalized nouns name one or many of the members of a class:

a St. Bernard, **an** Asian, **several** Catholics.

Study the following style sheet:

Style Sheet for Capitalization

CAPITALS	NO CAPITALS
Dr. Freda E. Watts	every doctor, my doctor
the War of 1812	a space war in 1999
English, Chinese, French	the language requirement
Harvard University	a university like Harvard
the U.S. Navy	a strong navy
December, Christmas	winter, holiday
the West, Westerners	to fly west, western regions
Canadian Nurses' Association	an association for Canadian nurses
Parkinson's disease	flu, asthma, leukemia
a Chihuahua, Ford trucks	a beagle, pickup trucks
two Liberal candidates	a liberal education
the Charter of Rights	a kind of charter of rights

■ **Exercise 1**   Write brief sentences correctly using each of the following words.

(1) professor (2) Professor (3) university (4) University (5) south (6) South (7) avenue (8) Avenue (9) theatre (10) Theatre

■ **Exercise 2**   Supply capitals wherever needed.

1. Trying to raise my grade average in both english and history, i spent my thanksgiving holidays reading articles on

recently proposed amendments to the canadian constitution.

2. The west offers grand sights for tourists: the dinosaur
trail, jasper national park, the rockies, the queen charlotte
islands, the pacific ocean.

3. At the end of her sermon on god's social justice as set forth
in the bible, she said, "we north americans really ought to
give more support to the united nations' children's fund."

4. The full title of jonathan swift's essay is "a modest proposal
for preventing the children of poor people in ireland, from
being a burden to their parents or country; and for making
them beneficial to the public."

Italics

10

Use underlining to indicate italics in accordance with customary practices. Use italics sparingly for emphasis.

In handwritten or typewritten papers, italics are indicated by underlining. Printers set underlined words in italic type.

TYPEWRITTEN   PRINTED

It was on <u>The Journal</u>.   It was on *The Journal*.

10a

Titles of separate publications (books, magazines, newspapers, pamphlets, long musical works) and titles of plays, films, radio and television programs, cassettes and software programs, and long poems are underlined (italicized).

As you study the following examples, note that punctuation which is a part of the title is underlined (italicized).

BOOKS   *Where Are the Children?*
                         A Caribbean Mystery
MAGAZINES   *Saturday Night*
                         The Atlantic OR the *Atlantic*

NEWSPAPERS	the *Ottawa Citizen* OR the Ottawa *Citizen*
	Le Devoir
MUSICAL WORKS	*Moonlight Sonata*
	Verdi's *Aida*
PLAYS, FILMS	*Saltwater Moon*
	My American Cousin
SOFTWARE PROGRAMS	*The Caret Patch*
	WordStar

Occasionally quotation marks are used for titles of separate publications and of radio and television programs. The usual practice, however, is to reserve quotation marks for titles of the individual parts of longer works (such as short stories, essays, songs, short poems) and for titles of episodes of a radio or television series. See **16b**.

> "Can Anything Be Done?" is the most thought-provoking section of David Burnham's *The Rise of the Computer State*.
>
> Jane Alexander starred in "Testament" on *American Playhouse*.

Exceptions: Neither italics nor quotation marks are used in references to the Bible and its parts or to legal documents.

> The Bible begins with the Book of Genesis.
>
> How many Canadians have actually read the Charter of Rights and Freedoms?

10b

Foreign words and phrases are usually underlined (italicized) in the context of an English sentence.

> The maxim of the French Revolution still echoes in our ears: *liberté, egalité, fraternité*.   —MORTIMER J. ADLER
>
> The beluga whale (*Delphinapterus leucas*) is an endangered species in the St. Lawrence River region.

Countless words borrowed from other languages are a part of the English vocabulary and are therefore not italicized:

amigo (Spanish)   karate (Japanese)   shalom (Hebrew)
blasé (French)   pizza (Italian)   non sequitur (Latin)

Dictionaries that label certain words and phrases as foreign are fairly dependable guides to the writer in doubt about the use of italics. The labels, however, are not always up to date, and writers must depend on their own judgment after considering current practices.

10c

Names of specific ships, aircraft, satellites, and spacecraft as well as works of art are underlined (italicized).

H.M.C.S. *Halifax*   the space shuttle *Challenger*
Michelangelo's *Pietà*   Tom Thomson's *Tea Lake Dam*

Names of trains and names of a general class or a trademark are not italicized: Royal Hudson, a Boeing 767, CF-18s, Anik, ICBMs.

10d

Words, letters, or figures spoken of as such or used as illustrations are usually underlined (italicized).

In no other language could a foreigner be tricked into pronouncing *manslaughter* as *man's laughter*.   —MARIO PEI

The letters *qu* replaced *cw* in such words as *queen*, *quoth*, and *quick*.   —CHARLES C. FRIES

The first *3* and the final *0* of the serial number are barely legible.

10e

Use underlining (italics) sparingly for emphasis. Do not underline the title of your own paper.

Writers occasionally use italics to show stress, especially in dialogue, or to emphasize the meaning of a word.

> When he sees the child dragging a rotten tomato on a string, Bill Cosby asks, "What *are* you doing?"
>
> If they take offence, then that's *their* problem.
>
> No one can imagine a *systematic* conversation.
>
> —JACQUES BARZUN

Overuse of italics for emphasis (like overuse of the exclamation point) defeats its own purpose. If you overuse italics, study Section **29**. When you are tempted to underline, try substituting a more precise or forceful word.

A title is not italicized when it stands at the head of a book or article. Accordingly, the title at the head of your paper (unless it is the title of a book or it includes the title of a book) should not be underlined. See also **8b(4)**.

■ **Exercise**   Underline all words in the following sentences that should be italicized.

1. While waiting for the doctor, I thumbed through an old issue of Maclean's and scanned an article called "Canadians Who Made a Difference."
2. On the Queen Mary from New York to London, Eleanor said she was so bored that she read all three books of Dante's The Divine Comedy!
3. Spelling errors involving the substitution of d for t in such words as partner and pretty reflect a tendency in pronunciation.
4. In Paris my young cousin attended a performance of Mozart's opera The Magic Flute, which she characterized in her letter as très magnifique.
5. Michelangelo's Battle of the Centaurs and his Madonna of the Steps are among the world's finest sculptures.

Abbreviations, Acronyms, and Numbers

11

Use abbreviations only when appropriate; at first use, spell out acronyms, and spell out numbers that can be expressed simply.

Abbreviations and figures are desirable in tables, notes, and bibliographies and in some kinds of special or technical writing. In ordinary writing, however, only certain abbreviations and figures are appropriate. All the principles in this section apply to ordinary writing, which of course includes the kind of writing often required in college.

Abbreviations

11a

In ordinary writing, use *Ms.* (or *Ms*), *Mr.*, *Mrs.*, *Dr.*, and *St.* before a proper name. Use such designations as *Jr.*, *Sr.*, *II*, and *M.D.* after a proper name.

Ms. Janet Gray   Dr. Bell   St. Boniface
[Compare "the young doctor," "the early life of the saint"]
Hal Grant, Sr.   E.R. Ames III   Alice Chow, M.D.

Abbreviations of degrees are often used without a proper name, as in "a *B.A.* in languages."

Caution: Do not use redundant titles: NOT Dr. E.T. Fulton, M.D. BUT Dr. E.T. Fulton OR E.T. Fulton, M.D.

Note: Such abbreviations as *Prof., Sen., 1st Lt.,* or *Capt.* may be used before full names or before initials and last names, but not before last names alone.

Sen. Allan J. MacEachen   Senator MacEachen
Capt. P.T. Gaines   Captain Gaines

11b

Spell out names of provinces, states, countries, continents, months, days of the week, and units of measurement.

On Sunday, October 10, we spent the night in Calgary, Alberta; the next day we flew to South America.
Slightly over a metre tall, Timmy weighs forty-two kilograms.

Exception: The Canadian Standards Association, in co-operation with Metric Commission Canada, has published guidelines for the proper format and presentation of SI units (*Système international d'unités*). The standard reference on SI style is the *Canadian Metric Practice Guide* (Rexdale, Ontario: Canadian Standards Association, 1979). According to CSA guidelines, unit *symbols* (they are not referred to as abbreviations) must be used with numerals, and the full name of the unit must be given when numbers are spelled out. SI symbols are never pluralized and are written without a period.

The lake was 8.5 km long but only a few metres deep.

You will find, however, that in newspapers, magazines, and many general-interest books the use of the full name of the unit of measurement with a numeral is still quite common.

> An acre is 4047 square metres.

11c

Spell out *Street, Avenue, Road, Park, Mount, River, Company*, and similar words used as an essential part of proper names.

> University Avenue is west of Yonge Street.
> The Ford Motor Company does not expect a strike soon.

Note: Avoid the use of & (the ampersand) except in copying official titles or names of firms. The abbreviations *Inc.* and *Ltd.* are usually omitted in ordinary writing.

> U.S. News & World Report   Noranda   [NOT Noranda, Inc.]
> Alberta & Southern Gas

11d

Spell out the words *volume, chapter,* and *page* and the names of courses of study.

> The chart is on page 46 of chapter 9.
> I registered for physical education and for child psychology.

Permissible Abbreviations

In addition to the abbreviations listed in **11a**, the following abbreviations and symbols are permissible and usually desirable.

1. *Certain words used with dates or figures:*

> 58 B.C.   A.D. 70   8:00 A.M. OR a.m.
> 21:31 EST OR E.S.T.   No. 13 OR no. 13 $4.25
> 100 km/h   37°C   CF-18s

2. *The names of certain provinces used adjectivally:*

   Charlottetown, P.E.I.   the B.C. economy

   The District of Columbia and the United States used adjectivally:

   Washington, D.C.   the U.S. Navy

3. *The names of organizations, agencies, countries, persons, or things usually referred to by their capitalized initials:*

   RCMP   CLC   UBC   CTV   CFL   U.S.S.R.
   JFK   VCRs   IQ   TV

4. *Certain common Latin expressions* (although the English term is usually spelled out in formal writing, as indicated here in brackets):

cf. [compare]	etc. [and so forth]
e.g. [for example]	i.e. [that is]
et al. [and others]	vs. OR v. [versus]

For abbreviations in bibliographies, see pages 457–60.

Acronyms

11e

Spell out the meaning of any acronym that may not be familiar to your reader when you use it for the first time.

> Then there is the Canadian International Development Agency (CIDA). Consider CIDA's budget and mandate.
> OR
> Then there is CIDA (the Canadian International Development Agency).

Your reader will probably be familiar with such terms as *NHL*, *NATO*, *sonar*, and *LSAT scores*, but perhaps not with those like *IMF*, *CUSO*, *EURATOM*.

Note: Some clipped forms—such as *info*, *rep*, *execs*, or *porn*—are avoided in formal writing. Others—such as *math*, *lab*, and *Statscan*—are generally acceptable.

■ **Exercise 1**   Strike out any form that is not appropriate in formal writing.

1. Ms. Janet Hogan; a dr. but not a saint
2. 90 km/h; on TV; in Sask. and Man.
3. on Yonge St.; on Yonge Street
4. on Aug. 15; on August 15
5. for Jr.; for John Evans, Jr.
6. before 6 A.M.; before six in the A.M.

Numbers

11f

Although usage varies, writers tend to spell out numbers that can be expressed in one word or two; they regularly use figures for other numbers.

after twenty-two years	after 124 years
only thirty dollars	only $29.99
five thousand voters	5261 voters
ten million bushels	10 402 317 bushels
over three litres	3.785 litres

Special Usage Regarding Numbers

1. *Specific time of day*

    2 A.M. OR 2:00 A.M. OR two o'clock in the morning
    4:30 P.M. OR half-past four in the afternoon

2. *Dates*

> May 7, 1989   OR   7 May 1989   [NOT May 7th, 1989]
> May sixth   OR   the sixth of May   OR   May 6   OR   May 6th
> the nineties   OR   the 1990's   OR   the 1990s
> the twentieth century
> in 1900   in 1981–1982   OR   in 1981–82
> from 1980 to 1985   OR   1980–1985   OR   1980–85
> [NOT from 1980–1985, from 1980–85]

3. *Addresses*

> Apartment 301, 444 Vienna Crescent, North Vancouver, British Columbia V7M 1P2
> [OR Apt. 301, 444 Vienna Cres., North Vancouver, BC V7M 1P2]

> Apartment 3C, 8 Redwood Drive, Prescott, Arizona 86301, United States of America
> [OR Apt. 3c, 8 Redwood Dr., Prescott, AZ 86301, USA]

> 16 Tenth Street   P.O. Box 247   R.R. 2
> 350 West 114 Street   OR   350 West 114th Street

4. *Identification numbers*

> Channel 13   Highway 99   Henry VIII   Room 10

5. *Pages and divisions of books and plays*

> page 30   chapter 6   part 4
> in act 3, scene 2   OR   in Act III, Scene ii

6. *Decimals and percentages*

> a 2.5 average $12\frac{1}{2}$ percent
> 0.907 t   [t is the symbol for *tonne*]

7. *Numbers in series and statistics*

> two cows, five pigs, and forty-two chickens
> 37.5 m long, 15 m wide, and 3.6 m deep
> 125 feet long, 50 feet wide, and 12 feet deep

scores of 17 to 13 and 42 to 3   OR   scores of 17–13 and
42–3

The members voted 99 to 23 against the motion.

8. *Large round numbers*

four billion dollars   OR $4 billion   OR $4 000 000 000
[Figures are used for emphasis only.]

12 500 000   OR   12.5 million

9. *Numbers beginning sentences*

Six percent of the students voted.   [NOT 6 percent of the
students voted.]

10. *Repeated numbers (in legal or commercial writing)*

The agent's fee will not exceed one hundred (100) dollars.
OR
The agent's fee will not exceed one hundred dollars ($100).

■ **Exercise 2**   Using desirable abbreviations and figures, change
each item to an acceptable shortened form.

1. on the fifteenth of June
2. Ernest Threadgill, a doctor
3. thirty million dollars
4. Brenda Szeto, a certified public accountant
5. one o'clock in the afternoon
6. by the first of December, 1985
7. at the bottom of the fifteenth page
8. four hundred years before Christ
9. in the second scene of the first act
10. a five-year plan (from 1990 to 1995)

PUNCTUATION

The Comma

12

Learn to apply the basic principles governing comma usage.

Just as pauses and variations in voice pitch help to convey the meaning of spoken sentences, commas help to clarify the meaning of written sentences.

> When the lightning struck, James Harvey fainted.
> When the lightning struck James, Harvey fainted.

Notice how the commas below contribute to ease in reading:

> All ball games feature hitting and socking, chopping and slicing, smashing, slamming, stroking, and whacking, but only in football are these blows diverted from the ball to the opponent.   —WRIGHT MORRIS

The use of the comma depends primarily on the structure of the sentence. If you understand sentence structure (see Section **1**) and if you study the rules and examples in this section, you can learn to follow the usual practices of the best modern writers. According to the four basic principles that follow, commas

a precede co-ordinating conjunctions when they link main clauses;

b follow introductory adverb clauses and, often, introductory phrases;
c separate items in a series (including co-ordinate adjectives);
d set off non-restrictive and other parenthetical elements.

Before Co-ordinating Conjunctions between Main Clauses

12a

A comma ordinarily precedes a co-ordinating conjunction that links main clauses.

```
                        ⎧ and ⎫
                        ⎪ but ⎪
   MAIN CLAUSE          ⎪ for ⎪     MAIN CLAUSE
   Subject + predicate, ⎨ or  ⎬     subject + predicate.
                        ⎪ nor ⎪
                        ⎪ so  ⎪
                        ⎩ yet ⎭
```

We are here on the planet only once, and we might as well get a feel for the place. —ANNIE DILLARD

The house was dying, but someone had been hastening its death. —JOHN LE CARRÉ

They are hopeless and humble, so he loves them.
—E.M. FORSTER

The rule also applies to co-ordinating conjunctions that link the main clauses of a compound-complex sentence:

Although I do have talent, I have not yet painted a perfect scene , nor do I ever expect to do so , for I can never get on the canvas exactly what I see in my mind.   [three main clauses and two subordinate clauses]

Especially when the clauses are short, the comma may be omitted before *and* or *or* (but seldom before *but, for, nor, so, yet*).

The next night the wind shifted and the thaw began.
—RACHEL CARSON

Sometimes, especially when the second main clause reveals a contrast or when one main clause contains commas, a semicolon is used instead of the usual comma.

It is one thing to read in a textbook that the footprints of an arctic wolf measure six inches in diameter ; but it is quite another thing to see them laid out in all their bald immensity.   —FARLEY MOWAT

We do not , most of us , choose to die ; nor do we choose the time or conditions of our death.   —JOSEPH EPSTEIN

Historically, French Canadians have not really believed in democracy for themselves ; and English Canadians have not really wanted it for others.   —PIERRE ELLIOTT TRUDEAU

Note: As a rule, do not use a comma before a co-ordinating conjunction that links parts of a compound predicate.

Colonel Cathcart had courage and never hesitated to volunteer his men for any target available.   —JOSEPH HELLER
[compound predicate—no comma before *and*]

Only occasionally do writers use a comma to emphasize a distinction between the parts of the predicate, as in E.M. Forster's "Artists always seek a new technique , and will continue to do so as long as their work excites them."

■ **Exercise 1**   Using the punctuation pattern of **12a**, link the sentences in the following items with an appropriate *and, but, or, nor, for, so*, or *yet*.

EXAMPLE
We cannot win the battle. We cannot afford to lose it.
We cannot win the battle , nor can we afford to lose it.

1. A scandal arises. Another judicial inquiry is convened.
2. The new leash law did not put all dogs behind bars. It did not make the streets safe for cats.
3. Motorists may admit their guilt and pay a fine immediately. They may choose to appear in court within thirty days and plead not guilty.
4. They decided not to take a vacation. They needed the money to remodel their kitchen.
5. The band leader can sing and dance and whistle. She cannot play the trombone.

■ **Exercise 2**   Follow rule **12a** as you insert commas before connectives linking main clauses in these sentences. (Remember that not all co-ordinating conjunctions link main clauses and that *but, for, so*, and *yet* do not always function as co-ordinating conjunctions.)

1. The students had finished taking the various tests and answering the long questionnaires and they had gone to lunch.
2. There are now special shoes for someone to fill for Jan has resigned and is going to business school.
3. I decided to withdraw from that eight-o'clock class so that I could sleep later but I plan to enrol again for the same class in January.
4. We had seen the stage play and the movie and the University Players' performance was the best of all.
5. Everyone in our group was invited to the party but Gary and Irene decided to go to the hockey game.

12b   , /

*After Adverb Clauses
and Introductory Phrases*

12b

A comma usually follows adverb clauses that precede main clauses. A comma often follows introductory phrases.

(1) Adverb clauses before main clauses

> ADVERB CLAUSE , MAIN CLAUSE .

When you write, you make a sound in the reader's head.
> —RUSSELL BAKER

If thought corrupts language, language can also corrupt thought. —GEORGE ORWELL

While writing his last novel, James recognized and faced his solitude. —LEON EDEL [an elliptical adverb clause—compare "While he was writing. . . . "]

The Meech Lake Accord is a simple document, but if it is ratified, life in Canada may become complicated. [adverb clause preceding the second main clause]

A writer may omit the comma after an introductory adverb clause, especially when the clause is short, if the omission does not make for difficult reading.

> When we talk to people we always mean something quite different from what we say. —ANTHONY BURGESS

Note: When the adverb clause follows the main clause, there is usually no need for a comma. Adverb clauses in this position, however, may be preceded by a comma if they are loosely connected with the rest of the sentence.

> Henry is now in good health, although he has been an invalid most of his life.

(2) Introductory phrases before subjects of verbs

> INTRODUCTORY PHRASE, SUBJECT + PREDICATE.

Prepositional phrases:

> In the next decade, the greenhouse effect will begin to influence the global climate.

The comma is often omitted after introductory prepositional phrases when no misreading would result:

> In 1980 Terry Fox began his Marathon of Hope. In 1981 he died of cancer.

> After months of listening for some meagre clue he suddenly began to talk in torrents. —ARTHUR L. KOPIT

In the next two examples the commas are needed to prevent misreading:

> Because of this, beauty differs radically from truth and goodness in one very important aspect. —MORTIMER J. ADLER

> In a country with a frontier tradition and a deep-rooted enthusiasm for hunting and target shooting, firearms have long been part of the national scene. —TREVOR ARMBRISTER

Other types of phrases:

> Having attempted nothing, I had no sense of my limitations; having dared nothing, I knew no boundaries to my courage. —TREVANIAN [participial phrases before both main clauses]

> Even more important, we now have a workable plan. [transitional expression—see the list on page 37.]

> All things considered, Third World debt is a serious threat to the global economy. [absolute phrase—see also **12d(3)**]

Note: A comma also follows an introductory interjection or an introductory *yes* or *no*:

Well, move the ball or move the body. —ALLEN JACKSON

Yes, I know that every vote counts. No, I didn't vote.

Caution: Do not use a comma after phrases that begin inverted sentences like these. (See also **29f**.)

With prosperity came trouble. —MALACHI MARTIN

Of far greater concern than censorship of ''bad'' words is censorship of ideas. —DONNA WOOLFOLK CROSS

■ **Exercise 3**   Decide whether to use a comma after adverb clauses or after phrases that begin the following sentences. Put a check mark after any sentence in which a comma would be incorrect.

1. If you have been thinking of making a fortune by working for someone else forget it.
2. As far as I know the flight will arrive on schedule.
3. At the same time I recognize that they had good intentions.
4. Before noon the voting lines were two blocks long.
5. Trying to pass three gravel trucks going downhill the driver lost control of his car.
6. Learning to think logically is the concern of almost every university student.
7. With about as much sensitivity as a brick wall the members of the government ignored the petition from the homeless.
8. Under the back seat is an extra heater as well as some storage space.
9. The election far from over the media began to announce the results.
10. When you can help someone less fortunate than yourself.

Between Items in a Series

12c

Commas separate items in a series (including co-ordinate adjectives).

Consisting of three or more items, a series is a succession of parallel elements. See Section **26**. The punctuation of a series depends on its form:

> The air was *raw, dank,* and *grey.* [**a, b,** and **c**—a preferred comma before *and*]
>
> The air was *raw, dank* and *grey.* [**a, b** and **c**—an acceptable omission of comma before *and* when there is no danger of misreading]
>
> The air was *raw, dank, grey.* [**a, b, c**]
>
> The air was *raw* and *dank* and *grey.* [**a** and **b** and **c**]

(1) Words, phrases, and clauses in a series

> Student reactions were swift and intense: delight, disbelief, fear, horror, anticipation. —ALVIN TOFFLER
>
> Garfield lives. His likeness looks up from beach thongs, out from coffee mugs, down from wall posters and across the room from the morning newspaper. —HOLLY G. MILLER
>
> He reported that shoppers fumed, babies wailed, clerks looked flustered, and so on.
>
> Life at the top is financially rewarding, spiritually draining, physically exhausting, and short. —PETER C. NEWMAN

Exceptions: If items in a series contain internal commas, the semicolon is used instead of commas for clarity: see **14b**. For special emphasis, commas are sometimes used even when all the items in a series are linked by co-ordinating conjunctions.

> We cannot put it off for a month, or a week, or even a day.

(2) Co-ordinate adjectives

Adjectives are co-ordinate when they modify the same noun (or nominal). Use a comma between co-ordinate adjectives not linked by a co-ordinating conjunction:

It is a waiting , silent , limp room. —EUDORA WELTY [*Waiting, silent*, and *limp* all modify *room*. Compare "It is a silent , limp waiting room."]

They are young , alert social workers. [*Young* and *alert* modify the word group *social workers*. Compare "They are young , social , alert workers."]

It was a solid , red-brick house with an eye-catching , sky-blue door. It stood at the end of a short , quiet street in a sleepy suburb lying in a rich , green valley.

■ **Exercise 4**   Using commas as needed, supply co-ordinate adjectives to modify any six of the following twelve word groups.

EXAMPLE
metric system   *the familiar, sensible metric system*

1. apple pie
2. social climbers
3. electronic music
4. pop art
5. minimum wage
6. traveller's cheques
7. snowy owl
8. rhetorical question
9. apartment buildings
10. major oil companies
11. blue cheese
12. secondary school

With Parenthetical and Miscellaneous Elements

12d

Commas set off non-restrictive and other parenthetical elements as well as contrasted elements, items in dates, and so on.

To set off a word or a word group with commas, use two commas unless the element is placed at the beginning of the sentence or at the end. (Expressions that come at the beginning of a sentence are treated by both **12b** and **12d**.)

"History is a pact ," *as Edmund Burke observed* , "between the dead, the living, and the yet unborn."

As Edmund Burke observed, "history is a pact between the dead, the living, and the yet unborn."

"History is a pact between the dead, the living, and the yet unborn," *as Edmund Burke observed.*

Caution: When two commas are needed to set off an element, do not forget one of the commas.

CONFUSING	An experienced driver generally speaking, does not fear the open road.
CLEAR	An experienced driver, generally speaking, does not fear the open road.

(1) Non-restrictive clauses or phrases and non-restrictive appositives are set off by commas. Restrictive elements are not set off.

ADJECTIVE CLAUSES OR PHRASES

Adjective clauses or phrases are non-restrictive when they describe (rather than limit the meaning of) the noun or pronoun they modify: set off by commas, they are non-essential parenthetical elements that may be omitted. Restrictive clauses or phrases are limiting (rather than descriptive) adjectivals: not set off by commas, they identify the noun or pronoun they modify by telling *which one* (or *ones*) and are essential elements that may not be omitted.

As you study the following examples, read each sentence aloud and notice not only meaning but also your pauses and intonation.

NON-RESTRICTIVE	RESTRICTIVE OR ESSENTIAL
Clauses:	
My mother**, who listened to his excuses,** smiled knowingly.	Any mother **who listened to such excuses** would smile knowingly.

We will explore Peggy's Cove, **which is the most photographed spot in Nova Scotia**.	We will explore a cove **that is the most photographed spot in Nova Scotia**.

Phrases:

In July these mountains, **covered with snow,** seem unreal.	In July mountains **covered with snow** seem unreal.
The old Renault, **glistening in the rain,** looked brand new.	An old car **glistening in the rain** looked brand new.
Such noise, **too loud for human ears,** can cause deafness.	A noise **too loud for human ears** can cause deafness.

Note: Although some writers prefer to use *that* at the beginning of restrictive clauses, *which* is also acceptable.

Sometimes only the omission or the use of commas indicates whether an adjectival is non-restrictive or restrictive and thus conveys the exact meaning intended by the writer.

The party opposed taxes, **which would be a burden to working Canadians**.   [*Non-restrictive*: the party opposed levying taxes of any kind, all of which would be a burden to working Canadians.]

The party opposed taxes **which would be a burden to working Canadians**.   [*Restrictive*: the party opposed levying taxes of a certain kind.]

She spent months teaching the children, **who were unable to read**.   [*Non-restrictive*: she taught all the children to read; they were all unable to do so.]

She spent months teaching the children **who were unable to read**.   [*Restrictive*: some of the children were unable to read; she taught only those children.]

APPOSITIVES

Appositives are either non-restrictive (set off by commas) or restrictive (not set off by commas). A non-restrictive appositive supplies additional but non-essential details about the noun or pronoun to which it refers. A restrictive appositive limits the meaning of the noun or pronoun to which it refers by pointing out *which one* (or *ones*).

NON-RESTRICTIVE	RESTRICTIVE OR ESSENTIAL
Even Paul Underhill **, my very best friend ,** let me down.	Even my friend **Paul Underhill** let me down.
Voyager photographed Saturn **, the ringed planet**.	*Voyager* photographed the planet **Saturn**.

Abbreviations after names are treated like non-restrictive appositives:

Was the letter from Frances Evans **, Ph.D. ,** or from F.H. Evans **, M.D.**?

■ **Exercise 5**   Use commas to set off non-restrictive adjective clauses or phrases and non-restrictive appositives in the following sentences. Put a check mark after any sentence that needs no commas.

1. I will interview Mary Smith who manages the bank.
2. I will interview the Mary Smith who manages the bank.
3. Vanessa Berry sitting near the window saw the accident.
4. Coho salmon served with bannock bread is my favourite meal.
5. Few people around here have ever heard of my hometown a little place called Marystown.
6. All players who broke the rules had to sit on the bench.
7. The word *malapropism* is derived from the name of a character in Sheridan's *The Rivals* a Mrs. Malaprop.

8. The coach who is chewing gum and clapping his hands is Teddy.
9. The telephone which was invented in 1876 is now a household necessity.
10. Martin Luther King Jr. and Archbishop Desmond Tutu won Nobel Peace Prizes for their efforts to promote non-violent social change.

(2) **Contrasted elements, geographical names, and most items in dates and addresses are set off by commas.**

CONTRASTED ELEMENTS

Racing is supposed to be a test of skill**, not a dice game with death**. —SONNY KLEINFIELD

His phrases dribbled off**, but not his memories**.
—JAMES A. MICHENER

Human beings**, unlike oysters,** frequently reveal their emotions. —GEORGE F. WILL

Note: Usage is divided regarding the placement of a comma before *but* in such structures as the following:

Other citizens who disagree with me base their disagreement not on facts different from the ones I know, but on a different set of values. —RENÉ DUBOS

Today the Black Hills are being invaded again, not for gold but for uranium. —PETER MATTHIESSEN

GEOGRAPHICAL NAMES, ITEMS IN DATES AND ADDRESSES

Geneva**,** Switzerland**,** is the site for the next round of disarmament talks.

The letter was addressed to Ms. J.N. Dang**,** Vancouver**,** BC V6T 1W5.

Leslie applied for the job in October**,** 1988**,** and accepted it on Friday**,** March 5**,** 1989.
OR

Leslie applied for the job in October 1988 and accepted it on Friday, 5 March 1989.
[Note that commas may be omitted when the day of the month is not given or when the day of the month precedes rather than follows the month.]

■ **Exercise 6**   Insert commas where needed in the following sentences.

1. Those are wolves not dogs.
2. The newspaper's address is 444 Front Street West Toronto Ontario M5V 2S9.
3. On 30 April 1987 Canada's first ministers met at Meech Lake Quebec to amend the Constitution.
4. Norman Bethune was born in Gravenhurst Ontario on March 3 not on March 23.
5. According to the February 1989 issue of *Report on Business*, a wave of corporate mergers will sweep the global economy in the 1990s.

(3) Parenthetical words, phrases, or clauses (inserted expressions), mild interjections, words in direct address, and absolute phrases are set off by commas.

PARENTHETICAL EXPRESSIONS

Language, **then,** sets the tone of our society.
—EDWIN NEWMAN

To be sure, beauty is a form of power.   —SUSAN SONTAG

Immanuel Kant suggested, **in the eighteenth century,** that tidal friction slowed the rotation of the Earth.   —ISAAC ASIMOV

It's healthy to admire, **I suppose,** but destructive to idolize.   —TIM WHITAKER

"The trouble with ministers," **said Mrs. Emerson,** "is that they're not women."   —ANNE TYLER   [See also **16a(2).**]

> Guard your enthusiasms, **however frail they may be**.
> —ARDIS WHITMAN [parenthetical clause]

> The Age of Television has dawned in China, **a generation later than in the West**. —LINDA MATHEWS [appended element]

When they cause little or no pause in reading, expressions such as *also, too, of course, perhaps, at least, therefore,* and *likewise* are frequently not set off by commas.

> The times **also** have changed in ways that soften the rhetoric. —HENRY FAIRLIE

> Study circles are **therefore** the most pervasive method of bringing education to Swedes of all ages and walks of life.
> —WILLIAM L. ABBOTT

MILD INTERJECTIONS AND WORDS USED IN DIRECT ADDRESS

> **Ah**, that's my idea of a good meal. [interjection]

> Now is the time, **animal lovers**, to protest. [direct address]

ABSOLUTE PHRASES

> **His temper being what it is**, I don't want a confrontation.

> He was thumping at a book, **his voice growing louder and louder**. —JOYCE CAROL OATES

12e

Occasionally a comma (although not required by any of the major principles already discussed) may be needed to prevent misreading.

Without commas the following sentences would confuse the reader, if only temporarily.

> Still, water must be transported to dry areas.
> The day before, I had talked with her on the phone.

In 1986, 19.5 million Canadians were in the work force.

Those who can, pay and forego consumption of other essential goods.   —ERIK P. ECKHOLM

The earth breathes, in a certain sense.   —LEWIS THOMAS

■ **Exercise 7**   Commas have been deleted from the following sentences. Insert commas where they are needed. Prepare to explain the reason for each comma used. Also prepare to point out where optional commas might be placed as a matter of stylistic preference.

1. When I was two we moved to the Gold Coast but by then it was known as Ghana.
2. It was a major uprising not a minor incident; there was civil disobedience anarchy violence.
3. My guess is as the Soviet Union changes cultural exchange programs will flourish.
4. But alas I do not control airline schedules and that I regret is the story of my life—always delayed never on time.
5. If all laws fail try drafting new ones for situations that defy resolution.
6. To commemorate the bicentennial of the revolution a crowd of people gathered in the streets on the night of July 14 1989.
7. Living in Canada's North is very expensive some families having been known to spend two-thirds of their income on accommodation.
8. The chess player's concentration at the tournament never flagged nor did it disappear at the press conference following his winning match.
9. "I wanted to see the Governor General's residence at Rideau Hall" said the young tourist his eyes shining with genuine interest.
10. Canada and the United States have a long-standing relationship harmonious and friendly much of the time but tense when it comes to negotiating disputes over trade.

■ **Exercise 8**   For humorous effect, the writer of the following paragraph deliberately omits commas that can be justified by rules

12a, b, or **d**. Be prepared for a discussion of the paragraph. Where could commas be inserted to contribute to ease in reading?

The commas are the most useful and usable of all the stops. It is highly important to put them in place as you go along. If you try to come back after doing a paragraph and stick them in the various spots that tempt you you will discover that they tend to swarm like minnows into all sorts of crevices whose existence you hadn't realized and before you know it the whole long sentence becomes immobilized and lashed up squirming in commas. Better to use them sparingly, and with affection, precisely when the need for each one arises, nicely, by itself.

—LEWIS THOMAS, *The Medusa and the Snail*

Superfluous Commas

13

Do not use superfluous commas.

Unnecessary or misplaced commas are false or awkward signals that may confuse the reader. If you tend to use too many commas, remember that although the comma ordinarily signals a pause, not every pause calls for a comma. As you read each sentence in the following paragraph aloud, you may pause naturally at places other than those marked by a period, but no commas are necessary.

> Springboard divers routinely execute manoeuvres in which their body rotates in space. The basic manoeuvres are the somersault and the twist. In the somersault the body rotates head over heels as if the athlete were rotating about an axis extending from his left side to his right side through his waist. In the twist the body spins or pirouettes in midair as if the athlete were rotating about an axis extending from his head to his toes.
>
> —CLIFF FROHLICH, "The Physics of Somersaulting and Twisting"

To avoid using unnecessary commas, first review Section **12** and then study and observe the following rules.

13a

Do not use a comma to separate the subject from its verb or the verb from its object.

The circled commas should be omitted:

> Many nations with low growth rates⊙ cannot sustain high birth rates. [needless separation of subject and verb]
> The man said⊙ that the old laws were antiquated. [needless separation of verb and object (a noun clause)]

13b

Do not misuse a comma before or after a co-ordinating conjunction. See **12a.**

The circled commas should be omitted:

> The facts were selected⊙ and organized with care.
> The film captured our attention, but⊙ others in the audience simply left before the end.

13c

Do not use commas to set off words and short phrases (especially introductory ones) that are not parenthetical or that are very slightly so.

The circled commas should be omitted:

> Teresa Stratas made her opera debut⊙ in *La Bohème*⊙ in 1960.
> Maybe⊙ the battery cables needed replacing.

13d

Do not use commas to set off restrictive (necessary) clauses, restrictive phrases, and restrictive appositives.

The circled commas should be omitted:

> Everyone⊙ who smokes cigarettes⊙ risks losing about ten
> years of life. [restrictive clause: see **12d(1)**]
> For years she has not eaten anything⊙ seasoned with onions
> or garlic. [restrictive phrase: see **12d(1)**]
> The word⊙ *nope*⊙ is a colloquial substitute for *no*. [restrictive appositive: see **12d(1)**]

13e

Do not use a comma before the first item or after the last item of a series (including a series of co-ordinate adjectives).

The circled commas should be omitted:

> Field trips were required in a few courses, such as⊙ botany,
> geology, and sociology.
> The company hires talented, smart, ambitious⊙ women.

■ **Exercise 1**   Study the structure of the following sentence; then answer the question that follows by giving a specific rule number (such as **13a, 13d**) for each item. Be prepared to explain your answers in class.

> Now when you say "newly rich" you picture a middle-aged and corpulent man who has a tendency to remove his collar at formal dinners and is in perpetual hot water with his ambitious wife and her titled friends.   —F. SCOTT FITZGERALD

Why is there no comma after (1) *Now*, (2) *say*, (3) *middle-aged*, (4) *man*, (5) *collar*, (6) *dinners*, or (7) *wife*?

■ **Exercise 2**   Change the structure and the punctuation of the following sentences according to the pattern of the examples.

EXAMPLE

A motorcyclist saw our flashing lights **,** and he stopped to offer aid. [an appropriate comma: see **12a**]

A motorcyclist saw our flashing lights and stopped to offer aid. [second main clause reduced to part of a compound predicate—comma no longer needed]

1. The hail stripped leaves from trees, and it pounded early gardens.
2. Some science fiction presents newly discovered facts, and it predicts the future accurately.
3. Rob likes the work, and he may make a career of it.

EXAMPLE

If any students destroyed public property **,** they were expelled. [an appropriate comma: see **12b**]

Any students who destroyed public property were expelled. [introductory adverb clause converted to restrictive clause—comma no longer needed]

4. When people lead rather than demand, they often get good results.
5. If a boy is willing to work, he can get a job here.

■ **Exercise 3**   In the following paragraph some of the commas are needed and some are superfluous. Circle all unnecessary commas. Prepare to explain (see Section **12**) each comma that you allow to stand.

¹There are, at least, three kinds of fishermen. ²First, is the boat owner. ³He usually gets up at 4 a.m., grabs a thermos of coffee, picks up his favourite, fishing buddy, and goes to the exact spot, where the trout or bass are striking. ⁴Fishing for a certain kind of fish, is his specialty, and he, generally, gets exactly the kind he goes after. ⁵Next is the person, who fishes with friends on a crowded pier, jetty, or barge. ⁶He expects the fish to come to him, and is happy to catch anything, fit to eat,

such as, perch or carp. [7]The third type is the loner, the one who fishes in some out-of-the-way place on the bank, by himself. [8]After he anchors one, great big, wad of bait on his hook, he throws his line out, and props up his pole, so that he doesn't have to hold it. [9]Then, he leans back, watches the cloud formations, or lazily examines a leaf or flower. [10]He, sometimes, dozes. [11]Also, he daydreams. [12]Lounging there with a kind of half smile on his face, he enjoys his solitude. [13]His fishing pole is merely an excuse for being there. [14]He forgets to watch his line, and, to rebait his hook.

The Semicolon

14

Use the semicolon between main clauses not linked by a co-ordinating conjunction and between co-ordinate elements containing commas.

Having the force of a co-ordinator, the semicolon is used chiefly between main clauses that are closely related. Compare the following structures.

> Some philosophers offer practical wisdom. Others do not. I prefer to study the former.   [three simple sentences]
> Some philosophers offer practical wisdom; others do not. I prefer to study the former.   [a semicolon linking the more closely related ideas]

If you can distinguish between main and subordinate clauses and between phrases and clauses (see **1d** and **1e**), you should have little trouble using the semicolon. As you study the rules in this section, notice that the semicolon is used only between closely related co-ordinate elements.

14a

Use the semicolon between two main clauses not linked by a co-ordinating conjunction. See also **12a**.

The co-ordinating conjunctions are *and, but, for, or, nor, so, yet.*

> MAIN CLAUSE   MAIN CLAUSE
> Subject + predicate ; subject + predicate.

No person is born arrogant; arrogance must be taught.
—CLARA M. DOBAY

Small mammals tick fast, burn rapidly, and live for a short time; large mammals live long at a stately pace.
—STEPHEN JAY GOULD

Rule **14a** also applies in compound-complex sentences:

If the new business is a success, I'll take my share of the profits; if it isn't, I think I'll leave the country.

COMPARE If the new business is a success, I'll take my share of the profits. If it isn't, I think I'll leave the country.

Keep in mind that *however, therefore, for example, on the contrary*, and so on (see the list of conjunctive adverbs and transitional expressions on page 37) are not co-ordinating conjunctions. Often appearing at the beginning of a sentence, such adverbials frequently serve as transitional devices between sentences: see **32b(4)**. When placed between main clauses, they are preceded by the semicolon: see **3b**.

At the 1988 Olympics, sprinter Ben Johnson won a gold medal; however, he lost it when he failed a drug test.

COMPARE At the 1988 Olympics, sprinter Ben Johnson won a gold medal. However, he lost it when he failed a drug test.

> For years he planned to sail around the world; therefore, he
> worked hard to develop his sailing skills.
>
> COMPARE   For years he planned to sail around the world.
>   Therefore, he worked hard to develop his sailing
>   skills.

The comma after a conjunctive adverb or transitional expression is often omitted when the adverbial is not considered
parenthetical or when the comma is not needed to prevent
misreading.

> Glenn Gould was unusual among Canadian musicians; indeed
> in many ways he was in a class all his own.

Sometimes, a semicolon (instead of the usual comma)
precedes a co-ordinating conjunction when the writer wishes
to make a sharp division between the two main clauses. See
also **12a**, page 124.

> The female bees feed these lazy drones for a while; but they
> let them starve to death after the mating of the queen bee.

Note: Occasionally, a comma separates short, very closely
related main clauses.

> We are strengthened by equality, we are weakened by it; we
> celebrate it, we repudiate it.   —THOMAS GRIFFITH   [a semi-
> colon used between pairs of main clauses separated by
> commas]

When the second main clause explains or amplifies the first,
a colon may be used between main clauses. See **17d**, page
167.

Caution: Do not overwork the semicolon: see **14c**. Often it
is better to revise compound sentences according to the
principles of subordination: see **24**.

■ **Exercise 1**   Use semicolons where needed to eliminate errors
in punctuation.

1. An engagement is not a marriage a family quarrel is not a broken home.
2. All members of my family save things they will never use, for example, my sister saves old calendars and bent or rusty nails.
3. Many nations now have heterogeneous populations, in Canada for instance, many new citizens come from Asia, Africa, and Europe.
4. He took a course in the art of self-defence, later, during a class demonstration, he broke his wrist.
5. The motor in my car blew up, as a result, I had to take the bus for a month.

14b

Use the semicolon to separate a series of items which themselves contain commas.

> At our benefit flea market we sold cracked plates, cups, vases; rusty garden tools; discarded, rickety TV tables; and half-used tubes of lipstick.

■ **Exercise 2** Substitute a semicolon for any comma that could result in misreading.

1. Prepared for a lively argument, the three debaters on the stage were Bob White, prominent labour leader, June Callwood, writer and social activist, and Pat Carney, former minister of trade.
2. On the talk shows are entertainers, such as actors or comedians, experts from various fields, such as educators or religious leaders, and authors of bestselling books.

14c

Do not use a semicolon between parts of unequal grammatical rank.

Not between a clause and a phrase:

NOT   Along came Gaetan; the dormitory clown.
BUT   Along came Gaetan, the dormitory clown.   [appositive phrase]

NOT   We took a detour; the reason being that the bridge was under construction.
BUT   We took a detour, the reason being that the bridge was under construction.   [absolute phrase]

NOT   Lucy has three topics of conversation; her courses, her career, and her travels.
BUT   Lucy has three topics of conversation: her courses, her career, and her travels.   [noun phrases]

Not between a main clause and a subordinate clause:

NOT   If this report is true; then we should act now.
BUT   If this report is true, then we should act now.   [introductory adverb clause]

NOT   We heard about the final decision; which really surprised us.
BUT   We heard about the final decision, which really surprised us.   [adjective clause]

NOT   The truck needed repairs; although it would still run.
BUT   The truck needed repairs, although it would still run.   [adverb clause]

■ **Exercise 3**   Find the semicolons used between parts of unequal rank and substitute a correct mark of punctuation. Do not change properly placed semicolons.

1. Don went jogging one afternoon; never returning; then he was numbered among the tens of thousands who disappear every year.
2. Although the educational TV channel is sometimes a bore; at least tedious commercials do not interrupt the programs.
3. I have two main pet peeves; jokes that are pointless and animals that get on furniture.

4. Many times I've pushed the up button; after I've waited for as long as five minutes; the doors of two elevators roll open at once.

5. The tormented bull lowered his head in readiness for another charge; the one-sided contest not being over yet.

■ **Exercise 4**　Compose four sentences to illustrate various uses of the semicolon.

General Exercise on the Comma and the Semicolon

■ **Exercise 5**　Study the following examples, which illustrate rules in Sections **12** and **14**. Using these examples as guides, punctuate sentences 1–10 on the following page appropriately.

12a　Pat poured chlorine into the crucible, for he had not read the warning in his lab manual.

12b　Since Pat had not read the warning in his lab manual, he poured chlorine into the crucible.

12c　Pat did not read the lab manual, observe the warning, or wait for the solution to cool.

Pat was a rash, impatient young chemist.

12d　Pat did not read his lab manual, which warned against pouring chlorine into a hot crucible.

Pat, a careless young man, poured chlorine into the hot crucible.

First, warnings should be read.

12e　A week before, he had glanced at the manual.

14a　Pat ignored the warning in the lab manual; he poured chlorine into the hot crucible.

Pat poured chlorine into the hot crucible; thus he caused the explosion.

14b　At the hospital Pat said that he had not read the warning; that he had, of course, been careless; and that he would never again, under any circumstances, pour chlorine into a hot crucible.

1. Many patients in the mid-eighties deliberately declined elective surgery for they did not wish to wait months to be admitted to hospital.

2. Dr. Chiang a visiting professor from China says that the Cultural Revolution strengthened the Red Guard but that it did so at a high price.

3. The stalls of the open market along the wharf were filled with tray after tray of glassy-eyed fish slender stalks of pink rhubarb mounds of home-grown tomatoes and jars of bronze honey.

4. Two or three scrawny mangy-looking hounds lay sprawled in the shade of the cabin.

5. While Diana was unpacking the camping gear and Grace was gathering firewood I began to pitch the tent.

6. After attending a preview of the new play the audience left the theatre in utter silence.

7. Still in high school we had to memorize dates and facts such as 1066 the Battle of Hastings 1914–1918 World War I 1939–1945 World War II and 1969 the first moon landing.

8. The dream home that they often talk about is a retreat in the Rockies to tell the truth however they seem perfectly happy in their mobile home on the outskirts of Fredericton.

9. The criminal was asking for mercy his victim was pleading for justice.

10. Chris and I felt that our blustery argument would never end however my weather-watching roommate reminded us that thunderstorms are usually of short duration.

The Apostrophe

15

Use the apostrophe to indicate the possessive case (except for personal pronouns), to mark omissions in contractions, and to form certain plurals.

15a
Use the apostrophe to indicate the possessive case of nouns (including acronyms) and indefinite pronouns.

The possessive (or genitive) case shows ownership or a comparable relationship: *Kelsey's* car, two *weeks'* pay. The possessive case of nouns and of indefinite pronouns may be indicated by the use of *'s* or by the apostrophe alone.

everybody's friend   the students' laughter

Occasionally, the idea of the possessive is indicated by the use of both an *of*-phrase and *'s*:

that tie **of** Al's   [often called a double possessive]

COMPARE   this description of Al   [Al is described.]
this description of Al's   [Al did the describing.]

A possessive may follow the word it modifies:

Is that old broken-down baby buggy **Frank's** or **Jane's**? [Compare "Frank's or Jane's baby buggy."]

(1) For singular nouns (including acronyms) and indefinite pronouns, add the apostrophe and s.

Sue's idea   a day's work   OPEC's aim   anyone's guess

Option: If a singular noun ends in *s*, add the apostrophe and *s* or only the apostrophe: Keats's poetry OR Keats' poetry.

(2) For plural nouns ending in s, add only the apostrophe. For plurals not ending in s, add the apostrophe and s.

her sons' room   ten dollars' worth   the Ameses' home
BUT
men's watches   women's names   children's rights

(3) For compounds, add the apostrophe and s only to the last word.

my sister-in-law's shop   someone else's turn
the minister of trade's idea   George Heming, Jr.'s reply
[Notice that no comma follows *Jr.'s* although *Jr.* is normally set off by commas.]

(4) To indicate individual ownership, add the apostrophe and s to each name.

the doctor's and the dentist's offices
Al's and Sue's cars [Note that *cars* is plural.]

Option: To indicate joint ownership, add the apostrophe and *s* only to the last name or to each name.

Al and Sue's car   OR   Al's and Sue's car

Note: Proper names (organizations, geographical locations, and so on) sometimes do not have the apostrophe or the apostrophe and *s*.

Devil's Island   Devils Tower   Devil Mountain

■ **Exercise 1**   Change the modifier after the noun to a possessive form before the noun, following the pattern of the examples.

EXAMPLES
the laughter of the crowd   *the crowd's laughter*
suggestions made by James   *James's suggestions* OR
                                                  James' suggestions

1. the acreage belonging to John L. Field III
2. the boat bought by the Weinsteins
3. the voices of Tess and Mary
4. the efforts of the editor-in-chief
5. the strategy that Doris uses
6. worth a quarter
7. ideas of somebody else
8. stories by Dickens
9. shoes for women
10. a song written by Robyn and Joan

15b
Use the apostrophe to mark omissions in contracted words and numbers.

didn't   he'll   they're   there's   she'd
class of '91   o'clock   [contraction of "of the clock"]

"Well, Curley's pretty handy," the swamper said skeptically.
"Never did seem right to me. S'pose Curley jumps a big guy an' licks him. Ever'body says what a game guy Curley is." —JOHN STEINBECK [See also **19b**.]

15c
Use the apostrophe and s to form certain plurals.

Use the apostrophe and *s* for the plural forms of lower-case letters and of abbreviations followed by periods.

his *e*'s and *o*'s   no more *ibid.*'s   two V.P.'s
[The '*s* following an italicized letter or word is not italicized
(underlined). See also **10d.**]

When needed to prevent confusion, the '*s* is used for the
plural of capital letters and of words referred to as words.

too many *I*'s   several *A*'s   two *plus*'s   the *ha ha*'s

Options:

the 1900's OR the 1900s   his 7's OR his 7s
two *B*'s OR two *B*s   the &'s OR the &s
her *and*'s OR her *and*s   the MLA's OR the MLAs

15d

**Do not use the apostrophe with the pronouns *his, hers,
its, ours, yours, theirs,* or *whose* or with plural nouns
not in the possessive case.**

A friend of **theirs** knows a cousin of **yours**.
Some **architects** design **offices** for **lawyers**.

Caution: Do not confuse *its* with *it's* or *whose* with *who's*:

Its motor is small.   **It's** [It is] a small motor.
Whose responsibility is it?   **Who's** [Who is] responsible?

■ **Exercise 2**   Insert apostrophes where needed.

1. Many students attitudes changed in the mid-1980s.
2. Two of Mr. Hughes students won awards for their essays.
3. Those newsstands sell Marian Rosss homemade candy.
4. Theyre not interested in hockey; its roughness repels them.
5. Snapshots of the class of 92 cover bulletin board.
6. "Its just one C.P.A.s opinion, isnt it?" Sean commented.
7. There are four *i*s and four *s*s in *Mississippi*.
8. Theres a difference between her attitude and theirs.
9. OPECs decision took a few economic analysts by surprise.
10. The computer confused my account with somebody elses.

Quotation Marks

16

Use quotation marks for direct quotations (other than those set off from the text), for some titles, and for words used in a special sense. Place other marks of punctuation in proper relation to quotation marks.

Quotation marks (like scissors) are always used in pairs. The first mark indicates a beginning (meaning *quote*) and the second an ending (*unquote*). Do not carelessly omit or misplace the second quotation mark.

16a
Use quotation marks for direct quotations and in all dialogue. Set off long quotations by indention.

(1) Use double quotation marks for direct quotations. Use single quotation marks to enclose a quotation (or a minor title—see also 16b) within a quotation.

Double quotation marks:

> "If we believe absurdities," said Voltaire, "we shall commit atrocities." [Quotation marks enclose only the quota-

tion, not expressions like *she said* or *he replied.* Quotation
marks are not used for indirect quotations: Voltaire said that
believers in absurdities commit atrocities.]

According to Disraeli, Gladstone was a person who did not
have "a single redeeming defect." [The quoted phrase
is an integral part of the sentence.]

Disraeli once said, "He [Gladstone] has not a single redeeming defect." [Not a part of the direct quotation, the information inserted in brackets contributes to clarity.]

Single quotation marks:

"Earl keeps calling my idea 'the impossible dream,'" she
said. [a quotation within a quotation]

"Roch Carrier's 'The Hockey Sweater' is one of the funniest
short stories I've ever read!" Tony exclaimed. [a title
within a quotation]

**(2) Use quotation marks for dialogue (directly quoted
conversation).**

In dialogue the standard practice is to write what each person
says, no matter how short, as a separate paragraph. Expressions such as *he said*, as well as closely related bits of
narrative, are included in the paragraph along with the direct
quotations.

Through an interpreter, I spoke with a Bedouin man tending
nearby olive trees.

"Do you own this land?" I asked him.

He shook his head. "The land belongs to Allah," he said.

"What about the trees?" I asked. He had just harvested a
basket of green olives, and I assumed that at least the trees
were his.

"The trees, too, are Allah's," he replied.

I marveled at this man who seemed unencumbered by material considerations . . . or so I was thinking when, as if in
afterthought, he said, "Of course, I own the *olives!*"

—HARVEY ARDEN, "In Search of Moses"

(3) Set off long quotations of prose and poetry by indention.

PROSE

When you quote one paragraph or less, all lines of a long quotation (generally more than four lines) are indented ten spaces from the left margin and are double-spaced. When you quote two or more paragraphs, indent the first line of each complete paragraph thirteen spaces rather than the usual ten. Quotation marks are used only if they appear in the original.

Metal coins replaced bartering. Then paper money became more convenient to use than metal coins not only because it is easy to handle but also because it has other advantages. As Cetron and O'Toole say in Encounters with the Future,

> Printing more zeroes is all it takes on a bill to increase its value. Careful engraving makes it easy to recognize and difficult to counterfeit. The fact that private individuals cannot create it at will keeps it scarce. Karl Marx once said that paper money was valued "only insofar as it represents gold" but that may never have been true. (188)

Today, cheques and credit cards are even more con-venient than paper money.

An omission within a quotation is indicated by the use of ellipsis points: see **17i**.

For the proper documentation of sources in a research paper, see Section **34**.

POETRY

Except for very special emphasis a quotation of three (or fewer) lines of poetry is handled like other short quotations—run in with the text and enclosed in quotation marks. A slash indicates the divisions between lines: see **17h**. Passages of more than three lines are set off from the text—double-spaced and indented ten spaces from the left margin. (Within the quotation the pattern of indention in the original should be followed as closely as possible.) Quotation marks are used only if they appear in the original. (Numbers in parentheses are often used to indicate the line numbers of the poem.)

Wordsworth deeply reveres nature. In "My Heart
Leaps Up," he expresses a hope that his reverence
for its beauty will not diminish as he grows older:

> My heart leaps up when I behold
>
> A rainbow in the sky;
>
> So was it when my life began,
>
> So is it now I am a man,
>
> So be it when I shall grow old
>
> Or let me die! (1-6)

■ **Exercise 1** Change each indirect quotation to a direct quotation and each direct quotation to an indirect one.

1. Doris said that she had a theory about me.

2. He says that he has read David Baltimore's "The Brain of a Cell."
3. A Weight Watcher, Eileen explained that she could eat as much as she wanted—of vegetables like spinach, eggplant, and zucchini.
4. Lucie asked, "Will you go to the opera with me?"
5. Last night Paolo said that he thought that Amanda's favourite expression was "Tell me about it!"

16b

Use quotation marks for minor titles (short stories, essays, short poems, songs, episodes of a radio or television series, articles in periodicals) and subdivisions of books.

Coral Browne starred in "An Englishman Abroad," part of the *Great Performances* series.

On the subway, I scanned Adrian Forsyth's "The Golden Alphabet" in an old issue of *Equinox*.

Margaret Laurence's *Heart of a Stranger* contains essays like "Down East" and "Where the World Began."

Use double quotation marks to enclose a minor title appearing in a longer italicized (underlined) title, and single marks for one within a longer title that is enclosed in double quotation marks.

Modern Interpretations of "My Last Duchess"
"An Introduction to 'My Last Duchess'"

Note: Quotation marks are sometimes used to enclose titles of books, periodicals, and newspapers, but italics are generally preferred: see **10a**.

16c

Words used in a special or an ironic sense are sometimes enclosed in quotation marks.

His "castle" was a cozy little rat-trap.
OR
His so-called castle was a cozy little rat-trap. [The use of *so-called* eliminates the need for quotation marks.]

And I do mean good and evil, not "adjustment and deviance," the gutless language that so often characterizes modern discussions of psychological topics. —CAROL TAVRIS

Note: Either quotation marks or italics may be used in definitions such as the following. See also **10d**.

"Ploy" means "a strategy used to gain an advantage."
Ploy means "a strategy used to gain an advantage."
Ploy means *a strategy used to gain an advantage.*

16d

Do not overuse quotation marks.

In general, do not enclose in quotation marks common nicknames, bits of humour, technical terms, or trite or well-known expressions (see **20c**). Instead of using slang and colloquialisms within quotation marks, try to use more formal English. Avoid the use of quotation marks for emphasis, for a *yes* or *no* in indirect discourse, or for diction that you may consider questionable.

REVISE   A "wimp" can't say "no" to anyone.
TO   A wimp can't say no to anyone.

Do not use quotation marks around the titles that head your own compositions.

■ **Exercise 2**   Insert quotation marks where needed in the following sentences.

1. In a short story entitled Cloning, scientists turn one Einstein into three Einsteins.
2. Here, bushed means suffering from cabin fever.

3. David enjoyed reading the short story The Progress of Love.
4. *The Great Cat Massacre* opens with a chapter entitled Peasants Tell Tales: The Meaning of Mother Goose.
5. Theresa said, My grandmother often said, When poverty comes in the door, love goes out the window.

16e

When using various marks of punctuation with quoted words, phrases, or sentences, follow the conventions of North American printers.

(1) Place the period and the comma within the quotation marks.

"Jenny," he said, "let's have lunch."
She replied, "OK, but first I want to finish 'The Machine Stops.' "

Exception:

The author states: "Time alone reveals the just" (471).
[The period follows the parenthetical reference to the source of the quotation.]

(2) Place the colon and the semicolon outside the quotation marks.

She spoke of "the protagonists"; yet I remembered only one in "The Tell-Tale Heart": the mad murderer.

(3) Place the question mark, the exclamation point, and the dash within the quotation marks when they apply only to the quoted matter. Place them outside when they do not.

Within the quotation marks:

Pilate asked, "What is truth?"
Gordon replied, "No way!"

"Achievement—success!—," states Heather Evans, "has become a national obsession."

Why do children keep asking "Why?" [a question within a question—one question mark inside the quotation marks]

Outside the quotation marks:

What is the meaning of the term "half-truth"?

Stop whistling "All I Do Is Dream of You"!

The boss exclaimed, "No one should work for the profit motive!"—no exceptions, I suppose.

■ **Exercise 3**   Insert quotation marks where they are needed.

1. Were you humming the song from the musical *Oliver!* called Where Is Love?
2. Get aholt, instead of get hold, is still used in that region.
3. Have you read Judy Syfers' essay Why I Want a Wife?
4. Last spring I discovered Frost's poem The Road Not Taken.
5. No, Peg said, I didn't agree to do that. I may be a softie, but I haven't gone bananas yet!
6. One of the prettiest songs in recent years is I Just Called to Say I Love You.
7. We were listening to Author's Choice, a regular feature of CBC Radio's weekly program, *Sunday Morning*.
8. His favourite short story is Ivy Day in the Committee Room; mine is From the Fifteenth District.
9. Why cry over spilled milk? my grandmother used to ask. Be glad you have the milk to spill.
10. Catherine said, Do the townspeople ever say to me You're a born leader? Yes, lots of times, and when they do, I just tell them my motto is Lead, follow, or get the heck out of the way!

The Period and Other Marks

17

Use the period, question mark, exclamation point, colon, dash, parentheses, brackets, slash, and ellipsis points appropriately. For the use of the hyphen, see **18f.**

Notice how the marks in colour below signal meaning and intonation.

> The days are dark **.** Why worry **?** The sun never stops shining **!**
>
> In *Lady Windermere's Fan* **(** 1892 **)** is this famous line **:** ''I **[** Lord Darlington **]** can resist everything except temptation **.** ''
>
> According to *Consumer Reports*, ''The electronic radio **/** clock **. . .** is extremely complicated **—** enough so to require five pages of instructions in the owner's manual **.** ''

The Period

17a
Use the period as an end mark and with some abbreviations.

---

(1) **Use the period to mark the end of a declarative sentence and a mildly imperative sentence.**

Everyone should drive defensively. [declarative]
Learn how to drive defensively. [mild imperative]
She asks how drivers can cross the city without driving offensively. [declarative sentence containing an indirect question]
"How can drivers cross the city without driving offensively?" she asked. [declarative sentence containing a direct question]
"Don't do it!" he hollered. [declarative sentence containing an exclamation]

(2) **Use periods after some abbreviations.**

Mrs., Jr.   A.D., B.C.   A.M., P.M.   vs., etc., et al.

Periods are not used with most abbreviations in ordinary writing (for example, *SSW, MVP, FM, km/h*—see also pages 115–16). The period is not used after clipped or shortened forms (*premed, lab, 12th*) or after modern postal abbreviations of provinces (*AB, ON, SK*) and states (*NJ, TX, KY*). (See also page 517.)

When in doubt about punctuating an abbreviation, consult a good college dictionary. Dictionaries often list options, such as *USA* or *U.S.A.*, *DST* or *D.S.T.*

Caution: When an abbreviation ending in a period appears last in the sentence, do not add a second period:

Someday I hope to be an R.N.

The Question Mark

17b

Use the question mark after direct (but not indirect) questions.

Who started the rumour ? [direct question]

BUT She asked who had started the rumour . [indirect question]

Did you hear her ask, "Are you accusing me of starting the rumour ?" [a direct question within a direct question—followed by one question mark inside the quotation marks]

Declarative sentences may contain direct questions:

"Who started the rumour ?" he asked. [No comma follows the question mark.]

He asked, "Who started the rumour ?" [No period follows the question mark.]

She told me—did I hear her correctly ?—who started the rumour. [interpolated question]

Questions are sometimes used between parts of a series:

Did they clean the attic ? the basement ? the whole house ?

COMPARE Did they clean the attic ? The basement ? The whole house ?

Note: A question mark within parentheses is used to express the writer's uncertainty as to the correctness of the preceding word, figure, or date:

Chaucer was born in 1340 (?) and died in 1400.

The Exclamation Point

17c

Use the exclamation point after an emphatic interjection and after other expressions to show strong emotion, such as surprise or disbelief.

Boo ! What a game ! Look at that windshield !

Use the exclamation point sparingly. Use a comma after

mild interjections; use a period after mildly exclamatory expressions and mild imperatives.

Oh, look at that windshield.   How quiet the lake was.

Caution: Do not use a comma or a period after an exclamation point.

"Watch out!" he yelled.   Mi exclaimed, "It's snowing!"

■ **Exercise 1**   Illustrate the chief uses of the period, the question mark, and the exclamation point by composing and correctly punctuating brief sentences of the types specified.

1. a direct question
2. a mild imperative
3. a declarative sentence containing a quoted exclamation
4. a declarative sentence containing an indirect question
5. a declarative sentence containing an interpolated question

The Colon

17d
Use the colon as a formal introducer to call attention to what follows and as a mark of separation in scriptural and time references and in certain titles.

(1) The colon may direct attention to an explanation or summary, a series, or a quotation.

The government wanted a tax increase, but of a certain type: a "value-added tax," to be tacked on to every item and service, from food to haircuts.

So this was her kingdom: an octagonal house, a roomful of books, and a bear.   —MARIAN ENGEL

Of all the distinctions between man and animal, the characteristic gift which makes us human is the power to work with symbolic images: the gift of imagination.   —JACOB BRONOWSKI

David Suzuki points to a dangerous modern assumption: "It is a delusion to think that we know enough to control, manipulate and manage nature." [A quoted sentence after a colon begins with a capital.]

The colon may separate two main clauses when the second clause explains or amplifies the first:

The American conceives of fishing as more than a sport: it is his personal contest against nature. —JOHN STEINBECK

Similarly, a colon is occasionally used after one sentence to introduce the next sentence. (Capitalization of the first letter following the colon is optional.)

The electorate was volatile: In two consecutive polls, the results were contradictory.

(2) Use the colon between figures in scriptural and time references and between titles and subtitles.

Then he quoted John 3:16.
At 13:35 the factory whistle blew.
At 2:15 A.M. the phone rang.
Read *Metamorphosis: Stages in a Life*.

Note: The colon is also used after the salutation of a business letter and in bibliographical data: see **35a(1)** and **34e(2)**.

(3) Do not use superfluous colons.

Be especially careful not to use an unnecessary colon between a verb and its complement or object, between a preposition and its object, or after *such as*.

NOT The winners were: Pat, Lydia, and Jack.
BUT The winners were Pat, Lydia, and Jack.
   OR There were three winners: Pat, Lydia, and Jack.
   OR The winners were as follows: Pat, Lydia, Jack.

NOT   Many vegetarians do not eat dairy products, such as: butter, cheese, yogurt, or ice cream.

BUT   Many vegetarians do not eat dairy products, such as butter, cheese, yogurt, or ice cream.

Exercise 2   Punctuate the following sentences by adding colons. Put a check mark after any sentence that needs no change.

1. At 1530, he began the class with his favourite quotation "Mind without heart is nothing."
2. The downtown streets are narrow, rough, and dirty.
3. Three scientists noted for their engaging writing are these Stephen Jay Gould, Jay Ingram, and Lewis Thomas.
4. During our tour of the library, our guide recommended that we find one of the following periodicals *Canadian Forum, Commentary,* or *Queen's Quarterly*.
5. All their thoughts were centred on equal pay for equal work.

Exercise 3   Decide whether to use a colon or a semicolon between the main clauses of the following sentences. See also **14a**.

1. These laws all have the same purpose they protect us from ourselves.
2. Some of these laws have an obvious purpose others seem senseless.
3. Few things are certain perhaps we could count them on one hand.
4. One thing is certain the future looks bright.

The Dash

17e

Use the dash to mark a break in thought, to set off a parenthetical element for emphasis or clarity, and to set off an introductory series.

On the typewriter, the dash is indicated by two hyphens

without spacing before, between, or after. In handwriting, the dash is an unbroken line about the length of two hyphens.

(1) Use the dash to mark a sudden break in thought, an abrupt change in tone, or faltering speech.

A hypocrite is a person who— but who isn't? —DON MARQUIS

When I was six I made my mother a little hat— out of her new blouse. —LILLY DACHÉ

Aunt Esther replied, ''I put the key on the— in the— no, under the doormat, I think.''

(2) Use the dash to set off a parenthetical element for emphasis or (if it contains commas) for clarity.

Lightning is an electrical discharge— an enormous spark.
—RICHARD E. ORVILLE

Recently, there has been a great deal of news in the press about the consequences— all bad— of high cholesterol levels.

Sentiments that human shyness will not always allow one to convey in conversation— sentiments of gratitude, of apology, of love— can often be more easily conveyed in a letter.
—ARISTIDES

(3) Use the dash after an introductory list or series.

Notice that in the main part of each of the following sentences a word like *all, these, that, such,* or *none* points to or sums up the meaning of the introductory list.

Keen, calculating, perspicacious, acute and astute— I was all of these. —MAX SHULMAN

Muddy, messy, muddled— that is a brief description of life in the trenches during World War I.

Caution: Use the dash carefully in formal writing. Do not use dashes as awkward substitutes for commas, semicolons, or end marks.

Parentheses

17f

Use parentheses to set off parenthetical, supplementary, or illustrative matter and to enclose figures or letters when used for enumeration.

> They call this illness Seasonal Affective Disorder (SAD).
> —LOWELL PONTE [a first-time use of an acronym in an article—see **11e**]

> Bernard Shaw once demonstrated that, by following the rules (up to a point!), we could spell *fish* this way: *ghoti*.
> —JOHN IRVING [an exclamatory parenthetical expression]

> In contrast, a judgment is subject to doubt if there is any possibility at all (1) of its being challenged in the light of additional or more accurate observations or (2) of its being criticized on the basis of more cogent or more comprehensive reasoning. —MORTIMER J. ADLER [In long sentences especially, the enumeration contributes to clarity.]

Notice in the next examples that the writer may choose between a parenthetical main clause and a parenthetical sentence. See also **9e**.

> The book examined political patronage in Canada (patronage does have a long history in Canadian political life).
> The book examined political patronage in Canada. (The author argued that patronage began when Canada did.)

Punctuation of Parenthetical Matter

Dashes, parentheses, commas—all are used to set off parenthetical matter. Dashes set off parenthetical elements sharply and usually emphasize them:

> Man's mind is indeed—as Luther said—a factory busy with making idols. —HARVEY COX

Parentheses usually de-emphasize the elements they enclose:

> Man's mind is indeed (as Luther said) a factory busy with making idols.

Commas are the most frequently used separators:

> Man's mind is indeed, as Luther said, a factory busy with making idols.

Brackets

17g
Use brackets to set off interpolations in quoted matter and to replace parentheses within parentheses.

> The *Home Herald* printed the beginning of the mayor's speech: "My dear fiends [sic] and fellow citizens." [A bracketed *sic*—meaning "thus"—tells the reader that the error appears in the original.]
> Mozart once said, "Some day he [Beethoven] will make quite a noise in the world."
> Some of Marshall McLuhan's writings should be required reading for prospective teachers. (See, for example, *City as Classroom* [Agincourt: The Book Society of Canada, 1977].)

The Slash

17h
Use the slash between terms to indicate that either term is applicable and to mark line divisions of quoted poetry. See also **16a(3)**.

Note that the slash is used unspaced between terms, but with a space before and after it between lines of poetry.

Today visions of the checkless/cashless society are not quite as popular as they used to be. —KATHRYN H. HUMES

Equally rare is a first-rate adventure story designed for those who enjoy a smartly told tale that isn't steeped in blood and/ or sex. —JUDITH CRIST

When in "Mr. Flood's Party" the hero sets down his jug at his feet, "as a mother lays her sleeping child / Down tenderly, fearing it may awake," one feels Robinson's heart to be quite simply on his sleeve. —WILLIAM H. PITCHARD

■ **Exercise 4**   Correctly punctuate each of the following sentences by supplying commas, dashes, parentheses, brackets, or the
slash. Prepare to explain the reason for all marks you add, especially
those you choose for setting off parenthetical matter.

1. Gordon Gibbs or is it his twin brother? plays the drums.
2. Joseph who is Gordon's brother is a lifeguard at English Bay.
3. "I admit that I" he began, but his voice broke; he could say no more.
4. This organization needs more of everything more money, brains, initiative.
5. Some of my courses for example, French and biology demand a great deal of work outside the classroom.
6. During his life, René Lévesque 1922–1987 worked as a jour-nalist, a broadcaster, and a politician.
7. This ridiculous sentence appeared in the school paper: "Because of a personal fool sic the Cougars failed to cross the goal line during the last seconds of the game."
8. Body language a wink or yawn nose-rubbing or ear-pulling folded arms or crossed legs can often speak much louder than words.
9. Gently rolling hills, rich valleys, beautiful lakes these things impress the tourist in New Zealand.
10. Some innovations for example the pass fail system did not contribute to grade inflation.

Ellipsis Points

17i

Use ellipsis points (three spaced periods) to mark an omission from a quoted passage and to mark a reflective pause or hesitation.

(1) Use ellipsis points to indicate an omission within a quoted passage.

Original:

> If—or is it when?—these computers are permitted to talk to one another, when they are interlinked, they can spew out a roomful of data on each of us that will leave us naked before whoever gains access to the information. (From Walter Cronkite, Foreword, *The Rise of the Computer State* by David Burnham [New York: Random, 1983], viii.)

OMISSION WITHIN A QUOTED SENTENCE

> As Walter Cronkite has observed, "If . . . these computers are permitted to talk to one another . . . , they can spew out a roomful of data on each of us that will leave us naked before whoever gains access to the information." [The comma after the second group of ellipsis points could be omitted, but it marks the end of an introductory adverb clause and contributes to the grammatical integrity of the sentence.]

OMISSION AT THE END OF A QUOTED SENTENCE

If an omission at the end of the quoted sentence coincides with the end of your sentence, use a period before the three ellipsis points, leaving no space before the period. If a parenthetical reference is cited, however, place the period after the second parenthesis.

> According to Walter Cronkite, "If—or is it when?—these computers are permitted to talk to one another, when they are

interlinked, they can spew out a roomful of data on each of us. . . . ''   [OR "each of us . . . " (viii).]

OMISSION OF A SENTENCE OR MORE

Original:

> There's an uncertainty in our minds about the engineering principles of an elevator. We've all had little glimpses into the dirty, dark elevator shaft and seen the greasy cables passing each other. They never look totally safe. The idea of being trapped in a small box going up and down on strings induces a kind of phobia in all of us.   (From Andrew A. Rooney, *Pieces of My Mind* [New York: Atheneum, 1984], 121.)

Use a period before ellipsis points to mark the omission of a sentence or more (even a paragraph or more) within a quoted passage.

> Andrew A. Rooney writes about everyday experiences—for example, riding an elevator: ''There's an uncertainty in our minds about the engineering principles of an elevator. . . . The idea of being trapped in a small box going up and down induces a kind of phobia in all of us.''   [A sentence comes both before and after the period and ellipsis points.]

To indicate the omission of a full line or more in quoted poetry, use spaced periods covering a whole line.

> All I can say is—I saw it!
>
> .   .   .   .
>
> Impossible! Only—I saw it!   —ROBERT BROWNING

(2) Use ellipsis points to mark a reflective pause or hesitation.

> Love, like other emotions, has causes . . . and consequences.   —LAWRENCE CASLER

It's a bird . . . it's a plane . . . well, it's the Gossamer Penguin, a 68-pound flying machine fueled only by the sun. —CATHLEEN McGUIGAN

"It's well for you . . . " began Lucille. She bit the remark off. —ELIZABETH BOWEN [a deliberately unfinished statement]

Ellipsis points to show a pause may also come after the period at the end of a sentence:

All channels are open. The meditation is about to begin . . . .
—TOM ROBBINS

■ **Exercise 5** Beginning with *According to John Donne*, or with *As John Donne has written*, quote the following passage, omitting the words placed in brackets. Use three or four periods as needed to indicate omissions.

No man is an island [entire of itself;] every man is a piece of the continent, a part of the main. [If a clod be washed away by the sea, Europe is the less, as well as if a promontory were, as well as if a manor of thy friend's or of thine own were]. Any man's death diminishes me because I am involved in mankind [and therefore never send to know for whom the bell tolls; it tolls for thee]. —JOHN DONNE

■ **Exercise 6** First, observing differences in meaning and emphasis, use ellipsis points in place of the dash, commas, and italicized words in the following sentences. Then write two sentences of your own to illustrate the use of ellipsis points to mark a pause or hesitation.

1. The journey had ended—*and, I wondered*, what would happen to us?
2. Our lives would have been different if *the journey had not ended*.

■ **Exercise 7** Punctuate the following sentences by supplying appropriate end marks, commas, colons, dashes, and parentheses. Do not use unnecessary punctuation. Be prepared to explain the reason for each mark you add, especially when you have a choice of correct marks (for example, commas, dashes, or parentheses).

1. Houses in this neighbourhood are all alike two storeys red brick white picket fences
2. "Is it is it a baby girl then" was all he managed to say
3. I tell you again What is new and different and challenging in this job is the opportunity to live in Japan
4. Matters aren't made easier by the following error "An increase in tuition fees to $30 000 per year isn't beyond the means of most students"
5. "John" she exclaimed "John you mustn't give up" She reached out to touch her son but he turned away
6. The Duke of Windsor formerly Edward VIII left Britain in 1936 after abdicating the throne and declaring his intention to marry Wallis Simpson
7. At last they had seen what they had long wished to see Mikhail Barishnikov dancing with Karen Kain
8. Her own estimate is that political leaders will continue to ignore pleas from economic experts and aid workers who argue that Third World debt must be erased
9. As one woman put it "Office politics party politics and international politics all are gutter politics to me"
10. "User friendly" means "easy to operate" "This software is user friendly" and "a fresh pot of tea" means that the tea not the pot is fresh

SPELLING AND DICTION

Spelling and Hyphenation

18

Spell every word according to established usage as shown by your dictionary. Hyphenate words in accordance with current usage.

Spelling

Because problems with spelling are usually highly individual, one of the best ways to improve your spelling is to keep, for study and reference, a record of those words (correctly spelled) that you have misspelled: see **8f**.

Always proofread to detect misspellings, many of which are slips of the pen or errors in typing. If you have access to a computer that singles out such mistakes for you to correct, use it as a time-saving tool, but be aware of its limitations—for example, its inability to recognize a misspelling that spells some other word, such as *hole* for *whole*.

If you have any doubt about a correct spelling, consult your dictionary. Note the syllabication, pronunciation, and any form changes. Check the meaning to be sure you have found the word you have in mind. Be mindful of restrictive labels such as *British* or *Chiefly British* in American dictionaries (for example, *The Random House College Dictionary*) and *U.S.* or *Chiefly U.S.* in British dictionaries (for example, *The Concise Oxford Dictionary*).

BRITISH	connexion	humour	centre	offence	realise
AMERICAN	connection	humor	center	offense	realize

Canadian writers should note that Canadian spelling patterns are the product of both British and American practices. It is not uncommon, for example, to find writers in this country using such British spellings as *traveller's cheques* and *catalogue centre* as well as such American spellings as *connection, program,* and *plow.* At present, neither practice dominates completely, but at least one expert has suggested that the simplified and usually phonetic American spellings have begun to edge out the formerly more prevalent British forms.

Dictionaries designed to meet the needs of the Canadian market (see page 198) will list variant and preferred spellings. Unless otherwise directed, you should use the preferred spelling (listed first in an entry) and maintain consistency within classes of words.

In ordinary writing, do not use spellings or words labelled *obsolete* or *archaic* (*compleat* for *complete*); *dialectal* or *regional* (*heighth* for *height*, *boughten* for *bought*); or *nonstandard* or *slang* (*weirdo*). Words and spellings labelled *informal* or *colloquial* (*kind of*, *kids*) are acceptable in informal writing.

If your dictionary lists two unlabelled spellings, either form is correct—for example, *fulfil* or *fulfill*, *symbolic* or *symbolical*, *tornadoes* or *tornados*, *likable* or *likeable*.

18a

Do not allow mispronunciation to cause you to misspell a word.

Although pronunciation is often not a dependable guide to spelling, mispronunciation does frequently lead to misspelling. In the following words, trouble spots are in boldface.

athlete	drowned	modern	represent
barbarous	everyone	perspire	surprise
candidate	gratitude	quantity	umbrella

As you check pronunciations in the dictionary, give special attention to /ə/, the symbol for a neutral vowel sound in unaccented syllables, usually an indistinct *uh* sound (as in *confidence*). Be especially careful not to omit letters representing /ə/. (The term *schwa* is used to refer to this vowel sound or to its phonetic symbol.)

A word that is difficult to spell may have alternate pronunciations. Of these, one may be a better guide to spelling. Here are examples of such words:

| arctic | government | literature | veteran |
| February | interest | sophomore | where |

Do not misspell words like *and* or *than* because they are not stressed in speech.

> We had ham and [NOT *an*] eggs.
> The movie is even more exciting than [NOT *then*] the book.

18b

Distinguish between words of similar sound and spelling; use the spelling required by the meaning.

Words such as *forth* and *fourth* or *sole* and *soul* sound alike but have vastly different meanings. Be sure to choose the right word for your context.

A number of frequently confused spellings may be studied in groups:

Contractions and possessive pronouns:

It's best to wait.	The team did **its** best.
You're required to attend.	**Your** attendance is required.
There's a change in plans.	**Theirs** have changed.

Single words and two-word phrases:

It's an **everyday** event.	It happens nearly **every day**.
Maybe that is true.	That **may be** true.
I ran **into** trouble.	I ran **in to** get it.
Nobody cared.	The ghost had **no body**.

*Singular nouns ending in **nce** and plural nouns ending in **nts**:*

not much **assistance**	too many **assistants**
for **instance**	just **instants** ago
even less **patience** with	several **patients**

As you study the following list, use your dictionary to check the meaning of words not thoroughly familiar to you. You may find it helpful to devise examples of usage such as these:

breath—a deep breath	**breathe**—to breathe deeply
passed—had passed	**past**—in the past

Words Frequently Confused

accept, except	altar, alter
access, excess	altogether, all together
adapt, adopt	always, all ways
advice, advise	angel, angle
affect, effect	ascent, assent
aisles, isles	assistance, assistants
alley, ally	baring, barring, bearing
allude, elude	birth, berth
allusion, illusion	board, bored
10 already, all ready	20 born, borne

break, brake
breath, breathe
buy, by
canvas, canvass
capital, capitol
censor, censure, sensor
choose, chose
cite, site, sight
clothes, cloths
30 coarse, course

complement, compliment
conscience, conscious
council, counsel
credible, creditable
cursor, curser
dairy, diary
decent, descent, dissent
desert, dessert
detract, distract
40 device, devise

dominant, dominate
dual, duel
dyeing, dying
elicit, illicit
envelop, envelope
fair, fare
faze, phase
formerly, formally
forth, fourth
50 forward, foreword

gorilla, guerrilla
hear, here
heard, herd
heroin, heroine
hole, whole
holy, wholly
horse, hoarse
human, humane
instance, instants
60 its, it's

later, latter
led, lead
lesson, lessen
licence, license
lightning, lightening
lose, loose
maybe, may be
minor, miner
moral, morale
70 of, off

passed, past
patience, patients
peace, piece
persecute, prosecute
perspective, prospective
personal, personnel
plain, plane
practice, practise
pray, prey
80 precede, proceed

predominant, predominate   straight, strait
presence, presents   taut, taunt
principle, principal   than, then
prophecy, prophesy   their, there, they're
purpose, propose   through, thorough
quiet, quite   to, too, two
respectfully, respectively   100 tract, track
right, rite, write
road, rode
90 sense, since   waist, waste
                             weak, week
                             weather, whether
shown, shone   were, where
stationary, stationery   who's, whose
statue, stature, statute   your, you're

18c
Distinguish between the prefix and the root.

The root is the base to which prefixes and suffixes are added.
Notice in the following examples that no letter is added or
dropped when the prefix is added to the root.

dis- disagree, disappear   **mis-** misspent, misspell
im-   immortal, immoral   **re-**   reelect [OR re-elect]
un-   unnecessary, unnoticed **ir-**   irrational, irregular

18d
Apply the rules for adding suffixes.

(1) Dropping or retaining a final unpronounced _e_
Drop the -_e_ before a suffix beginning with a vowel:

engage   engaging   scarce   scarcity
desire   desirable   fame   famous

Retain the -e before a suffix beginning with a consonant:

care	careful	safe	safety
mere	merely	manage	management

Options: *judgment* or *judgement*, *likable* or *likeable*

Some exceptions: *acreage*, *mileage*, *argument*, *ninth*, *truly*, *wholly*

To keep the sound /s/ of -*ce* or /j/ of -*ge*, do not drop the final *e* before -*able* or -*ous*:

noticeable   changeable   outrageous   courageous

Similarly, keep the *e* before -*ance* in *vengeance*.

■ **Exercise 1**   Practise adding suffixes to words ending in an unpronounced *e*.

EXAMPLES
-*ing*: rise, lose, guide   *rising, losing, guiding*
-*ly*, -*er*, -*ness*: late   *lately, later, lateness*

1. -*ly*: like, safe, sure
2. -*able*, -*ing*, -*ment*: excite
3. -*ing*: come, notice, hope
4. -*ing*, -*less*: use
5. -*ous*: continue, courage
6. -*ful*: care, hope, use
7. -*ing*, -*ment*, -*able*: argue
8. -*ly*, -*ing*: complete
9. -*able*: desire, notice
10. -*ing*, -*ment*: manage

(2) Doubling a final consonant before a suffix

Double a final consonant before a suffix beginning with a vowel if both (a) the consonant ends a stressed syllable or a one-syllable word and (b) the consonant is preceded by a single vowel.

One-syllable words:		*Words stressed on last syllable:*	
drag	dragged	abhor	abhorrent
hid	hidden	begin	beginning
shop	shoppers	occur	occurrence
stun	stunning	regret	regrettable
wet	wettest	unwrap	unwrapped

Compare benefited, reference [stressed on first syllable]

Exception: Following British practice, accepted Canadian usage doubles the consonant *l* in words stressed on the first syllable:

counsellor   travelled   labelling   marvellous

■ **Exercise 2**   Write the present participle (*-ing* form) and the past tense of each verb: *rob—robbing, robbed.*

admit	conceal	hope	plan	stop
brag	grip	jog	rebel	audit

(3) Changing or retaining a final *y* before a suffix

Change the *-y* to *i* before suffixes—except *-ing.*

apply → applies, applied, appliance BUT applying
study → studies, studied BUT studying
happy → happily, happiness, happier, happiest

Exceptions: Verbs ending in *y* preceded by a vowel do not change the *y* before *-s* or *-ed: stay, stays, stayed.* Following the same pattern of spelling, nouns like *joys* or *days* have *y* before *s*. The following irregularities in spelling are especially troublesome:

lays, laid   pays, paid [*Compare* says, said.]

(4) Retaining a final *l* before *-ly*

Do not drop a final *l* when you add *-ly*:

real—really   usual—usually   cool—coolly   formal—formally

■ **Exercise 3**   Add the designated suffixes to the following words.

1. *-able*: vary, ply
2. *-er*: funny, carry
3. *-ous*: vary, luxury
4. *-ly*: easy, final
5. *-ed*: supply, stay
6. *-ing*: study, worry
7. *-d*: pay, lay
8. *-hood*: lively, likely
9. *-ness*: friendly, lonely
10. *-ly*: usual, cool

(5) Adding *-s* or *-es* to form the plural of nouns

Form the plural of most nouns by adding *-s* to the singular:

two boys   many nations   a few scientists
several safes   three cupfuls   all the radios

both sisters-in-law   [chief word pluralized]
the Dudleys and the Itos   [proper names]

Note: To form the plural of some nouns ending in *f* or *fe*, change the ending to *ve* before adding the *s: a thief, two thieves; one life, our lives.*

Add *-es* to singular nouns ending in *s, ch, sh,* or *x*:

many loss**es**   these mailbox**es**   the Roger**ses**
two approach**es**   a lot of ash**es**   two Doris**es**

[Note that each plural above makes an extra syllable.]

Add *-es* to singular nouns ending in *y* preceded by a consonant, after changing the *y* to *i*:

eighty—eight**ies** industry—industr**ies**
company—compan**ies**

Note: Although *es* is often added to a singular noun ending in *o* preceded by a consonant, usage varies:

echoes	heroes	potatoes	vetoes [-es only]
autos	memos	pimentos	pros [-s only]
nos/noes	mottos/mottoes		zeros/zeroes [-s or -es]

Exceptions: Irregular plurals (including retained foreign spellings) are not formed by adding s or es.

SINGULAR	woman	goose	analysis	alga	species
PLURAL	women	geese	analyses	algae	species

■ **Exercise 4** Supply plural forms (including any optional spelling) for the following words, applying rule **18d(5)**. (If a word is not covered by the rule, use your dictionary.)

1. belief
2. theory
3. church
4. genius
5. Kelly
6. bath
7. hero
8. story
9. wish
10. forty
11. radius
12. scarf
13. wife
14. speech
15. tomato
16. phenomenon
17. halo
18. child
19. handful
20. video

18e
Apply the rules to avoid confusion of *ei* and *ie*.

When the sound is /ē/ (*ee*), write *ie* (except after *c*, in which case write *ei*).

chief, grief, pierce, wield, field, niece, relief, yield
BUT, after *c*:
ceiling, deceive, conceit, perceive

When the sound is other than /ē/ (*ee*), usually write *ei*.

counterfeit, foreign, heifer, heir, sleigh, vein
forfeit, freight, height, neighbour, stein, weigh

Exceptions: friend, mischief, seize, sheik

■ **Exercise 5** Fill in the blanks in the following words with the appropriate letters, *ei* or *ie*.

18e sp

1. p____ce
2. ach____ve
3. rec____ve
4. n____gh
5. fr____ght

6. ap____ce
7. bel____f
8. conc____ve
9. th____r
10. dec____t

11. n____ce
12. sh____ld
13. w____rd
14. shr____k
15. pr____st

Words Frequently Misspelled

You may find it helpful to study the following list in units of ten or twenty words at a time. Consult your dictionary for the exact meanings of any words you are not sure of.

	absence		affected		apology
	acceptable		affectionately		apparent
	accessible		aggravate		appearance
	accidentally		aggressive		appoint
	accommodate		alcohol		appreciate
	accompanied		allotted		appropriate
	accomplish		all right		approximately
	accumulate		a lot of		arguing
	accuracy		always		argument
10	achievement	30	amateur	50	arrangement
	acquaintance		among		arrest
	acquire		analysis		article
	acquitted		analyze		aspirin
	across		annihilate		assassination
	actually		announcement		associate
	address		annual		athlete
	admission		anxiety		athletics
	adolescent		anywhere		attacked
	advice		apartment		attendance
20	advised	40	apiece	60	attendant

authentic
average
awkward
bachelor
balance
bargain
basically
beginning
belief
70 believed

beneficial
benefited
biscuit
boundaries
breath
breathe
brilliant
bulletin
bureaucracy
80 burglar

business
busy
cafeteria
calendar
candidate
career
category
ceiling
cemetery
90 certain

challenge
changeable
changing
characteristic
chief
children
chocolate
choice
choose
100 chosen

coarsely
column
coming
commercial
commission
commitment
committed
committee
comparative
110 compelled

competence
competition
completely
conceited
conceivable
concentrate
condemn
confidence
conscience
120 conscientious

conscious
consensus
consistency
consistent
contradict
control
controlled
controlling
controversial
130 convenience

convenient
coolly
correlate
counterfeit
courteous
criticism
criticize
cruelty
curiosity
140 curious

dealt
deceive
decided
decision
defence
defensible
define
definitely
definition
150 descend

Frequently Misspelled Words   189

describe
description
desirable
despair
desperate
destroy
develop
dictionary
difference
160 different

dilemma
dining
disagree
disappearance
disappoint
disapprove
disastrous
discipline
discussion
170 disease

dispensable
disturbance
divide
divine
dormitory
ecstatic
effect
efficiency
eighth
180 elaborately

eligible
eliminate
embarrass
emphasis
emphasize
empty
enemy
entirely
environment
190 equipment

equipped
escape
especially
everything
evidently
exaggerate
exceed
excellence
excellent
200 except

exercise
exhaust
existence
exonerate
expense
experience
explanation
extraordinary
extremely
210 familiar

fascinate
favourite
February
finally
financially
forehead
foreign
foreword
forfeit
220 forty

forward
friend
gauge
generally
government
governor
grammar
grammatically
grief
230 guaranteed

guard
guerrilla
guidance
happened
harass
height
hero
heroes
hindrance
240 humour

hypocrisy
hypocrite
idiosyncrasy
ignorant
illogical
imaginary
imagine
imitate
immediately
250 immense

incalculable
incidentally
incredible
independent
indispensable
inevitable
infinite
influential
initiative
260 innocence

innocuous
innumerable
inoculate
intellectual
intelligence
intelligent
interest
interpret
interrupt
270 introduce

irrelevant
irresistible
irritated
jewellery
knowledge
laboratory
legitimate
leisure
liable
280 library

licence
license
lightning
literature
lively
loneliness
lonely
lose
lying
290 magazine

maintenance
manageable
manoeuvre
manual
manufacture
marriage
material
mathematics
meant
300 medicine

mere
messenger
miniature
minutes
mischievous
missile
morning
mortgage
muscles
310 mysterious

naturally
necessary
nickel
niece
ninety
ninth
noticeable
noticing
nuclear
320 nuisance

occasionally
occur
occurred
occurrence
omission
omitted
opinion
opponent
opportunity
330 opposite

optimism
organize
origin
original
paid
pamphlet
parallel
particular
pastime
340 peculiar

prejudiced
preparation
prepare
presence
prevalent
privilege
probably
procedure
proceed
370 profession

receipt
receive
receiving
recognize
recommend
reference
referred
referring
regular
400 rehearsal

performance
perhaps
permanent
permissible
personal
phase
physical
physician
pigeon
350 planned

professor
prominent
pronunciation
propaganda
prophecy
prophesy
psychology
publicly
pumpkin
380 purpose

relieve
religious
remembrance
reminisce
repetition
representative
reproduce
resemblance
resistance
410 resources

pleasant
poison
possess
possession
possible
possibly
practically
prairie
precede
360 preferred

pursue
pursuit
quandary
quantity
questionnaire
quiet
quite
quizzes
realize
390 really

restaurant
rhythm
ridiculous
roommate
sacrifice
safety
salary
scarcity
scenery
420 schedule

secede
secretary
seize
separate
sergeant
severely
sheriff
shining
similar
430 simply

since
sincerely
skiing
sophomore
specimen
speech
sponsor
strength
strenuous
440 strict

stubbornness
studying
subtlety
succeed
successful
succession
sufficient
suicide
summary
450 superintendent

supersede
suppose
suppress
surely
surprise
surround
susceptible
suspicious
swimming
460 symbol

sympathize
technique
temperament
temperature
tendency
tenet
than
their
themselves
470 then

therefore
thorough
thought
through
till
tobacco
together
tomorrow
tournament
480 traffic

trafficked
tragedy
transferred
tremendous
tried
tries
trouble
truly
twelfth
490 tyranny

unanimous
unconscious
undoubtedly
unmistakably
unnecessary
until
usage
useful
useless
500 using

usually
vacuum
valuable
varies
various
vegetable
vengeance
venomous
vice
510 view

vigilance	weird	woman
villain	where	women
violence	wherever	worshipped
visible	whether	wreck
vitamins	whichever	write
waive	wholly	writing
warrant	whose	written
warring	wield	yield
weather	wintry	
520 Wednesday	530 withdrawal	

Hyphenation

18f

Hyphenate words to express the idea of a unit and to avoid ambiguity. For the division of words at the end of a line, see **8d**.

Notice in the following examples that the hyphen links (or makes a compound of) two or more words that function as a single word.

> We planted forget–me–nots and Johnny–jump–ups. [nouns]
> He hand–fed them. I double–parked. Hard–boil an egg.
> [verbs]
> Was it a head–to–head confrontation? [adjectival]

Consult a good recent dictionary when you are not sure of the form of compounds, since some are connected with hyphens (*eye-opener, cross-examine*), some are written separately (*eye chart, cross street*), and others are written as one word (*eyewitness, crossbreed*).

(1) Use the hyphen to join two or more words serving as a single adjective before a noun.

a well-known surgeon
BUT   a surgeon who is well known

chocolate-covered peanuts
BUT   peanuts covered with chocolate

a ten-year-old plane
BUT   a plane that is ten years old

"I reject get-it-done, make-it-happen thinking," he says.
—THE ATLANTIC

In a series, hyphens are carried over:

second-, third-, or fourth-class mail

Note: The hyphen is generally omitted after an adverb ending in *-ly*:

a brand-new product   BUT   a completely new product
soft-spoken words   BUT   softly spoken words

■ **Exercise 6**   Convert the following word groups according to the pattern of the examples.

EXAMPLES
an initiation lasting two months   *a two-month initiation*
ideas that shake the world   *world-shaking ideas*

1. a house with six rooms
2. sharks that eat people
3. fingers stained with ink
4. cheese two years old
5. a person who loves cats
6. books costing twenty dollars
7. vigils that last all night
8. parents who solve problems
9. ponds covered with lilies
10. a highway with two lanes

18f sp

(2) **Use the hyphen with spelled out compound numbers from twenty-one to ninety-nine (or twenty-first to ninety-ninth).**

forty–six, fifty–eighth BUT three hundred twenty

Note: Usage varies regarding the hyphenation of spelled out fractions. The hyphen is required, however, only when the fraction functions as a compound modifier. See also **18f(1)**.

almost one–half full BUT eating only one half of it
a two–thirds vote BUT two thirds of the voters

(3) **Use the hyphen to avoid ambiguity or an awkward combination of letters or syllables between prefix and root or suffix and root.**

a dirty movie–theatre [Compare "a dirty-movie theatre."]
to re–sign a petition [Compare "to resign a position."]
semi–independent, shell–like BUT semifluid, childlike

(4) **Use the hyphen with the prefixes *ex-* ("former"), *self-, all-;* with the suffix *-elect;* and between a prefix and a capitalized word.**

ex–wife   self–help   all–inclusive   mayor–elect
mid–September   pre–Renaissance   anti–American

Note: The hyphen is also used with figures or letters such as *mid–1980s* or *T–shirt*, as well as with codes having more than five numbers: ISBN 0–03–921811–3.

■ **Exercise 7**   Refer to **18f** and to your dictionary as you convert each phrase (or words within each phrase) to a compound or to a word with a prefix. Use hyphens when needed.

EXAMPLES

glasses used for water	*water glasses* OR *waterglasses*
not Christian	*non-Christian*
a job that pays $45 000 a year	*a $45 000-a-year job*

1. respect for oneself
2. people who smoke cigarettes
3. ham cured with sugar
4. a latch used at night
5. in the shape of a V
6. a wax for all purposes
7. streets covered with snow
8. flights from Calgary to L.A.
9. a sale lasting one or two days
10. cars fifteen years old

Good Usage and Glossary

19

Use a good dictionary to help you select the words that express your ideas exactly.

You can find valuable information about words in a good concise or college dictionary, such as one of the following:

> *The Concise Oxford Dictionary*
> *Funk & Wagnalls Standard College Dictionary*,
>   Canadian edition
> *Gage Canadian Dictionary*
> *The Random House College Dictionary*
> *Webster's New Collegiate Dictionary*
> *Webster's New World Dictionary*

Several other texts may also be helpful to you because of their special features. For example, the *Oxford Advanced Learner's Dictionary of Current English* and *Collins Cobuild English Language Dictionary* offer useful information to students studying English as an additional language.

When buying a dictionary, you should keep in mind that only a Canadian dictionary or a Canadian edition of a dictionary will provide detailed information about Canadian words, weights and measures, and preferred spellings.

Occasionally you may need to refer to an unabridged dictionary or to some other special dictionary: see the two lists on pages 420–21.

19a

Use a good dictionary intelligently.

Examine the introductory matter as well as the arrangement and presentation of material in your dictionary so that you can easily find the information you need. Note meanings of any special abbreviations your dictionary uses.

Two sample dictionary entries follow. Note the definitions of *empty* as an adjective, as a transitive verb, as an intransitive verb, as a noun, and as part of an idiomatic phrase (with *of*). Observe the examples of usage. Note that the second

Pronunciation

Syllabication

Forms as adjective (with spelling)

Forms as verb (with spelling)

Spelling

emp·ty (emp′tē), *adj.,* **-ti·er, -ti·est,** *v.,* **-tied, -ty·ing,** *n., pl.* **-ties.** —*adj.* **1.** containing nothing; void of the usual or appropriate contents: *an empty bottle.* **2.** vacant; unoccupied: *an empty house.* **3.** without burden or load. **4.** destitute of people or human activity: *empty streets.* **5.** destitute of some quality or qualities; devoid (usually fol. by *of*): *a life empty of happiness.* **6.** without force, effect, or significance; hollow; meaningless: *empty compliments; empty pleasures.* **7.** hungry. **8.** without knowledge or sense; frivolous; foolish: *an empty head.* **9.** completely spent of emotion. — *v.t.* **10.** to make empty; discharge the contents of. **11.** to discharge (contents): *to empty the water out of a bucket.* —*v.i.* **12.** to become empty. **13.** to discharge contents, as a river. —*n.* **14.** something that is empty, as a box, bottle, can, etc. [ME (with intrusive *-p-*); OE *æm(et)-tig (æmett(a)* leisure + *-ig-*Y¹)] —**emp′ti·a·ble,** *adj.* —**emp′·ti·er,** *n.* —**emp′ti·ly,** *adv.* —**emp′ti·ness,** *n.* —**Syn. 1.** vacuous. EMPTY, VACANT, BLANK denote absence of content or contents. EMPTY means without appropriate or accustomed contents: *empty barrel; The house is empty* (has no furnishings). VACANT is usually applied to that which is temporarily unoccupied: *vacant chair; vacant* (uninhabited) *house.* BLANK applies to surfaces free from any marks or lacking appropriate markings, openings, etc.: *blank paper; a blank wall.* **6.** delusive, vain. **10.** unload. —**Ant. 1.** full.

—Etymology

—Antonym

Synonyms with definitions and distinctions

Hyphenation of compound form

emp·ty-hand·ed (emp′tē han′did), *adj., adv.* **1.** having nothing in the hands, as in doing no work. **2.** having gained nothing: *to come back from fishing empty-handed.*

entry defines a hyphenated compound form, *empty-handed*. Finally, note the various other kinds of information (labelled in colour) that the dictionary provides.

(1) Spelling, syllabication, and pronunciation

Your dictionary describes both written and spoken language: you can check spelling and word division as well as pronunciation of unfamiliar words. Notice above the way words are divided into syllables (syllabication) by the use of dots or sometimes accent marks. (For end-of-line division of words, see **8d**.) A key to the sound symbols is provided at the bottom of the entry pages as well as in the front of the dictionary. A primary stress mark (') normally follows the syllable that is most heavily accented. Secondary stress marks follow lightly accented syllables.

■ **Exercise 1**   With the aid of your dictionary, write out the words below using sound symbols and stress marks to show the correct pronunciation (or a correct one if options are given).

1. performance
2. incongruous
3. harass
4. Mozart
5. nuclear
6. interest
7. chalet
8. patois
9. advertisement
10. minutia

(2) Parts of speech and inflected forms

Your dictionary labels the possible uses of words in sentences—for instance, *adj.* (adjective), *adv.* (adverb), *v.t.* (verb, transitive). It also lists ways that nouns, verbs, and modifiers change form to indicate number, tense, or comparison or to serve as other parts of speech (for example, under *repress*, *v.t.*, you may also find *repressible, adj.*).

■ **Exercise 2**   With the aid of your dictionary, classify each of the following words as a verb (transitive or intransitive), a noun, an

adjective, an adverb, a preposition, or a conjunction. Give the principal parts of each verb, the plural (or plurals) of each noun, and the
comparative and superlative of each adjective and adverb. (Note
that some words are used as two or more parts of speech.)

1. permit	3. sweet-talk	5. subtle	7. late	9. crisis
2. lonely	4. tattoo	6. for	8. bring	10. fine

(3) Definitions and examples of usage

Observe whether your dictionary gives the most common
meaning of a word first or arranges the definitions in historical order. Notice also that examples of a word used in phrases
or sentences are often given to clarify each definition.

■ **Exercise 3** Study the definitions of any five of the following
pairs of words, paying special attention to any examples of usage
in your dictionary; then write sentences to illustrate the shades of
difference in meaning.

1. rot—putrefy	6. inspire—motivate
2. sensual—sensuous	7. contradict—deny
3. lethargy—lassitude	8. brutal—cruel
4. insolent—rude	9. jaded—a jade
5. mercy—clemency	10. draw—draft

(4) Synonyms and antonyms

Lists and discussions of synonyms in dictionaries often help
to clarify the meaning of closely related words. Studying
denotations and connotations of words with similar meanings
will help you choose words more exactly and convey more
subtle shades of meaning. Lists of antonyms are also helpful
because they provide words that mean the opposite of a
word.

Note: For more complete lists of synonyms, antonyms, and
related and contrasted words, refer to a special dictionary or
a thesaurus. A sample thesaurus entry follows.

empty *adj.* **1** *Our voices echoed in the empty house:*
vacant, unoccupied, uninhabited, bare, void. **2** *He didn't
want to retire and lead an empty life:* aimless, meaningless, without substance, vacuous, insignificant, worth-
less, purposeless, futile, unfulfilled, idle, hollow; shallow, banal, trivial, inane, insipid, frivolous. —*v.* **3**
*Empty the glass before putting it in the dishwasher. The
Mississippi empties into the Gulf of Mexico:* pour out,
drain, dump, void, evacuate; discharge, flow, debouch.
Ant. 1 full, stuffed, crammed, packed, jammed; occupied, inhabited. **2** meaningful, significant, substantial,
useful, valuable, worthwhile, purposeful, fulfilled,
busy, full, rich, vital, interesting, serious. **3** fill, pack,
put in, stuff, cram, jam; receive.

Before choosing a synonym or closely related word from
such a list, look it up in the dictionary to make sure that it
expresses your meaning exactly. Although *void, idle,* and
inane are all listed as synonyms of *empty,* they have different
meanings.

■ **Exercise 4**   With the aid of your dictionary or thesaurus, list
two synonyms and one antonym for each of the following words.

1. ugly   2. pleasure   3. defy   4. support   5. stingy

(5) Origin: development of the language

In college dictionaries the origin of a word—also called its
derivation or *etymology*—is shown in square brackets. For
example, after *expel* might be this information:

[<L *expellere* <*ex-* out + *pellere* to drive, thrust]

This means that *expel* is derived from (<) the Latin (L) word
expellere, which is made up of *ex-,* meaning ''out,'' and
pellere, meaning ''to drive or thrust.'' Breaking up a word,
when possible, into *prefix—root—suffix* will often help to
get at the basic meaning of a word.

	prefix		root		suffix
interruption	**inter-** between	+	**rupt** to break	+	**-ion** act of
transference	**trans-** across	+	**fer** to carry	+	**-ence** state of

The bracketed information given by a good dictionary is especially rich in meaning when considered in relation to the historical development of our language.

The parenthetical abbreviations for languages here and on the next few pages are those commonly used in bracketed derivations in dictionaries. English is one of the Indo-European (IE) languages, a group of languages apparently derived from a common source. Within this group of languages, many of the more familiar words are remarkably alike. Our word *mother*, for example, is *mater* in Latin (L), *meter* in Greek (Gk.), and *matar* in ancient Persian and in the Sanskrit (Skt.) of India. Such words, descended from or borrowed from the same form in a common parent language, are called *cognates*. The large number of cognates and the many correspondences in sound and structure in most of the languages of Europe and some languages of Asia indicate that they are derived from the common language that linguists call Indo-European, which it is believed was spoken in parts of Europe about six thousand years ago. By the opening of the Christian era the speakers of this language had spread over most of Europe and as far east as India, and the original Indo-European had developed into eight or nine language families. Of these, the chief ones that influenced English were the Hellenic (Greek) group on the eastern Mediterranean, the Italic (Latin) on the central and western Mediterranean, and the Germanic in northwestern Europe. English is descended from the Germanic.

Two thousand years ago the Hellenic, the Italic, and the Germanic branches of Indo-European each comprised a more or less unified language group. After the fall of the Roman

Empire in the fifth century, the several Latin-speaking divisions developed independently into the modern Romance languages, chief of which are Italian, French, and Spanish. Long before the fall of Rome the Germanic group was breaking up into three families: (1) East Germanic, represented by the Goths, who were to play a large part in the history of the last century of the Roman Empire before losing themselves in its ruins; (2) North Germanic, or Old Norse (ON), from which modern Danish (Dan.), Swedish (Sw.), Norwegian (Norw.), and Icelandic (Icel.) derive; and (3) West Germanic, the direct ancestor of English, Dutch (Du.), and German (Ger.).

The English language may be said to have begun about the middle of the fifth century, when the West Germanic Angles, Saxons, and Jutes began the conquest of what is now England and either absorbed or drove out the Celtic-speaking inhabitants. (Celtic—from which Scots Gaelic, Irish Gaelic, Welsh, and other languages later developed—is another member of the Indo-European family.) The next six or seven hundred years are known as the Old English (OE) or Anglo-Saxon (AS) period of the English language. The fifty or sixty thousand words then in the language were chiefly Anglo-Saxon, with a small mixture of Old Norse words as a result of the Danish (Viking) conquests of England beginning in the eighth century. But the Old Norse words were so much like the Anglo-Saxon that they cannot always be distinguished.

The transitional period from Old English to Modern English—about 1100 to 1500—is known as Middle English (ME). The Norman Conquest began in 1066. The Normans, or "Northmen," had settled in northern France during the Viking invasions and had adopted Old French (OF) in place of their native Old Norse. Then, crossing over to England by the thousands, they made French the language of the king's court in London and of the ruling classes—both French and English—throughout the land, while the masses continued to speak English. Only toward the end of the fifteenth century did English become once more the common language of all classes. But the language that emerged at that time had lost most of its Anglo-Saxon inflections and had taken on thousands of French words (derived originally from Latin). Nonetheless, it was still basically English, not French, in its structure.

The kinds of changes that occurred during the development of the English language (until it was partly stabilized by printing, introduced in London in 1476) are suggested by the following passages, two from Old English and two from Middle English.

Hē ǣrest gescēop   eorðan bearnum
He first created   *for earth's children*

heofon tō hrōfe,   hālig Scyppend.
heaven as a roof,   *holy creator.*

From the "Hymn of Caedmon"
about eighth century

Ǣlc þāra þe þās mīn word gehīerþ, and þā wyrcþ, biþ gelīc
Thus each who hears these my words, and does them, is like

þǣm wīsan were, sē his hūs ofer stān getimbrode. Þā cōm þǣr
a wise man, who builds his house on a stone. Then there came

regen and micel flōd, and þǣr blēowon windas, and āhruron on
rain and a great flood, and blowing winds, and a roaring in

þæt hūs, and hit nā ne fēoll: sōþlīce hit wæs ofer stān getimbrod.
that house, and it did not fall: truly it was built on stone.

Matthew 7:24–25
tenth century

Therefor ech man that herith these my wordis, and doith hem, shal be maad lijk to a wise man, that hath bildid his hous on a stoon. And reyn felde doun, and flodis camen, and wyndis blewen, and russchiden into that hous; and it felde not doun, for it was foundun on a stoon.

Matthew 7:24–25
fourteenth century

Use of Dictionary   205

A knight ther was, and that a worthy man,
That fro the tyme that he first bigan
To ryden out, he loved chivalrye,
Trouthe and honour, fredom and curteisye.

From Chaucer's Prologue to the
Canterbury Tales, about 1385

A striking feature of Modern English (that is, English since 1500) is its immense vocabulary. As already noted, Old English used some fifty or sixty thousand words, very largely native Anglo-Saxon; Middle English used perhaps a hundred thousand words, many taken through the French from Latin and others taken directly from Latin; and unabridged dictionaries today list over four times as many. To make up this tremendous word hoard, we have borrowed most heavily from Latin, but we have drawn some words from almost every known language. English writers of the sixteenth century were especially eager to interlace their works with words from Latin authors. And, as the English pushed out to colonize and to trade in many parts of the globe, they brought home new words as well as goods. Modern science and technology have drawn heavily from the Greek. As a result of all this borrowing, English has become one of the richest and most cosmopolitan of languages.

In the process of enlarging our vocabulary we have lost most of our original Anglo-Saxon words. But those that are left make up the most familiar, most useful part of our vocabulary. Practically all our simple verbs, our articles, conjunctions, prepositions, and pronouns are native Anglo-Saxon; and so are many of our familiar nouns, adjectives, and adverbs. Every speaker and writer uses these native words over and over, much more frequently than the borrowed words. Indeed, if every word is counted every time it is used, the percentage of native words runs very high—usually between 70 and 90 percent. Milton's percentage was

81, Tennyson's 88, Shakespeare's about 90, and that of the King James Bible about 94. English has been enriched by its extensive borrowings without losing its individuality; it is still fundamentally the *English* language.

■ **Exercise 5**   With the aid of your dictionary, give the etymology of each of the following words:

1. aspirin	5. laser	8. quasar
2. geriatrics	6. laugh	9. tariff
3. hallmark	7. OK	10. veal
4. ketchup		

(6) Special usage labels

In your dictionary, you will find special usage labels for words or particular definitions of words that differ from general (or unlabelled) usage. Here is a sampling of labels frequently used, each of them found in two or more college dictionaries:

unalienable	*Archaic, Obsolete*	inalienable
lift	*Informal, Colloquial*	plagiarize
codder	*Non-standard, Dialect, Colloquial*	a boat used for cod fishing
Spud Island	*Slang*	Prince Edward Island

The classification of usage is often difficult and controversial because our language is constantly changing. Good writers try to choose the words, whatever their labels, that exactly fit the audience and the occasion, informal or formal.

■ **Exercise 6**   Classify the following words and phrases according to the usage labels in your dictionary. If a word has no special usage label, classify it as *General*. If a given definition of a word has a usage label, give the meaning after the label.

EXAMPLES
job—general
murther—dialectal for *murder*
nutty—informal for *silly*, slang for *insane*

1. smog
2. mukluk
3. rink rat
4. gofer

5. holler
6. lout
7. macho

8. snigger
9. unto
10. sleazy

19b

Use informal words only when appropriate to the audience.

Words or expressions labelled *Informal* or *Colloquial* in college dictionaries are standard English and are used by writers every day, particularly in informal writing, especially dialogue. On occasion, informal words can be used effectively in formal writing, but they are usually inappropriate. Unless an informal expression is specifically called for, use the general English vocabulary, the unlabelled words in your dictionary.

| INFORMAL | dopey | gypped | bellybutton |
| GENERAL | stupid | swindled | navel |

Contractions are common in informal English, especially in dialogue: see the examples on page 153. But contracted forms (like *won't* or *there's*) are usually written out (*will not*, *there is*) in a formal composition—which is not as casual or spontaneous as conversational English.

■ **Exercise 7** Make a list of ten words or phrases you would consider informal. Then check your dictionary to see how (or if) each definition you have in mind is labelled.

19c
Use slang only when appropriate to the audience.

Slang words, including certain coinages and figures of speech, are variously considered as breezy, racy, extremely informal, non-standard, facetious, taboo, offbeat, or vigorous. On occasion, slang can be used effectively, even in formal writing. Below is an example of the effective use of the word *spiel*, still labelled by dictionaries as *Slang*:

> Here comes another Question Period. Here come the backbenchers, the frontbenchers, the barbs, the spiels, the catcalls, the hoopla. Here comes another difficult day for the Speaker of the House.

A few years ago the word *hoopla* was also generally considered as slang, but now dictionaries disagree: one classifies this word *Standard* (unlabelled); another, *Colloquial (Informal)*; still another, *Slang*. Like *hoopla*, words such as *spiel, spiffy, uptight, raunchy, schlep*, and *party pooper* have a particularly vivid quality; they soon may join former slang words such as *sham* and *mob* as part of the general English vocabulary.

But much slang is trite, tasteless, and inexact. For instance, when used to describe almost anything disapproved of, *gross* becomes inexact, flat.

Caution: As you avoid the use of ineffective slang in your writing, remember that many of the most vivid short words in our language are general, standard words. Certain long words can be as inexact and as drab as trite slang. For examples of the ineffective use of big words, see Exercise 9, page 212.

■ **Exercise 8**   Replace the italicized words in the following sentences with more exact words or specific phrases.

1. After dress rehearsal the whole cast *goofed off*.
2. Lately the weather has been *lousy* on weekends.
3. This movie is *awesome*.
4. That *wisecrack ticked* him *off*.

19d

Use regional words only when appropriate to the audience.

Regional or dialectal usages (also called localisms or provincialisms) should normally be avoided in writing outside the region where they are current. Speakers and writers may, however, safely use regional words known to the audience they are addressing.

REGIONAL   He slung the **nunny-bag** over his shoulder.
GENERAL   He slung the **knapsack** over his shoulder.

19e

Avoid non-standard words and usages.

Words and expressions labelled by dictionaries as *Non-standard* or *Illiterate* should be avoided in most writing—for example, ''He don't know how'' for ''He doesn't know how.'' Many expressions of this kind are not listed in college dictionaries.

19f

Avoid archaic and obsolete words.

All dictionaries list words (and meanings for words) that have long since passed out of general use. Such words as *ort* (fragment of food) and *yestreen* (last evening) are still found in dictionaries because these words, once the standard vocabulary of great authors, occur in our older literature and must be defined for the modern reader.

A number of obsolete or archaic words—such as *worser* (for *worse*) or *holp* (for *helped*)—are still in use but are now non-standard.

19g
Use technical words and jargon only when appropriate to the audience.

When writing for the general reader, avoid all unnecessary technical language. The careful writer will not refer to a mechanical computational process as an *algorithm* or a need for bifocals as *presbyopia*. (Of course, the greater precision of technical language makes it desirable when the audience can understand it, as when one physician writes to another.)

Jargon is technical slang that is tailored specifically for a particular occupation. It can be an efficient shortcut for specialized concepts, but you should use jargon only when you can be sure that all your readers understand it.

19h
Avoid overwriting, an ornate or flowery style, or distracting combinations of sounds.

Overwriting, as well as distracting combinations of sounds, calls attention to words rather than to ideas. Such writing makes for slow, difficult reading.

ORNATE	The majority believes that the approbation of society derives primarily from diligent pursuit of allocated tasks.
BETTER	Most people believe success results from hard work.

| DISTRACTING | The use of catalytic converters is just one contribution to the solution of the problem of air pollution. |
| BETTER | The use of catalytic converters is just one way to help solve the problem of air pollution. |

Also avoid the overuse of alliteration (repetition of the same consonant sound), as in "Some people **sh**un the **sea**shore."

■ **Exercise 9**   Using simple, formal, straightforward English, rewrite the following sentences (cited by Edwin Newman in *A Civil Tongue*).

1. We have exceptional game plan capabilities together with strict concerns for programming successful situations.
2. In order to improve security, we request that, effective immediately, no employees use the above subject doors for ingress and egress to the building.
3. We will also strategize with the client on ways to optimize usage of the spots by broadcast management.
4. Muzak helps human communities because it is a non-verbal symbolism for the common stuff of everyday living in the global village.
5. These precautions appeared to be quite successful in dissuading potential individuals with larcenous intent.

Glossary of Usage

19i

Consider your purpose and your audience as you consult the following glossary to determine appropriate usage.

The following short glossary covers only the most common usage problems. See **18b** for a supplementary list of frequently confused words.

The entries in this glossary are authoritative only to the extent that they describe current usage. The usage labels included do not duplicate the description in any one dictionary, but justification for each label can usually be found in at least two of the leading dictionaries. For a discussion of the restrictive labels used in dictionaries, see **19a(6)**.

As you study the descriptions of usage in this glossary, keep in mind the following categories:

GENERAL	Words or expressions in the Standard English vocabulary—listed in dictionaries without special usage labels.
INFORMAL	Words or expressions that dictionaries label *Informal* or *Colloquial*—used in speech and in informal writing.
STANDARD	All general and informal words or expressions.
NON-STANDARD	Words or expressions labelled in dictionaries as *Archaic, Illiterate, Non-standard, Obsolete, Slang,* or *Substandard*—words not considered a part of the standard English vocabulary. See also **19c, e,** and **f**.

a, an   Use *a* before the sound of a consonant: **a** yard, **a** U-turn, **a** one-base hit. Use *an* before a vowel sound: **an** empty can, **an** M.D., **an** axe, **an** X-ray, **an** hour, **an** NHL game.

above   Acceptable as a modifier or as a noun in such references as "in the paragraph above" or "none of the above." Some writers, however, avoid "the above."

accidently, accidentally   *Accidentally* is the correct form.

ad, advertisement   Use the full word in your formal writing.

adverse, averse   *Adverse* describes something as "hostile, antagonistic": **adverse** criticism. *Averse* means "having feelings of hostility against or repugnance for": He is **averse** to criticism.

advise   Non-standard as a substitute for the noun *advice*: the doctor's **advice** [NOT advise].

affect, effect   The verb *affect* means "to influence, attack" or "to touch the emotions." The noun *effect* means "result of a cause."

> Smoking **affects** the heart.   His tears **affected** her deeply.
> Drugs have side **effects**.   The **effect** on sales was good.

When used as a verb, *effect* means "to produce as an effect": The medicine **effected** a complete cure.

aggravate   Widely used for *annoy* or *irritate*. Many writers, however, restrict the meaning of *aggravate* to "intensify, make worse": Noises **aggravate** a headache.

a half a   Omit one of the *a*'s: half a loaf, a half loaf.

ahold of   Informal for "a hold of, a grasp upon something," as in "to get ahold of a rope."

ain't   A non-standard contraction generally avoided in writing, unless used in dialogue or for humorous effect.

alibi   Appropriate in a legal context but informal when used in place of "to give an excuse" or for the noun *excuse.*

allusion, illusion   An *allusion* is a casual or indirect reference. An *illusion* is a false idea or an unreal image.

> The author's **allusion** to a heaven on earth amused me.
> The author's concept of a heaven on earth is an **illusion**.

a lot   Sometimes misspelled as *alot.*

already, all ready   *Already* means "before or by the time specified." *All ready* means "completely prepared."

> The theatre was **already** full by seven o'clock.
> The cast was **all ready** for the curtain call.

alright   Not yet a generally accepted spelling of *all right.*

altogether, all together   *Altogether* means "wholly, thoroughly." *All together* means "in a group."

> That law is **altogether** unnecessary.
> They were **all together** in the lobby.

A.M., P.M. (OR a.m., p.m.)   Use only with figures.

> NOT   The wedding begins at ten thirty in the **a.m.**
> BUT   The wedding begins at 10:30 A.M. [OR at ten thirty in the morning]

among, between   Prepositions with plural objects (including collective nouns). As a rule, use *among* with objects denoting three or more (a group), and use *between* with those denoting only two (or twos).

> walked **among** the crowd, quarrelling **among** themselves
> a choice **between** war and peace, reading **between** the lines

amount of, number of   *Amount of* is followed by singular nouns; *number of*, by plural nouns.

> an **amount of** money, light, work, or postage [singular]
> a **number of** coins, lights, jobs, or stamps [plural]

See also **a number, the number**.

an   See **a, an**.

and etc.   *Etc.* is an abbreviation of *et* ("and") *cetera* ("other things"). Omit the redundant *and*. See also **etc.**

and/or   Now acceptable in general writing. Some writers, however, avoid the form because they consider it distracting.

and which, and who   Do not use *and* before only one *which* or *who* clause. The *and* may be used to link two subordinate clauses.

> They are competent volunteers **who** [NOT and who] work overtime.
> OR   They are volunteers *who are competent* **and** *who work overtime.* [two subordinate clauses]

a number, the number   As subjects, *a number* is generally plural and *the number* is singular. Make sure that the verb agrees with the subject.

> **A number** of options **are** available.
> **The number** of options **is** limited.

anyone, any one; everyone, every one   Distinguish between each one-word and two-word compound. *Anyone* means "any person at all"; *any one* refers to one of a group. Similarly, *everyone* means "all," and *every one* refers to each one in a group.

> Was **anyone** hurt? Was **any one** of us prepared?
> **Everyone** should attend. **Every one** of them should attend.

anyways   Non-standard for *anyway*.

as   (1) Do not use *as* instead of the preposition *like* in making a comparison: Natalie, **like** [NOT as] her mother, is a smart shopper.
(2) In your formal writing, do not use *as* instead of *if*, *that*, or *whether* after such verbs as *feel*, *know*, *say*, or *see*: I do not know **if** [NOT as] my adviser is right.
(3) To avoid even a slight chance of ambiguity, many writers prefer not to use *as* for *because*, *since*, or *while*.

> PREFERRED   **While** [NOT As] it was raining, we watched TV.
> OR   **Because** [NOT As] it was raining. . . .

as far as   Not acceptable as a substitute for the phrasal preposition *as for*: **As for** fasting [NOT As far as fasting], many doctors discourage it for weight loss.

at   Redundant after *where*. See **where . . . at, where . . . to**.

awful   Overworked for *ugly*, *shocking*, *very bad*. Informal as a substitute for *very*, as in "awful important."

awhile, a while   *Awhile*, an adverb, is not used as the object of a preposition: We rested **awhile**.   COMPARE We rested for **a while**.

back of   Informal for *behind* or *in back of*.

backwards   Use *backward* [NOT backwards] as an adjective: a **backward** motion.

bad, badly   The adverb *badly* is preferred after most verbs. But either *bad* or *badly* is now standard in the sense of "ill" or "sorry," and some writers now prefer *bad* after such verbs as *feel* or *look*.

> The organist plays **badly**.   Charles feels **bad**.

because   See **reason . . . because**.

beef, bellyache   Slang for *complain* or *grumble*.

being as, being that   Non-standard for *since, because*.

beside, besides   Always a preposition, *beside* usually means "next to," sometimes "apart from." As a preposition meaning "in addition to" or "other than," *besides* is now more common in writing than *beside*. When used adverbially, *besides* means "also" or "moreover."

> Martin was sitting **beside** Jenny.
> **Besides** countless toys, these children have their own TV set.
> The burglars stole our silver—and my stereo **besides**.

better, had better   Do not omit the *had* in your formal writing.

> We **had** better consider history as we plan for our future.

between   See **among, between**.

bias, prejudice   Synonyms in the sense of "a preconceived opinion" or "a distortion of judgment." But a bias may be in favour of or may be against, whereas a prejudice is against. Many writers do not use *bias* for *discrimination* because they consider the usage bureaucratic jargon.

borrow off, borrow from   Use *borrow from* in your writing.

bottom line   An overworked term for "outcome, upshot," or "the final result."

brass   Slang for "high-ranking officials" and informal for "insolence, impudence."

bug   Slang as a verb for *annoy* or *spy on* and as a noun for *fanatic* or *hidden microphone*.

bunch   Informal if used to refer to a group of people.

burger, hamburger   In your formal writing, use the full word.

bursted   Archaic for *burst*.

but what   Informal after *no* or *not* following such expressions as "no doubt" or "did not know."

> INFORMAL   There was no doubt but what they would win.
> GENERAL   There was no doubt **that** they would win.

but which, but who   Do not use *but* before one *which* or *who* clause. *But* may be used to link two subordinate clauses.

> It is a needed change which [NOT but which] will not be accepted.
>
> OR   It is a change *which is needed* but *which will not be accepted.* [two subordinate clauses]

can, may   Interchangeable when permission is sought. But formal English distinguishes between *can* referring to ability and *may* referring to permission in such sentences as these:

> **Can** student nurses give injections? [Are they able to?]
> **May** student nurses give injections? [Are they permitted to?]

can't hardly, can't scarcely   Use *can hardly, can scarcely.*

cause of . . . on account of, due to   Redundant. Omit the *on account of* or *due to*; or recast to avoid wordiness.

> WORDY   One cause of misunderstandings is on account of lack of communication.
> BETTER   One cause of misunderstandings is lack of communication.
> CONCISE   Lack of communication causes misunderstandings.

centre about, centre around   Informal for ''to be focussed on or at'' or for ''centre on.''

compare to, compare with   Formal English prefers *compare to* for the meaning ''regard as similar'' and *compare with* for the meaning ''examine to discover similarities or differences.''

> The speaker **compared** the earth **to** a lopsided baseball.
> Putting one under the other, the expert **compared** the forged signature **with** the authentic one.

complementary, complimentary   *Complementary* means ''completing'' or ''supplying needs.'' *Complimentary* means ''expressing praise'' or ''given free.''

> His talents and hers are **complementary**.
> Admiring the performance, he made several **complimentary** remarks.

conscious, conscience   An adjective, *conscious* means "aware, able to feel and think." A noun, *conscience* means "the sense of right and wrong."

> When I became **conscious** of my guilt, my **conscience** started bothering me.

consensus of opinion   Redundant. Omit the *of opinion*.

could of   Non-standard for *could have*. See **of**.

couple, couple of   Informal for *two* or for *several* in such phrases as "a couple aspirin," "a couple more litres of paint," or "in just a couple of seconds."

different from   In formal English the preferred preposition after *different* is *from*. But the less formal *different than* is accepted by many writers if the expression is followed by a clause.

> The Stoic philosophy is **different from** the Epicurean.
> The outcome was **different from** what I expected.
> OR   The outcome was **different than** I had expected.

differ from, differ with   *Differ from* means "to be unlike." *Differ with* means "to disagree."

disinterested   *Disinterested* means "impartial" or "lacking prejudice": a **disinterested** referee; *uninterested* means "indifferent, lacking in interest."

don't   Unacceptable when used for *doesn't*: He **doesn't** [NOT don't] agree.

due to   Usually avoided in formal writing when used as a preposition in place of *because of* or *on account of*: **Because of** [NOT Due to] holiday traffic, we arrived an hour late.

each other   Not used as the subject of a verb in formal writing.

> NOT   We hoped each other would keep in touch.
> BUT   Each of us hoped the other [OR others] would keep in touch.

effect   See **affect, effect**.

emigrate from, immigrate to   The prefix *e-* (a variant of *ex-*) means "out of"; *im-* (a variant of *in-*) means "into." To *emigrate* is to go out of one's own country to settle in another. To *immigrate* is to come into a different country to settle there. The corresponding adjective or noun forms are *emigrant* and *immigrant*. (Compare *export, import*.)

> Many families **emigrated from** Iran. The number of **emigrants** increased during the 1980s.
> Many Iranians **immigrated to** Canada. These **immigrants** contributed to the growth of our economy.

eminent, imminent   *Eminent* means "distinguished." *Imminent* means "about to happen, threatening."

> Charlotte is an **eminent** scientist.
> Bankruptcy seemed **imminent**.

enthuse   Informal for "to show enthusiasm."

etc.   Appropriate informally but used sparingly in formal writing. Many writers prefer to substitute *and so on* or *and so forth*. (Since *etc.* means "and other things," *and etc.* is redundant.)

> NEEDLESS   Ordinary games like Monopoly, backgammon, etc., did not interest these electronics hobbyists.
> REVISED   Ordinary games like Monopoly and backgammon did not interest these electronics hobbyists.

ever so often, every so often   *Ever so often* means "very often, frequently." *Every so often* means "every now and then, occasionally."

everyone, every one   See **anyone, any one**.

except, accept   To *except* is to exclude or make an exception of. To *accept* is to approve or receive.

> These laws **except** [exclude] juveniles.
> These schools **accept** [admit] juveniles.

expect   Informal for *suppose, surmise*, or *presume*.

explicit, implicit   *Explicit* means "expressed directly or precisely." *Implicit* means "implied or expressed indirectly."

The advertisement was **explicit**: "All sales final."
Reading between the lines, I understood the **implicit** message.

fantastic   Informal—overworked for "extraordinarily good" or "wonderful, remarkable."

farther, further   Used interchangeably. Some writers, however, prefer *farther* in references to geographic distance: six kilometres **farther**. *Further* is used as a synonym for *additional* in more abstract references: **further** delay, **further** proof.

fewer, less   Formally, *fewer* (used with plural nouns) refers to *how many*, and *less* (used with singular nouns) to *how much*.

> **fewer** noises, **fewer** hours, **fewer** children
> **less** noise, **less** time

figure   Informal for *believe, think, conclude*, or *predict*.

flunk   Informal for *fail*, as in an examination or test.

folks   Informal for *parents, relatives*.

former   Refers to the first named of two. If three or more items are named, use *first* and *last* instead of *former* or *latter*.

> Manawaka and Deptford are two fictional settings: Margaret Laurence created **the former**, and Robertson Davies created the latter.

fun   Informal if used adjectivally, as in "a fun person," "a fun car."

further   See **farther, further**.

get   Useful in numerous idioms but not appropriate formally in such expressions as "get with the times," "always gets in with his instructors," and "a stubborn attitude that gets me."

go, goes   Informal for *say, says*.

> INFORMAL   I go, "Hello there!" Then he goes, "Glad to see you!"
>
> GENERAL   I **say**, "Hello there!" Then he **says**, "Glad to see you!"

good   In your formal writing, do not use *good* as an adverb.

Watson played **well** [NOT good] under pressure.

great   Overworked informally for *skilful, good, clever, enthusiastic,* or *very well,* as in "really great at guessing the answers" or "with everything going great for us."

guy(s)   Informal for *any person(s).*

had of, had have   Non-standard for *had.*

NOT   I wish I had of [OR had have] said that.
BUT   I wish I **had** said that.

had ought, hadn't ought   Use *ought, ought not,* or *oughtn't.*

half a, a half, a half a   Use *half a* or *a half* in your writing.

hang   Useful in numerous idioms but slang in such expressions as "a hang-up about sex" and "to hang out in video arcades."

hanged, hung   Informally interchangeable in the sense of "put to death by hanging." Formally, it is *hanged* (often used figuratively nowadays) that refers to such an act.

When my parents supplied enough rope, I usually **hanged** myself—but not always.

hardly, scarcely   Words with negative force, usually considered non-standard if used with an unnecessary negative like *not, nothing,* or *without.*

I **could hardly** quit then. [NOT couldn't hardly]
Hardly anything went right today. [NOT hardly nothing]
The motion passed **with scarcely** a protest. [NOT without scarcely]

hisself   Non-standard for *himself.*

hooked on   Slang for *addicted to* or *obsessed with.*

hopefully   Still questionable for *I hope* or *it is hoped.*

how come   Informally used as a substitute for *why.*

illusion   See **allusion, illusion.**

immigrate   See **emigrate from, immigrate to**.

implicit   See **explicit, implicit**.

imply, infer   Most writers carefully distinguish between *infer* (meaning "draw a conclusion based on evidence") and *imply* ("suggest without actually stating").

> His attitude **implies** that money is no problem.
> I **infer** from his attitude that money is no problem.

incidently, incidentally   *Incidentally* is the correct form.

include   When precisely used, *include (includes, included)* precedes an incomplete rather than a complete list.

> Precipitation **includes** sleet and hail.   COMPARE Precipitation has four forms: rain, snow, sleet, and hail.

inferior than   Use *inferior to* or *worse than*.

ingenious, ingenuous   *Ingenious* means "clever, resourceful"; *ingenuous* means "open, frank; artless."

> This electric can opener is an **ingenious** device.
> Don's **ingenuous** smile disarms the critics.

input   Useful as a computer term but questionable in the sense of "a voice in" or "an active role," as in "Students had no input in these decisions."

in regards to, with regards to   Non-standard for *in regard to, with regard to*, or *as regards*.

into   Informal for "interested in" or "involved with," as in "We are into computers now."

irregardless   Non-standard for *regardless*.

its, it's   *Its* is a possessive pronoun ("for *its* beauty"). *It's* is a contraction of *it is* ("*It's* beautiful!") or of *it has* ("*It's* been a beautiful day!").

kick   Slang or very informal in such expressions as "to kick in my share," "just for kicks," "on another kick," "just kicking around town."

kind, sort   Singular forms, which may be modified by *this* or *that*. The use of *these* or *those* is increasingly common but is still questionable.

> QUESTIONABLE   These kind of arguments are deceptive.
> PREFERRED   **These kinds** of arguments are deceptive.
> OR   **This kind** of argument is deceptive.

kind of, sort of   Informal when used adverbially in the sense of "to a degree, somewhat, a bit" or "in a way" (as in "kind of silly," "sort of hesitated," or "kind of enjoying it").

kind of a, sort of a   Omit the *a* in your formal writing: NOT "this kind of a tour" BUT "this *kind of* tour."

later, latter   Comparative forms of *late* often confused in writing. In modern English, *later* (like *sooner*) refers to time; *latter* (like *former*) refers to one of two—to the second one (but not to the last of several).

> We set a **later** date. They arrived **later** than usual.
> She wrote a song and a play. The **latter** won a prize.

See also **former**.

lay (laid, laying)   Non-standard for *lie (lay, lain, lying)* in the sense of "to rest or recline."

> I should **lie** down [NOT lay]. Had he **lain** down [NOT laid]? The truck **was lying** [NOT laying] on its side.

learn   Non-standard for *teach, instruct, inform*.

leave   Non-standard for *let* except when followed by an object and *alone*, as in "*Leave* [OR let] them alone."

> **Let** sleeping dogs lie.   **Let** her go.   **Let** the baby be.

less   See **fewer, less**.

let's us   Redundant. Use *let's* or *let us*.

liable to   Informally used in place of *likely to* in reference to mere probability. Formally, *liable to* not only denotes likelihood or possibility but also suggests the idea of harm or danger.

> INFORMAL   It's liable to be cooler soon. [mere likelihood]

GENERAL   The roof is **liable** to collapse. [likelihood + danger]

lie (lay, lain, lying)   Non-standard for *lay (laid, laying)* in the sense of "put, place."

> Onion slices are then **laid** [NOT lain] on the fillet.
> Last night I **laid** [NOT lay] my homework aside.

like   Widely used as a conjunction (in place of *as, as if* or *as though*) in conversation and in public speaking. Formal English, however, still rejects the use of *like* as a conjunction.

FORMAL   He drives **as** [NOT like] I did before my accident.
   OR   He drives **the way** I did before my accident.
FORMAL   They acted **as though** [NOT like] they owned the town.

lose, loose   *Lose* is a verb: did **lose**, will **lose**. *Loose* is chiefly an adjective: a **loose** belt.

may be, maybe   Do not confuse the verb phrase *may be* with the adverb *maybe*.

> The story **may be** [OR might be] true.
> **Maybe** [OR Perhaps] the story is true.

me and   Non-standard as part of a compound subject.

NON-STANDARD   Me and Jeanne took an early flight.
STANDARD   Jeanne and I took an early flight.

mighty   Informal for *very* or *extremely* (as in "mighty fine" or "mighty big").

militate, mitigate   *Militate* means "to act, work, or operate *against* (rarely, *in favour of*) something." *Mitigate* means "to make less unpleasant, serious, or painful; to soften or moderate."

> Excessive noise can **militate** against learning.
> A good doctor tries to **mitigate** a patient's suffering.

morale, moral   *Morale* (a noun) refers to mood or spirit. *Moral* (chiefly an adjective) refers to right conduct or ethical character.

the **morale** of our team, affecting **morale**, low **morale**
a **moral** person, **moral** judgments, an im**moral** act

most   Informal if used instead of *almost*, as in ''most everyone.''

Ms. (OR Ms)   Correctly used before a woman's name but not before her husband's name: **Ms.** Martha Jamison OR **Ms.** Jamison [NOT Ms. Philip Jamison].

much   Use *many* [NOT much] to modify plural nouns: **many** children, too **many** facts. See also **fewer, less**.

myself   Not acceptable formally and still questionable informally as a replacement for the subjective form *I* or the objective *me*.

My sister and **I** [NOT myself] prefer soccer.
He confided in Hayden as well as **me** [NOT myself].

nauseous   Generally avoided in writing as a substitute for *nauseated*.

no . . . nor   Use *no . . . or* in compound phrases: ''They had **no** water **or** food.'' BUT ''They had **neither** water **nor** food.''

not . . . no/none/nothing   Non-standard when the two negatives have a negative meaning.

NOT   We didn't have no fun.
        We could not do nothing about it.
BUT   We didn't have any fun.
        We could do nothing about it.

number   See **amount of, number of; a number, the number**.

of   Do not write *of* for an unstressed *have*.

COMPARE	I could have it done. [stressed]
	I could have done it. [unstressed]
NON-STANDARD	I might of [may of, could of, would of, must of, should of, ought to of] said that.
STANDARD	I might **have** [may *have*, could *have*, would *have*, must *have*, should *have*, ought to *have*] said that.

off of   In formal writing, omit the *of* after *off* in such phrases as "fell off of the ladder."

OK, O.K., okay   All three are acceptable spellings. However, a more specific word usually replaces *OK* in a formal context.

parameter   Informal for *boundary* or *perimeter*.

party   Unacceptable in general writing when used for *person*.

per   Used especially in commercial writing. Many authors prefer to use *per* only in Latinisms ("per capita," "per se," or "per cent/percent").

plenty   Informal when used adverbially to mean *quite* or *sufficiently* (as in "plenty good enough").

plus   Many writers do not use or accept *plus* as a substitute for *and* between main clauses (see **12a**)—or for conjunctive adverbs like *moreover, besides,* or *in addition* placed between main clauses or sentences.

P.M.   See **A.M., P.M.**

prep   Informal for *prepare, preparation,* or *preparatory*. Use the full word in your formal writing.

principal, principle   Distinguish between *principal,* an adjective or noun meaning "chief" or "chief official," and the noun *principle,* meaning "fundamental truth."

> A **principal** factor in his decision was his belief in the **principle** that men and women are born equal.

raise, rise   *Raise (raised, raising)* means "to lift or cause to move upward, to bring up or increase." *Rise (rose, risen, rising)* means "to get up, to move or extend upward, ascend." *Raise* (a transitive verb) takes an object; *rise* (an intransitive verb) does not.

> Retailers **raised** prices.   Retail prices **rose** sharply.

rarely ever   In formal writing, either omit the *ever,* or use *hardly* instead of *rarely*.

> He **rarely** mentions money. OR He **hardly ever** mentions it.

real   In non-standard and some informal use, an adverb meaning *very*, as in "real tired."

reason... is because   Formal usage prefers *that* instead of *because*.

> The reason why he missed the test was that he overslept.
> OR   He missed the test because he overslept.

reckon   Informal for *guess, think.*

relate to   Overworked in the sense of "be sympathetic with, understand" or "respond to in a favourable manner," as in "I don't relate to algebra."

respectively, respectfully   *Respectively* means "in the order designated." *Respectfully* means "showing respect."

> I considered becoming a farmer, a landscape artist, and a
>   florist, **respectively**.
> They considered the rabbi's suggestion **respectfully**.

rise   See **raise, rise**.

says   Avoid the use of *says* for *said* after a past-tense verb: stood up and **said** [NOT says].

scarcely   See **hardly, scarcely**.

seldom ever   Omit the *ever* in your formal writing.

sit   Occasionally misused for *set* (put, place): to **set** something [NOT to sit something].

so, so that   *So that* is preferred in formal writing when there is even a remote possibility of ambiguity.

> AMBIGUOUS   We stay with Uncle Ed so we can help him out.
>   [Does *so* mean *therefore* or *so that*?]
> PREFERRED   We stay with Uncle Ed **so that** we can help him
>   out.

someone, some one   See **anyone, any one**.

sort   See **kind, sort**.

sort of a   Omit the *a* in your formal writing.

stationary, stationery   *Stationary* means "in a fixed position"; *stationery* means "writing paper and envelopes."

subsequently   Do not confuse with *consequently. Subsequently* means "afterward, occurring later." *Consequently* means "as a result, therefore."

> The last three pages of the novel are missing; **consequently**, [NOT subsequently] I do not know the ending.

suppose to, supposed to   Be sure to add the *-d*: was **supposed** to do that.

sure   Informal for *surely* or *certainly.*

their, there, they're   *Their* is the possessive form of *they; there* is ordinarily an adverb or an expletive; *they're* is a contraction of *they are.*

> **There** is no explanation for **their** refusal.
> **They're** installing a traffic light **there**.

theirself, theirselves   Non-standard for *themselves.*

them   Non-standard when used adjectivally: **those** apples OR **these** apples [NOT them apples].

then   Sometimes incorrectly used for *than.* Unlike *then, than* does not relate to time.

> Last summer, we paid more **than** that. [Compare "We paid more *then.*"]
> Other **than** a pension cheque, they had no income.

these kind, these sort, those kind, those sort   See **kind, sort**.

this here, that there, these here, them there   Non-standard expressions. Use *this, that, these, those.*

thusly   Grammatically redundant. Write *thus* (already an adverb without the *-ly*).

to   Redundant after *where.* See **where . . . at, where . . . to**.

to, too   Distinguish the preposition *to* from the adverb *too.*

> If it isn't **too** cold Saturday, let's go **to** the state fair.

try and   Informal for *try to*.

type   Informal for *type of* (as in "that type program").

use to, used to   Be sure to add the *-d* to *use* unless the auxiliary is accompanied by *did* in questions or in negative constructions.

> He **used** to sail.   We **used** to argue about trifles.
> Did he **use** to sail?   We didn't **use** to argue about trifles.

very   Omit when superfluous (as in "very unique" or "very terrified"). If you tend to overuse *very* as an intensifier, try using more exact words; in place of "very strange," for example, try *outlandish, grotesque*, or *bizarre*.

want in, want out   Informal for "want to enter, want to leave."

ways   Informal for *way* when referring to distance, as in "It's a long ways to Halifax."

where   Informal for *that* in such sentences as "I saw in the paper where the strike had been settled."

where . . . at, where . . . to   Omit the superfluous *at, to*.

> NOT   Where is she at? Where is she going to?
> BUT   Where is she? Where is she going?

which   Use *who* or *that* to refer to persons.

-wise   An overused adverb-forming suffix. Such recent coinages as *computerwise, advertisingwise*, or *cost-benefit-analysiswise* are generally unacceptable in college writing.

with regards to   Use *with regard to* or *as regards*.

would of   Non-standard for *would have*. See **of**.

your, you're   *Your* is the possessive of *you*: on **your** desk. *You're* is a contraction of *you are*: **You're** a winner.

zap   Slang for *destroy, jolt*.

Exactness

20

Choose words that are exact, idiomatic, and fresh.

Strive to choose words that express your ideas and feelings exactly. If you can make effective use of the words you already know, you need not have a huge vocabulary. Good writing often consists of short, familiar words:

> You can't teach your children anything important. You can teach them the sounds of consonants, how to tie shoelaces, the rules of chess or the manual gearshift. You can give them your recipe for date squares, your dentist's phone number and your barber's name and preference in Christmas gifts. You can enroll them in the schools you went to, introduce them to your best teachers, give them subscriptions to your favourite magazines and keep them up late at night playing excerpts from your cherished collection of records. But no matter how great your efforts and how profound your love, they will learn nothing from what you *try* to teach them. They will, of course, *assimilate* from you—your mannerisms, your gestures, your laugh, your bad habits. They will walk like you and you will see parts of yourself, and hear echoes, every time you are with them, but which parts those are, and which echoes— which they have chosen and which they have rejected—will be irrelevant to those you have tried to impart.
>
> —PETER GZOWSKI, *The Morningside Papers*

Adding to your vocabulary, however, will help you become a better writer. When you discover a valuable new word, make it your own by mastering its spelling, meaning, and exact use.

20a
Select the word that expresses your idea exactly.

(1) Choose the word that precisely denotes what you have in mind.

WRONG	A loud radio does not detract me when I am reading a good novel. [*Detract* means "to subtract a part of" or "to remove something desirable."]
RIGHT	A loud radio does not **distract** me when I am reading a good novel. [*Distract* means "to draw the attention away."]
INEXACT	Arnold was willing to pay the bill, and his billfold was empty. [*And* adds or continues.]
EXACT	Arnold was willing to pay the bill, **but** his billfold was empty. [*But* contrasts.]
WRONG	They acted out of prejudism. [non-standard]
RIGHT	They acted out of **prejudice**.
WRONG	She never reverts to herself as an expert.
RIGHT	She never **refers** to herself as an expert.
	OR
	She never **reminds** anyone that she is an expert.

■ **Exercise 1**   The italicized words in the following sentences are wrong or inexact. Correct the errors and replace inexact words with exact ones.

1. Every gardener should have a *compote* bin.
2. My father's curly hair and dimples gave him a *childish* appearance.
3. Todd *flouts* his wealth.
4. Their behaviour was *unhuman*.

5. The lyrics are perfectly *adopted* to the music.
6. Perhaps she just missed getting that job by some *misfortunate* chance.
7. I frequently consult the classified ads, *and* I can seldom find what I want.
8. She didn't say it but she *intimidated* it.
9. Hurricanes are *seasonable*.
10. Liquor *effects* the brain and nervous system.

■ **Exercise 2**   With the aid of your dictionary, give the exact meaning of each italicized word in the quotations below. (Italics have been added.)

1. Ignorance of *history* is dangerous. —JEFFREY RECORD

   Those who cannot remember *the past* are condemned to repeat it. —GEORGE SANTAYANA

2. The capacity for rage, spite and aggression is part of our endowment as *human beings*. —KENNETH KENISTON

   Man, all down his history, has defended his uniqueness like a point of honor. —RUTH BENEDICT

3. Travel is no cure for melancholia; space-ships and time machines are no *escape* from the human condition.
   —ARTHUR KOESTLER

   Well, Columbus was probably regarded as an *escapist* when he set forth for the New World. —ARTHUR C. CLARKE

4. Once, a full high school education was the best achievement of a minority; today, it is the *barest minimum* for decent employment or self-respect. —ERIC SEVAREID

   Study and planning are an *absolute prerequisite* for any kind of intelligent action. —EDWARD BROOKE

5. We had a *permissive* father. He *permitted* us to work.
   —SAM LEVENSON

(2) **Choose the word with the connotation, as well as the denotation, appropriate to the idea you wish to express.**

The *denotation* of a word is what the word actually refers to in the physical world. According to the dictionary, the word *beach* denotes "the shore of a body of water, especially when sandy or pebbly." The *connotation* of a word is what the word suggests or implies. *Beach*, for instance, may connote natural beauty, warmth, surf, water sports, fun, sunburn, crowds, or even gritty sandwiches.

A word may be right in one situation, wrong in another. *Female parent*, for instance, is a proper expression in a biology laboratory, but it would be very inappropriate to say "John wept because of the death of his female parent." *Female parent* used in this sense is literally correct, but the connotation is wrong. The more appropriate word, *mother*, conveys not only the meaning denoted by *female parent* but also the reason why John wept. The first expression simply implies a biological relationship; the second includes emotional suggestions.

■ **Exercise 3**   Give one denotation and one connotation for each of the following words.

1. golden
2. mountain
3. star
4. Yukon
5. liberal
6. computer
7. jogging
8. law
9. success
10. snake

■ **Exercise 4**   Prepare for a class discussion of word choice. After the first quotation below are several series of words that the author might have used but did not select. Note the differences in meaning when an italicized word is substituted for the related word at the head of each series. Be prepared to supply your own alternatives for each of the words that follow the other four quotations.

1. Creeping gloom hits us all. The symptoms are usually the same: not wanting to get out of bed to start the day, failing to smile at ironies, failing to laugh at oneself.

—CHRISTOPHER BUCKLEY

a. gloom: *sadness, depression, melancholy*
b. hits: *strikes, assaults, infects, zaps*
c. usually: *often, frequently, consistently, as a rule*
d. failing: *too blue, unable, neglecting, too far gone*

2. Our plane rocked in a rain squall, bobbed about, then slipped into a patch of sun. —THEODORE H. WHITE

   a. rocked   b. bobbed   c. slipped   d. patch

3. The morning tides are low, the breeze is brisk and salty, and the clams squirt up through the sand and tunnel back down almost faster than you can dig. —ANN COMBS

   a. morning   b. brisk   c. squirt   d. tunnel

4. Stereotypes economize on our mental effort by covering up the blooming, buzzing confusion with big recognizable cut-outs. —ROBERT L. HEILBRONER

   a. economize   b. effort   c. blooming
   d. recognizable   e. cut-outs

5. No emotion is so corrosive of the system and the soul as acute envy. —HARRY STEIN

   a. corrosive   b. system   c. soul   d. acute   e. envy

(3) Choose the specific and concrete word rather than the general and abstract one.

A *general* word is all-inclusive, indefinite, sweeping in scope. A *specific* word is precise, definite, limited in scope.

GENERAL	SPECIFIC	MORE SPECIFIC / CONCRETE
food	fast food	pizza
prose	fiction	short stories
place	city	Edmonton

An *abstract* word deals with concepts, with ideas, with what cannot be touched, heard, or seen. A *concrete* word has to do with particular objects, with the practical, with what can be touched, heard, or seen.

ABSTRACT WORDS	democracy, loyal, evil, hate, charity
CONCRETE WORDS	mosquito, spotted, crunch, wedding

Exact Words   235

Often, writers tend to use too many abstract or general words, leaving their writing drab and lifeless. As you select words to fit your context, be as specific and concrete as you can. For example, instead of the word *bad*, consider using a more precise adjective.

bad planks: rotten, warped, scorched, knotty, termite-eaten

bad children: rowdy, rude, ungrateful, selfish, perverse

bad meat: tough, tainted, overcooked, contaminated

To test whether or not a word is specific, ask one or more of these questions about what you want to say: Exactly who? Exactly what? Exactly when? Exactly where? Exactly how? As you study the following examples, notice what a difference specific, concrete words can make in the expression of an idea. Notice, too, how specific details can be used to expand or develop ideas.

VAGUE   I always think of a good museum as one that is very big.

SPECIFIC   I always think of a good museum as one I get lost in.   —EDWARD PARKS

VAGUE   The discontented people debated the matter and finally found a suitable leader in William Lyon Mackenzie.

SPECIFIC   The malcontents argued on the platforms and in the end they found a leader to their hearts in William Lyon Mackenzie, a Scot, arrived in 1820, editing the *Colonial Advocate*, as honest as daylight, and as uncompromising as the Westminster Catechism.   —STEPHEN LEACOCK

VAGUE   I remember my pleasure at discovering new things about language.

SPECIFIC   I remember my real joy at discovering for the first time how language worked, at discovering, for example, that the central line of Joseph Conrad's *Heart of Darkness* was in parentheses.

—JOAN DIDION

Notice in the second sentence below how specific details can be used to develop an idea.

> Much of a Cuban's day is spent waiting. People wait for taxis, for buses, for newspapers, for ice cream, for cakes, for restaurants, for movies, for picture postcards.
>
> —STANLEY MEISLER

All writers use abstract words and generalizations when these are vital to the communication of ideas, as in the following sentence:

> He is immortal, not because he alone among creatures has an inexhaustible voice, but because he has a soul, a spirit capable of compassion and sacrifice and endurance.
>
> —WILLIAM FAULKNER

To be effective, however, the use of these words must be based upon clearly understood and well-thought-out ideas.

■ **Exercise 5** Replace the general words and phrases in italics with specific ones.

1. I always think of a shopping mall as *very big*.
2. *A lot of people* are threatened by *pollution*.
3. The *movie* was *great*.
4. Aunt Grace served *the same thing* every Sunday.
5. I explained my overdraft to my parents by telling them I had bought *some things I needed*.
6. Backpacking has *numerous advantages*.
7. The *dog walked* over to his *food*.
8. My friend looked at my history essay and said *what I least expected to hear*.
9. *Various aspects of the television show* were criticized *in the newspaper*.
10. *Cities* have their *problems*.

(4) Use figurative language appropriately.

A *figure of speech* is a word or words used in an imaginative rather than in a literal sense. The two chief figures of speech are the *simile* and the *metaphor*. A *simile* is an explicit comparison between two things of a different kind or quality, usually introduced by *like* or *as*. A *metaphor* is an implied comparison of dissimilar things. In a metaphor, words of comparison, such as *like* or *as*, are not used.

SIMILES

Writers who choose domicile in a foreign place, for whatever reason, usually treat their native language like a delicate time-piece, making certain it runs exactly and that no dust gets inside. —MAVIS GALLANT

His death was like the flash of his gun, sudden, accurate and—since one must die—merciful. —GEORGE WOODCOCK

The whole place is silent as an empty classroom, like a house suddenly without children. —W.P. KINSELLA

The two men passed through the crowd as easily as the Israelites through the Red Sea. —WILLIAM X. KIENZLE

He was like a piece of rare and delicate china which was always being saved from breaking and which finally fell.
—ALICE WALKER

METAPHORS

Dress is language. —LANCE MORROW

Successful living is a journey toward simplicity and a triumph over confusion. —MARTIN E. MARTY

A North American supermarket is market place, temple, palace, and parade all rolled into one. —MARGARET VISSER

We are born princes and the civilizing process turns us into frogs. —ERIC BERNE

Wolf pups make a frothy ribbon of sound like fat bubbling.
—EDWARD HOAGLAND   [a metaphor and a simile]

Single words are often used metaphorically:

These roses must be **planted** in good soil.   [literal]

A man's feet must be **planted** in his country, but his eyes should survey the world. —GEORGE SANTAYANA [metaphorical]

We always **sweep** the leaves out of the garage.   [literal]

She was letting her imagination **sweep** unchecked round every rock and cranny of the world that lies submerged in the depths of our unconscious being.   —VIRGINIA WOOLF   [metaphorical]

Similes and metaphors are especially valuable when they are concrete and point up essential relationships that cannot otherwise be communicated. (For faulty metaphors, see **23c**.) Similes and metaphors can also be extended throughout a paragraph of comparison. See **32d(10)**.

Two other frequently used figures of speech are *hyperbole* and *personification*. *Hyperbole* is deliberate overstatement or fanciful exaggeration.

I, for one, don't expect till I die to be so good a man as I am at this minute, for just now I'm fifty thousand feet high—a tower with all the trumpets shouting.   —G.K. CHESTERTON

Personification is the attribution to the non-human (objects, animals, ideas) of characteristics possessed only by the human.

Time talks. It speaks more plainly than words. . . . It can shout the truth where words lie.   —EDWARD T. HALL

■ **Exercise 6**   Complete each sentence with an effective simile, metaphor, hyperbole, or personification.

EXAMPLES
The grass rolls out to the bleachers like a *freshly brushed billiard table*.   —JAY WRIGHT

The sentence is a *bridge* we build and cross to reach one another.   —ROBIN ENDRES

1. Sightseers flocked around the TV crew like _____ .
2. Viewed from outer space, the earth is _____ .
3. The mosquitoes in those weeds _____ .
4. The third hurricane of the season slashed through Jamaican towns _____ .

5. Death in a hovel or in a penthouse is _____ .
6. Like _____ , the class sat speechless.
7. The lecture was as as _____ .
8. Her eyes looked like _____ .
9. Surging forward, the crowd _____ .
10. Constant bickering is as _____ .
11. She was as self-confident as _____ .
12. The alarm sounded like _____ .

20b

Choose expressions that are idiomatic.

Be careful to use idiomatic English, not unidiomatic approximations. *She talked down to him* is idiomatic. *She talked under to him* is not. Occasionally the idiomatic use of prepositions may prove difficult. If you are uncertain which preposition to use with a given word, check the word in the dictionary. For instance, *agree* may be followed by *about, on, to,* or *with.* The choice depends on the context. Writers often have trouble with expressions such as these:

> according **to** the plan   [NOT with]
> accuse **of** perjury   [NOT with]
> comply **with** rules   [NOT to]
> conform **to/with** standards   [NOT in]
> die **of** cancer   [NOT with]
> in accordance **with** policy   [NOT to]
> independent **of** her family   [NOT from]
> inferior **to** ours   [NOT than]
> jealous **of** others   [NOT for]

Many idioms—such as *kick the bucket, put up a fight,* and *in full swing*—defy literal interpretation. That is, their meanings cannot be understood from the individual meanings of their elements. As you encounter idioms that are new to you, master their meanings just as you would any new word.

■ **Exercise 7**   Write sentences using each of the following idioms correctly. Use your dictionary as necessary.

1. agree with, agree to, agree on
2. differ from, differ with, differ about
3. wait on, wait for
4. necessity for, necessity of
5. part from, part with
6. pick on, pick out, pick up
7. put on, put off, put by

20c
Choose fresh expressions instead of trite, worn-out ones.

Such expressions as *to the bitter end, lazy as the day is long,* and *dead as a doornail* were once striking and effective. Excessive use, however, has drained them of their original force and made them clichés. Some euphemisms (pleasant-sounding substitutions for more explicit but possibly offensive words) are not only trite but wordy—for example, *laid to rest* for *buried* or *pecuniary difficulties* for *debt.* Many political slogans and the catchy phraseology of advertisements soon become hackneyed. Faddish or trendy expressions like *interface, impacted, viable, input,* or *be into* (as in "I am into dieting") are so overused that they quickly lose their force.

Nearly every writer uses clichés from time to time because they are so much a part of the language, especially of spoken English, and do contribute to the clear expression of ideas in written English.

> We feel free when we escape—even if it be but **from the frying pan into the fire**.   —ERIC HOFFER

It is often possible to give a fresh twist to an old saying or a well-known literary passage.

If a thing is worth doing, it is worth doing badly.
—G.K. CHESTERTON

Into each life a little sun must fall.   —L.E. SISSMAN

Washington is Thunder City—full of the sound and fury signifying power.   —TOM BETHELL   [Compare Shakespeare's "full of sound and fury, / Signifying nothing."—*Macbeth*]

Proverbs and familiar expressions from literature or the Bible, many of which have become a part of everyday language, can often be used effectively in your own writing.

Our lives are empty of belief. They are **lives of quiet desperation**.   —ARTHUR M. SCHLESINGER, JR.   [Compare Thoreau's *Walden*: "The mass of men lead lives of quiet desperation."]

Slowly but steadily, in the following years, a new vision began gradually to replace the dream of political power—a powerful movement, the rise of another ideal to guide the unguided, another **pillar of fire by night** after a clouded day.
—W.E.B. DU BOIS   [Compare Exodus 13:21: "And the Lord went before them . . . by night in a pillar of fire, to give them light."]

Good writers, however, do not rely too heavily on the words of others; they choose their own words to communicate their own ideas.

■ **Exercise 8**   From the following list of trite expressions—only a sampling of the many in current use—select ten that you often use or hear, and replace them with carefully chosen words or phrases.

EXAMPLES
a bolt from the blue   *a shock*
beyond the shadow of a doubt   *undoubtedly*

1. a chip off the old block
2. a crying shame
3. abreast of the times
4. after all is said and done
5. as cold as ice
6. as happy as a lark
7. at the crack of dawn
8. at one fell swoop
9. bored to tears/death
10. follow in the footsteps of
11. hoping against hope
12. in the last analysis
13. in this day and age
14. little bundle of joy

15. over and done with
16. selling like hotcakes
17. slept like a log
18. stick to your guns
19. straight from the shoulder/hip
20. the depths of despair
21. the powers that be
22. the spitting image of
23. the picture of health
24. working like a Trojan
25. nipped in the bud

■ **Exercise 9** Choose five of the ten items below as the basis for five original sentences. Use language that is exact, idiomatic, and fresh.

EXAMPLES
the appearance of her hair

Her hair poked through a broken net like stunted antlers.

—J.F. POWERS

OR   *Her dark hair was gathered up in a coil like a crown on her head.* —D.H. LAWRENCE

1. the look on her face
2. his response to fear
3. the way he walks
4. the condition of the streets
5. spring in the air
6. the noises of the city
7. the appearance of the room
8. the scene of the accident
9. the final minutes of play
10. the approaching storm

■ **Exercise 10** Read the two passages that follow in preparation for a class discussion of the authors' choice of words, their use of concrete, specific language, and their use of figurative language.

[1]The days were short, and often sombre, but we kept a good fire going in the house, we ate pumpkin pie, we sorted walnuts and corn.   [2]We also set tomatoes to ripen on the window sills, and on certain days the whole house was permeated with the odour of pickles cooking over a gentle fire in large pans.   [3]The saw could be heard singing in the yard; its two-toned song, first clear, then deeper and heavier as it bit into the wood, seemed to me to promise us joyfully, "I'm cutting you fine logs, fine logs for the whole winter."   [4]All this time the house, like a ship ready to weigh anchor or a city about to undergo a siege, was being filled with provisions—sauerkraut, maple syrup from Quebec, red apples from British Columbia, plums from Ontario.   [5]Soon

also we began to receive from our uncles in the country fat geese and turkeys, dozens of chickens, hams and salt bacon, cases of fresh eggs and farm butter. ⁶To help ourselves we only had to go into our summer kitchen, now transformed into a storehouse, where the frost preserved our stock. ⁷Such were the joys of autumn, based upon abundance and a feeling of security that I think I appreciated even then.

—GABRIELLE ROY

¹They say, too, that nature did its best to co-operate. ²A wind came up from somewhere, bending trees, shaking the house. ³You could hear the screech of giant trunks grinding against each other. ⁴You could hear the squeal of nails wrenched in the lumbered walls and the cedar roof above you. ⁵The water in the strait was churned up into waves that smashed against the cliff, and leapt upwards high enough to spray the windows and toss driftwood logs like sticks across the yard. ⁶A door flew open in the wind, crashed against the wall, and was forced shut again by someone whose face was streaming with rain and salt water and strips of kelp. ⁷Sticks and bits of limbs were flying across the floor. ⁸Dead pine needles clotted like hairballs in the corner. ⁹Keneally's voice rose above the tumult to include it.

¹⁰He would be transformed, Keneally said, his voice suddenly heavy with importance. ¹¹He would be transformed from flesh into spirit this night. ¹²He would, in fact, be dead. ¹³The organ music spiralled upward into a final impossible note that lay across the sudden silence like a clear metallic lid, though frightened Kathleen's feet kept pumping madly still and her forehead pressed against the elaborately carved wood of the instrument like a cyclist against the wind. ¹⁴Logs crashed on the verandah; men whimpered; bladders weakened; a light in the ceiling dimmed.

—JACK HODGINS

Wordiness and Needless Repetition

21

Avoid wordiness. Repeat a word or phrase only when it is needed for emphasis or clarity.

Wordiness is the use of more words than necessary to express an idea.

WORDY   In the early part of the month of January, a blizzard was moving threateningly toward St. John's.

REVISED   In early January, a blizzard was threatening St. John's.

Needless repetition of words or phrases distracts the reader and blurs meaning.

REPETITIOUS   This **interesting** instructor knows how to make an un**interesting** subject **interesting**.

REVISED   This instructor knows how to make a dull subject interesting.

For the effective use of repetition in parallel structures, for emphasis, and as a transitional device, see **26b**, **29e**, and **32b(3)**, respectively.

Wordiness

21a

Make every word count; omit words or phrases that add nothing to the meaning.

(1) Avoid tautology (the use of different words that say the same thing).

WORDY	Commuters going back and forth to work or school formed carpools.
CONCISE	Commuters formed carpools.
WORDY	Each writer has a distinctive style, and he or she uses this in his or her own works.
CONCISE	Each writer has a distinctive style.

Notice the useless words in brackets below:

yellow [in colour]	circular [in shape]
at 21:45 [that night]	return [back]
[basic] essentials	rich [and wealthy] nations
bitter [-tasting] salad	small [-size] potatoes
but [though]	to apply [or utilize] rules
connect [up together]	[true] facts

Avoid grammatical redundancy—such as a double subject (subject + subjective pronoun), double comparison, or double negative.

my sister [she] is	[more] easier than	could[n't] hardly

(2) Do not use many words when a few will express the idea well. Omit unnecessary words.

WORDY	**In the event that** the grading system is changed, expect complaints **on the part of** the students.
CONCISE	**If** the grading system is changed, expect complaints **from** the students. [Two words take the place of eight.]

WORDY   **As far as sexism is concerned, it seems to me that** a woman can be as guilty of sexism as a man.

CONCISE   A woman can be as guilty of sexism as a man.
[Unnecessary words are deleted.]

One or two words can replace expressions such as these:

at this point in time	**now**
has the capability of working	**can work**
made contact by personal visits	**visited**
on account of the fact that	**because**
somewhere in the neighbourhood of $2500	**about $2500**

One exact word can say as much as many. (See also **20a**.)

spoke in a low and hard-to-hear voice	**mumbled**
persons who really know their particular field	**experts**

Notice below that the words in brackets are not necessary.

because [of the fact that]	was [more or less] hinting
[really and truly] fearless	by [virtue of] his authority
fans [who were] watching TV	the oil [that exists] in shale

■ **Exercise 1**   Revise each sentence to eliminate tautology.

1. The exact date has not been set and is not known to us.
2. During the last two innings, many senseless mistakes occurred without any apparent reason for them.
3. Long lines of starving refugees in need of food were helped by the Red Cross volunteer people.
4. Perhaps maybe the chief cause or reason for obesity in people who are overweight is lack of exercise.
5. The tall skyscraper buildings form a dark silhouette against the evening sky.

■ **Exercise 2**   Substitute one or two words for each item.

1. in this day and age
2. has the ability to sing
3. was of the opinion that
4. in a serious manner

5. prior to the time that
6. did put in an appearance
7. located in the vicinity of
8. has a tendency to break
9. during the same time that
10. involving too much expense

■ **Exercise 3**   Delete unnecessary words below.

1. It seems to me to be obvious.
2. Because of the fact that Larry was there, the party was lively.
3. Other things being equal, it is my opinion that all of these oil slicks, whether they are massive or not so big, do damage to the environment to a greater or lesser degree.
4. As for the nature of biassed newscasts, I can only say that I realize that reporters have to do some editing, though they may not use the finest type of judgment when they are underscoring, as it were, some of the stories and downplaying others.

21b

Eliminate needless words by combining sentences or by simplifying phrases and clauses.

Note differences in emphasis as you study the following examples.

WORDY   The grass was like a carpet. It covered the whole playground. The colour of the grass was blue-green.

CONCISE   A carpet of blue-green grass covered the whole playground.

WORDY   A few of the listeners who had become angry called in so that they would have the opportunity of refuting the arguments set forth by the host.

CONCISE   A few angry listeners called in to refute the host's arguments.

■ **Exercise 4**   Condense the following sentences based on the patterns of the examples provided.

EXAMPLE
These were theories which were, in essence, concerned with politics.
These were political theories.

1. These are pitfalls that do, of course, pose a real danger.
2. This is an act which, in truth, partakes of the nature of aggression.

EXAMPLE
It was a house built with cheap materials.
It was a cheaply built house.

3. It was a garden planned with a great deal of care.
4. It was a speech delivered with a lot of passion.

EXAMPLE
The stories written by Alice Munro are different from those composed by Jack Hodgins.
Alice Munro's stories are different from Jack Hodgins'.

5. The dishes prepared by her husband are not as good as those fixed by her father.
6. The ideas shared by the students were different from those promoted by the advertiser.

EXAMPLE
It is unfortunate. A few come to college so that they can avoid work.
Unfortunately, a few come to college to avoid work.

7. It is inevitable. Corporations produce goods so that they can make a profit.
8. It is predictable. Before an election legislators reduce taxation so that they can win the approval of voters.

EXAMPLE
The forces that were against censorship ran an advertisement that covered two pages.
The anti-censorship forces ran a two-page advertisement.

9. A group that is in favour of labour wants contracts that last twelve months.
10. One editorial supporting day-care stressed the need for centres that are government funded.

■ **Exercise 5**   Restructure or combine sentences to reduce the number of words.

1. These hazards are not visible, and they cause accidents, many of which are fatal ones.
2. The countryside was being invaded. What I mean by that is a takeover of land. Urban developers were buying up farms.
3. In spite of the fact that my parents did not approve of it, I was married to Evelyn last June.
4. The fire chief made the recommendation saying that wooden shingles should not be used on homes now being built or in the future.

Needless Repetition

21c
Avoid needless repetition.

NEEDLESS	His uncle is not like her uncle. Her uncle takes more chances.
REVISED	His uncle is not like hers. Hers takes more chances.
NEEDLESS	I think that he knows that that woman is not the one for him to marry.
REVISED	I think he knows he should not marry that woman.

Note: Avoid the distracting repetition of a word (or part of a word) used in different senses.

CARELESS	Even at the graveside services, the brothers kept quarrelling. It was a grave situation.
BETTER	. . . It was a **serious** situation.

Do not unintentionally use jingles like ''compared the fare there.'' A repetition of sounds can be distracting: see **19h**.

21d

Eliminate needless repetition by using pronouns and elliptical constructions.

Use a pronoun instead of needlessly repeating a noun or substituting a clumsy synonym. If the reference is clear, several pronouns may refer to the same antecedent.

NEEDLESS   The hall outside these offices was empty. The hall had dirty floors, and the walls of this corridor were full of gaudy portraits.

REVISED   The hall outside these offices was empty. It had dirty floors, and its walls were full of gaudy portraits.

The writer of the following sentence uses an elliptical construction. The omitted words (shown here in brackets) will be understood by the reader without being repeated.

Prosperity is the goal for some people, fame [is the goal] for others, and complete independence [is the goal] for still others. . . . —RENÉ DUBOS

Sometimes, as an aid to clarity, commas are used to mark omissions that avoid repetition.

Family life in my parents' home was based upon a cosmic order: Papa was the sun; Mamma, the moon; and we kids, minor satellites. —SAM LEVENSON

For effective use of the repetition of words or phrases, see **29e**.

■ **Exercise 6**   Revise each sentence to eliminate wordiness and needless repetition.

1. The manager returned the application back because of illegible handwriting that could not be read.
2. In this day and time, it is difficult today to find in the field of science a physicist who shows as much insight into the field of space and time as Stephen Hawking shows.
3. From time to time during one's life, one needs to remember that one who is learning to walk has to put one foot before the other one.
4. When the fans in the stadium shout and yell, the shouting and yelling is deafening, and so the total effect of all this is that it is a contributing factor in decisions to stay home and watch the games on TV.
5. A distant hurricane or a seaquake can cause a tidal wave. This wave can form when either occurs.
6. A comedy of intrigue (or a situation comedy) is a comedy that relies on action instead of characterization for its comedy.
7. In my family, schoolwork came first, chores came second, fun and games came next, and discussions came last.
8. Numerous products can be made from corn. The oil from this plant is used in soap. A starch extracted from corn helps make gravy without lumps.

Omission of Necessary Words

22

Do not omit a word or phrase necessary to the meaning of the sentence.

If you omit necessary words in your compositions, your mind may be racing ahead of your pen, or your writing may reflect omissions in your spoken English.

> The analyst talked about the tax dollar goes.   [The writer thought "talked about where" but did not write *where*.]
> You better be there on time!   [When speaking, the writer omits *had* before *better*.]

To avoid omitting necessary words, proofread your compositions carefully and study **22a–c**.

22a
Do not omit a necessary article, pronoun, conjunction, or preposition. See also **26b**.

(1) Omitted article or pronoun

> INCOMPLETE   The first meeting was held on other campus.
> COMPLETE   The first meeting was held on **the** other campus.

| INCOMPLETE | I know a man had a horse like that. |
| COMPLETE | I know a man **who** had a horse like that. |

To avoid ambiguity, it is often necessary to repeat a pronoun or an article before the second part of a compound.

AMBIGUOUS	A friend and helper stood nearby. [One person or two?]
CLEAR	A friend and **a** helper stood nearby. [two persons clearly indicated by repetition of *a*]
ALSO CLEAR	My mother and father were there. [clearly two persons—repetition of *my* before *father* not necessary]

(2) Omitted conjunction or preposition

CONFUSING	Fran noticed the passenger who was sleeping soundly had dropped his wallet in the aisle. [The reader may be momentarily confused by "noticed the passenger."]
BETTER	Fran noticed **that** the passenger who was sleeping soundly had dropped his wallet in the aisle.
INFORMAL	I had never seen that type movie before.
GENERAL	I had never seen that type **of** movie before.

When two verbs requiring different prepositions are used together, do not omit the first preposition. See also **20b**.

| INCOMPLETE | Such comments neither contribute nor detract from his reputation. |
| COMPLETE | Such comments neither contribute **to** nor detract from his reputation. |

In sentences such as the following, if you omit the conjunction, use a comma in its place.

The English used the paints chiefly on churches at first **,** then later on public buildings and the homes of the wealthy. —E.M. FISHER [Compare "on churches at first *and* then later on public buildings."]

The fact is, very few people in this society make a habit of thinking in ethical terms. —HARRY STEIN [Compare "The fact is *that* very few people. . . . "]

■ **Exercise 1**   Insert needed words below.

1. Lars reminded Sheila Richard might not approve.
2. What kind course to take is the big question.
3. Winter and spring breaks the campus is dead.
4. She lent me a dollar then decided to take it back.
5. The trouble was my good pair shoes got stolen.
6. Don will not ask nor listen to any advice.
7. Fires had burned for weeks were still not out.
8. The book which he referred was not in our library.
9. It is the exception proves the rule.
10. The recipe calls for a variety spices.

22b

Avoid awkward omission of verbs and auxiliaries.

AWKWARD	Scott has never and cannot be wholly honest with himself.
BETTER	Scott has never **been** and cannot be wholly honest with himself.
INCOMPLETE	Since I been in college, some of my values have changed.
COMPLETE	Since I **have** been in college, some of my values have changed.
INCOMPLETE	This problem easy to solve.
COMPLETE	This problem **is** easy to solve.
INCOMPLETE	As far as the speed limit, many drivers think they have to drive that fast.
COMPLETE	As far as the speed limit **is concerned**, many drivers think they have to drive that fast.
LESS WORDY	**As for** the speed limit, many drivers think they have to drive that fast.

Option: In sentences such as the following, the omission or inclusion of the second verb is optional.

> The sounds were angry, the manner violent. —A.E. VAN VOGT
> [omission of second verb]
> The sounds were angry, the manner **was** violent. [inclusion of second verb]

22c
Do not omit words needed to complete comparisons.

INCOMPLETE	Broken bottles around a swimming area are more dangerous than picnic tables.
COMPLETE	Broken bottles around a swimming area are more dangerous than **around** picnic tables.
INCOMPLETE	Snow here is as scarce as Fiji.
COMPLETE	Snow here is as scarce as **it is in** Fiji.
CONFUSING	Sometimes counsellors help an alcoholic less than the rest of the family.
CLEAR	Sometimes counsellors help an alcoholic less than **they do** the rest of the family.
	OR
	Sometimes counsellors help an alcoholic less than the rest of the family **does**.
INCOMPLETE	The amateur's performance was as good, possibly even better than, the professional's.
COMPLETE	The amateur's performance was as good **as**, possibly even better than, the professional's.

In a comparison such as the following, the word *other* may indicate a difference in meaning:

> O'Brien runs faster than any player on the team. [O'Brien is apparently not on the team. In context, however, this may be an informal sentence meaning that O'Brien is the fastest of the players on the team.]

O'Brien runs faster than any **other** player on the team.   [*Other* clearly indicates that O'Brien is on the team.]

■ **Exercise 2**   Supply needed words in verb phrases and in comparisons.

1. They been trying to make small cars safe.
2. The consumers better listen to these warnings.
3. Ed's income is less than his wife.
4. Bruce admires Cathy more than Aline.
5. Fiberglass roofs are better.
6. The scenery here is as beautiful as any place.
7. I always have and always will like to read the comics.
8. One argument was as bad, maybe even worse than, the other.
9. The ordinance never has and never will be enforced.
10. The crusty old man irritates his roommate more than the cranky young nurse.

22d

When used as intensifiers in formal writing, *so, such*, and *too* are generally (but not always) followed by a completing phrase or clause.

The line was **so** long that we decided to skip lunch.
Bill has **such** a hearty laugh that it is contagious.
Laura was **too** angry to think straight.

■ **Exercise 3**   Insert words where needed.

1. I had my senior year a strange type virus.
2. As far as Victoria, I could see the people were proud of their history.
3. The group is opposed and angered by these attempts to amend the Constitution.
4. It good to talk with a person has a similar problem.

5. In our province the taxes are as high as Quebec.
6. The mystery of the stolen jewels reminds me mysteries like Sherlock Holmes.
7. The lawyer had to prove whatever the witness said was false.
8. Here is the hole which the rabbit escaped.
9. If Jack gets a job which he is not trained, he will fail.
10. The stadium was already filled with people and still coming.

EFFECTIVE SENTENCES

Sentence Unity

23

Write unified sentences.

Good writing is unified: it sticks to its purpose. Whether in sentences, paragraphs (see **32**), or whole compositions (**33**), unity is achieved when all the parts contribute to fulfilling the writer's aim. A sentence may lack unity because it combines unrelated ideas (see **23a**) or may have excessive details (**23b**) or may contain mixed metaphors, mixed constructions (**23c**), or faulty predication (**23d**). Clear, precise definitions (**23e**) often depend upon careful attention to sentence unity.

23a

Make the relationship of ideas in a sentence immediately clear to the reader.

UNRELATED	The St. Elias Range has majestic glaciers, but most Canadians must travel great distances. [unity thwarted by a gap in the thought]
RELATED	The St. Elias Range has majestic glaciers, but to see them most Canadians must travel great distances.

■ **Exercise 1**   All the sentences below contain ideas that are apparently unrelated. Adding words when necessary, rewrite each of the sentences to indicate clearly a relationship between ideas. If you cannot establish a close relationship, put the ideas in separate sentences.

1. There are many types of bores at social gatherings, but I prefer a quiet evening at home.
2. A telephone lineman who works during heavy storms can prove a hero, and cowards can be found in any walk of life.
3. Jones was advised to hire a tutor in French immediately, but the long hours of work at the florist shop kept his grades low.
4. Macbeth was not the only man to succumb to ambition, and Professor Stetson, for example, likes to draw parallels between modern men and literary characters.
5. Birds migrate to the warmer countries in the fall and in the summer get food by eating worms and insects that are pests to the farmer.

23b

Do not allow excessive detail to obscure the central thought of a sentence.

> EXCESSIVE DETAIL   In 1789, when Sir Alexander Mackenzie set out to chart the major river that ran out of Great Slave Lake and when he discovered it flowed to the Arctic instead, he was a partner in the fur firm of Gregory, McLeod and Company and second in command to Peter Pond, a famous explorer in his own right who believed the river flowed to the Pacific Ocean.
>
> ADEQUATE DETAIL   In 1789, when Sir Alexander Mackenzie charted the course of the river running out of Great Slave Lake, he found that it led to the Arctic Ocean, not the Pacific as the explorer Peter Pond had theorized.

As you strive to eliminate excessive detail, remember that length alone does not make a sentence ineffective. Your purpose sometimes requires a long, detailed sentence. Even a sentence of paragraph length can be unified by parallel structure, balance, rhythm, effectively repeated connectives, and careful punctuation. Consider this sentence about a Newfoundland outport kitchen and its furnishings.

> [The kitchen] always contains at least one "day bed" (a combination of sofa and single bed) which provides a place for the man to stretch out for a few minutes before his meal; a place for the woman to sit with the children beside her as she knits, sews, or spins; a place for a gaggle of neighbours' children to perch in owl-eyed silence; a place for a grandfather or an aging aunt to rest and reminisce; a place where young lovers come together when the rest of the house lies sleeping.
>
> —FARLEY MOWAT, *This Rock within the Sea*

■ **Exercise 2**   Revise each sentence to eliminate excessive detail.

1. The fan that Joan bought for her brother, who frets about any temperature that exceeds twenty and insists that he can't stand the heat, arrived today.
2. Flames from the gas heater that was given to us three years ago by friends who were moving to Regina licked at the chintz curtains.
3. After finishing breakfast, which consisted of oatmeal, toast, and coffee, Sigrid called the tree surgeon, a cheerful man approximately fifty years old.
4. At last I returned the book that I had used for the report which I made Tuesday to the library.
5. A course in business methods helps undergraduates to get jobs and in addition helps them to find out whether they are fitted for business and thus to avoid postponing the crucial test, as so many do, until it is too late.

23c
Avoid mixed metaphors and mixed constructions.

(1) Do not mix metaphors. See also **20a(4).**

MIXED	Playing with fire can get you into deep water.
BETTER	Playing with fire can result in burned fingers.
MIXED	Her climb up the ladder of success was nipped in the bud.
BETTER	Her climb up the ladder of success was soon halted.
	OR
	Her promising career was nipped in the bud.

(2) Do not mix constructions.

MIXED	When Howard plays the hypochondriac taxes his wife's patience. [adverb clause + predicate]
REVISED	When Howard plays the hypochondriac, he taxes his wife's patience. [adverb clause, main clause]
	OR
	Howard's playing the hypochondriac taxes his wife's patience. [subject + predicate]
MIXED	It was an old ramshackle house but which was quite livable.
REVISED	It was an old ramshackle house, but it was quite livable.
	OR
	It was an old ramshackle house which was quite livable. [noun + adjective clause]

Note: Sometimes a sentence is flawed by the use of a singular noun instead of a plural one: "Hundreds who attended the convention drove their own **cars** [NOT car]."

23d

Avoid faulty predication.

Faulty predication occurs when the subject and predicate do not fit each other logically.

FAULTY	One book I read believes in eliminating subsidies. [A person, not a thing, believes.]

REVISED   The author of one book I read believes in eliminating subsidies.
OR
One book I read says that subsidies should be eliminated.

FAULTY   An example of discrimination is an apartment owner, especially after he has refused to rent to people with children.   [The refusal, not the owner, is an example of discrimination.]

REVISED   An example of discrimination is an apartment owner's refusal to rent to people with children.

■ **Exercise 3**   Revise each sentence to eliminate faulty predication, a mixed construction, or a mixed metaphor.

1. Another famous story from Canadian history is Laura Secord.
2. One example of a rip-off would be a butcher, because he could weigh his heavy thumb with the steak.
3. When people avoid saying or doing something tactless shows they have good manners.
4. Like a bat guided by radar, Jane was always surefooted in her business dealings.
5. Could anyone be certain why George resigned or where did he find a better job?
6. For Don, money does grow on trees, and it also goes down the drain quickly.
7. Because his feet are not the same size explains the difficulty he has finding shoes that fit.
8. I felt like a grain of sand crying out in the wilderness.
9. When children need glasses causes them to make mistakes in reading and writing.
10. The forecast of subnormal temperatures in late March was predicted by Environment Canada.

23e

Avoid awkward definitions. Define a word or an expression clearly and precisely. See also **32d(7)**.

(1) Avoid faulty *is-when* or *is-where* definitions.

FAULTY   Banishing a man is where he is driven out of his
country. [Banishing is an act, not a place.]

REVISED   Banishing a man is driving him out of his country.

FAULTY   Unlike a fact, a value judgment is when you express
personal opinions or preferences.

REVISED   Unlike a fact, a value judgment is a personal opinion
or preference.

(2) Write clear, precise definitions.

A short dictionary definition may be adequate when you
need to define a term or a special meaning of a word that
may be unfamiliar to your reader.

Here *galvanic* means "produced as if by electric shock."
[See also the note on page 160.]

Giving a synonym or two may clarify the meaning of a
term. Often such synonyms are used as appositives.

A dolt is a dullard, a blockhead.

Magendo, or black-market corruption, is flourishing.
—KEN ADELMAN

If you press your forefinger gently against your closed eyelid
for a minute or less, you will probably start to see phosphenes:
shapes and colors that march and swirl across your darkened
field of view. —JEARL WALKER [word substitutions with
restrictive details]

Writers frequently show—rather than tell—what a word
means by giving examples.

Many homophones (*be* and *bee*, *in* and *inn*, *see* and *sea*) are
not spelling problems.

A "formal definition" first states the term to be defined
and puts it into a class, then differentiates the term from
other members of its class.

A phosphene [term] is a luminous visual image [class] that results from applying pressure to the eyeball [differentiation].

You may formulate your own definitions of the concepts you wish to clarify.

Questions are windows to the mind.   —GERARD I. NIERENBERG
[use of a metaphor—see also **20a(4)**]

Clichés are sometimes thought of as wisdom gone stale.
—JOSEPH EPSTEIN

■ **Exercise 4**   Define any two of the following terms.

1. blintz
2. uncanny
3. love
4. peer
5. neurotic

6. Bren gun
7. stupid
8. Francophone
9. humanism
10. integrity

Subordination and Co-ordination

24

Use subordination to relate ideas concisely and effectively. Use co-ordination to give ideas equal emphasis.

One of the marks of mature writing is the ability to relate ideas effectively by subordination and co-ordination.

Subordinate means "being of lower structural rank." In the following sentence, the italicized subordinate elements are grammatically dependent on the sentence base (subject + compound predicate) in boldface.

> *Since I was sixteen years old at the time and had been graduated from high school,* **I knew a great deal and had opinions** *on a variety of subjects that I thought anyone else in the office would consider it a privilege to hear.*
>
> —EDWIN NEWMAN

As this example shows, grammatically subordinate structures may contain very important ideas.

Co-ordinate means "being of equal structural rank." Co-ordination gives equal grammatical emphasis to two or more ideas. In the following sentence, each main clause (subject + predicate) is a co-ordinate element.

> **These are mysteries performed before our very eyes; we
> can see every detail, and yet they are still mysteries.**
> —ANNIE DILLARD

Co-ordination gives equal emphasis not only to two or more
clauses but also to two or more words, phrases, or sentences.
See also Section **26**.

> *tactless, abrasive* language   [co-ordinate adjectives]
> *on the roof* or *in the attic*   [compound prepositional phrases]
> *I have not gone on a diet.* Nor *do I intend to.*   [sentences
>   linked by co-ordinating conjunction]

A study of this section should help you to use subordination effectively when you revise a series of short, choppy
simple sentences (see **24a**) or stringy compound ones
(**24b[1]**). It should also help you use co-ordination to secure
the grammatical emphasis you want (**24b[2]**) and to eliminate faulty subordination (**24c**). If you cannot distinguish
between phrases and clauses and between subordinate and
main clauses, see **1d** and **1e**.

24a

**Use subordination to combine a series of related short
sentences into longer more effective units.**

CHOPPY   He stood there in his buckskin clothes. One felt in
          him standards and loyalties. One also felt a code.
          This code is not easily put into words. But this code
          is instantly felt when two men who live by it come
          together by chance.

BETTER   As he stood there in his buckskin clothes, one felt
          in him standards, loyalties, a code which is not eas-
          ily put into words, but which is instantly felt when
          two men who live by it come together by chance.
                                              —WILLA CATHER

When combining a series of related sentences, first choose
a sentence base (subject + predicate); then use subordinate

elements to relate the other ideas to the base. (Co-ordination is also used to combine short sentences, but inexperienced writers tend to use too much of it: see **24b**.)

(1) Use adjectives and adjective phrases.

CHOPPY   The limbs were covered with ice. They sparkled in the sunlight. They made a breathtaking sight.

BETTER   *Sparkling in the sunlight*, the *ice-covered* limbs made a breathtaking sight.   [participial phrase and hyphenated adjectival]

(2) Use adverbs or adverb phrases.

CHOPPY   Season the chicken livers with garlic. Use a lot of it. Fry them in butter. Use very low heat.

BETTER   Season the chicken livers *heavily* with garlic, and *slowly* fry them in butter.   [Note the use of both subordination and co-ordination.]
OR
After seasoning the chicken livers heavily with garlic, slowly fry them in butter.

CHOPPY   His face was covered with white dust. So were his clothes. The man looked like a ghost.

BETTER   *His face and clothes white with dust*, the man looked like a ghost.   [first two sentences combined in an absolute phrase]

(3) Use appositives and contrasting elements.

CHOPPY   These kindnesses were acts of love. They were noticed. But they were not appreciated.

BETTER   These kindnesses—*acts of love*—were noticed *but not appreciated*.

(4) Use subordinate clauses.

Subordinate clauses are linked and related to main clauses by such markers as *who, that, when*, and *if*. See the lists of these markers (subordinating conjunctions and relative pronouns) on page 20.

CHOPPY   The blizzard ended. Then helicopters headed for the mountaintop. It looked dark and forbidding.

BETTER   *As soon as the blizzard ended*, helicopters headed for the mountaintop, *which looked dark and forbidding*.   [adverb clause and adjective clause]

Caution: Do not use *but* or *and* before *which, who,* or *whom* when introducing a single adjective clause, as in ''Irene is a music major who can play several instruments   [NOT and who].'' See also **23c(2)**.

■ **Exercise 1**   Combine the following short sentences into longer sentences by using effective subordination and co-ordination. (If you wish, keep a short sentence or two for emphasis: see **29h**.)

¹I have just read "The Idea of a University" by John Henry Newman.   ²I am especially interested in his views regarding knowledge.   ³He says that knowledge is its own reward.   ⁴It is not just a means to an end.   ⁵Newman says knowledge is a treasure in itself.   ⁶I had looked upon knowledge only in terms of practical results.   ⁷One result would be financial security.   ⁸But that was before I read this essay.   ⁹Now I accept Newman's definition of knowledge.   ¹⁰Such knowledge is worth pursuing for its own sake.

24b

Do not string main clauses together when some ideas should be subordinated. Use co-ordination to give ideas equal emphasis.

Do not overwork co-ordinating connectives like *and, then, and then, so, and so, but, however, therefore*. For ways to revise stringy or loose compound sentences, see **30c**. Methods of subordination that apply to combining two or more sentences also apply to revising faulty or excessive co-ordination in a single sentence: see **24a**.

(1) **Do not blur your emphasis with stringy compound sentences; subordinate some ideas to others.**

AWKWARD I wanted to go to college, so I mowed and trimmed lawns all summer, and that way I could earn my tuition.

BETTER *Because I wanted to go to college*, I mowed and trimmed lawns *to earn my tuition*.

AWKWARD Burns won, and it was a landslide vote, but he had rigged the election.

BETTER Burns, *who had rigged the election*, won by a landslide vote.
OR
Having rigged the election, Burns won by a landslide vote.

(2) **Use co-ordination to give ideas equal emphasis.**

The offer was tempting, but I didn't accept it. [equal grammatical stress on the offer and the refusal]

COMPARE Although the offer was tempting, I didn't accept it. [stress on the refusal]
Although I didn't accept it, the offer was tempting. [stress on the offer]

■ **Exercise 2** Revise each sentence by using effective subordination and co-ordination.

1. First she selected a lancet and sterilized it, and then she gave the patient a local anesthetic and lanced the infected flesh.
2. Yesterday I was taking a shower, so I did not hear the telephone ring, but I got the message in time to go to the party.

3. Two ambulances tore by, and an oncoming bus crowded a truckload of labourers off the road, but nobody got hurt.
4. Jean Henri Dunant was a citizen of Switzerland, and he felt sorry for Austrian soldiers wounded in the Napoleonic Wars; therefore, he started an organization, and it was later named the Red Cross.
5. The administrators stressed career education, and not only did they require back-to-basics courses, but they also kept students informed about job opportunities.

24c

Avoid faulty or excessive subordination.

FAULTY   I have never before known a person like Ernie, who is ready to help anybody who is in trouble that involves finances.

BETTER   I have never before known a person like Ernie, who is ready to help anybody in financial trouble.   [one subordinate clause reduced to a phrase, another reduced to an adjective]

■ **Exercise 3**   Observing differences in emphasis, convert each pair of sentences to (a) a simple sentence, (b) a compound sentence consisting of two main clauses, and (c) a complex sentence with one main clause and one subordinate clause.

EXAMPLE
Male sperm whales occasionally attack ships. These whales jealously guard their territory.

a. *Jealously guarding their territory, male sperm whales occasionally attack ships.*
b. *Male sperm whales occasionally attack ships; these whales jealously guard their territory.*
c. *Since male sperm whales jealously guard their territory, they occasionally attack ships.*

1. The men smuggled marijuana into Spain. They were sentenced to six years in prison.

2. The council first condemned the property. Then it ordered the owner's eviction.
3. Aunt Elinor applied for a patent on her invention. She learned of three hundred such devices already on the market.
4. The border guards delayed every tourist. They carefully examined passports and luggage.

■ **Exercise 4**   Prepare for a discussion of the subordination and the co-ordination of ideas in the paragraph below.

¹Going by canoe is often the best—and sometimes the only—way to go.   ²Some difficult country can't be reached any other way, and once you arrive, the aches of paddling and sitting unsupported on a canoe seat seem a small price to pay for being there.   ³One such place is the Boundary Waters area along the border of northeastern Minnesota and Ontario.   ⁴The terrain is rolling and pocked by thousands of glacier lakes.   ⁵Some are no more than bowls of rock that hold the accumulated clear green water; others are spring-fed and dark.   ⁶The maze of lakes, islands, and portage trails is inhabited by all sorts of wildlife: beaver, otter, loons, and bear.   ⁷It is a landscape suited to the canoe and has in fact been canoe country since the time of the fur-trading voyageurs—hard Frenchmen whose freighters were up to twenty-five feet long and required eight paddlers.

—GEOFFREY NORMAN, "Rapid Transit"

Misplaced Parts, Dangling Modifiers

25

Avoid needless separation of related parts of the sentence. Avoid dangling modifiers.

25a
Avoid needless separation of related parts of the sentence.

As a rule, place modifiers near the words they modify. Note how the meaning of the following sentences changes according to the position of modifiers:

> Rex **just** died with his boots on.
> Rex died with **just** his boots on.
> **Just** Rex died with his boots on.

> The woman **who drowned** had tried to help the child.
> The woman had tried to help the child **who drowned**.

(1) **In formal English, modifiers such as** *almost, only, just, even, hardly, nearly*, **and** *merely* **are regularly placed immediately before the words they modify.**

> The truck costs **only** $450.   [NOT only costs]
> He works **even** during his vacation.   [NOT even works]

■ **Exercise 1**   Circle each misplaced modifier; draw an arrow to show its proper position.

1. The explosion only killed one person.
2. The transistor nearly cost fifty dollars.
3. On Thanksgiving Day the guests almost ate all the turkey.
4. Compulsive talkers hardly show any interest in what other people may have to say.

(2) **The position of a modifying prepositional phrase should clearly indicate what the phrase modifies.**

MISPLACED	A garish poster attracts the visitor's eye **on the east wall**.
BETTER	A garish poster **on the east wall** attracts the visitor's eye.
MISPLACED	One student said that such singing was not music but a throat ailment **in class**.
BETTER	**In class** one student **said** that such singing was not music but a throat ailment.
	OR
	One student **said in class** that such singing was not music but a throat ailment.

■ **Exercise 2**   Circle each misplaced prepositional phrase below; draw an arrow to show its proper position.

1. Newspapers carried the story of the quarterback's fumbling in every part of the country.
2. Lucille bakes date muffins just for her friends with pecans in them.
3. At the picnic Sharon and Michael served sundaes to hungry guests in paper cups.
4. The professor made it clear why plagiarism is wrong on Monday.

(3) **Adjective clauses should be placed near the words they modify.**

MISPLACED	We bought gasoline in Manitoba at a small country store **which cost $10.25**.
BETTER	At a small country store in Manitoba, we bought gasoline **which cost $10.25**.

(4) Avoid "squinting" constructions—modifiers that may refer to either a preceding or a following word.

SQUINTING	Jogging **often** relaxes her.
BETTER	**Often**, jogging relaxes her.
	OR
	It relaxes her to jog **often**.

(5) Avoid the awkward separation of the sentence base and the awkward splitting of an infinitive.

AWKWARD	**I had** in spite of my not living in a neighbourhood as fine as Jane's a healthy **measure** of pride. [awkward separation of a verb from its object]
BETTER	In spite of my not living in a neighbourhood as fine as Jane's, **I had** a healthy **measure** of pride.
AWKWARD	Longpré is the person **to**, if we can, **nominate** for councillor. [awkward splitting of an infinitive]
BETTER	Longpré is the person **to nominate** for councillor if we can.

Splitting an infinitive is often not only natural but desirable.

For her to **never** complain seems unreal.
I wished to **properly** understand programming.

■ **Exercise 3**   Revise the sentences to eliminate squinting modifiers or needless separation of related sentence parts.

1. An official warned the hunter not to carry a rifle in a car that was loaded.
2. Selby said in the evening he would go.
3. Kuniko wanted to, because she was winning, finish the game.
4. Darren promised when he was on his way home to stop at the library.

5. The car advertised in last night's paper which is only two years old is in excellent condition.

25b

Avoid dangling modifiers.

Although any misplaced word, phrase, or clause can be said to dangle, the term *dangling* is applied primarily to verbal phrases that do not refer clearly and logically to another word or phrase in the sentence.

To correct a dangling modifier, rearrange the words in the sentence to make the modifier clearly refer to the right word, or add words to make the meaning clear and logical.

(1) Avoid dangling participial phrases.

DANGLING **Discouraged by low grades**, dropping out seemed to make sense.

REVISED **Because I was discouraged by low grades**, dropping out seemed to make sense.
OR
Discouraged by low grades, I thought dropping out made sense.

Placed after the sentence base, the participial phrase in the revision below refers to the subject.

DANGLING The evening passed very pleasantly, **playing backgammon and swapping jokes**.

REVISED **They** passed the evening very pleasantly, **playing backgammon and swapping jokes.**

(2) Avoid dangling phrases containing gerunds or infinitives.

DANGLING **Instead of watching the late show**, a novel was read.

REVISED **Instead of watching the late show**, Hilary read a novel.

DANGLING   **Not able to swim that far**, a lifeguard came to my rescue.

REVISED   **I was not able to swim that far**, so a lifeguard came to my rescue.

OR

Because I was not able to swim that far, a lifeguard came to my rescue.

(3) Avoid dangling elliptical adverb clauses.

Elliptical clauses have words that are implied rather than stated.

DANGLING   **When confronted with these facts**, not one word was said.

REVISED   **When confronted with these facts, nobody** said a word.

OR

When they were confronted with these facts, not one word was said.

DANGLING   **Although only a small boy**, my father expected me to do a man's work.

REVISED   **Although I was only a small boy**, my father expected me to do a man's work.

Note: Sentence modifiers (see page 554) are considered standard usage, not danglers.

To judge from reports, all must be going well.

His health is fairly good, **considering his age**.

■ **Exercise 4**   Revise the following sentences to eliminate dangling modifiers. Put a check mark after any sentence that needs no revision.

1. While wondering about this phenomenon, the sun sank from view.
2. By standing and singing the anthem, the ceremony came to an end.
3. Once made, you must execute the decision promptly.

4. Prepare to make an incision in the abdomen as soon as completely anesthetized.
5. After sitting there awhile, it began to snow, and we went indoors.
6. Darkness having come, we stopped for the night.
7. Having taken his seat, we began to question the witness.
8. Ready to pitch camp, the windstorm hit.
9. The prisoners did not yield, thinking they could attract the support of the press.
10. Burned to the ground, the Rosellis had to build a new house.

■ **Exercise 5** Combine the two sentences in each item below into a single sentence. Use an appropriately placed verbal phrase or elliptical clause as an introductory parenthetical element.

EXAMPLES

We were in a hurry to leave Banff. The dented fender was not noticed.
Being in a hurry to leave Banff, we did not notice the dented fender.

People may sometimes be confused. At such times they ought to ask questions.
When confused, people ought to ask questions.

1. The statue has a broken arm and nose. I think it is an interesting antique.
2. James sometimes worried about the world situation. At such times working for CUSO seemed to him a good idea.
3. I read the first three questions on the test. The test covered materials that I had not studied.
4. Leona was only twelve years old. Her teachers noticed her inventive abilities.
5. I turned on the flashers and lifted the hood. A passing motorist, I thought, might see my predicament, slow down, and offer me a ride.

Parallelism

26

Use parallel structure to express matching ideas.

Parallel (grammatically equal) sentence elements regularly appear in lists or series, in compound structures, in comparisons using *than* or *as*, and in contrasted elements. As the examples below illustrate, parallelism contributes to clarity, rhythm, and ease in reading.

> Music expresses, at different moments, **serenity or exuberance, regret or triumph, fury or delight**.   —AARON COPLAND

> **Listening** is as much a persuasive technique as **speaking**.
> —GERARD I. NIERENBERG   [a comparison with *as . . . as*]

Many parallel elements are linked by a co-ordinating conjunction (such as *and, or, but*) or by correlatives (such as *neither . . . nor, whether . . . or*). Others are not. In the following examples, verbals used as subjects and complements are parallel in form.

> **To define** flora is **to define** climate.   —NATIONAL GEOGRAPHIC

> **Seeing** is **deceiving**. It's **eating** that's **believing**.
> —JAMES THURBER

Parallel structures are also used in topic outlines: see **33f**, page 385.

Faulty parallelism disrupts the balance of co-ordinate elements:

FAULTY   We are not so much **what we eat** but **the thoughts we think**. [The co-ordinate elements differ in grammatical form.]

REVISED   We are not so much **what we eat** but **what we think**.

OR

We are not so much **the food we eat** but **the thoughts we think**.

If you cannot readily distinguish between parts of speech and between types of phrases and clauses, study Section **1**.

26a

For parallel structure, balance nouns with nouns, prepositional phrases with prepositional phrases, main clauses with main clauses, and so on.

As you study the parallel words, phrases, clauses, and sentences that follow, notice that repetition can be used to emphasize the balanced structure.

(1) Parallel words and phrases

People begin to feel ‖ **faceless**
and ‖ **insignificant.**   —S.L. HALLECK

Freedom is ‖ **the right to be wrong,**
not ‖ **the right to do wrong.**   —JOHN G. DIEFENBAKER

She had ‖ **no time to be human,**
‖ **no time to be happy.**   —SEAN O'FAOLAIN

(2) Parallel clauses

Almost all of us want things ‖ **that we do not need**
and fail to want things ‖ **that we do need.**
—MORTIMER J. ADLER

|| **Let us be English** or
|| **let us be French**, but above all
|| **let us be Canadians.** ———SIR JOHN A. MACDONALD

(3) Parallel sentences

|| **There's no story so fantastic that I cannot imagine**
|| **myself the hero.** And
|| **there's no story so evil that I cannot imagine myself**
|| **the villain.**

———LEONARD COHEN

|| **The danger of the past was that men became slaves.**
|| **The danger of the future is that men may become**
|| **robots.**

———ERICH FROMM

■ **Exercise 1** Underline the parallel structures. Then write sentences containing parallel (1) words, (2) phrases, (3) clauses, and (4) sentences.

1. Many plants are pollinated by animals, such as bees, birds, or bats. ———NATIONAL GEOGRAPHIC
2. Carpets are bought by the yard and worn by the foot.
   ———A.R. SPOFFORD
3. We are all sick, all lonely, all in need of love. ———JEAN VANIER
4. Style in writing, as in painting, is the author's thumbprint, his mark. ———MAVIS GALLANT
5. Reading through *The Origin* is like eating Cracker Jacks and finding an I O U note at the bottom of the box.
   ———JOHN FLUDAS
6. The earth's nearest neighbor has mountains taller than Everest, valleys deeper than the Dead Sea rift, and highlands bigger than Australia. ———NEWSWEEK
7. There might be some people in the world who do not need flowers, who cannot be surprised by joy, but I haven't met them. ———GLORIA EMERSON

8. Top soil, once blown away, can never be returned; virgin prairie, once plowed, can never be reclaimed.

—MARILYN COFFEY

9. Think before you speak. Read before you think.

—FRAN LEBOWITZ

26b

To make the parallel clear, repeat a preposition, an article, the *to* of the infinitive, or the introductory word of a phrase or clause.

The reward rests not ‖ **in** the task
but ‖ **in** the pay.   —JOHN K. GALBRAITH

Life is ‖ **a** mystery
and ‖ **an** adventure
which he shares with all living things.

—JOSEPH WOOD KRUTCH

It is easier ‖ **to love humanity as a whole**
than ‖ **to love one's neighbor.**   —ERIC HOFFER

It is the things we think we know—
‖ **because** they are so elementary
or ‖ **because** they surround us—
that often present the greatest difficulties when we are
actually challenged to explain them.   —STEPHEN JAY GOULD

■ **Exercise 2**   Insert words needed to bring out the parallel structure in the following sentences.

1. They would lie on the battlefield without medical attention for an hour or day.
2. Two things I intend to do: to try and succeed.
3. I told him politely that I could not go and I had reasons.
4. I finally realized that one can learn much more by studying than worrying.
5. On the safari Eva took photographs of a tiger and elephant.

26c

Use parallel structures with correlatives (*both . . . and; either . . . or; neither . . . nor; not only . . . but also; whether . . . or*).

FAULTY   Either they obey the manager or get fired.

PARALLEL   Either ‖ **they obey the manager**
           or ‖ **they get fired.**

PARALLEL   They either ‖ **obey the manager**
             or ‖ **get fired.**

FAULTY   Whether drunk or when he was sober, he liked
               to pick a fight.

PARALLEL   Whether ‖ **drunk**
            or ‖ **sober,**
       he liked to pick a fight.

FAULTY   Not only jogging at 6 a.m. during the week,
               but Jason also works out on Sunday afternoons.

PARALLEL   Jason
       not only ‖ **jogs at 6 a.m. during the week**
       but also ‖ **works out on Sunday afternoons.**
       OR
       Not only does Jason jog at 6 a.m. during the
       week, but he also works out on Sunday after-
       noons. [The *also* may be omitted.]

■ **Exercise 3**   Revise each sentence by using parallel structure to express parallel ideas.

1. Shirley not only likes to play tennis but watching basketball.
2. Our personalities are shaped by both heredity and what type of environment we have.
3. My friend asked me whether the trip would be delayed or to be ready to start on Friday as planned.
4. He was quiet and in a serious mood after the lecture.
5. People fall naturally into two classes: the workers and those who like to depend on others.

■ **Exercise 4**   First study the parallelism in the sentences below. Then use three of the sentences as structural models for sentences of your own.

1. There are three things wrong with *Love in Albania*: the play, the direction, and the casting.   —NATHAN COHEN
2. What is true of coral and of all other forms of marine life is also true of whales.   —JACQUES-YVES COUSTEAU
3. We have seen that the capacity to be alone is a valuable resource. It enables men and women to get in touch with their deepest feelings; to come to terms with loss; to sort out their ideas; to change attitudes.   —ANTHONY STORR
4. Calm, relaxed people get ulcers as often as hard-pressed, competitive people do, and lower-status workers get ulcers as often as higher-status ones.   —CAROL TAVRIS
5. Each word has been weighed, each thought has been evaluated, and each point carefully considered.   —ZIG ZIGLAR
6. But it is the human mind that can summon up the power to resist, that can imagine a better world than the one before it, that can retain memory and courage in the face of unspeakable suffering.   —MARGARET ATWOOD

Shifts

27

**Avoid needless shifts in grammatical struc-
tures, in tone or style, and in viewpoint.**

Abrupt, unnecessary shifts—for example, from past to present, from singular to plural, from formal diction to slang,
from one perspective to another—obscure meaning and
make for difficult reading.

27a

Avoid needless shifts in tense, mood, and voice. See
also Section **7**.

SHIFT   During their talk Pierre **argued** against overkill while
        his brother **discusses** the dangers of unprepared-
        ness.   [shift from past to present tense]

BETTER During their talk Pierre **argued** against overkill while
        his brother **discussed** the dangers of unprepared-
        ness.   [both verbs in the past tense]

SHIFT   If I **were** rich and if my father **was** still alive, my
        life would be different.   [shift from subjunctive to
        indicative mood]

BETTER If I **were** rich and if my father **were** still alive, my
        life would be different.   [verbs in the subjunctive
        mood]

SHIFT   The old man finally **had to enter** a nursing home, but it **was** not **liked** by him.   [The voice shifts from active to passive.]

BETTER   The old man finally **had to enter** a nursing home, but he **did** not **like** it.   [Both verbs are active.]

When using the literary present, as in summarizing plots of novels and plays, avoid slipping from the present into the past tense.

Romeo and Juliet fall in love at first sight, marry secretly, and die [NOT *died*] together in the tomb within the same hour.

27b

Avoid needless shifts in person and in number. See also **6b.**

SHIFT   **One** reads for pleasure during **our** spare time.   [shift from third person to first person]

BETTER   **We** read for pleasure during **our** spare time.   [first person]

OR

You read for pleasure during **your** spare time.   [second person]

OR

People read for pleasure during **their** spare time. [third person]

SHIFT   The drama class **is** planning to ask six faculty members to **their** spring production.   [shift in number]

BETTER   The drama class **is** planning to ask six faculty members to **its** spring production.

■ **Exercise 1**   Correct all needless shifts in tense, mood, voice, person, and number.

1. After their easy victory, Kurt and Marla strutted over to me and asks a smart-aleck question.

2. Martinez recommended that property taxes be raised and spend wisely for the poor.
3. Kevin added meat to the frozen pizza, and then it was baked fifteen minutes by him.
4. Every bystander was suspect, so they were taken away for questioning.
5. I was told that billions of germs live on one's skin and that you should bathe often.

27c

Avoid needless shifts from indirect to direct discourse. See also **26a**.

SHIFT   The Gordons wonder **how the thieves got the tape deck out** and **why didn't they steal the tapes?** [shift from indirect to direct discourse]

BETTER   The Gordons wonder **how the thieves got the tape deck out** and **why they didn't steal the tapes**. [two indirect questions]

OR

The Gordons asked, "**How did the thieves get the tape deck out? Why didn't they steal the tapes?**"

SHIFT   The secretary said **that he was sick** and **would I please read the minutes**. [shift from indirect to direct discourse]

BETTER   The secretary said **that he was sick** and **asked me to read the minutes**. [indirect discourse]

27d

Avoid needless shifts in tone or style.

INAPPROPRIATE   Journalists who contend that the inefficiency of our courts will lead to the total elimination of the jury system are **nuts**. [Replace *nuts* (slang) with a word like *wrong* or *uninformed*.]

INAPPROPRIATE The darkness of the auditorium, the monotony of the ballet, and the strains of music drifting sleepily from the orchestra aroused in me a desire to **sack out**. [Replace *sack out* (slang) with a word like *doze* or *sleep*.]

27e
Avoid needless shifts in perspective or viewpoint.

FAULTY PERSPECTIVE The underwater scene was dark and mysterious; the willows lining the shore dipped gracefully into the water. [The perspective abruptly shifts from beneath the surface of the water to above it.]

BETTER The underwater scene was dark and mysterious; **above**, the willows lining the shore dipped gracefully into the water.

■ **Exercise 2** Correct all needless shifts. Put a check mark after any sentence that needs no revision.

1. A woman stepped forward, grabs the mugger's belt, snatches the purses, and got lost in the crowd.
2. A vacation is enjoyed by everyone because it refreshes the mind and body.
3. Hilary spent her summers in Ontario but flew to Florida for the winters.
4. Jim wondered whether Jack had left and did he say when he would return?
5. Every cook has their own recipes for making chili.
6. She told them that there is somebody in the room.
7. If Louis really likes someone, he would make any sacrifice for them.
8. Take your raincoat. They will be needed.
9. The outside of the building looks like a fortress; the comfortable furnishings seem out of place.
10. The instructor asked me why I missed class and will I take the make-up quiz on Tuesday?

■ **Exercise 3**   Revise the following paragraph to eliminate all needless shifts.

¹He was a shrewd businessman, or so it had always seemed to me.   ²He has innocent-looking eyes, which are in a baby face, and swaggered when he walks.   ³When questioned about his recent windfall, he up and says, "I'm lucky enough to have the right contacts."   ⁴Not one name was mentioned by him; moreover, his reluctance to discuss his business transactions was evident.   ⁵Take these comments for what they are worth; they may help one in your dealings with this big shot.

Reference of Pronouns

28

Make a pronoun refer unmistakably to its antecedent. See also **6b.**

Each boldfaced pronoun below clearly refers to its italicized antecedent, a single word or a word group:

> *Languages* are not invented; **they** grow with our need for expression.   —SUSANNE K. LANGER

> There is no *country* in the world **whose** population is stationary.   —KENNETH BOULDING

> Thus, *being busy* is more than merely a national passion; **it** is a national excuse.   —NORMAN COUSINS

Without any loss of clarity, a pronoun can often refer to a noun that follows:

> Unlike **their** predecessors, today's *social workers* cannot exclusively seek middle-class, home-owning, two-parent, one-career families for the children they want to place.
> —MARSHA TRUGOT

As you edit your compositions, check to see that the meaning of each pronoun is immediately obvious. If there is any chance of confusion, repeat the antecedent, use a synonym for it, or recast your sentence.

28a

Avoid an ambiguous reference.

When a pronoun could refer to either of two possible antecedents, the ambiguity confuses, or at least inconveniences,
your reader. (A pronoun, of course, may clearly refer to two
or more antecedents: "*Jack* and *Jill* met *their* Waterloo.")

AMBIGUOUS	Lisa wrote to Jennifer every day when she was in the hospital.
CLEAR	When Lisa was in the hospital, she wrote to Jennifer every day.
	OR
	When Jennifer was in the hospital, Lisa wrote to her every day.
AMBIGUOUS	After listening to Ray's proposal and to Avram's objections, I liked his ideas better.
CLEAR	I agreed with Avram after listening to his objections to Ray's proposal.

28b

Avoid a remote or an awkward reference.

Placing a pronoun too far away from its antecedent may
force your reader to backtrack to get your meaning. Making
a pronoun refer to a modifier can obscure your meaning.

REMOTE	A first-year student found herself the unanimously elected president of a group of animal lovers, **who** was not a joiner of organizations. [*Who* is too far removed from the antecedent *student*. See also **25a(3)**.]
BETTER	A first-year student **who** was not a joiner of organizations found herself the unanimously elected president of a group of animal lovers.
OBSCURE	Before Ellen could get to the jewellery store, **it** was all sold. [reference to a modifier]

BETTER   Before Ellen could get to the jewellery store, all
            the **jewellery** was sold.

Note: As a rule, writers avoid using a pronoun like *it*, *this*,
or *he* to refer to the title of a composition or to a word in the
title.

                    Title: Justice with Mercy

AWKWARD FIRST SENTENCE   How can this ever be?
BETTER   How can justice be merciful?

■ **Exercise 1**   Revise each sentence below to eliminate ambiguous, remote, or obscure pronoun reference.

1. The Kemps' tiff with the Leongs did not end until they invited them over for a swim in their new pool.
2. On the dashboard the various buttons and knobs seldom confuse the driver that are clearly labelled.
3. In Jane's letter she did not mention the robbery.
4. The lake is peaceful. Near the shore, water lilies grow in profusion, spreading out their green leaves and sending up white blossoms. It is well stocked with fish.
5. Meg waved to Mrs. James as she was coming down the ramp.

28c
Use broad or implied reference only with discretion.

Pronouns such as *it*, *this*, *that*, *which*, and *such* may refer
to a specific word or phrase or to the sense of a whole clause,
sentence, or paragraph.

SPECIFIC REFERENCE   His nose was absolutely covered with
            warts of different sizes; it looked like a sponge, or some
            other kind of marine growth.   —DAN JACOBSON   [*It* refers
            to *nose*.]

BROAD REFERENCE   Some people think that the fall of man had
something to do with sex, but that's a mistake.
—C.S. LEWIS [The pronoun *that* refers to the sense of the
whole clause.]

When used carelessly, however, broad reference can inter-
fere with clear communication.

(1) Avoid broad reference to an expressed idea.

VAGUE   Although the story referred to James, Henry misap-
plied it to himself, which is true in real life.

CLEAR   Although the story referred to James, Henry misap-
plied it to himself. Such mistakes occur in real life.

**(2) As a rule, do not refer to a word or an idea not
expressed but merely implied.**

VAGUE   Lois said that she would stay in Rome for at least a
year. This suggests that she is happy there.   [*This*
has no expressed antecedent.]

CLEAR   Lois said that she would stay in Rome for at least a
year. This remark suggests that she is happy there.

VAGUE   He wanted his teachers to think he was above average, as he could have been if he had used it to
advantage.   [*It* has no expressed antecedent.]

CLEAR   He wanted his teachers to think he was above average, as he could have been if he had used his ability
to advantage.

28d

Avoid the awkward use of *you* or *it*.

AWKWARD   When one cannot swim, you fear deep, stormy
waters.   [The pronoun *you* (second person) refers
to *one* (third person). See also **27b**.]

REVISED   The person who cannot swim fears deep, stormy
waters.

| AWKWARD | In the book **it** says that many mushrooms are edible. [The pronoun *it* clumsily refers to *book*.] |
| REVISED | The book says that many mushrooms are edible. |

In some contexts, the use of the impersonal, or indefinite, *you* is both natural and acceptable. Notice in the following example that *you* is equivalent in meaning to "people in general" or "the reader."

> The study of dreams has become a significant and respectable scientific exploration, one that can directly benefit **you**.
>
> —PATRICIA GARFIELD

Some writers, however, prefer not to use *you* in a formal context.

Note: Avoid the awkward placement of *it* near another *it* with a different meaning.

AWKWARD	Although it was very hot on the beach, it was a beautiful place. [The first *it* is the indefinite or unspecified *it*. The second *it* refers to *beach*.]
REVISED	Although it was very hot on the beach, the place was beautiful.
AWKWARD	It would be unwise to buy the new model now, but it is a superior machine. [The first *it* is an expletive. The second *it* refers to *model*.]
REVISED	Buying the new model now would be unwise, but it is a superior machine.

■ **Exercise 2**   Revise the following sentences as necessary to correct faults in reference. Put a check mark after any sentence that needs no revision.

1. At the Chinese restaurant, the Meltons had a hard time eating with chopsticks, but that is their favourite food.
2. Apparently the dishwasher was out of order; it leaked all over the kitchen floor.

3. Copiers and other fine modern office machines enable business executives to accomplish more work because their assistants can manage them easily and quickly.

4. In the article it states that Sable Island in Nova Scotia is the only breeding site of the rare Ipswich sparrow.

5. Our language is rich in connectives that express fine distinctions of meaning.

6. I did not even buy a season ticket, which was very disloyal to my school.

7. Mary told Ann that she had to read *Pride and Prejudice*.

8. When building roads the Romans tried to detour around valleys as much as possible for fear that flood waters might cover them and make them useless.

9. The extra fees surprised many students that seemed unreasonably high.

10. In Frank's suitcase he packs only wash-and-wear clothes.

Emphasis

29

Write sentences that will give emphasis to important ideas.

You may emphasize ideas by using exact diction (see Section **20**), concise language (**21**), and appropriate subordination and co-ordination (**24**). This section presents other ways to gain emphasis.

29a

Gain emphasis by placing important words at the beginning or end of the sentence—especially at the end.

UNEMPHATIC   Total deafness is worse than total blindness, however, in many ways.   [Parenthetical elements in an important position weaken the sentence.]

EMPHATIC   Total deafness, however, is in many ways worse than total blindness.
OR
However, total deafness is in many ways worse than total blindness.   [Introductory transitional expressions do not ordinarily weaken a sentence beginning.]

| UNEMPHATIC | There was an underground blast that rocked the whole area.   [Unemphatic words begin the sentence.] |
| EMPHATIC | An underground blast rocked the whole area. |

Since the semicolon, sometimes called a weak period, is a strong punctuation mark when used between main clauses, the words placed immediately before and after a semicolon tend to receive emphasis.

The colon and the dash often precede an emphatic ending.

> I would like to point out to these people a type of labour from which they are certain to profit: an expedition by canoe.
> —PIERRE TRUDEAU

> *The Coast* meant only one thing—British Columbia.
> —MARGARET LAURENCE

■ **Exercise 1**   Giving special attention to the placement of important words, revise the following sentences to improve emphasis.

1. Music has the power to hypnotize, so they say.
2. In fact, only one person could have written all these articles because of their same political slant, I am convinced.
3. There is one stunt woman who earns five thousand dollars for two hours of work.
4. It had never before entered her mind to resent her husband's complacent ignorance or to ignore his unreasonable demands, however.

29b

Gain emphasis by occasionally changing loose sentences into periodic sentences.

In a *loose* sentence, the main idea (grammatically a main clause or sentence base) comes first; less important ideas or details follow. In a *periodic* sentence, however, the main idea comes last, just before the period.

LOOSE	Such sticky labels do not accurately describe any generation—for example, labels like *lost, beat, now, silent,* or *me.*
PERIODIC	Such sticky labels as *lost, beat, now, silent,* or *me* do not accurately describe any generation.

LOOSE	Hair has always been a statement for men, variously representing strength (Samson), fashionable virtue (King Charles I of England, whose wigs were long-locked and elaborate), bravado (General Custer), and genius (Einstein).
	—OWEN EDWARDS [The main idea comes first.]

PERIODIC	When you die, when you get a divorce, when you buy a house, when you have an auto accident, not to mention the hundreds of times during your lifetime when you are fleeced in your role as a consumer, a lawyer either must or should be involved. —DAVID HAPGOOD [The main idea comes last.]

Both types of sentences can be effective. The loose sentence is, and should be, the more commonly used. Although the periodic sentence is often the more emphatic, you should take care in your writing not to overuse it.

■ **Exercise 2**   Convert the loose sentences to periodic sentences, and the periodic to loose. Notice how your revisions make for varying emphasis.

1. Italy remains cheerful, despite everything.
   —AUBERON WAUGH
2. Even where people want better relations, old habits and reflexes persist.   —HEDRICK SMITH
3. The Milky Way Galaxy is entirely unremarkable, one of billions of other galaxies strewn through the vastness of space.   —CARL SAGAN
4. And then she was sweet and apologetic, as always, as she had been all her life, nervously backing away from the

arguments she should have had with my father, turning aside from the talks she should have had with me.

—JOYCE CAROL OATES

5. By the time the production studios moved from New York to Hollywood, the movie Mountie was a fixture on the screens of the nation.   —PIERRE BERTON

29c

Gain emphasis by arranging ideas in the order of climax.

Notice in the following examples that the ideas are arranged in an order that places the writer's most dramatic or important idea last.

Urban life is unhealthy, morally corrupt, and fundamentally inhuman.   —RENÉ DUBOS   [adjectives in the series arranged in climactic order]

Give me a good canoe, a pair of Jibway snowshoes, my beaver, my family and ten thousand square miles of wilderness and I am happy.   —GREY OWL   [nouns in the series arranged in climactic order]

In the language of screen comedians four of the main grades of laugh are the titter, the yowl, the belly laugh and the boffo. The titter is just a titter. The yowl is a runaway titter. Anyone who has ever had the pleasure knows all about a belly laugh. The boffo is the laugh that kills.   —JAMES AGEE   [First, words are placed in climactic order, then sentences.]

Note: Anticlimax—an unexpected shift from the dignified to the trivial or from the serious to the comic or ironic—is sometimes used for special effect.

John Crosbie was the gold medallist when he graduated from Queen's University. He was the gold medallist when he graduated from Dalhousie Law School, the top law student in Canada and winner of a scholarship to the London School of

Economics. Unfortunately, he did not receive a degree in common sense. —ALLAN FOTHERINGHAM

■ **Exercise 3** Arrange the ideas in the following sentences in what you consider to be the order of climax.

1. Franklin used the ant as a symbol of industry, wisdom, and efficiency.
2. Among the images in the poem are sun-drenched orchards, diamond-eyed children, and golden-flecked birds.
3. He left the city because his health was failing, his taxes were going up, and his pet dog was tired of the leash.
4. Something must be done at once. Unless we act now, the city will be bankrupt in five years. The council is faced with a deficit.
5. The would-be prime minister attended a community church supper, spoke at a rally, promised new jobs, and visited homes for senior citizens.

29d

Gain emphasis by using the active voice and by using verbs more forceful than *have* or *be*.

(1) Use the active voice instead of the passive voice.

UNEMPHATIC Little attention is being paid to cheap, nutritious foods by the average shopper.

EMPHATIC The average shopper is paying little attention to cheap, nutritious foods.

Exception: If the receiver of the action is more important than the doer, the passive voice is more effective.

There in the tin factory, in the first moment of the atomic age, a human being was crushed by books. —JOHN HERSEY

Freedom can be squashed by the tyrant or suffocated by the bureaucrat. —WILLIAM F. RICKENBACKER

(2) Use an action verb or a linking verb more forceful than a form of *have* or *be*.

UNEMPHATIC   Our student society is always the winner of the debates.

EMPHATIC   Our student society always wins the debates.

UNEMPHATIC   The meat has a rotten smell.

EMPHATIC   The meat smells rotten.

■ **Exercise 4**   Make each sentence more emphatic by substituting the active for the passive voice or by substituting a more forceful verb for a form of *have* or *be*.

1. Pennies are often thrown into the fountain by tourists.
2. My brother is a manipulator of other people.
3. Every Saturday, TV is being watched by easily influenced children.
4. Bad pizza has a taste like cardboard.
5. It is greatly feared by the citizens that the judge will have too harsh a sentence for the defendant.

29e

Gain emphasis by repeating important words.

Note the repetitions in the following excerpt, in which Hugh MacLennan recalls his conversation with an editor who asked him to write about Canada using certain stereotypical images.

> [He] explained that this would be what he called a "duty piece." His magazine sold several hundred thousand copies in Canada every month, and occasionally the management felt it a duty to print some Canadian material. I must have made a comment about there being no Eskimos, trappers, or husky dogs within fifteen hundred miles of where we were sitting, for he cut me short with a gesture.

"No, they're imperative. In an African duty-piece you stress the heat and the jungle. In an English duty-piece you stress how old everything is. A French duty-piece has got to be romantic, but at the same time we like an angle showing the French are also practical and getting themselves orientated to the up-to-date. But in a Canadian duty-piece you simply have to go heavy on the snow and the cold."

—HUGH MACLENNAN, "On Living in a Cold Country"

■ **Exercise 5** First make each sentence below more emphatic by substituting repetition for the use of synonyms; then write two sentences of your own using repetition for emphasis.

1. Sometimes we lie to avoid hurting someone's feelings; occasionally we prevaricate to make another person like us.
2. He gripes all the time: he complains about the weather, fusses in heavy traffic, grumbles about high prices, and is critical of his meals.

29f

Gain emphasis by occasionally inverting the word order of a sentence. See also **30b**.

At the feet of the tallest and plushiest offices lie the crummiest slums. —E.B. WHITE [Compare "The crummiest slums lie at the feet of the tallest and plushiest offices."]

Then come all the greens in the spectrum—doubly welcome after a long winter. —HAL BORLAND

Caution: This method of gaining emphasis, if overused, will make the style distinctly artificial.

29g

Gain emphasis by using balanced sentence construction.

A sentence is balanced when grammatically equal structures—usually main clauses with parallel elements—are
used to express contrasted (or similar) ideas: see Section **26**.
A balanced sentence emphasizes the contrast (or similarity)
between parts of equal length and movement.

> To be French is to be like no one else; to be American is to
> be like everyone else.   —PETER USTINOV

> Love is positive; tolerance negative. Love involves passion;
> tolerance is humdrum and dull.   —E.M. FORSTER

> A compliment is a statement of an agreeable truth; flattery is
> the statement of an agreeable untruth.
> —SIR JOHN A. MACDONALD

■ **Exercise 6**   Write emphatic sentences using balanced construction to show the contrast between the following:

1. summer and winter   3. town and city
2. youth and age   4. hypocrisy and candour

29h

Gain emphasis by abruptly changing sentence length.

> In the last two decades there has occurred a series of changes
> in American life, the extent, durability, and significance of
> which no one has yet measured. No one can.   —IRVING HOWE
> [The short sentence, which abruptly follows a much longer one,
> is emphatic.]

> I suppose each painter has his own way of launching into the
> adventures in shape, colour, texture and space that we call
> painting. I mostly fall into them.   —DAVID MILNE

■ **Exercise 7**   Write a short, emphatic sentence to follow each of
the two long sentences. Then write another pair of sentences—one
long and one short—of your own.

1. According to some minor prophets of doom, the next century will be a push-button era, a computer-controlled and robot-dominated one with life dependent on the movement of a forefinger.
2. In sequined costumes the skaters glide into the huge arena, smile at the applauding spectators, strike a brief pose, and then race into a series of intricate leaps and spins, their feet perfectly balanced on thin wedges of shining steel.

■ **Exercise 8**   Prepare for a class discussion of emphasis in the following passages.

1. No one reads anymore—blame television. Families are breaking up—blame television. High culture is being despoiled—blame television. . . . What a splendid all-purpose explanation television has become.   —ARISTIDES
2. In fantasy, the timid can be bold and aggressive, the weak are strong, the clumsy are full of grace, the tongue-tied discover vast verbal resources. In the privacy of the mind, we can all rise up in righteous wrath, and vengeance is ours.   —ADELAIDE BRY
3. Contained within the Arctic lands of Canada is the vast inland sea of Hudson Bay, in which the British Isles could be sunk without a trace.   —FARLEY MOWAT

■ **Exercise 9**   Revise each sentence for emphasis.

1. I think that replacing human organs with animal organs should stop, even if it might extend a person's life.
2. Such jokes are offensive to many people because they have references to minorities or to religion.
3. Fields of wild flowers were all around us.
4. Fools talk about each other; ideas fill the conversations of the wise.
5. At any rate, the gun fired when the fleeing youth tripped over the patrolman's foot.

6. The storm broke in all its fury at the close of a hot day.

7. A fast pass was caught by Milburn, and a thirty-yard gain was made by him before the whistle was blown by the referee.

8. I asked her to marry me, two years ago, in a shop on Tremont Street, late in the fall.

9. The art of the people was crude, but a great deal of originality was shown by some of them.

10. I can identify the guilty person in every Agatha Christie novel by the simple device of choosing the least likely suspect whose alibi is airtight.

Variety

30

Vary the structure and the length of your sentences.

Inexperienced writers tend to rely too heavily—regardless of content or purpose—on a few comfortable, familiar structures. Seek sentence variety in your writing.

Compare the two paragraphs below. Both express the same ideas in virtually the same words; both use acceptable sentence patterns. It is the variety in sentence structure and length that makes the difference.

NOT VARIED

Most Canadians highly value their freedom to do this or that. They value their ability to own this or that. Freedom to them means the right to become something or other. But I have a different point of view. I prize most the freedom not to do, not to have, and not to become. I can, as a Canadian, choose not to vote, and I don't have to buy. Moreover, I can also choose not to be ambitious; I don't have to be successful. I can pursue my own kind of happiness. I prize this freedom the most.   [nine sentences, seven simple and two compound— all except two beginning with the subject]

VARIED

To do this or that, to own this or that, to become something or other—these freedoms are what most Canadians value highly. But I have a different point of view. What I prize most is the freedom not to do, not to have, not to become. As a Canadian, I can choose not to vote, and I can choose not to buy. Although I am free to be ambitious and successful, I can choose not to be either. To pursue happiness—as I define it— is the freedom I prize most.   [six sentences: four complex, one compound, and one simple—two beginning with the subject]

Note: If you have difficulty distinguishing various types of structures, review the fundamentals of the sentence treated in Section **1**, especially **1d**.

30a

As a rule, avoid a series of short simple sentences. Vary the length. See also **29h**.

Rather than present your ideas in a series of choppy, ineffective sentences, learn how to relate your ideas precisely in a longer sentence. See Section **24**.

CHOPPY   In some ways the Gulf Islands and Cape Breton look very much alike. The houses by the sea, however, are different. It's a matter of architectural style.

EFFECTIVE   Although the Gulf Islands and Cape Breton look very much alike in some ways, the architectural styles of the houses by the sea are different.   [use of subordination to combine sentences]

CHOPPY   Some people simply put coffee in an enamel saucepan. Next, they pour very hot water over it. Then they wait until flavour develops. Finally, they add eggshell or a small amount of cold water. The idea is to get the floating grounds to settle to the bottom.

EFFECTIVE   Some people simply put coffee in an enamel saucepan, pour very hot water over it, wait until flavour develops, and get the floating grounds to settle to the bottom by adding eggshell or a small amount of cold water. [use of co-ordination to combine sentences]

Note: Occasionally, as the example below illustrates, a series of brief, subject-first sentences may be used for special effect:

He stumbled, recovered, picked up his pace. Now he was running. He broke out of the ring. People were throwing things at him. An egg hurtled past his head. A tomato hit someone nearby and splattered onto his suit. —GERRY NADEL [The short sentences suggest staccato action.]

■ **Exercise 1**   Study the structure of the sentences below, giving special attention to the variety of sentence lengths.

As she picked her way toward the garden chairs beside the front porch, she poured out a customary torrent of complaint. Her eyesight was failing. She found herself swatting raisins on the kitchen table, thinking they were flies, and bringing her stick down on spiders that turned out to be scurrying tufts of lint. Her hearing was going, and she suffered from head noises. She imagined she heard drums beating. —PETER DE VRIES

■ **Exercise 2**   Convert each of the following series of short simple sentences to one long sentence in which ideas are carefully related.

1. There were thirty seconds of play left. Harrison intercepted the pass and raced downfield. He dropped the ball at the five-yard line.
2. Her speech had an interesting thesis. Salespersons should solve the existing problems of their customers. They should also point out new problems in order to solve them.
3. Bennett's Comet appeared in 1969. It disappeared again in 1970. It will not be visible again for thousands of years.
4. Ellen Dolan did not buy a second car. She bought a Piper.

It is a small airplane. It flies at just under two hundred kilometres an hour.

5. Paula Blanchard is the author of *The Life of Emily Carr.* In her book Blanchard describes Carr's struggles to record the Indian art of the West Coast. Carr worked in isolation. She travelled to remote Indian villages. She did this even the year she turned sixty.

30b

Avoid a long series of sentences beginning with the subject. Vary the beginnings.

Most writers begin about half their sentences with the subject—far more than the number of sentences begun in any other one way. But overuse of the subject-first beginning results in monotonous writing.

(1) Begin with an adverb or an adverb clause.

Suddenly a hissing and clattering came from the heights around us.   —DOUGLAS LEE [adverb]

Even though baseball is essentially the same, the strategy of play then and now is different.   —JAMES T. FARRELL [adverb clause]

(2) Begin with a prepositional phrase or a verbal phrase.

For the writer, the wild dream is the first step to reality.
—NORMAN COUSINS [prepositional phrase]

To produce small boys quicker than you can say "kite,"
fly one.   —P.K. PAGE [infinitive phrase]

Travelling on a special train of war brides from Halifax as a young and ignorant reporter, I kept asking them to comment on what they saw.   —MAVIS GALLANT [participial phrase]

(3) **Begin with a sentence connective—a co-ordinating conjunction, a conjunctive adverb, or a transitional expression.**

Notice how each sentence connective relates the ideas in each set of sentences. See also **32b(4)**.

> Transitory popularity is not proof of genius. **But** permanent popularity is.   —STEPHEN LEACOCK   [The co-ordinating conjunction *but* marks a contrast.]

> All human cultures seek to realize and protect their identity. **And** identity is definable only by reference to former times.   —HUGH BRODY

> Engine speed also affected the heater's output. **Nonetheless**, the system did manage to keep us warm enough throughout a New England winter.   —CONSUMER REPORTS   [conjunctive adverb]

> The nuclei of atoms become radioactive when they absorb neutrons. **That is**, they decay by giving off some kind of radiation.   —ROBERT HOFSTADTER   [transitional expression]

(4) **Begin with an appositive, an absolute phrase, or an introductory series.**

> **A city of ancient origins**, Varna lies on the Black Sea coast.   —COLIN RENFREW   [appositive referring to the subject]

> **His eyebrows raised high in resignation**, he began to examine his hand.   —LIONEL TRILLING   [absolute phrase]

> **Logging, sawmilling, mixed farming, commercial fishing, and sport fishing**—these are the bases of Bella Coola's economy.   [See also **17e(3)**.]

Note: An occasional declarative sentence with inverted word order can contribute to sentence variety. See **29f**.

■ **Exercise 3**   Prepare for a class discussion of the types of sentence beginnings in the following paragraph.

¹Whenever the east-west context of the Canadian outlook begins to weaken, separatism, which is always there, emerges as a political force.   ²Every part of Canada has strong separatist feelings: there is separatism of the Pacific Coast, of the Prairies, of the Maritimes, of Newfoundland, as well as of Quebec.   ³Ontario, of course, began with a separatist movement from the American Revolution.   ⁴But since the rise of the great ideological revolutionary movements of our time, whether communist, fascist, imperialist, Islamic or what not, separatism has been an almost wholly destructive force.   ⁵The successful separatings, like that of Norway and Sweden in 1905, took place before the rise of these movements.   ⁶In India and Pakistan, in the Arab-Jewish world, and in many other centres divided by language, colour or religion, separatism has seldom if ever stabilized the prejudices which gave rise to it, but has steadily increased them.   ⁷Even where there is no political affiliation, the separation of Cuba from the American sphere of influence, or of Yugoslavia from the Russian one, cannot be a politically neutral act.

—NORTHROP FRYE

■ **Exercise 4**   Recast each sentence twice to vary the beginning.

EXAMPLE
Two businessmen dropped by the dean's office and discussed the co-operative education program.
a. *Dropping by the dean's office, two businessmen discussed the co-operative education program.*
b. *In the dean's office, two businessmen discussed the co-operative education program.*

1. Reporters interviewed the newly appointed Minister of External Affairs and asked him some very tricky questions about world affairs.
2. Many people today are concerned about the quality of life but not about a reverence for life.
3. Jesse enjoyed the course in science-fiction literature most of all.
4. The green fireballs travelled at great speed and fascinated sky watchers throughout the Maritimes.

30c

Avoid loose, stringy compound sentences. See also **24b**.

To revise an ineffective compound sentence, try one of the following methods.

(1) Make a compound sentence complex.

COMPOUND	The Mississippi River is one of the longest rivers in the world, and in the springtime it often overflows its banks, and the lives of many people are endangered.
COMPLEX	The Mississippi River, which is one of the longest rivers in the world, often overflows its banks in the springtime, endangering the lives of many people.

(2) Use a compound predicate in a simple sentence.

COMPOUND	He put on his coat, and next he picked up his keys, and then he dashed out of the house.
SIMPLE	He put on his coat, picked up his keys, and dashed out of the house.

(3) Use an appositive in a simple sentence.

COMPOUND	Emma Lake is north of Prince Albert in Saskatchewan, and it is a summer camp, and it is the site of an influential artists' workshop.
SIMPLE	A summer camp north of Prince Albert in Saskatchewan, Emma Lake is the site of an influential artists' workshop.
COMPOUND	Her ability to listen is an acquired skill, and it attracts many friends.
SIMPLE	Her ability to listen, an acquired skill, attracts many friends.

(4) Use a prepositional or verbal phrase in a simple sentence.

COMPOUND	The streets were icy, and we could not drive the car.
SIMPLE	Because of the icy streets, we could not drive the car.
COMPOUND	He arrived in Calgary at 1:30 A.M., and then he made the toll-free call.
SIMPLE	After arriving in Calgary at 1:30 A.M., he made the toll-free call.
COMPOUND	The town was north of the Red River, and a tornado struck it, and it was practically demolished.
SIMPLE	The town, located north of the Red River, was struck by a tornado and practically demolished.

■ **Exercise 5** Using the methods illustrated in **30c**, revise the loose, stringy compound sentences below.

1. The small car hugs the road, and it is easy to drive in traffic, but it is not comfortable.
2. The Johnsons grew tired of city smog and noise pollution, so they moved to the country, but there they had no fire department or police protection.
3. North Americans at first traded their products, and then they began to use money and bank cheques, and now they use the all-inclusive plastic credit card.
4. Harvey kept criticizing middle-class values, and he mentioned such things as marriage and two-car garages, but he did not define upper-class or lower-class values.

30d

Vary the conventional subject–verb sequence by occasionally separating subject and verb with words or phrases.

Each subject and verb below is in boldface.

SUBJECT–VERB   **The auditorium is** across from the park, and **it is** a gift of the alumni. [compound sentence]

VARIED   **The auditorium**, across from the park, **is** a gift of the alumni. [simple sentence]

SUBJECT–VERB   **The crowd sympathized** with the visitors **and applauded** every good play.

VARIED   **The crowd**, sympathizing with the visitors, **applauded** every good play.

■ **Exercise 6**   Using the methods illustrated in **30d**, vary the conventional subject–verb sequence.

1. Roger is like his mother; he is an excellent conversationalist.
2. St. John's is the capital of Newfoundland, and it lies over 900 km east of Halifax and lies about 1900 km east of New York.
3. My grandparents valued strong family ties and encouraged us young ones "to always keep in touch."
4. Margaret was racing back to the library to avoid getting wet, and she fell broadside into a big puddle of water.
5. Niagara-on-the-Lake is now recognized as an architectural and historical treasure house, but it was a forgotten town until the early sixties.

30e

Occasionally, instead of the usual declarative sentence, use a question, an exclamation, or a command.

How can anybody assert that "growth" is a good thing? If my children grow, it is a very good thing; if I should suddenly start growing, it would be a disaster.   —E.F. SCHUMACHER
[Here a rhetorical question is followed by the usual declarative statement.]

Now I stare and stare at people, shamelessly. Stare. It's the way to educate your eye. —WALKER EVANS [A one-word imperative sentence provides variety.]

■ **Exercise 7**   Prepare for a class discussion of sentence variety in the following paragraph.

¹Our host has a very scientifically managed pig farm and he provides information for anyone wanting to start one (and those who don't!) ²For instance, we learned how to keep flies out of our sties by putting mounds of pig excrement on grids over pans of water at strategic spots. ³Why? ⁴Flies like pig excrement for laying their eggs in better than anything else. ⁵When the maggots hatch, they burrow away from the light and drown in the water. ⁶We also learned how to get the largest litters per sow. ⁷How? ⁸Import Swedish sows. ⁹They have been bred longer in the back and, miraculously, given additional teats to fill up the extra space.

—P.K. PAGE, *Brazilian Journal*

LARGER ELEMENTS

Logical Thinking

31

Base your writing on logical thinking. Avoid common fallacies.

Logical thinking involves the natural reasoning processes of induction and deduction. As you study **31a** and **31b**, keep in mind that both kinds of reasoning help you win your reader's confidence. One kind of reasoning often leads to the other. The most important thing is to ensure that your reader confidently follows your thinking.

31a
Learn how to use inductive reasoning in your writing.

Whenever you interpret evidence, you reason inductively. Every time you flick the light switch, the lights come on, and so you conclude that they will do so the next time you flick the switch. But inductive reasoning can never lead to absolute certainty. The next time you flick the switch, the lights may not come on. This is the basic method of science: a phenomenon is observed so often that scientists feel confident in reaching a conclusion.

Inductive reasoning is useful not only for arriving at conclusions, but for persuading others to accept conclusions you have already reached. An inductive argument is built on facts; as evidence mounts, your reader arrives at the conclusion you intend. It is crucial that the amount of evidence be sufficient (see Hasty Generalization, page 322). You also need to be sure that the conclusions you draw fit the facts (see *Post Hoc, Ergo Propter Hoc*, page 323). Be sure that you have not inadvertently ignored evidence that might invalidate your conclusion (''neglected aspect''). Also resist the temptation to present only the evidence that supports a predetermined conclusion (''slanting'').

When you use induction in your writing, the organizational strategy can vary with the situation. You may wish to state the logical conclusion first and then present the evidence on which it is based. On the other hand, you may wish to present the evidence first and let your reader draw the conclusion. This strategy works well when your conclusion is one your reader may resist.

31b
Learn how to use deductive reasoning in your writing.

Although the terminology may be new to you, you are already familiar with deductive reasoning. For example, you know that the only prerequisite for enrolling in honours history is a B+ average. You have a B+ average. Therefore, you can conclude, with certainty, that you are eligible for honours history. This kind of reasoning is based on a logical structure called a syllogism. A syllogism has three terms: a major premise (usually a generalization), a minor premise (a specific fact), and a conclusion that fits both the major premise and the minor premise.

When the major premise and the minor premise are correctly related to form a conclusion, the syllogism is valid. Even if it is valid, however, the conclusion may be false if one of the premises is false. In the example just given, if your assumption that the honours history requirement is a B+ were not true, or if you had miscalculated your own average, your conclusion might be false even though your reasoning was valid. But when both premises are true and the syllogism is valid, then the conclusion must be true.

Deductive reasoning can be a powerful tool in argumentative papers. However, when you argue deductively, you must think about your premises very carefully to be sure your argument is sound—both true and valid (see Non Sequitur, page 321; Either . . . or, page 323; Circular Reasoning, page 322; and Equivocation, page 323).

When you write a deductive argument, it is important to frame a premise which you not only consider to be true but with which your reader is likely to agree. For instance, if you want to convince a reader that vivisection should be outlawed, you might think of a premise such as this:

> Anything that inflicts pain on living creatures should be outlawed.

But on further consideration it may occur to you that this premise might be difficult for your reader to accept. After all, sometimes pain is inflicted on living creatures for a benefit; if you have appendicitis, you willingly submit to the pain of surgery to have your appendix removed. So the premise needs to be qualified:

> Anything that inflicts pain on living creatures *needlessly* should be outlawed.
> Vivisection inflicts pain on living creatures *needlessly*.
> Vivisection should be outlawed.

In other situations you may decide to limit your objectives. You may be able to succeed in getting a reader to agree that anything that inflicts pain on living creatures needlessly is morally wrong, but not necessarily to agree that a law should be enacted to prohibit every moral wrong. You could alter your premise like this:

Anything that inflicts pain on living creatures needlessly *is morally wrong*.
Vivisection inflicts pain on living creatures needlessly.
Vivisection is morally wrong.

Although you always need to think carefully about both of your premises and be able to state them correctly for yourself, you do not always have to express both of them in your writing.

Because vivisection inflicts pain on living creatures needlessly, it is morally wrong. [major premise unstated]

■ **Exercise 1**   Prepare for a class discussion of the premises and conclusions in the following items.

1. First, many situations in real life have unhappy endings; therefore, if fiction is to illuminate life, it must present defeat as well as triumph.   —LAURENCE PERRINE

2. Universities must stop using students as an important part of the process of evaluating teachers. Evaluation of teaching performance should be done by peers who know what good teaching is and who can separate good teaching from mere entertainment.
   —DAVID BERCUSON, ROBERT BOTHWELL, and J.L. GRANATSTEIN,
   The Great Brain Robbery: Canada's Universities on the Road to Ruin

31c
Avoid fallacies.

Fallacies are faults in reasoning. They may result from misusing or misrepresenting evidence, from relying on faulty premises or omitting a needed premise, or from distorting the issues.

(1) **Non Sequitur:**   A statement that does not follow logically from what has just been said—a conclusion that does not follow from the premises.

FAULTY   Victor is honest; therefore, he will get a good job.
[Many honest people do not have good jobs.]

(2) Hasty Generalization: A generalization based on too little evidence or on exceptional or biassed evidence.

FAULTY   Teenagers are reckless drivers.
[Many teenagers are careful drivers.]

(3) *Ad Hominem:*   Attacking the person who presents an issue rather than dealing logically with the issue itself.

FAULTY   His arguments might impress us if we were not aware of his unbroken record of selfishness.
[The man's alleged selfishness need not invalidate his arguments.]

(4) Bandwagon: An argument saying, in effect, "Everyone's doing or saying or thinking this, so you should too."

FAULTY   Everyone else is cheating, so why shouldn't I?
[The majority is not always right.]

(5) Circular Reasoning: An assertion that restates the point just made. Such an assertion "begs the question" by drawing as a conclusion a point stated in the premise.

FAULTY   He is lazy because he just doesn't like to work.
[Being lazy and not liking to work mean essentially the same thing.]

(6) Red Herring: Dodging the real issue by drawing attention to an irrelevant issue.

FAULTY   Why worry about a few terrorists when we ought to be doing something about acid rain?
[Acid rain has nothing to do with the actions of terrorists.]

(7) *Post Hoc, Ergo Propter Hoc:* "After this, so because of this"—the mistake of assuming that because one event follows another, the first must be the cause of the second.

> FAULTY   The new mayor took office last January and crime in the streets has already increased 25 percent.
> [The assumption is that having the new mayor caused the increase in crime, an assumption unlikely to be true.]

(8) **Either . . . or Fallacy:**   Stating that only two alternatives exist when in fact there are more than two.

> FAULTY   We have only two choices: ban nuclear weapons, or destroy the earth.
> [In fact, other possibilities exist.]

(9) **False Analogy:**   The assumption that because two things are alike in some ways, they must be alike in other ways.

> FAULTY   Since the books are about the same length and cover the same material, one is probably as good as the other.
> [The length and coverage of the books cannot predict whether one is as good as the other.]

(10) **Equivocation:**   An assertion that falsely relies on the use of a term in two different senses.

> FAULTY   You have a right to vote, so do what is right and vote.
> [The word *right* means both "a just claim" and "correct."]

■ **Exercise 2**   Prepare for a class discussion of the faulty logic in the following sentences.

1. A person who cannot spell should not become a journalist.

2. True, many citizens cheat on their income tax, but you should consider how much good they do for the economy by spending the money that they saved.

3. If you walk self-confidently, with your head high, you won't be attacked.

4. Our prisons are full because a lot of people don't have enough money to buy necessities.

5. I will not vote for him as my representative because he was not born in Canada.

6. Women just can't understand math.

7. Everybody likes Jacqueline, so she will be a good class president.

8. I've never met a German who didn't like opera; all Germans do.

9. Fred missed class twice last week; he must have been sick.

10. These electric razors give the smoothest shave; all successful executives use them.

11. After that oil spill, the fish I caught tasted greasy. Those fish are contaminated.

12. There are only two kinds of politicians: those interested in their own welfare and those interested in the welfare of the people.

The Paragraph

32

Write paragraphs that are unified, coherent, and adequately developed.

An essential unit of thought in writing, the paragraph usually consists of a group of related sentences, though occasionally no more than one sentence. The first line of a paragraph is indented, about $2\frac{1}{2}$ cm (one inch) when handwritten and five spaces when typewritten.

Good paragraphs are unified, coherent, and well developed. As you read the following paragraph, observe the unity—how all of the sentences in the paragraph relate to a single main idea. Notice also the easy, natural progression of ideas from sentence to sentence (coherence), and the use of plenty of specific information, appropriately arranged to support the main idea (development). (For easy reference, the paragraphs in this section are numbered—except for those in need of revision.)

1   The modern typewriter keyboard was deliberately designed to be as inconvenient as possible. On earlier models of the typewriter, the keyboard was arranged so that the most common letters in the English language were located in the middle row. Typists soon became so quick that they continually jammed the primitive machines. The inventor solved the problem by scrambling the letters on the keyboard and creating a deliberately inconvenient arrangement. This slowed down the typists and thus prevented them from accidentally jamming

the typewriter. Although modern typewriters are virtually jam-proof, they still have the deliberately inefficient keyboard arrangement designed for the first primitive typing machines.

—PAUL STIRLING HAGERMAN,
The Odd, Mad World of Paul Stirling Hagerman

2   My scholastic career got off to a good start when I was very young. I received a special diploma in the second grade for being the outstanding boy student, and in the third and fifth grades I was moved ahead so suddenly that I was the smallest kid in the class. Somehow, I survived the early years of grade school, but when I entered junior high school, I failed everything in sight. High school proved not much better. There was no doubt that I was absolutely the worst physics student in the history of St. Paul Central High School. It was not until I became a senior that I earned any respectable grades at all. I have often felt that some semblance of maturity began to arrive at last. I saved that final report card because it was the only one that seemed to justify those long years of agony.   —CHARLES M. SCHULZ, *Peanuts Jubilee*

Paragraphs have no set length. Typically, they range from 50 to 250 words, averaging perhaps 100 words. Paragraphs intended for books are on average longer than those written for the narrow columns of newspapers and magazines. The shortest paragraphs generally occur in dialogue (see also **16a[2]**).

Note: Modern writers generally avoid extremely long paragraphs, especially those that belabour one point or combine too many points.

32a
Construct unified paragraphs.

In a unified paragraph each sentence contributes to developing a central thought. Stating the central thought in a topic sentence will help you achieve unity.

(1) Make sure each sentence is related to the central thought.

Hold to the main idea; eliminate information that is unrelated or only vaguely related to it. Suppose, for instance, the main idea of one of your paragraphs is this: "Computers help students organize their time." In such a paragraph, if you include sentences about other benefits of computers you will disrupt the unity. Every statement should pertain to the usefulness of the computer for organizing time. Notice in paragraph 3 how each sentence helps to show exactly what the writer means by the curious experiences referred to in the first sentence.

> 3   A number of curious experiences occur at the onset of sleep. A person just about to go to sleep may experience an electric shock, a flash of light, or a crash of thunder—but the most common sensation is that of floating or falling, which is why "falling asleep" is a scientifically valid description. A nearly universal occurrence at the beginning of sleep (although not everyone recalls it) is a sudden, uncoordinated jerk of the head, the limbs, or even the entire body. Most people tend to think of going to sleep as a slow slippage into oblivion, but the onset of sleep is not gradual at all. It happens in an instant. One moment the individual is awake, the next moment not.
>
> —PETER FARB, *Humankind*

As you check your paragraphs for unity, if any information does not relate to your main idea, eliminate this irrelevant material. If any material is related to the main idea but not clearly so, revise to make the relationship clear. Sometimes, the problem is that the main idea itself needs to be more clearly formulated. (See also **32a[2]**.) Or there may be too many major ideas in a single paragraph. If so, the chances are that you should develop each in a separate paragraph. Occasionally, however, the best strategy is to formulate a new "umbrella" sentence, one expressing an idea that all the others will support.

■ **Exercise 1**   Revise the following faulty paragraph to improve unity. Be prepared to give the reasons for your revisions.

When I visited Vancouver Island's west coast last summer, I noticed that it looked very much like the coast of Oregon. It was very cold and rainy at Long Beach and we had to wear coats even though it was late July. The Island's coastline is rocky and in many places evergreens march straight to the water. In other places, bluffs lined with evergreens overlook the sea. One day we saw a large sailboat driving hard toward some half-submerged rocks. In Oregon, pine-rimmed bluffs usually overlook the ocean, but sometimes the trees extend to a partly submerged rocky ledge or a pebble beach. Small islands, called sea stacks, dot this coastline much as the wooded islands lie offshore in Barkley Sound. Lighthouses can be found here and there along both coastlines.

(2) State the main idea of the paragraph in a clearly constructed topic sentence.

A topic sentence embodies the central thought of a paragraph. Notice how the topic sentence of paragraph 4 (the first sentence) announces the idea of our reaction to eye behaviour; it also suggests the approach of the paragraph by establishing an expectation that the writer will go on to provide a number of examples.

4   Much of eye behavior is so subtle that we react to it only on the intuitive level. The next time you have a conversation with someone who makes you feel liked, notice what he does with his eyes. Chances are he looks at you more often than usual with glances a little longer than the normal. You interpret this as a sign—a polite one—that he is interested in you as a person rather than just in the topic of conversation. Probably you also feel that he is both self-confident and sincere.

—FLORA DAVIS, *Inside Intuition:*
What We Know about Nonverbal Communication

Notice in paragraph 5 how the phrase "two significant facts" in the topic sentence introduces the writer's approach.

5   Years of studying something as unremarkable as the shape of craters on the surface of Mars have turned up two significant facts about the planet and its satellites. One is that Phobos and Deimos, the two tiny moons of Mars, may be the last survivors of a family of ancient satellites—perhaps dozens of them—that once whirled around the red planet. The second fact is that the skin, or outer crust, of Mars underwent a dramatic change about 3 billion years ago.   —TERENCE DICKINSON, "Stars"

The main idea of a paragraph is most often stated at or near the beginning, as in examples 4 and 5, although it may appear anywhere in the paragraph. When the main idea is stated early, it is sometimes also restated at the end, to point up its importance.

6   In the towns and cities of Ulster, the intolerable has become normal. The civic environment is scarred. In Belfast and Derry, it is hard to find a shop with windows; shopkeepers have had so many broken that they are content to leave the boards up. Burned-out houses and shops are left as abandoned hulks. The army has run out its barbed wire, concrete and corrugated iron in dozens of checkpoints, barricades and gun emplacements. Ugliness is accepted, no longer even noticed.
—PAUL HARRISON, "The Dark Age of Ulster"

Occasionally, as in paragraph 7, the topic sentence is the last sentence, especially when the writer progresses from particulars—for instance, from a specific example—to a generalization.

7   In the warmth of the inner Solar System a comet releases clouds of vapor and dust that form the glowing head and then leak into the tail, which is the cosmic equivalent of an oil slick. Pieces of the dust later hit the Earth, as meteors. A few survivors among the comets evolve into menacing lumps of dirt in tight orbits around the Sun. For these reasons comets

are, in my opinion, best regarded as a conspicuous form of sky pollution. —NIGEL CALDER, *The Comet is Coming*

A single topic sentence (such as the first sentence below) may serve for a sequence of two or more paragraphs.

8   The world has always been divided into two camps: those who love garlic and onions and those who detest them. The first camp would include the Egyptian pharaohs who were entombed with clay and wood carvings of garlic and onions to ensure that meals in the afterlife would be well seasoned. It would include the Jews who wandered for 40 years in the Sinai wilderness, fondly remembering "the fish which we did eat in Egypt so freely, and the pumpkins and melons, and the leeks, onions and garlic." It would include Sydney Smith, the 19th-century essayist, whose "Recipe for Salad" includes this couplet: "Let onion atoms lurk within the bowl, / And, scarce-suspected, animate the whole."

9   The camp of the garlic and onion haters would include the Egyptian priests who, according to Plutarch, "kept themselves clear of the onion. . . . It is suitable neither for fasting nor festival, because in the one case it causes thirst, and in the other tears for those who partake it." The camp would include the ancient Greeks, who considered the odor of garlic and onions vulgar and prohibited garlic and onion eaters from worshiping at the Temple of Cybele. It would include Bottom, who in *A Midsummer Night's Dream* instructs his troupe of actors to "eat no onions nor garlic, for we are to utter sweet breath." —ERIC BLOCK, "The Chemistry of Garlic and Onions"

Occasionally, no topic sentence is needed because the details unmistakably imply the central idea.

10   Tennis has become more than the national sport; it is a rigorous discipline, a form of collective physiotherapy. Jogging is done by swarms of people, out onto the streets each day in underpants, moving in a stolid sort of rapid trudge, hoping by this to stay alive. Bicycles are cures. Meditation

may be good for the soul but it is even better for the blood pressure.   —LEWIS THOMAS, *The Medusa and the Snail*

■ **Exercise 2**   Write a paragraph with a topic sentence at the beginning, another with the topic sentence at the end, and a two-paragraph sequence containing a single topic sentence. Here are a few possible approaches.

1. Two kinds of . . .
2. Reasons for believing . . .
3. The things that happen when . . .
4. Examples of . . .

32b

Make paragraphs coherent by arranging ideas in a clear, logical order and providing appropriate transitions.

A paragraph has coherence when the relationship among ideas is clear and the progression from one sentence to the next is easy and natural for the reader to follow. To achieve coherence, arrange ideas in a clear, logical order. Also provide transitions between sentences (not only within the paragraph but between paragraphs) by the effective use of pronoun reference, repetition of key words and ideas, appropriate conjunctions and other transitional expressions, and parallel structure.

ARRANGEMENT OF IDEAS

(1) Arrange ideas in a clear, logical order.

There are many common, logical ways to arrange ideas in a paragraph. The choice depends on the context and on the writer's purpose. One of the simplest orders is **time order**.

11   As a tornado spins faster and faster, the atmospheric pressure within it drops, just as the pressure falls within any storm as the storm intensifies. When atmospheric pressure drops, air expands and cools. This causes the moisture in the air to condense into a cloud, much as a person's breath condenses on a cold day. As a tornado intensifies, the cloudiness of the parent thunderstorm snakes down along the tornado's length toward where it touches the ground.

—STEVE OLSON, "Year of the Tornado"

Descriptive passages are often arranged in **space order**, moving from east to west, from near to distant, from left to right, and so on.

In paragraph 12, Thomas Merton presents details in a near-far perspective, enabling the reader to share the experience of approaching the monastery that was to become his home.

12   I looked at the rolling country, and at the pale ribbon of road in front of us, stretching out as grey as lead in the light of the moon. Then suddenly I saw a steeple that shone like silver in the moonlight, growing into sight from behind a rounded knoll. The tires sang on the empty road, and, breathless, I looked at the monastery that was revealed before me as we came over the rise. At the end of an avenue of trees was a big rectangular block of buildings, all dark, with a church crowned by a tower and a steeple and a cross: and the steeple was as bright as platinum and the whole place was as quiet as midnight and lost in the all-absorbing silence and solitude of the fields. Behind the monastery was a dark curtain of woods, and over to the west was a wooded valley, and beyond that a rampart of wooded hills, a barrier and a defense against the world.   —THOMAS MERTON, *The Seven Storey Mountain*

Another useful arrangement of ideas is that of **order of importance**, from most important to least or from least to most. (See also **29c**.) In paragraph 13 Harrison focusses on a hierarchy of intelligence, moving from lower to higher forms of life.

13   An ant cannot purposefully try anything new, and any ant that accidentally did so would be murdered by his colleagues. It is the ant colony as a whole that slowly learns over the ages. In contrast, even an earthworm has enough flexibility of brain to enable it to be taught to turn toward the left or right for food. Though rats are not able to reason to any considerable degree, they can solve such problems as separating round objects from triangular ones when these have to do with health or appetite. Cats, with better brains, can be taught somewhat more, and young dogs a great deal. The higher apes can learn by insight as well as by trial and error.

—GEORGE RUSSELL HARRISON, *What Man May Be*

Sometimes the movement within the paragraph is from **general to specific**, or from **specific to general**. A paragraph may begin with a general statement or idea, which is then supported by particular details (as in paragraph 14). Reversing the order, it may begin with a striking detail or series of details and conclude with a summarizing statement (as in paragraph 15).

14   The *conventions* of a period are the inherited, invented, and prescribed formulas that the people who formed its culture generally understood. The traditional arrangement of areas and rooms in a temple or dwelling, the larger-than-life representations and rigid postures of gods and rulers, the appearance of a masked deity or hero to pronounce the prologue and epilogue of a Greek drama, the required fourteen lines of a sonnet, the repeated rhythmic patterns of dances, the way characters speak in rhymed meters in poetic drama and sing their lines in opera—all are conveniences that became conventions through their acceptance by a representative number of people whose commonly held values and attitudes formed a culture.   —WILLIAM FLEMING, *Arts and Ideas*

15   When we watch a person walk away from us, his image shrinks in size. But since we know for a fact that he is not shrinking, we make an unconscious correcting and ''see'' him as retaining his full stature. Past experience tells us what his true stature is with respect to our own. Any sane and dependable expectation of the future requires that he have the same stature when we next encounter him. Our perception is thus a prediction; it embraces the past and the future as well as the present.

—WARREN J. WITTREICH, "Visual Perception and Personality"

One common form of the general–specific pattern is **topic–restriction–illustration**. In this pattern, the writer announces the topic, restricts or qualifies it, and illustrates the restriction in the remaining sentences of the paragraph.

16   Perhaps the most mystifying of the habits peculiar to whales is their "singing." Humpback whales are the most renowned for a wide range of tones, and whole herds often join together in "songs" composed of complete sequences, which, repeated, can last for hours. Some evenings, we listened to the humpbacks starting to make a few sounds, like musicians tuning their instruments. Then, one by one, they began to sing. Underwater canyons made the sounds echo, and it seemed as though we were in a cathedral listening to the faithful alternating verses of a psalm.

—JACQUES-YVES COUSTEAU, "Jonah's Complaint"

In paragraph 16 the general topic "the singing of whales" begins the paragraph. The next sentence restricts the topic to "the singing of humpback whales," and two illustrations are given, "how the whales 'tune up' " and "what the singing sounded like."

In the **problem–solution** pattern the first sentence states a problem, and the solution follows:

17   Dinner is at eight, and so is your favorite television show. Solution? Tape the show on your video cassette recorder.

18   Two must-see shows are scheduled for the same hour? Watch one on your TV while taping the other on your VCR.

19   Want to see "Casablanca" tomorrow night? Rent a copy from your local video store, and pop it into your VCR.

—CONSUMER REPORTS

The topic sentence in the **question–answer** pattern asks a question and the supporting sentences answer it, as in paragraph 20.

20   What does he do, this business mogul, this multimillionaire, this comfortable man? He thinks up ways for people to dress. Fifty years ago he might have been a tailor or a dressmaker; if he had lived in France he would have been called a couturier. But to call Ralph Lauren a tailor is like calling the Bechtel Corporation a builder. The word does not convey the sheer size or the international scale of the operation. A tailor makes clothes; Lauren's corporation franchises manufacturers on four continents who turn out products that are sold in more than three hundred shops carrying his name, as well as in specialty boutiques in department stores in the United States, Canada, England, Italy, Switzerland, Scandinavia, Mexico, and Hong Kong. As it has grown, his business has also diversified. It started modestly, with neckties, but soon expanded to men's wear, then clothes for women, lately a special line for children. Now perfumes, soaps, cosmetics, shoes, luggage, belts, wallets, and eyeglasses all bear his imprimatur. Lauren's is that most modern of professions: he is the total fashion designer.

—WITOLD RYBCZYNSKI, *Home: A Short History of an Idea*

Paragraphs 11 through 20 illustrate seven of the many possible types of clear arrangement within the paragraph. Any order, or any combination of orders, is satisfactory as long as it makes the sequence of thought clear.

■ **Exercise 3**   Prepare to discuss how paragraphs with various arrangements of ideas might be developed by using (or building on) the information provided below.

COCKROACH
   Description: An urban grasshopper, cynical, corrupt, dissatisfied, dangerous.
   Habitat: Any city with more than a 50,000 population, and swank resort hotels in the tropics.

Habits: Defiance and survival. Likes to pop up from time to time to run across the tablecloths at really expensive restaurants.

Foods: Likes ethnic fare but will eat greedily anything that isn't tightly covered. Will take an occasional after-dinner cigar.

Comments: Cockroaches are perhaps the most unsung social force of all time. They were directly responsible for the great human migration to the suburbs in the 1950s and early 1960s, and thus they can be blamed for a wide variety of social ills.

—CHARLES A. MONAGAN, *The Reluctant Naturalist*

TRANSITIONS BETWEEN SENTENCES

The linking of sentences by transitional devices such as pronoun reference, repeated key words or ideas, appropriate conjunctions and other transitional expressions, and parallel structure helps create a coherent paragraph. Usually, several of these aids to coherence are found in a single paragraph:

21

key words and ideas

Civilized (peoples) are not alone in having grasped the [idea] of [superstitions]—[beliefs and practices] that are superseded but that still may evoke compliance. The [idea] is one that is familiar to every (people,) however primitive, that I have ever known. Every (society) has a core of transcendent [beliefs]—[beliefs] about the nature of the universe, the world, and man— that no one doubts or questions. Every (society) also has a [fund of knowledge] related to practical life—about the succession of day and night and of the

parallel construction

transitional expression

seasons; about correct ways of planting seeds so that they will germinate and grow; about the processes involved in making dyes or the steps necessary to remove the deadly poison from manioc roots so they become edible. Island (peoples) know how the winds shift and they know the star toward which they must point the prow of the canoe exactly so that as the sun rises they will see the first fringing palms on the shore toward which they are sailing.

pronoun repetition

—MARGARET MEAD, "New Superstitions for Old—January, 1966"

[Words and phrases relating to *people* are circled; those relating to *superstitions* are placed in boxes. Pronouns are underlined.]

(2) Link sentences by using pronouns.

In paragraph 22 the writer links sentences by using the pronouns *their* and *they*. Although these same two pronouns are used repeatedly, their referent, "the native people," is always clear.

22   Now the industrial system beckons to the native people. But it does not merely beckon: it has intruded into their culture, economy and society, now pulling, now pushing them towards another, and in many ways an alien, way of life. In the North today, the native people are being urged to give up their life on the land; they are being told that their days and their lives should become partitioned like our own. We have often urged that their commitment to the industrial system be entire and complete. Native people have even been told that they cannot compromise: they must become industrial workers, or go naked back to the bush.

—THOMAS BERGER, *Northern Frontier, Northern Homeland*

(3) Link sentences by repeating key words or ideas.

In paragraph 23, the repetition of the key words "sick and tired" links the sentences. (The repetition also provides emphasis: see **29e**.)

23   I was sick and tired of January, and sick and tired of February following January year after year like famine and pestilence following war. I was sick and tired of football, and sick and tired of football being followed by ice hockey and basketball as pestilentially as February followed January. I was especially sick and tired of people interrupting my grouch with commands to smile and cheer up. I was sick and tired of everything except being sick and tired of it all, which I enjoyed immensely.

—RUSSELL BAKER, "Confessions of a Three-Day Grouch"

(4) Link sentences by using conjunctions and other transitional expressions.

Here is a list of some frequently used transitional connectives arranged according to the kinds of relationships they establish.

1. *Alternative and addition*: or, nor, and, and then, moreover, further, furthermore, besides, likewise, also, too, again, in addition, even more important, next, first, second, third, in the first place, in the second place, finally, last.
2. *Comparison*: similarly, likewise, in like manner.
3. *Contrast*: but, yet, or, and yet, however, still, nevertheless, on the other hand, on the contrary, conversely,

even so, notwithstanding, for all that, in contrast, at the same time, although this may be true, otherwise, nonetheless.

4. *Place*: here, beyond, nearby, opposite to, adjacent to, on the opposite side.
5. *Purpose*: to this end, for this purpose, with this object.
6. *Cause, result*: so, for, hence, therefore, accordingly, consequently, thus, thereupon, as a result, then.
7. *Summary, repetition, exemplification, intensification*: to sum up, in brief, on the whole, in sum, in short, as I have said, in other words, that is, to be sure, as has been noted, for example, for instance, in fact, indeed, to tell the truth, in any event.
8. *Time*: meanwhile, at length, soon, after a few days, in the meantime, afterward, later, now, then, in the past.

(5) Link sentences by means of parallel structure.

Parallelism is the repetition of the sentence pattern or of other grammatical structures. See also Section **26**.

In paragraph 24, the author uses parallel constructions in almost every sentence. This, combined with repetition of the phrase "I have seen," strengthens the impression of repeated, first-hand experience and prepares the reader for the summing up in the final sentence.

24   On the Old Crow Flats, in the Mackenzie Delta, and along the Beaufort Sea coast I have seen the immense flocks of birds that migrate in their thousands to this arctic area each summer. I have seen the white whales swimming in the shallow coastal waters of the Beaufort Sea around the Mackenzie Delta. I have seen the Porcupine caribou herd in early summer at its calving grounds in the Northern Yukon, and the Bathurst herd at its wintering grounds north of Great Slave Lake. And in every native village I have seen the meat and fish, the fur and hides that the people have harvested from the land and water.
—THOMAS BERGER, *Northern Frontier, Northern Homeland*

■ **Exercise 4**   Prepare for a class discussion of the specific linking devices (pronouns, transitional words, repetition, parallelism) used in the following paragraph.

25   Electronic music is a new departure from orthodox, or generally accepted, music in that it is electrically originated or modified sound. This sound is the output of electric pianos, organs, synthesizers, saxophones, guitars, flutes, violins, trumpets, and many other instruments. It is the product of composers who use tape recorders and tape manipulation to distort, for better or worse, conventional sounds. Also, it is the sounds we hear in concerts and on records that use amplification to boost or alter the volume of instruments.

— MERRIL C. LEHRER, "The Electronic Music Revolution"

■ **Exercise 5**   Revise the sentences in the following paragraph so that the thought flows smoothly from one sentence to the next.

Cable television sounds like a good deal at first. All available local channels can be piped in to a television set for a relatively low cost per month. The reception is clear—a real bonus in fringe and rural areas—and in addition several channels for news and local access are in the basic monthly fee. A cable connection to a second or third TV set costs extra. In most places subscribers have to pay as much as thirty dollars a month extra to get the desirable channels like Arts & Entertainment, First Choice, and The Sports Network. Although the movies change each month, the pay-TV movie channels run the same films over and over during a month's time. Many of the films offered each month are box office flops or reruns of old movies that can be viewed on regular channels. Cable television isn't really a bargain.

(6) Provide clear transitions between paragraphs.

Clear writing depends upon clear transitions between paragraphs as well as between sentences.

For example, read paragraph 26 in which the economist Galbraith introduces Karl Marx's criticisms of capitalist theory. Then observe the types of transitional devices used in the first sentences of subsequent paragraphs that summarize Marx's views.

26

transitional expressions and parallel constructions

repetition of words/ideas

The vulnerable points in the capitalist system and its interpretation were, as he saw them, first, the distribution of power—which had been effectively and almost universally ignored by the classical economists.

Second, there was the highly unequal distribution of income. . . .

Third, there was the susceptibility of the economic system to crises and unemployment—in modern terms, to depression. . . .

Finally, there was monopoly, a flaw that was conceded by the classical tradition. But for Marx this was not an isolated phenomenon; it reflected a basic tendency, one that would be decisive in the final fate of capitalism.

—JOHN KENNETH GALBRAITH,
Economics in Perspective

The closely related words in each of the groups that follow are often placed at or near the beginnings of sentences to link ideas in separate paragraphs (as illustrated in paragraph 26) or within a paragraph.

1. First. . . . Second. . . . Third. . . .
2. First. . . . Then. . . . Next. . . . Finally. . . .
3. Then. . . . Now. . . . Soon. . . . Later. . . .
4. One. . . . Another. . . . Still another. . . .
5. Some. . . . Others. . . . Still others. . . .
6. A few. . . . Many. . . . More. . . . Most. . . .
7. Just as significant. . . . more important. . . . most important of all. . . .

Sometimes a transitional paragraph serves as a bridge between two paragraphs. Ordinarily, such a paragraph is short (often consisting of only one sentence) because the writer intends it to be merely a signpost. Notice below that the first noun phrase in the transitional paragraph 28 echoes the preceding key idea and that the second noun phrase points to a fact to be explained next.

27   Indeed, instead of seeing evolution as a smooth process, many of today's life scientists and archeologists are studying the "theory of catastrophes" to explain "gaps" and "jumps" in the multiple branches of the evolutionary record. Others are studying small changes that may have been amplified through feedback into sudden structural transformations. Heated controversies divide the scientific community over every one of these issues.

28   **But all such controversies are dwarfed by a single history-changing fact.**

29   One day in 1953 at Cambridge in England a young biologist, James Watson, was sitting in the Eagle pub when his colleague, Francis Crick, ran excitedly in and announced to "everyone within hearing distance that we had found the secret of life." They had. Watson and Crick had unraveled the structure of DNA. —ALVIN TOFFLER, *The Third Wave*

32c
Develop the paragraph adequately.

Many short paragraphs are adequately developed. A one-sentence paragraph such as the following supplies enough information to satisfy the reader.

30   The village contains a railway station which hasn't been used since 1965 when the CNR discontinued passenger service in that part of northwestern New Brunswick, a one-room school that was closed five years ago when the government began using buses to carry local children to the regional school in Cumberland Centre, a general store and two churches: St. Edward's Anglican, which used to be attended by the station agent, the teacher and the store-keeper, and the Fire-Baptized Tabernacle of the Living God, attended by practically every-one else in Indian River.

—ALDEN NOWLAN, *Miracle at Indian River*

Sometimes, however, short paragraphs (especially a series of them) are a sign of inadequate development of the idea. Sometimes the solution is to combine the paragraphs if they deal with the same idea. If not, each paragraph should be expanded so that the thought is adequately developed.

PARAGRAPHS THAT SHOULD BE COMBINED

The line of demarcation between capitalism and socialism is sharp and clear.

Capitalism is that form of organization in which the means of production—and by that is meant the machine and the funds required to use the machine—are controlled by private individuals or by privately owned organizations.

Under a socialist regime the control of the means of production, the control of capital—for even socialists concede the need for capital—is by the group. Under capitalism the profits accrue to the private individual; under socialism, to the group.

Taken separately, these three paragraphs are short and choppy; if combined, they would form a paragraph adequately developing an idea stated in the first sentence and clarified in the last.

The following paragraphs (from different compositions) stop before supplying enough information to satisfy an interested reader.

PARAGRAPHS THAT SHOULD BE EXPANDED

Many adoptees searching for their natural parents have similar experiences. A few of the stories they tell, however, are unique.

[Which kinds of experiences are similar? Which kinds unique?]

Forestry work is healthful, educational, and financially rewarding. For example, a forester soon learns how to prevent and to fight forest fires.

[The reader expects to find out about three aspects of forestry work, but the writer comments briefly on only the educational benefit. How is the work healthful? What else does a forester learn? What are the financial rewards?]

If the paragraphs in your compositions tend to be inadequately developed, study the methods of paragraph development described and illustrated in **32d**.

32d

Learn to use various methods of paragraph development.

You can learn to write good paragraphs by studying the various techniques professional writers use to develop ideas. All the strategies for developing paragraphs discussed in the following pages are equally useful for developing whole compositions. (See also Section **33**.)

The more you read, the more you will find that paragraphs are rarely developed by a single method; a combination of methods is more common. No one method, or no one combination, is better than another except insofar as it better suits the writer's purpose in a given paragraph. As you study the following illustrations of good paragraphs, notice how each main idea is worked out.

(1) Develop the main idea by supplying relevant specific details.

The main idea of a paragraph often brings specific details to mind. Consider, for example, ''Beatniks rebelled against what they considered to be the intellectually and socially stultifying aspects of 1950s America.'' This statement raises such questions as ''How did they rebel?'' and ''What exactly did they rebel against?'' By answering these questions and choosing details with care (omitting irrelevant details, no matter how interesting they are in themselves), the writer can develop the main idea effectively—as in the following paragraph.

31   Beatniks rebelled against what they considered to be the intellectually and socially stultifying aspects of 1950s America. They shunned regular employment. They took no interest in politics and public life. They mocked the American enchantment with consumer goods by dressing in T-shirts and rumpled khaki trousers, the women innocent of cosmetics and the intricate hairstyles of suburbia. They made a great deal of the lack of furniture in their cheap walk-up apartments, calling their homes ''pads'' after the mattress on the floor.

—JOSEPH CONLIN, *The American Past*

(2) Illustrate a generalization using several closely related examples or one striking example.

Examples are especially useful for illustrating a generalization that a reader might question or might not understand. A paragraph developed by examples begins with a statement which is followed by one or more examples to illustrate it.

32   The modern corporation has deep historical roots. One goes back to the Middle Ages and before, ever since substantial trade in goods has been carried out over a distance. This is the merchant caravan or, at sea, the convoy. In a caravan, merchants gained the strength of numbers and organization against predators such as highwaymen, toll collectors, locally entrenched business competitors, monopolistic suppliers, and tax-hungry politicians. The Silk Route from China to Damascus was traversed by such caravans, and so were the routes to leading market cities in Europe. In Renaissance Europe, the famous East India companies organized by the British, Dutch, and French provided merchant venturers with strength in oceangoing ventures. —ARTHUR FLEISCHER, GEOFFREY C. HAZARD, and MIRIAM Z. KLIPPER, *Board Games* [Numerous examples illustrate the generalization.]

33   He was one of the greatest scientists the world has ever known, yet if I had to convey the essence of Albert Einstein in a single word, I would choose *simplicity*. Perhaps an anecdote will help. Once, caught in a downpour, he took off his hat and held it under his coat. Asked why, he explained, with admirable logic, that the rain would damage the hat, but his hair would be none the worse for its wetting. This knack for going instinctively to the heart of the matter was the secret of his major scientific discoveries—this and his extraordinary feeling for beauty. —BANESH HOFFMAN, "My Friend, Albert Einstein" [A single example, an anecdote, illustrates Einstein's simplicity.]

(3) Narrate a series of events.

Narrative paragraphs present a series of events, normally in the order in which they occur. (Longer narratives often begin in the middle of a sequence of events and contain flashbacks to earlier events.)

In paragraph 34, Denis Waitley uses a narrative to illustrate his point about children acquiring their parents' habits.

34   It's amazing how parents continue to pass their own hang-ups on to their children. It reminds me of the story about the young bride who cooked a ham for her new husband. Before putting it in the pan, she cut off both ends. When her husband asked her why she did that, she replied that her mother had always done it that way. At a later date, when they were having baked ham dinner at her mother's home, he asked her, casually, why she cut both ends off the ham. The mother shrugged and said she really didn't know, except that her mother had always done it that way. Finally, he asked the grandmother why she always cut the ends off the ham before she baked it. She looked at him suspiciously, replying, "Because my baking dish is too small!"

—DENIS WAITLEY, *Seeds of Greatness*

(4) Explain a process.

Process paragraphs explain how something is done or made. For this reason, they often have a temporal element that makes a step-by-step chronological arrangement both possible and natural, as in paragraph 35.

35   The best of all scientific tricks with an egg is the well-known one in which air pressure forces a peeled hard-boiled egg into a glass milk bottle and then forces it out again undamaged. The mouth of the bottle must be only slightly smaller than the egg, and so you must be careful not to use too large an egg or too small a bottle. It is impossible to push the egg into the bottle. To get the egg through the mouth you must heat the air in the bottle. That is best done by standing the bottle in boiling water for a few minutes. Put the egg upright on the mouth and take the bottle off the stove. As the air in the bottle cools it contracts, creating a partial vacuum that draws the peeled egg inside. To get the egg out again invert the bottle so that the egg falls into the neck. Place the opening of the bottle against your mouth and blow vigorously. This will compress the air in the bottle. When you stop blowing, the air expands, pushing the egg through the neck of the bottle and into your waiting hands.

—MARTIN GARDNER, "Mathematical Games"

(5) Show cause and effect.

A paragraph developed by causal analysis must not only raise the question *why* (directly or indirectly) but answer it to the satisfaction of the reader. The cause or causes must satisfactorily explain the result.

Paragraph 36 shows how the constraint of writing in Chinese and the exclusion of Japanese women from higher studies accounted for the effect named in the opening sentence.

36   For one brief and shining moment in world literature, writing "in feminine" gave women an edge in creative expression. Japanese nobility during the tenth-century Heian period believed the Chinese language was superior to their own. They reserved Chinese for higher study barred to women, and they attempted to write their serious works in Chinese as well, in much the same manner that Western scholars used Latin and Greek. While they struggled to master the square, formal characters of a foreign language, women of the court were free to use *kana*, a simplified, phonetic script, to set down the language they actually spoke. Permitted a fluidity and a native idiom that men denied themselves, Murasaki Shikibu (Lady Murasaki), author of *The Tale of Genji*, and Sei Shonagon, author of *The Pillow Book*, produced the lasting masterworks of their age.   —SUSAN BROWNMILLER, *Femininity*

(6) Use classification to relate ideas.

To classify is to group things in categories. Classification is a method for understanding or explaining a large or diverse subject and discovering the relationships within it. For example, of a variety of trees, black oak, sycamore, and cottonwood may be classified as deciduous; cedar, fir, and pine as evergreen. In paragraph 37, White classifies three views of New York.

37   There are roughly three New Yorks. There is, first, the New York of the man or woman who was born there, who takes the city for granted and accepts its size and its turbulence as natural and inevitable. Second, there is the New York of the commuter—the city that is devoured by locusts each day and spat out each night. Third, there is the New York of the person who was born somewhere else and came to New York in quest of something. Of these three trembling cities the greatest is the last—the city of final destination, the city that is a goal. It is this third city that accounts for New York's high-strung disposition, its poetical deportment, its dedication to the arts, and its incomparable achievements. Commuters give the city its tidal restlessness, natives give it solidity and continuity, but the settlers give it passion. And whether it is a farmer arriving from Italy to set up a small grocery store in a slum, or a young girl arriving from a small town in Mississippi to escape the indignity of being observed by her neighbors, or a boy arriving from the Corn Belt with a manuscript in his suitcase and a pain in his heart, it makes no difference: each embraces New York with the intense excitement of first love, each absorbs New York with the fresh eyes of an adventurer, each generates heat and light to dwarf the Consolidated Edison Company.   —E.B. WHITE, "Here Is New York"

(7) Formulate a definition.

Paragraphs of definition explain. As in the following paragraph, a *formal* definition explains a thing (viruses) by putting it in a class (infectious agents) and then by distinguishing it from other members of that class (small size, simple composition, and so on).

38   Viruses are a unique group of infectious agents that are characterized by their small size, simple composition, and the need to grow in an animal, plant, or bacterial cell. In general, viruses are much smaller than bacteria, ranging in size from

20 to 400 nanometres (nm) in diameter (1 nanometre = 10^{-9} metre). They are composed of a core of nucleic acid, a coat of protein, and in some cases, lipid (fatty) and carbohydrate material. Viruses vary in their detailed morphology (form and structure) and in their specificity for different types of host cells.

—WILLIAM COFIELD SUMMERS,
"Viruses," *Britannica Macropaedia*, 15th edition, 1987

An *informal* definition differs from a formal definition in that it does not rely on the formula of class and differentiation. It defines by describing, narrating, comparing, or providing examples or synonyms. Paragraph 39 illustrates an informal definition that relies upon examples and synonyms. (See also **23d**.)

39   Biofeedback, Dr. Green said, means getting immediate, ongoing information about one's own biological processes or conditions—such as heart behavior, temperature, brainwave activity, blood pressure or muscle tension—and using the information to change and control voluntarily the specific process or response being monitored.

—THOMAS W. PEW, JR.,
"Biofeedback seeks new medical uses for concept of yoga"

(8) Describe by presenting an orderly sequence of sensory details.

An effective description presents carefully chosen details in some clear order, for instance, from near to far, from general to particular, from right to left, from top to bottom. Moving in such a way, it provides an orderly scheme so the reader can visualize what you are describing.

In paragraph 40, Peter Newman presents the details of the dress of the voyageurs, moving from footwear to headgear.

40   They [the Voyageurs] kept their hair long so that a shake of the head would help drive away the marauding summer

insects. Short and bulky like Belgian workhorses, they took the pride of dandies in their simple but distinctive dress code. They wore deer- or moose-skin moccasins with no socks, corduroy trousers and sky blue *capots* (hooded frock coats with brass buttons) over red-and-black flannel shirts. The pants were tied at the knees with beadwork garters and held around the waist with crimson handwoven sashes—the famous *ceintures fléchées*. One variation was an embroidered buckskin coat, its seams decorated with bear hair; when caught by the wind after a rainstorm, the garment would make a strange and desolate sound like the ground drumming of a grouse. Choice of hats expressed at least a touch of individuality. Some wore high, scarlet-tasselled night bonnets, others coarse blue cloth caps with peaks, or toques or colourful handkerchiefs wound into turbans. The Northmen proclaimed their vanity by sticking what they called "ostrich plumes" into their headgear, though these were usually dyed chicken feathers—and, sometimes, fox tails.

—PETER C. NEWMAN, *Caesars of the Wilderness*

(9) Analyze the parts of a subject.

Analysis breaks an object or idea into its elements and examines the relationships among them. In paragraph 41 the author analyzes the parts of a factory trawler.

41   Common to all factory trawlers are four essential elements that set them apart from the generations of fishing vessels that preceded them. These are a stern ramp or slipway for the rapid recovery of nets from astern (rather than over the side), a sheltered belowdecks factory section with assembly-line machines to gut and fillet fish (as opposed to cleaning by hand on an exposed main deck), an ammonia or freon refrigerating plant for the quick freezing and frozen storage of fish (in place of heavy and space-consuming chopped ice), and equipment to make fishmeal (to utilize both the factory leavings and trash or nonmarketable fish).

—WILLIAM W. WARNER,
Distant Water: The Fate of the North Atlantic Fisherman

Methods of Development   351

(10) Compare or contrast to develop a main idea.

A comparison points out similarities; a contrast points out differences. A comparison or contrast may be organized in either of two ways (or a combination of them), the choice depending on the writer's purpose. Paragraph 42 illustrates a part-by-part organization: it first identifies the two items being compared or contrasted (beggars and "respectable people"), and then it alternates between them as it considers various characteristics.

42   Yet if one looks closely one sees that there is no *essential* difference between a beggar's livelihood and that of numberless respectable people. Beggars do not work, it is said; but then, what is *work*? A navvy works by swinging a pick. An accountant works by adding up figures. A beggar works by standing out of doors in all weathers and getting varicose veins, chronic bronchitis, etc. It is a trade like any other; quite useless, of course—but, then, many reputable trades are quite useless. And as a social type a beggar compares well with scores of others. He is honest compared with the sellers of most patent medicines, high-minded compared with a Sunday newspaper proprietor, amiable compared with a hire-purchase tout—in short, a parasite, but a fairly harmless parasite. He seldom extracts more than a bare living from the community, and, what should justify him according to our ethical ideas, he pays for it over and over in suffering. I do not think there is anything about a beggar than sets him in a different class from other people, or gives most modern men the right to despise him.   —GEORGE ORWELL, *Down and Out in Paris and London*

Paragraph 43 illustrates a whole-by-whole organization, which treats all the pertinent qualities of one item being compared or contrasted (men's faces) before going on to treat the corresponding qualities in the next item (women's faces).

43   Women do not simply have faces, as men do; they are identified with their faces. Men have a naturalistic relation to

their faces. Certainly they care whether they are good-looking or not. They suffer over acne, protruding ears, tiny eyes; they hate getting bald. But there is a much wider latitude in what is esthetically acceptable in a man's face than what is in a woman's. A man's face is defined as something he basically doesn't need to tamper with; all he has to do is keep it clean. He can avail himself of the options for ornament supplied by nature: a beard, a mustache, longer or shorter hair. But he is not supposed to disguise himself. What he is "really" like is supposed to show. A man lives through his face; it records the progressive stages of his life. And since he doesn't tamper with his face, it is not separate from but is completed by his body—which is judged attractive by the impression it gives of virility and energy. By contrast, a woman's face is potentially separate from her body. She does not treat it naturalistically. A woman's face is the canvas upon which she paints a revised, corrected portrait of herself. One of the rules of this creation is that the face *not* show what she doesn't want it to show. Her face is an emblem, an icon, a flag. How she arranges her hair, the type of make-up she uses, the quality of her complexion—all these are signs, not of what she is "really" like, but of how she asks to be treated by others, especially men. They establish her status as an "object."

—SUSAN SONTAG, "The Double Standard of Aging"

Sometimes a concept can be vividly conveyed by an analogy, a kind of comparison in which one thing is explained in terms of its similarities to something more familiar. (See also **20a[4]**.) Notice in the next paragraph how Roger Shattuck compares literature and wine.

44   Literature has two advantages over wine. A good book ages forever; and you can read it as often as you wish without diminishing its substance. The devoted reader is like a wine lover whose dream has come true. His stock will never spoil or be consumed. He can sample, enjoy, and share his cellar without fear of depleting his reserve; it will grow as he grows. He need never go thirsty.

—ROGER SHATTUCK, "How to Rescue Literature"

(11) Use a combination of methods to develop the main idea.

Many good paragraphs are developed not by one specific method but by a combination of methods. Some good paragraphs almost defy analysis. The important consideration is not that a specific method is used to develop the paragraph, but that the development is clear, complete, and appropriate. Notice the combination of methods in each of the following paragraphs.

45   The question of why snowflakes are different remains one of the classic puzzles of science, but that they *are* different is part of our culture. Who has not heard, and believed without a thought, that no two snowflakes are alike? All snowflakes *look* very much alike; like little white dots. No doubt, if one examines them closely enough, there are differences to be found, but surely there is nothing remarkable about that. A single ice crystal might well contain some ten sextillion molecules: Considering all the ways those molecules can be arranged, the odds against any two completely identical snowflakes having fallen since the atmosphere formed some four billion years ago are enormous. But by the same analysis, no two grains of sand on the beach, no two waves in the ocean, no two hairs on the head are identical. Why all the fuss, then, over snowflakes?   —FRED HAPGOOD, "When Ice Crystals Fall from the Sky"   [The first sentence announces the topic which is developed by specific details and comparison.]

46   The ideal ballet body is long limbed with a small compact torso. This makes for beauty of line; the longer the arms and legs the more exciting the body line. The ideal ballet foot has a high taut instep and a wide stretch in the Achilles' tendon. This tendon is the spring on which a dancer pushes for his jump, the hinge on which he takes the shock of landing. If there is one tendon in a dancer's body more important than any other, it is this tendon. It is, I should say, the prerequisite for all great technique. When the heel does not stretch easily

and softly like a cat's, as mine did not, almost to the point of malformation, the shock of running or jumping must be taken somewhere in the spine by sticking out behind, for instance, in a sitting posture after every jump. I seemed to be all rusty wire and safety pins. My torso was long with unusually broad hips, my legs and arms abnormally short, my hands and feet broad and short. I was besides fat. What I did not know was that I was constructed for endurance and that I developed through effort alone a capacity for outperforming far, far better technicians. Because I was built like a mustang, stocky, mettlesome and sturdy, I became a good jumper, growing special compensating muscles up the front of my shins for the lack of a helpful heel. But the long, cool, serene classic line was forever denied me.   —AGNES DE MILLE, *Dance to the Piper*
[The paragraph is developed by definition, description, and cause and effect.]

■ **Exercise 6**   Prepare for a class discussion of the following paragraphs. Bear in mind unity, organization, coherence, and development.

47   In studies of perception, subjects were fitted with goggles that turned their visual image upside down. The goggles were worn constantly, the subjects having to adjust to an upside-down world as best they could. After several days, however, the visual process suddenly *righted* that upside-down vision of the world. After a time the goggles were removed. And immediately the world was seen *upside down* again. After about the same period of adjustment time, however, the inordinately complex relationship between eye-brain-mind again reversed the reversal, and turned that world view back upright.
—JOSEPH CHILTON PEARCE, *Exploring the Crack in the Cosmic Egg*

48   There are two basic kinds of literature. One helps you to understand, the other helps you to forget; the first helps you to be a free person and a free citizen, the other helps people to manipulate you. One is like astronomy, the other is like astrology.   —STEPHEN VIZINCZEY, *Truth and Lies in Literature*

49   What is the secret of Holmes's astonishing durability? It
has been said that Hamlet, Robinson Crusoe, and Sherlock
Holmes, in that order, are the most popular characters in
literature. The estimate needs revising. The agonizings of
Shakespeare's gloomy Dane are too cerebral for mass appeal.
Crusoe has been made laughably quaint by a crowded world;
footsteps on any strand today would lead a castaway to a resort
hotel not more than a mile down the beach. Holmes's striking
persona, however, has been undimmed by time or change.
And although Holmes is unique in literature, he did have a
real role model, Dr. Joseph Bell, a surgeon and medical
instructor at the University of Edinburgh. Bell's hobby was
deductive reasoning, and he entertained his students, often to
their dismay, by drawing character inferences from sharp
observations of their dress, habits, and mannerisms.

—KAY GARDELLA, "The Adventures of Sherlock Holmes"

50   Tall, gangling, black curls flopping about his neck, a banter-
ing, deprecating smile on his full lips, he looked more like a
provincial theatrical manager than a statesman. He was blest
with that rarest of political talents: a sense of humour. An
American senator's wife once found herself chatting with a
thin backwoodsy fellow who offered that he was from Canada.
She remarked that she had heard about "a smart man up
there," one John A. Macdonald, but that he was a "regular
rascal." Her acquaintance solemnly agreed. "Why do the
Canadians keep such a man in power?" the woman asked,
"They say he's a real scalawag." "Well," came the answer,
"they can't seem to get on without him." At this point the
Senator came up and introduced his wife formally to Macdonald. The Prime Minister laughed and soothed the lady's
confusion. "Don't apologize," he said. "All you have said
is perfectly true and well known at home."

—W.L. MORTON and L.F. HANNON, *This Land, These People*

51   Sound has shaped the bodies of many beasts. Noise tapped
away at the bullfrog until his ears became bigger than his
eyes. Now he hears so well that at the slightest sound of
danger he quickly plops to safety under a sunken leaf. The
rabbit has long ears to hear the quiet "whoosh" of the owl's

wings, while the grasshopper's ears are on the base of his abdomen, the lowest point of his body, where he can detect the tread of a crow's foot or the stealthy approach of a shrew.

—JEAN GEORGE, "That Astounding Creator—Nature"

52 Without doubt the most famous of all megalithic monuments is Stonehenge, on the Wiltshire plain of southern Britain. Visited by thousands yearly, it is second only to the Tower of London as a tourist attraction. It has a larger literature than any other archaeological site in the world, including the pyramids of Egypt and the great statues of Easter Island, as well as mythical sites such as Atlantis. The number of books on Stonehenge and on other megalithic monuments that have poured from the presses in the past decade or so is a measure of the continued interest in these antiquities.

—GLYN DANIEL, "Megalithic Monuments"

53 I feel . . . that there is a close connection among three aspects of language in our society. First is the associative squirrel-chatter that one hears on streets, and even in college halls, jerking along apologetically or defiantly in a series of unshaped phrases, using slang or vogue words for emphasis and punctuation. Second is the poetic illiteracy which regards anything in verse as a verbal puzzle, not even a puzzle to be worked out, but a disdainful and inscrutable puzzle without an answer. Third is the dead, senseless, sentenceless, written pseudo-prose that surrounds us like a boa constrictor, which is said to cover its victims with slime before strangling them. This last, under the names of jargon, gobbledygook, and the like, has often enough been recognized as a disease of contemporary language and ridiculed or deplored as such.

—NORTHROP FRYE, *The Well-Tempered Critic*

54 I thought of the country as a retreat, a quiet place, where life would be simple and pleasant and cheap, and where I could cut down on the need I have felt most of my adult life to make as much money as I could just to stay even. Well, quiet and simple and pleasant it has been, I assure you, but cheap? I might as well have bought a racehorse. I pay rent on my mailbox and tax on my trees. Fertilizer costs money so

the grass will grow long, and the local university student charges me to keep it, occasionally, short. The tomatoes I have tried to grow have been more expensive—if better—than those I could buy in a city supermarket, and I have not been able to put up the capital to buy equipment to do my own preserves. Even my daily newspaper, which I have to use gasoline to go to buy, costs me more than it would have cost in the city. At times I have looked at my city friends the way the have provinces have looked at the have-nots in a federal conference, as if I were subsidizing them and they didn't realize it.   —PETER GZOWSKI, *The Morningside Papers*

55   Alcatraz Island is covered with flowers now: orange and yellow nasturtiums, geraniums, sweet grass, blue iris, black-eyed Susans. Candytuft springs up through the cracked concrete in the exercise yard. Ice plant carpets the rusting catwalks. "WARNING! KEEP OFF! U.S. PROPERTY," the sign still reads, big and yellow and visible for perhaps a quarter of a mile, but since March 21, 1963, the day they took the last thirty or so men off the island and sent them to prisons less expensive to maintain, the warning has been only *pro forma*, the gun turrets empty, the cell blocks abandoned. It is not an unpleasant place to be, out there on Alcatraz with only the flowers and the wind and a bell buoy moaning and the tide surging through the Golden Gate, but to like a place like that you have to want a moat.   —JOAN DIDION, "Rock of Ages"

The Whole Composition

33

Learn to plan, draft, and revise your compositions effectively.

Whenever you write you engage, for some purpose (**33a**), in a process of developing an appropriate subject (**33b**) for a certain audience (**33c**). Focussing the subject (**33d**) and shaping a thesis statement (**33e**) will help you choose the information you will include, plan an appropriate arrangement (**33f**), and draft your essay (**33g**). You will probably revise several drafts (**33h**) before preparing a final version.

This process of planning, drafting, and revision is seldom as neat and straightforward as inexperienced writers may suppose. As you move through the process, you may need to engage in any of the activities several times. For example, you may need to go back and collect more ideas. Or you may write a draft only to discover that you have strayed from your main idea (or thesis). Such a discovery is not the catastrophe it may seem at first: writing is one of the best ways of clarifying your own views and gaining new insights. You may want to go back and change your thesis, or even throw it out and start with a new one. Whatever repetition of the steps in the process is necessary, the effort will be worthwhile if the result is a clear, coherent, unified essay.

As you read the following composition, observe how effectively Richard Preston marshals an abundance of sharply observed details to communicate his experience and knowledge of a commonplace subject—ice.

Ice

1   A pond sits in the middle of the woods on a windless night. The moon has set. A few leaves hang on emptied branches. Winter constellations gleam in the water. Molecules of water dance with each other. On the brink of becoming crystals, they break up, gather again. As the liquid skin of the pond cools below the freezing point, the pond's surface expands slightly. The surface becomes a wobbly lattice of water molecules, a kind of "flowing crystal." It is tensing itself. Now, in silence from rocks at the water's edge, needles of ice begin to grow. Pure water cannot freeze; it must build on a solid object. Ice can grow from a floating leaf, a root, the wing of a dead moth, a microscopic speck. Even a stray snowflake can start ice. If the snowflake happens to be a needle, it will send a spear shooting in a single direction; if the snowflake is a hexagonal star, it will throw a radiance of blades from all six points.

2   A trellis of ribs is growing toward the center of the pond. Sometimes the ice hisses as it moves. Meanwhile, crystals of ice that look like upside-down Christmas trees reach their way downward under the water. By morning, fish observe the sun as though through a cathedral window.

3   If the weather holds, the pond will soon reverberate with the whisk and click of skates. Why is ice so slippery? At normal temperatures, ice has a layer of water a few hundred molecules thick on its surface. Anything rubbed across it enlarges that liquid layer through frictional heating. A skate's blade *floats* on water.

4   Scientists like to speak of the "habits" of ice, as if ice were a creature. Nearly all substances, when they cool from liquid to solid, become denser, heavier. They form into a few predictable crystal shapes. Not water. It becomes lighter, emp-

tier, 9 per cent bigger by volume, able to float on itself. Water assumes a frenzy of solid forms. In addition to eighty known types of snow crystal, it becomes hoar, rime, silver thaw, depth hoar, subsoil lenses, bergs, mushrooms on the sea floor, glaciers that ooze like tar, arctic clouds 50 miles high that glow after midnight, and the labyrinth of frost on a window-pane. Two hundred billion balls of ice circle the sun outside the orbit of Pluto. The largest ice crystals on Earth are under Siberia, 2 feet in diameter and as old as the pyramids.

5   It is a lucky thing that ice floats. Otherwise, the oceanic abysses might gradually fill with sunken ice until the planet froze. But ice is an excellent insulator. It keeps lakes warm and fish alive. Ten million crystals in a cubic foot of snow trap dead air like goose down; a quilt wraps the earth in winter. Underneath a layer of fluffy snow, the ground temperature can be 50 degrees higher than the air above. Pheasants, grouse, rabbits, bears, meadow mice, spring peepers, beetle larvae, and many dormant plants depend on the snow's protection for survival.

6   According to its habits, ice plays with light. Arctic explorers have reported flashes in the darkness when sea ice moves. Plates of ice floating in water give off blue light when they snap. Nobody knows why. Hexagonal prisms in the upper air cleave light from the sun and moon into spots, pillars, arcs, and rings of iridescence. They portend snow.

7   To the Apollo astronauts Earth was a blue-and-white disk. The blue was water; the white was clouds and the polar caps— and many of those clouds were ice. Earth could be considered a fairly icy planet. Ice covers one quarter of the globe every year, including land and sea. Eighty per cent of the earth's fresh water is locked up in cold storage at the poles. It would melt into 8 billion *billion* gallons of water.

8   A melting pond adds only a drop to the planet's fresh water. As spring comes and sun warms the ice, water molecules spin away from their crystalline bonds. The pond's ice vanishes in a day. But it is still there, lurking hidden in the structure of water, as molecules dance with each other, waiting for the cold nights of next year. Ice keeps to its own habits.

—RICHARD M. PRESTON

Essays like Preston's, so natural and seemingly effortless, are the result of hard work. Experienced writers wrestle with the same writing activities inexperienced writers do: planning, drafting, and especially revising. For almost everyone, writing is a process of returning again and again to the various writing tasks, adjusting and fine-tuning until the result is a unified, coherent, and well-developed composition.

33a

Consider the purpose of your composition.

Writing is never done in a vacuum; the writer is always in a particular situation that involves some purpose—some reason for writing. The clearer the purpose is in the writer's mind, the more successful the writing is likely to be. The purposes of non-fiction writing are often classified as expressive, informative, and persuasive. Although these purposes are usually combined in an extended piece of writing, one of them almost always predominates.

Expressive writing emphasizes the writer's feelings and reactions to the world—to people, objects, events, and ideas. Some examples of expressive writing are journals and diaries, reminiscences, and, frequently, personal letters. The following example is a journal entry.

> Venice was wonderfully beautiful, quite unlike it is in the summer when it has the quality of painting with dark fissures, keyholes, patterns of clover, chimneys like halberds thrust into the sky, marble in the *palazzi* of the Grand Canal, which looks like stained leather. Last week it looked more drawn than painted, and geometrical: the vertical lines of *palazzi* windows, triangles, circles, semicircles, oblongs, squares. Buildings shone, subdued in colour as in a glow of dawn or sunset. Venice in bud, in spring, not the blown flowers, all pink and green of summer—the water a steely undulating mirror in which the reflections of buildings were strong and

clear. The *calle* [narrow streets] cool and shadowy in their near emptiness with light clear colour that cut like knives into the darkness above—and, overtopping all, the lid of blue sky. —STEPHEN SPENDER, *Journals 1939–1983*

Informative writing focusses the reader's attention upon the objective world, the objects, the events, and the ideas themselves rather than upon the writer's feelings or attitudes about them. Some examples of informative writing are news accounts, encyclopedia articles, laboratory and scientific reports, textbooks, and, usually, articles in professional journals and other publications directed to specialized audiences. Notice that in the following account the writer presents facts objectively.

When peat-digging was revived during and after World War II, bodies were unearthed in abundance—first in 1942 at Store Arden, then in 1946, 1947, and 1948 at Borre Fen. Artifacts found beside them positively identified them as people of Denmark's Early Iron Age, from 400 B.C. to A.D. 400. None, then, was less than 1500 years old, and some were probably much older. The first of the Borre Fen finds—a full-grown male—was to prove especially significant: Borre Fen man, too, had died violently, with a noose about his neck, strangled or hanged. And his last meal had consisted of grain.

—MAURICE SHADBOLT,
"Who Killed the Bog Men of Denmark? And Why?"

Persuasive writing aims to sway the reader's opinions or attitudes, arouse the reader to action, or in some other way bring about a particular response. Persuasive writing relies especially on the use of evidence and logical reasoning (see also Section **31**). The reader's perception of the writer's honesty and fair-mindedness is crucial. Persuasive writing may also depend on the skilful use of language to evoke an emotional response. For example, a defence lawyer's summation to a jury will rely upon documented evidence from which the lawyer draws logical conclusions, and it may also cite the testimony of authorities, and employ words and phrases that appeal to the jurors' emotions and sense of morality. Not least in this arsenal of techniques is the lawyer's stance as a seeker of truth and justice. Some other examples of persuasive writing are advertisements, political speeches, and editorials. In the following example, Margaret Laurence aims to persuade the reader to accept her belief that disarmament is essential to peace.

> Our lives and the lives of all generations as yet unborn are being threatened, as never before, by the increasing possibility of a nuclear war. I believe that the question of disarmament is the most pressing practical, moral and spiritual issue of our times. I'm not talking about abstractions. I'm talking about my life and your life and my kids' lives and the lives of people everywhere. If we value our own lives, and the lives of our children and all children everywhere, if we honour both the past and the future, then we must do everything in our power to work non-violently for peace. These beliefs are not only an integral part of my social and moral stance but of my religious faith as well. Human society now possesses the terrible ability to destroy all life on earth, and our planet itself. Can anyone who has ever marvelled at the miracle of creation—who has ever borne or fathered a beloved child, who has even looked closely at a tree or a plant or a river—fail to feel concerned and indeed anguished, every single day, at this thought?
>
> —MARGARET LAURENCE, "My Final Hour"

Although the purpose of college writing is usually informative, it may often be expressive or persuasive. Whenever you write, understand which aim a writing situation calls for. You might write an expressive essay on the impact of a personal encounter with poverty for an English course, an informative paper on the causes of poverty for an economics class, and a persuasive paper arguing for measures to eliminate poverty in a political science course. If you maintain an awareness of your purpose and your reader throughout the writing process, your writing will be clearer and more successful.

■ **Exercise 1**   Select two of the following subjects and explain how you could treat each (1) as expressive writing, (2) as informative writing, and (3) as persuasive writing.

a. finding an apartment   b. buying a car   c. applying for a job
d. accepting responsibilities   e. managing money

33b
Find an appropriate subject.

If you are assigned a subject to write about or if your situation clearly dictates a subject—as in most business writing, for example—you can move directly to a consideration of your audience (**33c**), of the particular aspect of the subject you will emphasize (**33d**), and of the ways you might organize your discussion (**33e**). Especially in college writing, however, you will sometimes be expected to choose a subject for yourself.

Often the best subject may be one drawn from your own experience—your personal knowledge, interests, and beliefs. Do you play a musical instrument? Climb mountains? Like to travel? Do you have a job? What classes are you taking? Can you think of a particular place that is important to you? An interesting character you have met? Something unusual about your family? What ambitions do you have for yourself? What strong convictions do you hold? When you are free to choose a subject, you can write an interesting paper on almost anything you care about.

Sometimes you will need to choose a subject outside your own experience because you want to extend your knowledge of a subject or because the situation dictates that you do so. If you have to write a term paper for a microbiology course, you may be free to write on any aspect of that discipline that interests you, but the instructor making the assignment wants a paper demonstrating your command of information, not your personal feelings about or experiences with microbes. No less than with writing about personal experience, however, you should take some trouble to find a subject that interests you. You can often find a subject by looking in your textbook, particularly in the sections listing suggestions for further reading and study. You can go through your lecture notes, examine books and articles in the library, look through the subject catalogue, or refer to encyclopedias. Sometimes talking to other students or to your instructor will help you find a subject.

Finally, remember that most writing situations have built-in constraints. For instance, the choice of a subject for a sociology paper is up to you, but the instructor has specified a length of ten to twelve pages. Obviously, a subject you can develop fully in two or three pages won't do. Or you have free choice of a subject for a political science paper, but the paper is due in a week. You will do well to choose a subject you already know something about rather than one on which you have to do extensive research. Choose a subject you can handle in the situation.

■ **Exercise 2** Be prepared to discuss in class one of the following:

1. Choose a personal experience you might want to write about. How was the experience meaningful to you? What reasons can you think of for sharing this experience with others?
2. Find a controversial subject you are interested in, one that you would like to know more about. What are the issues involved? What would you need to look up to write about it? What are the main points for it? Against it?

33c

Analyze your audience.

Before you begin to write, think as specifically as you can about who will read your writing—your audience. Understanding your audience will help you not only to define your subject and establish its scope but also to decide how technical you can be, what kinds of details you will use, and what tone you will take. You can distinguish between at least two kinds of audience, specialized and general.

SPECIALIZED AUDIENCES

A specialized audience has considerable knowledge of the subject about which you are writing and a keen interest in it. For example, if your subject is a new skiing technique, a group of ski instructors would obviously constitute a specialized audience. So would readers of *Ski* magazine, though in writing for this audience you would allow for a greater variation in knowledge and interest. (A specialized audience for one subject would be a general audience for another; the ski instructor, unless also a gifted chef, would probably constitute a general audience for an essay on cooking with a wok.)

It is often easier to write for specialized audiences because you have a specific idea of how much and what kinds of information, as well as what methods of presentation, are called for. You can adjust your tone and the kind of language you use as you tailor your presentation to their expertise and attitudes. The following example from the *Annual Review of Astronomy and Astrophysics* is written for a specialized audience that understands mathematical notation and expects scientific jargon to provide shortcuts to explanations.

> It is now generally believed that a cometary nucleus consists of some sort of conglomerate of ice and meteoric material, as was envisioned by Whipple (1950, 1951). As the comet

nears the Sun, the ices are sublimated, and the resultant gas and released meteoric dust become available for forming the coma and tail. Reaction of the comet to the ejection of this material then provides an explanation for the nongravitational effects in the motions of comets. The prevalence of strong outward radial components of the nongravitational forces ($A_1 \approx 10 \mid A_2 \mid$) is precisely to be expected from the icy-conglomerate model. The fact that there is any transverse component at all follows from the comet's rotation and a lag between the direction of maximum mass ejection and the subsolar meridian: $A_2 > 0$ corresponds to direct rotation of the comet, $A_2 < 0$ to retrograde rotation.

—BRIAN G. MARSDEN, "Comets"

GENERAL AUDIENCES

Think of a general audience as a reader or readers not exp rt on your topic but presumably willing to read what you have to say about it. It is possible to identify certain characteristics even in a general audience so that you can shape your presentation accordingly. For example, the audience for which your instructor usually wishes you to write is one made up of educated adults, intellectually alert and receptive to ideas (but with many different special interests of their own). This assumed audience is not very different from the one for which the articles in a general encyclopedia are written. Consider the following description from such an encyclopedia.

A comet is a generally nebulous celestial body of small mass revolving around the Sun. Its appearance and brightness vary markedly with its distance from the Sun. A comet far from the Sun is very faint, appears starlike, and consists of a small body or group of bodies reflecting sunlight, called the nucleus. As the comet approaches the Sun, a nebulosity called the coma develops around the nucleus; with the nucleus it constitutes the head of the comet. The coma contains dust and gas released from the nucleus through the action of solar radiation. When close enough to the Sun, a tail may develop, sometimes very long and bright, directed away from the Sun. Such a comet shines partly by scattering of solar radiation on dust particles and partly by re-emission of the gas of absorbed solar radiation (through processes called resonance or fluorescence).

—ENCYCLOPEDIA BRITANNICA

General audiences may be of quite different kinds. Consider the following passage from a fifth-grade science textbook. It describes a comet by using details (such as "flying frozen gravel pits") that appeal to ten-year-old readers and by using simple words in short, uncomplicated sentences.

Comets may be no more than a few miles across. They are made of bits of frozen gas and dust. They can be thought of as flying frozen gravel pits. Much of a comet's matter changes to vapor when the comet travels near the sun. As the comet "head" absorbs the sun's energy, the gas of the comet expands. So the comet takes up more space. A "tail" is formed. The tail may be as much as 500 million miles long. The matter of a comet is spread very thin.

—GEORGE MALLINSON et al.,
Science: Understanding Your Environment

When you are writing for a general audience, a useful technique is to imagine one specific reader whose background and expectations are typical; then adjust your choice of details and your tone accordingly.

MIXED AUDIENCES

Although in work-related writing situations you probably will write most often for a specialized audience, occasionally you will need to write for a mixed audience of specialized and general readers. For example, an engineer may prepare a technical report for an immediate supervisor who is also an engineer and therefore represents a specialized audience. But the report will also be read by executives who are not engineers. The engineer, therefore, has to design the report so that it conveys specialized information to the supervisor but is sufficiently clear to the others. Often in such situations it is simply not possible to serve all the members of a mixed audience equally well; a writer must then determine who the primary audience is and write mainly to that audience, doing the best he or she can for the others.

■ **Exercise 3**   Choose an experience you have had recently and write letters about it to all three of the following: (1) your parents or your employer, (2) your best friend, (3) *Maclean's* magazine.

TONE

A clear sense of audience is essential in determining the tone you should take when you write. What is your relationship to your reader? What is the reader's perception of the relationship? What is the reader's attitude toward the subject? How do you want your reader to react? The answers to such questions will help to determine whether you should be formal or informal, humorous, serious, or indignant. Suppose that as you were driving your new automobile down a busy street your brakes locked and caused you to slide into a parked car. In complaining to the company that manufactured your car with defective brakes, you would be writing to an unfamiliar audience, and your tone might reflect your indignation that the brakes were faulty. If you wrote to your insurance company to explain what happened, it would be inappropriate for you to take an indignant tone, though you would probably be serious and formal. A letter to your best friend would have an entirely different flavour. You might decide to express your indignation, even to do so humorously, but your tone would probably be informal.

The control of tone can be a subtle thing. Notice in the following essay how the author's serious, matter-of-fact approach to the subject and her stance as a person eager to be helpful to her reader contribute to the humorous effect.

Heat on the Hoof

1   As fuel costs continue to spiral upwards, the householder must continue his search for a reasonable and effective means of heating his establishment. Solar, or "passive," heating and woodburning stoves are popular alternatives to oil- and coal-burning systems; however, no discussion of modern heating methods would be complete without mention of the horse.

2   Horses may be used in a variety of ways as heating units. All of these are simpler than existing mechanical methods, and surprisingly effective. The average 1,200 pound horse has a caloric production rate of 600 therms per minute, and double that if he is angry or unsettled. The fuel-calorie conversion rate is extremely favorable, being about one to eight, which means that the standard four-bedroom house, with snacking center and media room, can be heated by one healthy horse and eight bales of hay per week: an appealing statistic and a soothing prospect. As there are a number of horse-heating methods available, it is wise to examine each to determine which will fit your particular needs the best.

3   One common practice is the installation of a very large horse (a Percheron or other heavy draft type is popular) in the basement of the house. Hot air ducts lead off the Percheron and act as conduits throughout the house. This is a safe and reliable method, as Percherons are mild and ruminative by nature, and fond of basements. In the event that your basement has been turned into a family recreation center, this should not adversely affect your Percheron system: many Percherons are ardent ping-pong spectators, and some are interested in taking up the game themselves. If the prospect of a blue-roan gelding playing round-robin in your basement unsettles you, remember this: even the most ineffectual efforts on the Percheron's part to join in family ping-pong games will raise the heat production in your home by a tremendous factor. Encouraging the horse in any sort of physical activity, even charades, should enable your entire family and the close neighbors of your choice to take hot showers as a result.

4   A drawback of the central-heating Percheron is that it heats the entire house regardless of which rooms are being used,

and some homeowners prefer a more adaptable system which will heat only the rooms that are routinely occupied. Many people find that stationing Thoroughbred mares throughout the house is an attractive alternative to the heavy draft cellar horse. The Thoroughbred is an extremely energetic breed, and its heat production is enormous, owing to its highly developed capillary system, which is a relatively new feature in equine design. The dainty Thoroughbred foot, another hallmark of this fine breed, ensures minimum damage to your flooring and fine carpets. Thoroughbreds are, however, emotionally unstable, and more care and attention must be paid them than the placid draft horse. This maintenance may be more than the average homeowner is willing to provide: soothing words must be used, idle or vicious gossip must be eschewed, and a friendly greeting must be offered daily, incorporating the correct name of the horse (not some jocular substitute), to maintain psychic order. Failure to follow these rules may result in ''sulk-outs,'' and a general lowering of temperature. Mares are more effusive than geldings, and they make particularly good heat producers, but they tend to shy at mice and violence, so geldings are recommended for kitchen and TV room use.

5   A third, and highly recommended, plan is to give each member of the family a Shetland pony of his own. These tiny ponies are docile creatures, with thick coats and long manes which will double as bathmats. If properly trained, these nimble creatures will follow their receptors eagerly and unselfishly about the house, producing a steady stream of therms. They can be trained as well to make beds and wash sweaters; the drawback is, of course, that they are such terrible liars.

6   Besides the practical attractions of the horse, there is his great aesthetic appeal. Durably made and skillfully designed, the horse is available in a handsome selection of coordinated earth tones, ranging from white to black and including brown. He also comes in a wide assortment of body styles, from the trim and compact Shetland, through the rugged, all-purpose Quarter horse, whose stylish white trim and abstract patterning make him a popular favorite with decorators, to the massive,

heavy-duty Percheron or Clydesdale, who can heat an entire convention without moving a fetlock.

7   The horse is clean, docile, thrifty, and cheerful. He is bio-degradable, non-carcinogenic, and produces no long-term side effects. His own needs are modest: he requires only sweet sun-cured timothy hay and a double-handful of dry oats daily. Clearly, the record of the horse as a reliable and valuable helpmate to man continues, and the horse takes his place beside the stove, the sun, and the furnace.

—ROXANNA BARRY

33d

Explore and focus the subject.

When you have a subject in mind—whether it is one assigned by an instructor, one dictated by some other writing situation, or one you have chosen for yourself—you will often need to explore the subject further in order to discover all the particular aspects of it which may be worth developing. And almost certainly you will benefit—make your writing task easier and the finished composition more effective—by taking at least a few minutes to limit the subject and get it sharply in focus before you start writing.

(1) Explore your subject.

Writers use many different methods to explore a subject. Some especially useful methods are listing, questioning, applying different perspectives, and surveying the possible development strategies. Use whatever methods seem to be productive for you. Different methods may work best for different subjects: if you run out of ideas using one method, switch to another. Sometimes, especially for an assigned subject remote from your own interests and knowledge, you may need to use several methods.

Listing Your mind already holds a variety of ideas about any subject you choose to write on. One way to dig these ideas out is to make an informal list. Jot down any ideas that come to you while you are thinking about your subject. Don't worry if the ideas seem to come without any kind of order, and don't worry about the form in which you write them down—grammar, spelling, and diction are not concerns at this stage. You can devote as much time to making your list as necessary—perhaps five minutes, perhaps an entire evening. The point is to collect as many ideas as you can about your subject.

If you were thinking about writing on home computers, you might make a list like the one below. This one took a student about five minutes.

> reasons people want home computers
> playing games
> keeping track of money
> helping to organize daily tasks
> what should you look for when you choose one?
> what size and price?
> what do you want it to do for you?
> what kinds of programs are available for it?
> cost of programs
> variety of programs
> ease of use—programs and computer
> any gadgets to attach—like printers, disk drives?
> what about monitors—colour, monochrome?
> can you use your TV?
> what kind of storage is best?
> what do you have to know before you can use one?
> do you need to know math?
> where can you learn?
> any hidden costs—higher electrical bills, repairs, etc.?
> do they break frequently?
> where do you get them fixed?
> where should you buy one?
> keeping records—addresses, Christmas cards, spending habits, tax

If you study the list, you can see that the writer was keeping her mind open, sometimes letting one idea lead to another, sometimes making a jump in an entirely new direction. Occasionally the greatest value of such a list is that it allows an idea to surface that can become the subject of a new list; consider, for example, the last item on the list and the fifth from the last.

Questioning   Another useful way to explore a subject is to ask yourself questions about it. The journalists' questions *who? what? when? where? how?* and *why?* are easy to use and can help you discover ideas about any subject. Using journalists' questions to explore the subject of home computers could lead you to think about *how* computers affect people, *what* they are and *what* kinds are available, *when* and *how* they were developed, *where* they are used or *who* uses them, *why* people want home computers, *how* computers work or *how* to decide which one to buy.

Applying perspectives   Sometimes it is helpful to consider a subject in three quite different ways—as static, dynamic, and relative. A *static* perspective would focus your attention on what a home computer is. You might define it, describe its physical characteristics, analyze its parts or its main uses, or give examples of home computers.

The *dynamic* perspective focusses on action and change. Thus you might examine the history or development of the computer, its workings or the processes involved in using it, and changes of all sorts resulting from its use.

The *relative* perspective focusses on relationships, on systems. You might examine relationships of the computer to other things and to people. You can view the home computer as a system in itself or as a part of a larger system of information management. You can also analyze it in relation to other kinds of computers such as mainframe computers, or to other kinds of information management tools such as library catalogues.

Surveying development strategies   The various development strategies (more fully discussed in **32d**) represent natural thinking processes, and so are especially useful for generating ideas about a subject. Here are some thoughts a writer might jot down using these strategies.

> *Narration*—Tell about my first experience using a home computer.

> *Process*—How do you buy one? How does it work?

> *Cause and Effect*—Why were home computers developed? What effects do they have on other things?

> *Description*—What does a home computer look like? What is a typical owner like?

> *Definition*—What is a home computer?

> *Analysis*—What are the parts of a computer? What are the various tasks it can do?

> *Classification*—What kinds of people buy these computers? What types are on the market?

> *Example*—Computers save time—name several ways.

> *Comparison and Contrast*—What similarities and differences are there between kinds of home computers? What are the differences between managing information with a computer and without? How is a computer like a library or like an office?

(2) Limit and focus the subject.

No matter how well you have explored your subject, almost certainly you will need to limit and focus it before you write. As you do so, keep your purpose and your audience in mind. A simple analogy helps explain why limiting and focussing are so important. When you take a picture of something, you decide what it is you want to photograph, and you aim your camera in that direction. But that's not all you do: you also look through the viewfinder to make sure the subject is correctly framed and in focus. You may decide to move in closer to eliminate distracting elements from the frame, and you may change your angle, using light and shadow to emphasize some features of your subject over others. You need to do something very similar when you write. When you have generated enough ideas about your subject, look at them carefully to see how to frame your subject and to make sure it is clearly in focus.

For example, "home computers" is too large and general a subject to make a good writing topic. However, some of the items that appear on the list about the home computer in **33d(1)** can be grouped to form a writing topic that might be manageable. Items about cost can be grouped, as can items about programs, about things the computer can do, or about learning to use the computer. Conceivably, an essay focussing on any one of these groups—eliminating all the other, irrelevant items—might be both workable and interesting.

However, chances are that still more focussing will be required. Suppose you have narrowed "home computers" to "learning to use a home computer." This is still a very big topic, one on which sizable books are written. For a short paper you would do better to focus on, for example, the ways such knowledge can be acquired. You might examine the relative merits of college courses, training sessions given by dealers, and self-instruction through reading manuals and other publications. Or you could focus your paper on the specific kinds of knowledge that are needed: how to turn the computer on and off, how to use disk drives, how to save information you have put into the computer, and so forth. The exact focus you finally choose will be determined by your purpose, your audience, and the time and space available.

■ **Exercise 4**   Taking one of the subjects from Exercise 2, explore it by using the journalists' questions (*who? what? when? where? why? how?*). Next explore the same subject using the three perspectives: What is it? How does it change or act? What is it related to—part of, different from, or like? Then explore the subject by surveying development strategies. Decide how you would limit and focus this subject.

33e
Construct a focussed, specific thesis statement containing a single main idea.

An effective thesis statement satisfies your reader's natural desire to know—usually early in the paper—what the central point or idea will be and how you are likely to go about presenting it. It contains a single idea clearly focussed and specifically stated.

A good thesis statement is useful to you as the writer as well as to your reader. It will help you maintain unity and will guide many decisions about what details to include. Sometimes you have information about your subject that is interesting but does not really help you make your point. When you are tempted to include such material simply because it is interesting, looking at your thesis statement can help you decide to leave it out. You can also use the thesis statement to guide your search for additional information that you may need to make your point.

As you write, refer to your thesis statement from time to time to see if you have drifted away from your main idea. However, do not hesitate to change your thesis if you find a more productive path, one you would rather pursue. Make whatever adjustments you need to ensure a unified essay.

A good thesis statement is often a declarative sentence with a single main clause—that is, either a simple or complex sentence. If your thesis statement announces two or more co-ordinate ideas, as a compound sentence does, be sure you are not in danger of having your paper lose direction and focus. If you wish to sharpen the thesis statement by adding information that qualifies or supports it, subordinate such material to the main idea. Beware of vague qualifiers such as *interesting, important*, and *unusual*. Often such words signal that you have chosen a subject that does not interest you much and you would do better to rethink your subject to come up with something you care about. In a thesis statement such as "My education has been very unusual" the vague word *unusual* may indicate that the idea itself is trivial and unproductive and that the writer needs to find a more congenial subject. On the other hand, this kind of vague thesis may disguise an idea of real interest that simply needs to be made specific: "Unlike most people, I received my high school education from my parents on a boat." Sometimes thesis statements containing such vague words can be made more effective by simply replacing the bland words with other, more meaningful ones. The following examples show ways to focus, clarify, and sharpen vague thesis statements.

VAGUE	Rock collecting can be an interesting hobby.
BETTER	Rock collecting fills empty time, satisfies a yen for beauty, and brings in a little extra cash.
VAGUE	I have trouble making decisions.
BETTER	Making decisions is difficult for me, especially when money is involved, and most of all when such decisions affect other people.
VAGUE	Summer is an interesting season.
BETTER	Summer is an infuriating season.

Thesis statements appear most often in the first paragraph although you may put them anywhere that suits your purpose—occasionally even in the conclusion. The advantage, however, of putting the thesis statement in the introductory paragraph is that your reader knows from the beginning what you are writing about and where the essay is going. If the thesis statement begins the introductory paragraph, the rest of the sentences in the paragraph usually support or clarify it with more specific information.

> Whether we like it or not—and many may disagree with my thesis because painting, or music, or some other art is more important to them—the art of the moving picture is the only art truly of our time, whether it is in the form of the film or television. The moving picture is our universal art, which comprises all others, literature and acting, stage design and music, dance and the beauty of nature, and, most of all, the use of light and color.
> —BRUNO BETTELHEIM, "The Art of Moving Pictures"

> In many ways a pool is the best place to do real swimming. Free water tends to be too tempestuous, while in a pool it is tamed and imprisoned; the challenge has been filtered out of it along with the bacteria.   —JOHN KNOWLES, "Everybody's Sport"

Frequently, you will want to give your reader some background on your subject, or to place it in a particular context, before stating your thesis.

> What is chance? Dictionaries define it as something fortuitous that happens unpredictably without discernible human intention. Chance is unintentional and capricious but we needn't conclude that chance is immune from human intervention. Indeed, chance plays several distinct roles when humans react creatively with one another and with their environment.   —JAMES H. AUSTIN, "Four Kinds of Chance"

Sometimes an essay has no explicit thesis statement. This is especially common in writing which is primarily narrative or descriptive. (The essay "Ice," pages 360–61, has none.) Sometimes, even in the kinds of writing where a thesis is most often explicitly stated (persuasive and informative), there may be special reasons for leaving the thesis statement out. Yet even when your thesis is implied, your readers should be able to sense a clear direction and focus in your paper. You can make sure that they will by writing a thesis statement for your own use and then testing each paragraph to make sure it is relevant to the thesis. What is important is to think about your thesis even if you never intend your readers to see it.

■ **Exercise 5**   Construct a clear and precise thesis statement for the subject you limited in Exercise 4.

33f

Choose an appropriate method or combination of methods of development for arranging ideas, and prepare a working plan.

The strategies discussed and exemplified in Section **32d** are more than simply methods for developing a paragraph and exploring a subject (see **33d**). They are the methods by which writers organize and develop longer pieces of writing as well.

Your choice of a particular method of development will depend to a great extent upon other choices you have already made—purpose, subject, focus, thesis. Whether your aim is expressive, informative, or persuasive, one of these methods or a combination of them can be used for organizing your paper: exemplification, narration, process, cause and effect, classification, definition, description, analysis, and comparison and contrast.

Most writers find that they need some kind of written working plan to keep their writing on course. Many think that making a formal outline interferes with the flow of their ideas, generally preferring to use lists or other kinds of jottings. Others find a formal outline useful, particularly when the project is long or when they have to produce under pressure. Choose a plan that works for you.

INFORMAL WORKING PLANS

An informal working plan need be little more than an ordered list that suggests a way of organizing your information. Such plans often grow out of lists similar to those used to explore subjects (see **33d**). A student who chose to write a paper on purple martins made the following list as he was exploring for ideas.

> favourite bird
> beautiful when they fly
> largest Canadian swallow
> season—February–August
> migrate to South America
> semi-tamed by Indians
> choosing nests
> nests in bottles, gourds, etc.
> mating
> building nests
> raising young
> division of labour
> behaviour similar to humans'

When you make a list such as this, ideas often overlap. Some are general, some specific. They appear in no particular order. But you have the beginning of a plan. Examine your list carefully to see if any items are repeated and if any particular plan suggests itself.

The student writing on purple martins examined his list and noticed that the habits of the birds kept coming up. Choosing to limit his essay to that, he noticed that one item on his list gave him a focus for his composition: in certain ways, the habits of purple martins mimic those of people. He formulated a thesis statement and decided that a chronological organization would present those habits naturally and effectively—birds fly in, find homes, mate, breed, raise young, then fly away again. He then prepared an informal working plan of how his paper would be organized:

Thesis Statement: The family life of the purple martin, a beautiful Canadian swallow, resembles that of people.

1. How purple martins find and choose homes.
2. How purple martins choose mates.
3. How purple martins divide household responsibilities.
4. How purple martins raise and educate their young.

FORMAL OUTLINES

A formal outline uses indention and numbers to indicate various levels of subordination. Thus it is a kind of graphic scheme of the logic of your paper. The main points form the major headings, and the supporting ideas for each point form the subheadings.

Thesis:
  I. Major idea
    A. Supporting idea
      1. Example or illustration for supporting idea
      2. Example or illustration for supporting idea
        a. Detail for example or illustration
        b. Detail for example or illustration
    B. Supporting idea
  II. Major idea

Headings and subheadings stand for divisions, and a division denotes at least two parts. Therefore, to be logical, each outline should have at least two main headings, I and II. If it has a subheading marked A, it should also have a subheading marked B; if it has a 1, it should also have a 2. Any intelligible system of notation is acceptable.

The types of outlines most commonly used are the topic outline and the sentence outline. When you write a topic outline, you express the major headings (those numbered I, II, III, and so on) and subdivisions in phrases. In topic outlines, the phrases that make up the major headings (I, II, III, and so on) should be grammatically parallel (see Section **26**) as should each group of subheadings. But it is unnecessary to strive for parallel structure between different groups of subheadings—for example, between A, B, and C under I and A, B, and C under II. When you write a sentence outline, you do not have to be concerned with parallel structure. Instead, express your headings and subdivisions in complete sentences.

The advantage of a sentence outline is that it helps you make sure that you become sufficiently specific about your subject rather than simply generalizing. The advantage of the topic outline, besides its brevity, is that its parallel structure reveals the logic you will follow in your paper. But regardless of what type of outline you choose, you will need to have enough major headings to develop your topic fully within the boundaries established by your thesis statement.

Sentence Outline

Thesis statement: The family life of the purple martin, a beautiful Canadian swallow, resembles that of people.

I. Martin scouts from South America search for suitable nesting places.
   A. Martins choose a variety of houses.
   B. The birds fight over individual nesting places.
II. Courtship is related to choosing a nesting place.
   A. Males lure the females with song and dance.
   B. Females make the decisions.
III. Purple martins divide household responsibilities.
   A. They build the nest together.
   B. They both watch over the eggs.
   C. Both partners feed the young.
   D. They both keep the nest clean.
IV. Purple martins educate their young and prepare them for migration.
   A. Adults teach youngsters to fly.
   B. They teach youngsters to hunt and catch food.
   C. A diet of insects makes young birds strong.

Topic Outline

Thesis statement: The family life of the purple martin, a beautiful Canadian swallow, resembles that of people.

I. Locating the nesting places
   A. Variety of nesting places
   B. Selection of individual nesting places
II. Choosing a mate
   A. Male courtship antics
   B. Female courtship behaviour
III. Dividing household responsibilities
   A. Building the nest
   B. Hatching the eggs
   C. Feeding the young
   D. Cleaning house
IV. Educating the young and preparing them for migration
   A. Teaching them to fly
   B. Teaching them to hunt and catch food
   C. Building strong bodies

■ **Exercise 6**   Follow your instructor's directions as you develop a working plan or an outline for the subject you limited in Exercise 4.

33g
Write the composition.

As you write the first draft of your composition, keep your plan in mind, but put your ideas on paper quickly without much concern for matters such as spelling, punctuation, and usage. Remember, this draft is one that only you will read. If you realize you have veered from your plan, you may find it helpful to stop drafting and reread what you have written to reorient yourself. If you find yourself stuck and uncertain where to go next, referring to your plan should help you discover how to continue. When you complete your draft, set it aside for a time, several days if possible.

Some writers find that they work best by writing chunks or blocks of their essay without worrying about the order in which the chunks will finally appear. For example, if writing the introduction is difficult for you, try starting with one of the supporting ideas you feel sure of and draft that idea through to a stopping point. You may find that once you are actually writing, your thinking processes will operate more efficiently. If that happens, you can move on to any part of the composition you think will be easy to write next— another supporting idea paragraph, even the introduction or conclusion. What is important is to begin writing and to write as quickly as you can. One word of caution: If you find that writing in chunks works best for you, you will later need to give special care to ensuring that you have clear transitions.

(1) Write effective introductions and conclusions.

An effective introduction arouses the reader's interest and indicates what the composition is about (see also page 378 and pages 379–80). Introductions have no set length; they can be as brief as a phrase or as long as a paragraph or more. To arouse interest, you might begin your introduction with a startling event, a cleverly phrased statement, or an anecdote. The first introductory paragraph below begins with an arresting sentence that makes you want to read more. The second introductory paragraph engages your attention with an interesting anecdote.

> It was hard to call it science when physician Peter Hackett dangled upside down on a sheer rock face 8,000 feet above his next stopping place. And it was hard to call it science when medical researcher Chris Pizzo misplaced his ice ax, grabbed a flimsy aluminum tent pole and marched toward the summit of Everest in a glorious quest for data. But science it was when the 1981 American Medical Research Expedition to Everest transformed the mountain into the highest research laboratory on Earth.   —ERIC PERLMAN, "For a Breath of Thin Air"

> What is intelligence, anyway? When I was in the army I received a kind of aptitude test that all soldiers took and, against a normal of 100, scored 160. No one at the base had ever seen a figure like that, and for two hours they made a big fuss over me. (It didn't mean anything. The next day I was still a buck private with KP as my highest duty.)
>
> —ISAAC ASIMOV, "What Is Intelligence, Anyway?"

Sometimes an interesting fact or unusual detail makes an introduction effective.

> Twenty-eight percent of the occupations that will be available to children born in 1976 were not in existence when those children were born.

Many introductions simply begin with general information as background about the subject and then focus specifically upon the thesis.

> It has just occurred to me that there are young people growing up today who have never had the experience of using a fountain pen. All they know is a ballpoint. I haven't used a fountain pen for many years myself, but I remember what it was like.   —RICHARD ARMOUR, "Fountain of My Youth"

If your essay is persuasive, you may want to begin with the proposition for which you intend to argue.

> The influence of the modern medical school on liberal-arts education in this country over the last decade has been baleful and malign, nothing less. The admission policies of the medical schools are at the root of the trouble. If something is not done quickly to change these, all the joy of going to college will have been destroyed, not just for that growing majority of undergraduate students who draw breath only to become doctors, but for everyone else, all the students, and all the faculty as well.
>
> —LEWIS THOMAS, "How to Fix the Premedical Curriculum"

Avoid using a cliché in an introduction unless you can give it a fresh twist (see **20c**). Also avoid unnecessary definitions, such as "Webster's dictionary defines *hate* as. . . . "

Finally, apologies generally have no place in an introduction. You may not know as much as you would like to about your subject or may find it difficult to write on, but apologizing for that fact will only undermine the effectiveness of your paper.

A composition should finish, not merely stop. Some effective conclusions, especially those that introduce a question for further thought or suggest directions for future study of the topic, do encourage the reader to continue thinking about the subject. To maintain the unity of your essay, however, avoid introducing a completely new subject in the conclusion. Other effective conclusions summarize, restate, or evaluate the information in the essay without encouraging the reader to think beyond the discussion. However, avoid simply repeating your thesis in the conclusion. If a summary of your thesis is useful, try to rephrase it to avoid unnecessary repetition. Anne Roiphe's conclusion evaluates the information she presented in her essay, but does not direct the reader beyond her discussion.

> Hard as it is for many of us to believe, women are not really superior to men in intelligence or humanity—they are only equal. —ANNE ROIPHE, "Confessions of a Female Chauvinist Sow"

Stephen Potter's conclusion directs the reader's attention to the larger concept of gamesmanship which develops from his discussion of the single game.

> That night I thought hard and long. Could not this simple gambit of Joad's be extended to include other aspects of the game—to include all games? For me, it was the birth of gamesmanship. —STEPHEN POTTER, *Gamesmanship*

Conclusions often clinch or stress the importance of the central idea by referring in some way to the introduction, as Russell Baker's does in the next example.

> INTRODUCTION   I read *The National Enquirer* when I want to feel exhilarated about life's possibilities. It

tells me of a world where miracles still occur. In the world of *The National Enquirer*, UFOs flash over the Bermuda Triangle, cancer cures are imminent, ancient film stars at last find love that is for keeps. Reached on The Other Side by spiritualists, Clark Gable urges America to keep its chin up. Of all possible worlds, I like the world of *The National Enquirer* best. . . .

CONCLUSION So I whoop with glee when a new edition of *The National Enquirer* hits the newsstands and step into the world where Gable can cheer me up from The Other Side.

—RUSSELL BAKER, "Magazine Rack"

As in an introduction, avoid apologizing in a conclusion. Finally, in very short essays where all the points can easily be kept in mind, a conclusion is often unnecessary because it is likely to unbalance the essay and, in any case, there is little more to be said.

(2) Develop a good title.

First impressions are important, and usually the first thing your reader sees is your title. An appropriate title fits the subject matter of the paper. Sometimes the title announces the subject simply and directly: "Ice," *Colombo's Concise Canadian Quotations*, Virginia Woolf's "Professions for Women." A good title may also arouse the reader's curiosity by asking a question, as does Maurice Shadbolt's "Who Killed the Bog Men of Denmark? And Why?" Sometimes a clever title, such as Farb and Armelagos' *Consuming Passions: The Anthropology of Eating* will reflect the writer's attitude and approach. A good way to begin developing a title is to try condensing your thesis statement without becoming too vague or general. Try to work in some indication of the attitude and approach you have taken in the paper.

Consider the following possible titles for the essay beginning on page 371:

GENERAL   A New Method of Heating   [only vague indication of subject, no indication of attitude or approach]

ADEQUATE   The Horse as Heater   [clearer indication of subject but still no suggestion of attitude or approach]

BETTER   Heat on the Hoof   [sharply focussed, indicates subject, attitude and approach, and tone]

33h
Revise the composition.

In one way or another you revise throughout the writing process. For example, even in the earliest planning stages, as you consider a possible subject and then discard it in favour of another, you are revising. Similarly, after choosing a subject, if you decide to change your focus to emphasize some new aspect of it, you are revising. And of course you are revising when, as you draft your paper, you realize that a sentence or a paragraph you have just written does not belong where it is and you pause to strike it out or mark it to be moved to an earlier or later place in the paper. But once you have finished a draft, you should set it aside for a time (preferably, if the situation permits, at least overnight) so that you will be able to see it freshly and objectively, and then you should revise it carefully and systematically as a whole. In scheduling your work, allow plenty of time for revising.

Consider large matters before you turn to smaller ones. Attending to the larger matters first is an efficient approach because as you revise paragraphs or reorganize the essay you often change or eliminate smaller elements—sentences, words, punctuation, mechanics, and so forth. Check to be sure that you have stuck to your purpose and your subject and that you have not lost sight of your audience anywhere in the draft. Is your focus consistent? Is everything governed by the central idea, or thesis? Are the major ideas in the most effective order? Is the reasoning logical?

Is every paragraph unified, coherent, and well developed? Is every sentence related to the paragraph's central idea? Are the sentences presented in the most natural and effective order? Are transitions adequate between paragraphs and between sentences?

Next, look at sentence structure. Are all of your sentences clear? Do short sentences give your essay a choppy, unconnected movement? Consider combining some of them. Rework long, overly complicated sentences. Do too many of your sentences begin with the same kind of grammatical structure? For example, if your essay contains many sentences that begin with prepositional phrases, try to rework some of those into other patterns. Have you avoided needless shifts in grammatical structures, tone, style, or point of view?

Examine your diction. Do you find vague words like *area, interesting,* or *unusual* where more precise words would be more effective? Watch for clauses and sentences in the passive voice. The active voice usually, though by no means always, makes your writing more direct and forceful. Is your writing wordy and repetitive? Cut any non-essential words, phrases, and sentences to make your writing tighter and more emphatic. Make sure sentences are grammatically correct. Check spelling, punctuation, and mechanics.

Sometimes while revising sentences you will find that you still have work to do on your paragraphs. Fuzzy sentences often obscure faults in reasoning or lapses in unity or coherence. Don't be discouraged. Many writers wrestle with the same problems. Keep in mind that many professionals consider revision the most important part of their writing. As one observed, "I'm not a very good writer, but I'm a terrific reviser!'' You will probably find that you too will need to revise your compositions several times, sharpening, rewriting, inserting, and deleting again and again to communicate with your reader and achieve your purpose as effectively as you can.

WORD PROCESSING

Access to a computer with word-processing capability puts a powerful revision tool at your fingertips. If you need to correct, change, or rearrange any part of your writing—from inserting or deleting a single letter to reorganizing large blocks of material—word-processing programs such as *MacWrite* or *Microsoft Works* (to name two of many) can help you do that. With these programs you can even delete or insert whole paragraphs or pages. Furthermore, you can rearrange words and blocks of writing by moving them to a part of the composition where you think they will be most effective. And word processing allows you to do this without having to retype anything. The computer simply makes room on the screen where you need it and takes space away where you don't.

When you have completed your drafting and revision, many word-processing programs will help you check spelling and even grammar before you finally print what you have written. Style-checking programs that can help you make your composition more unified and coherent are also becoming available. Such programs usually operate by highlighting or otherwise isolating on the screen any part of your composition that may contain a problem. You are offered the chance to reconsider what you have written and revise it if necessary. A word of caution: word-processing programs are only a mechanical means for manipulating language that you create yourself. They cannot think for you; they only remind you to think for yourself, and they make revision faster and easier. A further caution: because they are so easy to use, word processing systems can also reinforce natural but undesirable tendencies, making a wordy writer even wordier, for example, or a terse writer even less fluent.

AN ESSAY UNDERGOING REVISION

Following are two drafts of an essay on purple martins by Buck Strobeck, the first marked with Strobeck's notes for revision. Compare the drafts and observe all the ways in which Strobeck has made the final version more effective than the first.

First Draft and Revisions

The Purple Martin — Birds of Our Feather?

~~Another Side of the Coin~~

~~The Purple Martin—Our Domestic Wonder~~

Darwinians or not, we know that

~Sometimes people ~~act like~~ mimic ~~some of the~~ the behaviour of lower animals— evolution in reverse. They may act like, or wolves in sheep's clothing, be as as stubborn proud as as ~a~ mule,s or ~~as~~ dumb stupid as turkeys, or ~~They may be~~ peacocks, ~~snakes in the grass.~~

   I'm convinced, however, that there is

some animals act like people. ~~Take the purple martin, for~~ Consider

another side of the coin: Since childhood I've~ instance

closely observed the lifestyle of

~~watched~~ the purple martin (our largest and most

urban swallow), and I am amazed at the many ways

ours.

its behaviour resembles ~~that of human beings.~~

their winter resorts in

Martins

~~Some~~ birds ~~act like~~ arrive early each spring from South realtors ~~and work in~~ America

to scout available land and housing for the flock.

~~groups of two or three as they locate~~ (hoses) that

~~(the)~~ will later show to individuals. Arriving

from South America in early spring, two or three martin scouts look for suitable nesting places for the flocks that will follow. For these martins, the country's most desirable real estate stretches from a northern habitat that comprises southern Quebec and the adjacent area of New Brunswick, through southern Ontario, right across the southern Prairies, then into British Columbia. Some of the more ambitious might even venture as far north as the Peace River country in search of the right accommodation.

No longer for these up-to-date martins the old-style homes so very popular with the earlier generations. No more rural abodes, for them no more tree cavities! When the clients start arriving a little later, these scouts find a variety of houses is open and ready for occupancy: gourds or bottles with the right-size opening, wooden houses with eight or twelve holes, even fancy high-rise condominiums.

It isn't long, however, before fights break out among the males for the most desirable accommodations. Each winner arrogantly takes possession of the compartment, for he has established his (teritorial) rights.

The loser decides that he likes a different

compartment anyway and decides to be a good

neighbour. ~~Such power struggles resemble those of~~
~~human beings and such behaviour after the battle~~
~~reminds me of the attitudes of certain people who~~
~~win and who lose.~~

Like some humans, the martin male ~~shows off~~ flaunts his
~~In spring a young man's fancy does turn to~~
brains, ~~his~~ brawn, and ~~his~~ possessions to
~~thoughts of love and courtship and marriage.~~
~~When he finds the right woman, he often shows off~~
~~to get her attention and uses special tactics to~~
a wife a mate.
win ~~her affection.~~ ~~Once the male martin who does~~
~~not already have a mate is a property owner, he~~
~~starts flirting with his favourite female.~~ He
lures her to his compartment. ~~by~~ Singing liquid

notes and performing aerial acrobatics, ~~Usually,~~ But there's
nothing flighty about her; like today's practical woman,
~~like a woman who refuses to be swept off her~~
~~feet,~~ she takes plenty of time making up her mind
to move in. ~~with him.~~ ~~While he patiently waits~~
~~outside the entrance of his compartment, she goes~~
She looks over the compartment,
~~inside the place several times.~~ ~~Often she~~ pecks

at the flooring, notes the ventilation, and

checks the roof for leaks. If she approves, ~~of his~~

~~taste in housing and decides he is the male she~~
~~wants to father her offspring, she gives him the~~
~~nod and~~ they are mates––for life, according to a
number of bird–banding ornithologists.

Just as many married couples do today, the two birds
~~Like happy newlyweds I know,~~ the pair work
together to raise a family~~, and educate their~~
~~young. After the martins have mated, the~~
~~female's place is in the home, and so is the~~
~~male's.~~ Together they build the nest. They
select just
~~bring~~ the right twigs and leaves (sometimes after
a noisy squabble) and carry in the mud for the
mortar. ~~In time, the female lays the eggs and~~
~~incubates them.~~ For brief periods, ~~however~~ the
male martin stays with the eggs so that his mate
can stretch her wings and grab a bite to eat.

~~His consideration reminds me of the husband who~~
~~babysits while his wife goes to the beauty parlour.~~
~~washes the dishes every night.~~

no ¶   ~~In human communities the birth of babies is~~
~~an occasion for celebration and makes a vast~~
~~difference in the live~~s~~ of parents. So it is with~~
~~purple martins.~~ When the nestlings ~~(ugly little~~
~~creatures with big mouths and no feathers)~~ hatch,
both parents rejoice, along with *chattering* ~~noisy~~ neighbours

who drop by for a look~~-see~~. ~~(As they poke~~ *poking* insects

down ~~the babies'~~ *their* throats,) *And* the male works as hard

as the female~~.~~ *feeding the young,* Both parents also work together as

they get rid of garbage—the droppings—to keep

the nest clean.

~~Martins are~~ Like human parents, *martins* ~~for they~~

have problems with *a youngster now and then.* ~~their children.~~ For example,

when the fledglings are ready to leave the nest,

the parents sometimes have to throw out a lazy

freeloader ~~who is~~ reluctant to ~~leave~~ *give up the comforts of* home. ~~Of~~

~~course, they do this for the adolescent's own~~

~~good.~~

~~Again like many people, the adult~~ Martin~~s~~ *parents*

understand ~~fully~~ the value of a^n ~~good~~ education

and ~~realize~~ the ~~value of parental~~ *need for* guidance. ~~The~~

They ~~adult martins~~ teach the youngsters to fly, to

hunt food, to catch insects on the wing. The

parents fly ahead, capture a ~~bug~~, *dragonfly* and then put it

into the ~~student's~~ *youngster's* mouth. A *F*ast food fancier^s

from a tender age, *the* a hungry young martin^s catche~~s~~

on ~~to the idea~~ *O.K.* very quickly. *By late summer their* ~~The~~ heavy diet of

mosquitoes and other *flying* insects ~~will make him, in a~~ *has made them*

~~short time,~~ strong enough to fly *away from the colony* ~~long distances~~

when the leaders, ~~of the colony~~ <ins>restless for the resorts of the south,</ins> give the signal to depart <ins>for South America</ins>.

~~In late summer or early fall, the martins leave in groups.~~ In order to survive, the purple martins—like refugees who flee from a famine-ridden area or like hunters who have <ins>exterminated</ins> ~~exhausted~~ <ins>the buffalo</ins> ~~their food supply~~—purple martins must leave their home and follow their food supply. They return ~~to~~ summer and the flying insects ~~in South America.~~

<ins>Although this bird</ins> ~~The purple martin~~ may resemble us in remarkable ways, ~~However~~ the purple martin has ~~one~~ <ins>a</ins> gift ~~that~~ people do not share. ~~No other bird or creature is so beautiful as a purple martin in flight. I'll never forget what~~ <ins>As</ins> a friend of mine—a pilot—said when he first saw a purple martin soar, dip, and dive: "If only we could fly like that!" <ins>When</ins> ~~Every time~~ I ~~watch~~ <ins>see</ins> ~~these birds~~ <ins>this magnificent swallow</ins> ~~fly in the sky~~ in flight— ~~and they forage higher than any other member of the swallow family—I think of Wordsworth.~~ <ins>my heart leaps up.</ins> <ins>Wordsworth.</ins> ~~He~~ can have his ~~daffodils~~ <ins>rainbows.</ins> I'll take the purple martin.

Final Draft

The Purple Martin—Birds of Our Feather?

Darwinians or not, we all know that people sometimes mimic the behaviour of the lower animals. People may act like snakes in the grass or wolves in sheep's clothing, may be as proud as peacocks, as dumb as turkeys, or as stubborn as mules.

I'm convinced, however, that there is another side of the coin: some animals act like people. Consider the purple martin, our largest and most urban swallow. Since childhood I've closely observed the lifestyle of the purple martin, and I am amazed at the many ways its behaviour resembles ours.

Martin realtors arrive early each spring from their winter resorts in South America to scout the available land and housing for the flock. For these martins, the country's most desirable real estate stretches from southern Quebec and adjacent New Brunswick through Ontario right across the southern Prairies and then northwest into British Columbia. Some of the more ambitious might even venture as far north as the Peace River country in search of the right accommodation.

No longer for these up-to-date martins the old style homes so popular with the earlier generations. No more rural abodes, no more tree cavities for them! When the clients start arriving a little later, a variety of houses is open and ready for occupancy: gourds or bottles with the right-size opening, wooden or aluminum houses with eight or twelve holes, even fancy high-rise condominiums.

It isn't long, however, before fights break out among the males for the most desirable accommodations. Each winner arrogantly takes possession, for he has established his territorial rights. The loser decides that he liked a different compartment anyway.

Like some humans, the male martin flaunts his brains, brawn, and possessions to win a mate. Singing liquid notes and performing aerial acrobatics, he lures her to his compartment. But there's nothing flighty about her; like today's practical woman, she takes plenty of time making up her mind to move in. She looks over the compartment, pecks at the flooring, notes the ventilation, and checks the roof for leaks. If she approves, the two are mates—for life, according to a number of bird-banding ornithologists.

Just as many married couples do today, the two birds work together to raise a family. Together they build the nest. They select just the right twigs and leaves (sometimes after a noisy squabble) and carry in the mud for the mortar. For brief periods, the male martin stays with the eggs so that his mate can stretch her wings and grab a bite to eat. When the nestlings hatch, both parents rejoice, along with chattering neighbours who drop by for a look. And the male works as hard as the female feeding the young, poking insects down their throats. Both parents also work together as they dispose of household garbage, carrying away the droppings to keep the nest clean.

Like human parents, martins have problems with a youngster now and then. For example, when the fledglings are ready to leave the nest, the parents sometimes have to throw out a lazy freeloader reluctant to give up the comforts of home.

Martin parents understand the value of an education and the need for guidance. They teach the youngsters to fly, to hunt, to catch insects on the wing. The parents fly ahead, capture a dragonfly, and then put it into the youngster's mouth. Fast food fanciers from a tender age, the hungry young martins catch on to the idea very quickly. By late summer their heavy diet of mosquitoes and other flying insects has made them strong enough to fly away from the colony when the leaders, restless for the resorts of the south, give the signal to depart for South America.

Although this bird may resemble us in remarkable ways, the purple martin has a gift people do not share. As a friend of mine—a pilot—said when he first saw a purple martin

soar, dip, and dive: "If only <u>we</u> could fly like
that!" When I see this magnificent swallow in
flight my heart leaps up. Wordsworth can have
his rainbows. I'll take the purple martin.

Reviser's Checklist

The Essay as a Whole

1. Does the whole essay stick to the purpose (see **33a**) and the subject (see **33b**)?

2. Have you kept your audience clearly in mind? Is the tone appropriate and consistent? See **33c**. Do any terms require definition?

3. Is the focus consistent (see **33d**)? Do the ideas in the essay show clear relationships to the central idea, or thesis?

4. Is the central idea or thesis sharply conceived? Does your thesis statement (if one is appropriate) clearly suggest the position and approach you are taking? See **33e**.

5. Have you chosen an effective method or combination of methods of development? See **33f**.

6. Is the essay logically sound both as a whole and in individual paragraphs and sentences? See **31**.

7. Will the introduction arouse the reader's interest? Does it indicate what the paper is about? See **33g**.

8. Does the essay come to a satisfying close? See **33g**.

Paragraphs

1. Are all the paragraphs unified? Are there any ideas in any paragraph that do not belong? See **32a**.

2. Is each paragraph coherent? Are sentences within each paragraph in a natural and effective order? Are the sentences connected by repetition of key words or ideas, by pronoun reference, by parallel structure, or by transitional expressions? See **32b**.

3. Is the progression between paragraphs easy and natural? Are there clear transitions where needed? See **32b(6)**.

4. Is each paragraph adequately developed? See **32c**.

Sentences and Diction

1. Have you used subordination and co-ordination to relate ideas effectively? See **24**.

2. Are there misplaced sentence parts or dangling modifiers? See **25**.

3. Do you find any faulty parallelism? See **26**.

4. Are there any needless shifts in grammatical structures, in tone or style, or in viewpoint? See **27**.

5. Does each pronoun refer clearly to its antecedent? See **28**.

6. Are ideas given appropriate emphasis within the sentence? See **29**.

7. Are the sentences varied in length? in type? See **30**.

8. Are there any fragments? comma splices or fused sentences? See **2** and **3**.

9. Do all verbs agree with their subjects? pronouns with their antecedents? See **6**.

10. Have you used the appropriate form of the verb? See **7**.

11. Are any words overused? used imprecisely? vague? See **20**.

12. Have all unnecessary words and phrases been eliminated? See **21**. Have any necessary words been omitted? See **22**.

Punctuation, Spelling, Mechanics

1. Are commas (see **12**) and semicolons (see **14**) used where required by the sentence structure? Have superfluous commas been removed (see **13**)?

2. Is any end punctuation omitted? See **17**.

3. Are apostrophes (see **15**) and quotation marks (see **16**) placed correctly?

4. Are all words spelled correctly? See **18**.

5. Are capitals (see **9**), italics (see **10**), and abbreviations used correctly?

6. Is your manuscript in an acceptable form? Have all words been divided correctly at the ends of lines? See **8**.

Writing under Pressure

33i

Write well-organized answers to essay tests; write effective in-class essays.

Frequently in college or university, you will be required to write clearly and correctly in a brief time and under pressure—for example, when you write compositions in class and when you take essay examinations.

33i comp

(1) Write clear, concise, well-organized answers on essay tests.

When you write an answer to an essay question, you are conveying information, but you are also proving to your audience—the examiner—that you have mastered the information and can work with it. In other words, your purpose is both informative and persuasive. There are several things you can do in preparing for and taking an essay examination to ensure that you do the best job you can.

Prepare trial questions.

Perhaps the best way to get ready for an essay examination is to prepare yourself from the first day of class. Try to decide what is most important about the material you have been learning and pay attention to indications that your instructor considers certain material especially important. As you assimilate facts and concepts, attempt to work out questions that your instructor is likely to ask. Then plan how you would answer such a question.

Plan your time.

Although you will be working under severe pressure of time, take a few minutes to plan your time and your answer. Determine how many minutes you can devote to each answer. Answer the questions that are worth the most points first (unless your mind is a blank about them at that moment).

Read instructions and questions carefully.

During your examination, first read the question carefully. Most essay examination questions are carefully worded and contain specific instructions about how as well as what you are to answer. Always answer exactly the question asked without digressing to related areas unless they are called for.

Furthermore, if you are asked to define or identify, do not
evaluate. Instead, give clear, concise, and accurate answers.
If you are asked to explain, you must demonstrate that you
have a depth of understanding about the subject. If you are
asked to evaluate, you must decide what is important and
then measure what you plan to say against that yardstick. If
you are asked to compare and contrast, you will need to
have a thorough knowledge of at least two subjects and you
will need to show efficiently how they are similar and/or
different.

Plan your answer.

Jot down the main points you intend to make as you think
through how you plan to respond. This list of main points
can serve as a working plan to help you stay on target.

State main points clearly.

State your thesis in the first paragraph so that the instructor
will know what you intend. Make your main points stand
out from the rest of the essay by identifying them in some
way. For instance, you can use transitional expressions such
as *first, second, third;* you can underline each main point;
or you can create headings to guide the reader.

Support generalizations.

Be sure that you support any generalizations that you make
with specific details, examples, and illustrations. Write with
assurance to help convince the instructor that you have a
thorough knowledge of the subject. Make sure your answers
are complete; do not write one- or two-sentence answers
unless it is clearly specified that you should. Do not, however, pad your answers in an effort to make the instructor
think you know more than you do. A clearly stated, concise,

emphatic, and complete answer, though somewhat brief, will impress a reader much more than a fuzzy answer that is much longer.

Stick to the question.

Sometimes you may know more about a related question than you do about the question asked. Do not wander from the question asked by trying to answer a question you think you could handle better. Similarly, make sure that you follow your thesis as you answer the question and do not include material that is irrelevant.

Revise and proofread.

Finally, save a few minutes to reread your answer. Make whatever corrections and revisions you think are necessary. It is much better to cross out a paragraph that is irrelevant (and to replace it with a relevant one if time permits) than to allow it to stand. Similarly, consider whether your sentences are clear and correct. Check sentence structure, spelling, and punctuation; clarify any illegible scribbles.

(2) Write well-organized, clear in-class essays.

Writing an in-class essay is much like writing any other essay except that you are usually given the topic and you must produce the finished essay during one class period. Because the writing process is so compressed, you must plan to make the best use of your time that you can. Reserve a few minutes at the end of the class period for revising and proofreading. Take a few minutes at the beginning of the class period to consider your main idea, or thesis, and make at least a mental plan.

As you draft the essay, keeping your plan in mind will help you stay on track. Pace yourself so that you can cover all your major points. Don't forget transitions. It is just as important to support your generalizations and to stick to the point in an in-class essay as in an essay test or in an essay you write at home.

In the time you have saved for revision and proofreading, check your essay for unity and coherence. Strike out any unrelated matter and make any needed insertions. Unless you are instructed to do so, it is best not to use your revising time to make a clean copy of the essay. Make your revisions as neatly and clearly as possible (see also page 97). Proofread carefully.

■ **Exercise 7** Write and revise a composition from the work you did in Exercises 4 through 6.

■ **Exercise 8** Carefully read the following composition in preparation for a class discussion of (1) its title and thesis, (2) its purpose and audience, (3) its arrangement and development of main points, (4) its beginning and ending. Also be prepared to discuss how the word choice and the use of specific details contribute to the tone of the essay.

The "Miracle" of Technofix

Somehow this nation has become caught in what I call the mire of "technofix": the belief, reinforced in us by the highest corporate and political forces, that all our current crises can be solved, or at least significantly eased, by the application of modern high technology. In the words of former [U.S.] Atomic Energy Commission chairman Glenn Seaborg: "We must pursue the idea that it is more science, better science, more wisely applied that is going to free us from [our] predicaments."

Energy crisis? Try synfuels. Never mind that they will require billions—eventually trillions—of dollars transferred out of the public coffers into the energy companies' pockets, or that nobody has yet fully explored, much less solved, the problems of environmental damage, pollution, hazardous-waste disposal and occupational dangers their production will create. Never mind—it's technofix.

Food for the hungry world? Try the "Green Revolution." Never mind that such farming is far more energy- and chemical-intensive than any other method known, and therefore generally too expensive for the poor countries that are supposed to benefit from it, or that its principle of monoculture over crop diversity places whole regions, even whole countries, at the risk of a single breed of disease or pest. Never mind—it's scientific.

Diseases? Try wonder drugs. Never mind that few of the thousands of drugs introduced every year have ever been fully tested for long-range effects, or that they are vastly overprescribed and overused, or that nearly half of them prove to be totally ineffective in treating the ailments they are administered for and half of the rest produce unintended side effects. Never mind—it's progress.

And progress, God help us all, may be our most important product. —KIRKPATRICK SALE

The Research Paper

34

Learn how to use the library and how to write a research paper.

If you have read Section **33** on the whole composition and have written even a few essays, you are ready to begin the special kind of essay known as the research paper (or term paper). Planning, drafting, and revising a research paper involve the skills you have already developed. The distinctive feature of the research paper assignment is that it requires you to find and use information in library books and periodicals and to acknowledge your sources properly. Section **34** will help you develop these additional skills.

One of the best ways to begin a research assignment is with a question, with something you want to find out. You may also begin with a tentative *thesis* (**33e**), but if you do you must be willing to revise it if your research findings do not support it (see also **31a**). Once you have done some digging in your sources, you will be in a position to decide whether the *purpose* (**33a**) of your paper will be chiefly informative (to report, analyze, or explain) or persuasive (to prove a point). Your *audience* (**33b**) may or may not be an expert on your subject (this will depend on the assignment), but you may safely envision a reader who is intelligent, fair-minded, and interested in finding out what you have to say, and so your tone should be objective and businesslike.

A word of caution: Scheduling your time is especially important because the research paper assignment usually spans several weeks and the temptation to procrastinate is strong. Divide the amount of time you are given into blocks for various stages of completion: choosing a subject, preparing a preliminary bibliography, taking notes, drafting, and revising.

34a

Choose a subject for a research paper and limit it appropriately. See also **33b** and **33d**.

Occasionally, you may be assigned a specific subject. If so, you are ready to begin your search for sources (**34b**). Often, however, choosing a subject will be up to you. An inquiring mind is the best equipment you can bring to this task: choose a subject you would enjoy knowing more about. If you are stuck for an idea, consider some of the resources mentioned in **33b**. Four reference works in the library may be especially helpful for research paper subjects: try scanning the *Library of Congress Subject Headings* (see page 416) or the subject categories in the *Readers' Guide*, the *Canadian Periodicals Index*, and the *New York Times Index* (see pages 417–18).

Once you have a subject in mind, your exploration of it will evolve naturally as you do your research, but the exploration methods discussed in **33d**—listing, questioning, considering perspectives, surveying development strategies—will almost certainly help you limit your subject and find an interesting focus. Limiting is especially important with the research paper since one of your main objectives is to show that you can treat a subject in some depth within the constraints of time and (usually) a specified length. One basic test of any subject you may have in mind is the amount of pertinent material in the library. If you find dozens of relevant sources, you may be getting in over your head and you should probably narrow the subject to one with a more manageable scope. On the other hand, if you find only two or three sources, chances are that your subject is too narrow and needs to be made more inclusive.

■ **Exercise 1**   Select a subject that would be suitable for a research paper. Then check the availability of materials. (If you cannot find enough books, periodicals, and so on, try another subject.) As you skim through the information, perhaps beginning with an encyclopedia, single out facets of the subject that you would like to investigate further. Finally, limit the subject so that you can develop it in a paper of the assigned length.

34b

Learn to find the library materials you need and to prepare a working bibliography.

College and university libraries are organized to make research as efficient as possible. Most provide a map or diagram—either printed for handing out or posted on the wall—to show you where various kinds of materials are located. Reference books, encyclopedias, and indexes—materials that cannot usually be checked out of the library—are located in the *reference collection*. Other books are located in the *stacks* or at the *reserve desk* and may be checked out for a specified length of time. If your library has a closed-stack policy, you request the books you need by call number from the *circulation desk*. You can find the call number in the *main catalogue* (on cards, in microform, or on a computer). If the stacks are open, however, you may find it useful to browse among the books shelved near those you have located through the catalogue. *Periodicals* (magazines, journals, newspapers) and their indexes are usually stored in a special section of the library. Also bear in mind that many colleges and universities, especially those in the same geographic area, have arrangements for the exchange of books between libraries. You may also be entitled to use the facilities of other college and university libraries in your area. If you have difficulty locating or using any research materials, do not hesitate to ask a *reference librarian* for help.

(1) Learn to find books and periodicals.

Books

The first place to look is usually the *main catalogue*. This may be a traditional card catalogue, or it may be in microform or on a computer. Long-established libraries with extensive collections may combine these, so it is always wise to find out how the collections are catalogued.

The Card Catalogue   The card catalogue lists all books and, usually, all periodicals in the library's collection. In many libraries one general catalogue lists all books owned by the college or university and shows whether a book is in the general library or in a special collection in another building.

The card catalogue consists of cards arranged alphabetically in drawers. For each book, cards are filed alphabetically in at least three ways: by author, by title, and by subject or subjects. Major libraries may also have a location file to indicate where the book is kept or whether it is available in several locations. For example, a university library may have separate collections (sometimes in buildings spread across a large campus) for such fields as medicine, law, forestry, engineering, and music. Author and title cards are usually filed in the same cabinets. Subject cards are often filed separately. These cards are identical except that the title card and the subject card have extra headings. (See the following illustration.)

SAMPLE CATALOGUE CARDS

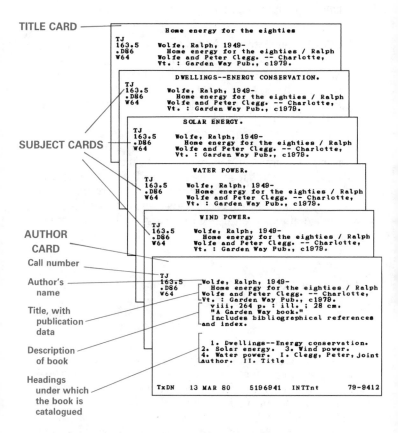

TITLE CARD

    Home energy for the eighties
TJ
163.5   Wolfe, Ralph, 1949-
.D86   Home energy for the eighties / Ralph
W64   Wolfe and Peter Clegg. -- Charlotte,
         Vt. : Garden Way Pub., c1979.

    DWELLINGS--ENERGY CONSERVATION.
TJ
163.5   Wolfe, Ralph, 1949-
.D86   Home energy for the eighties / Ralph
W64   Wolfe and Peter Clegg. -- Charlotte,
         Vt. : Garden Way Pub., c1979.

    SOLAR ENERGY.
TJ
163.5   Wolfe, Ralph, 1949-
.D86   Home energy for the eighties / Ralph
W64   Wolfe and Peter Clegg. -- Charlotte,
         Vt. : Garden Way Pub., c1979.

SUBJECT CARDS

    WATER POWER.
TJ
163.5   Wolfe, Ralph, 1949-
.D86   Home energy for the eighties / Ralph
W64   Wolfe and Peter Clegg. -- Charlotte,
         Vt. : Garden Way Pub., c1979.

    WIND POWER.
TJ
163.5   Wolfe, Ralph, 1949-
.D86   Home energy for the eighties / Ralph
W64   Wolfe and Peter Clegg. -- Charlotte,
         Vt. : Garden Way Pub., c1979.

AUTHOR CARD

Call number

Author's name

Title, with publication data

Description of book

Headings under which the book is catalogued

TJ
163.5   Wolfe, Ralph, 1949-
.D86   Home energy for the eighties / Ralph
W64   Wolfe and Peter Clegg. -- Charlotte,
         Vt. : Garden Way Pub., c1979.
         viii, 264 p. : ill. ; 28 cm.
         "A Garden Way book."
         Includes bibliographical references
         and index.

         1. Dwellings--Energy conservation.
         2. Solar energy. 3. Wind power.
         4. Water power. I. Clegg, Peter, joint
         author. II. Title

TxDN   13 MAR 80   5196941 INTTnt   79-9412

The Microfilm or Microfiche Catalogue   As book collections have grown, some libraries have turned to the microfilm or microfiche catalogue, essentially the card catalogue information reproduced in miniature on film, which is read on a special magnifying viewer. As with the card catalogue, you need to find out if author, title, and subject entries are alphabetized in the same listing or in separate listings.

The Computer Catalogue   Today, more and more college and university libraries are computerizing their catalogues. Students use terminals (located in the library and often elsewhere on campus) to query the computer. By pressing a few lettered keys, users have instant access to information about an author, a title, a subject, an editor, and so on.

Some libraries also subscribe to commercial data-base services which transfer information from printed indexes, abstracts, government documents, and other such material to computer files that give users immediate access to this information. Data-base searches offer the advantages of speed and comprehensiveness. However, they have the disadvantage of expense (the user is charged a fee), and much of the material listed may not be available to you except on interlibrary loan.

Library of Congress Subject Headings   If your library uses Library of Congress numbers for cataloguing books, there is an easy way to find out quickly what books your library has in your subject area. First, look for your subject in the *Library of Congress Subject Headings*. If your subject is one indexed by that catalogue, you will find a specific catalogue number for books on your subject as well as cross-references to related subject areas that may help you sharpen your focus. If you find a number indexed, write it down; then find that number in your library's own *shelf list*, which lists all the books in the library by call number. The first part of a call number indicates the subject of a book (for example, TJ163.5). Therefore, when you look up the call number of only one book, you will find adjacent to it call numbers of other books the library owns on that subject.

Other Indexes   You may wish to consult other standard references. The *Cumulative Book Index* lists books by author and subject. The standard references for books in print in Canada, Britain, and the United States are: *Canadian Books in Print; Whittaker's Books in Print* (British); and *Books in Print* and *Paperbound Books in Print* (American). All are arranged by author and title. All are updated annually, and all list publishers' addresses in their respective countries. In addition, a *Subject Index* and a *Subject Guide* are available for the Canadian and American catalogues.

Periodicals

Since periodicals (magazines, journals, newspapers) are published frequently (and much more quickly than books), they often contain the most recent information on your subject. A variety of the periodical indexes (usually located in the reference section of the library) do for articles what the main catalogue does for books. You may need to consult a number of these indexes to find the information you need since each index includes some publications not listed in the others.

General-Interest Periodicals   If your subject is one which may have been dealt with in popular or general-interest magazines or in newspapers, you will want to consult the *Readers' Guide to Periodical Literature*, published from 1900 to the present, the *Canadian Periodical Index*, and newspaper indexes, the best known of which is the *New York Times Index*, published since 1913.

The front pages of each issue of the *Readers' Guide* provide an explanation of a sample entry as well as a key to abbreviations.

SUBJECT ENTRY

Nineteen hundred and eighty-four
　Nineteen eighty-four [part of Orwell's original manuscript]
　　il *Hist Today* 34:61 Ag '84
　Nineteen eighty-four: the latest educational reform
　　proposal. G.D. Fenstermacher, il *Phi Delta Kappan*
　　65:323-6 Ja '84
　Not one of us [G. Orwell] A. Kazin, il *N Y Rev Books*
　　31:13-14+ Je 14 '84

This subject entry appears in the *Reader's Guide* year-end index for 1984. The first item listed is an illustrated article entitled "Nineteen Eighty-Four." Part of Orwell's original manuscript for *Nineteen Eighty-Four*, the article was published in Vol. 34 of the magazine *History Today*, on page 61 of the August 1984 issue.

PERSONAL NAME ENTRY

Orwell, George, 1903–1950
　George Orwell's America [excerpt from The collected
　　essays, journalism and letters of George Orwell] il
　　Am Herit 35:65-80 F/Mr '84
　　　　　about
　1984. E.J. Jensen, il *Horizon* 27:14-15 Ja/F '84
　Not one of us. A. Kazin. il *N Y Rev Books* 31:13-14+
　　Je 14 '84
　Of bafflegab and Newspeak. A. Fotheringham. il *Macleans*
　　97:56 Ja 16 '84

This entry for Orwell lists first an article by Orwell and then three articles about him. The article written by Orwell is taken from *The Collected Essays, Journalism and Letters of George Orwell*. This illustrated article appears in Vol. 35 of *American Heritage*, the February/March 1984 issue, on pages 65–80. One of the articles about Orwell is Allan Fotheringham's "Of Bafflegab and Newspeak"; it was printed on page 56 of the January 16, 1984, issue of *Maclean's*. This is Vol. 97 of the magazine.

For older articles of general interest you can consult *Poole's Index*, 1802–1907, or *Nineteenth Century Readers' Guide*, 1890–99.

Special-Interest Periodicals   Virtually every specialized field has its own periodicals. Some of the most useful indexes to them are listed below.

Applied Science and Technology Index. 1958–. Formerly *Industrial Arts Index*. 1913–57.
Art Index. 1929–.
Biography Index. 1946–.
Biological and Agricultural Index. 1964–. Formerly *Agricultural Index*. 1916–64.
Business Periodicals Index. 1958–.
Canadian Business Periodical Index. 1958–.
Canadian Essay and Literature Index. 1973–.
Canadian News Index. 1980–.
Current Index to Journals in Education. 1969–.
Education Index. 1929–.
Engineering Index. 1884–.
Government of Canada Publications/Publications du Gouvernement du Canada. (Revised quarterly)
Humanities Index. 1974–. Formerly *Social Sciences and Humanities Index*. 1965–73. *International Index*. 1907–65.
Index to Legal Periodicals. 1908–.
MICROLOG Index. 1979–. (Canadian research index, includes Canadian federal, provincial, and local government publications; bilingual; revised monthly.)
Music Index. 1949–.
Public Affairs Information Service (Bulletin). 1915–.
Social Sciences Index. 1974–. Formerly *Social Sciences and Humanities Index*. 1965–73. *International Index*. 1907–65.
United States Government Publications (Monthly Catalogue). 1895–.
See also the various abstracts, such as *Chemical Abstracts*, 1907–; *Abstracts of English Studies*, 1958–; *Abstracts of Popular Culture*, 1976–.

Reference Books

For a detailed list of reference books, with a short description of each, consult *Canadian Reference Sources: A Selected Guide* by Dorothy E. Ryder, *Guide to Basic Reference Materials for Canadian Libraries*, edited by Claire England, *Guide to Reference Books* (with supplements) by Eugene P. Sheehy, and *American Reference Books Annual (ARBA)*, edited by Bohdan S. Wynar and Anna G. Patterson. A few of the most important reference books are listed on the following pages (with abbreviated bibliographical information).

Another useful research tool is *Microform Research Collections: A Guide*, edited by Suzanne Cates Dodson. This book lists, in detail, available microform resources and describes each set as well as any associated indexes and bibliographies.

General dictionaries (unabridged)

A Dictionary of American English on Historical Principles. 4 vols. 1938–44.

Century Dictionary and Cyclopedia. 12 vols. 1911. 3 vols. 1927–33.

New Standard Dictionary of the English Language. 1947, 1952, 1966.

The Oxford English Dictionary. 20 vols. 1989. Originally issued as *A New English Dictionary on Historical Principles*. 10 vols. and supp. 1888–1933. Supplements.

The Random House Dictionary of the English Language. 2nd ed. 1987.

Webster's Third New International Dictionary. 1986.

Special dictionaries: language

Avis, Walter, et al. *A Dictionary of Canadianisms on Historical Principles*. 1967.

Cassidy, Frederic G. *Dictionary of American Regional English*. Vol. 1 (A–C)–. 1985–.

Cowie, A.P., and R. Mackin. *Oxford Dictionary of Current Idiomatic English*. Vol. I–. 1975–.

Fowler, H.W. *Dictionary of Modern English Usage*. 2nd ed. Rev. Sir Ernest Gowers. 1965.

Hayakawa, S.I., and the Funk and Wagnalls dictionary staff. *Modern Guide to Synonyms and Related Words*. 1968.

Mawson, C.O.S. *Dictionary of Foreign Terms*. 2nd ed. Rev. Charles Berlitz. 1975.

Morris, William, and Mary Morris. *Harper Dictionary of Contemporary Usage*. 1975.

Onions, C.T. *Oxford Dictionary of English Etymology*. 1967.

Partridge, Eric. *Dictionary of Catch Phrases*. 1979.

———. *Dictionary of Slang and Unconventional English*. 7th ed. 1970.

Random House Thesaurus. College ed. Ed. Jess Stein and Stewart Berg Flexner. 1984.

Roget's Thesaurus. New ed. Ed. Betty Kirkpatrick. 1987.

Wentworth, Harold, and Stuart B. Flexner. *Dictionary of American Slang*. 2nd ed. 1975.

Vinay, Jean-Paul. *The Canadian Dictionary: French-English/English-French*. 1962.

General encyclopedias

Academic American Encyclopedia. 21 vols. 1984.

Chamber's Encyclopaedia. New rev. ed. 15 vols. 1973.

Collier's Encyclopedia. 24 vols. 1976.

Encyclopaedia Britannica. 15th ed. 30 vols. 1979.

Encyclopedia Americana. Intl. ed. 30 vols. 1977.

Encyclopedia Canadiana. 10 vols. 1977.

Special encyclopedias and dictionaries

Adams, James T. *Dictionary of American History*. Rev. ed. 8 vols. 1976.

Cambridge Encyclopaedia of Astronomy. Ed. Simon Mitton. 1977.

Canadian Encyclopedia. 2nd ed. 4 vols. 1988.

Colombo, John Robert. *Colombo's Canadian References*. 1976.

Dictionary of the History of Ideas. Ed. Philip P. Wierner et al. 5 vols. 1973.

Encyclopedia of American Foreign Policy. Ed. Alexander DeConde. 3 vols. 1978.

Encyclopedia of Computers and Data Processing. Vol. I–. 1978–.

Encyclopedia of Philosophy. Ed. Paul Edwards et al. 4 vols. 1973.

Encyclopedia of Psychology. 2nd ed. Ed. Hans Jurgen Eysenck et al. 1979.

Encyclopedia of World Art. 15 vols. 1959–68. Supp. 1983.

Focal Encyclopedia of Photography. Rev. ed. 1980.

Grzimek's Animal Life Encyclopedia. 13 vols. 1972–75.

International Encyclopedia of Higher Education. Ed. Asa K. Knowles. 10 vols. 1977.

International Encyclopedia of the Social Sciences. Ed. D.E. Sills. 17 vols. 1968. Supplements.

Kallmann, Helmut, et al. *Encyclopedia of Music in Canada*. 1981.

Klein, Barry, and D. Icolari. *Reference Encyclopedia of the American Indian*. 3rd ed. 1978.

Kurian, George Thomas. *Encyclopedia of the Third World*. 2 vols. 1978.

Langer, William L. *An Encyclopedia of World History*. 5th ed. 1972.

McGraw-Hill Encyclopedia of Science and Technology. 15 vols. 4th ed. 1977. Yearbooks.

Munn, Glenn G. *Encyclopedia of Banking and Finance*. 7th rev. ed. Ed. Ferdinand L. Garcia. 1973.

The New Grove Dictionary of Music and Musicians. Ed. Stanley Sadie. 20 vols. 1980.

Stierlin, Henri. *Encyclopedia of World Architecture*. 2 vols. 2nd ed. 1979.

Story, Norah. *Oxford Companion to Canadian History and Literature*. 1967. Supplement, 1973.

Thompson, Oscar. *International Cyclopedia of Music and Musicians*. 10th ed. Rev. ed. [Ed. Bruce Bohle.] 1975.

Atlases

Commercial Atlas and Marketing Guide (Rand McNally). 1981.

Cosmopolitan World Atlas (Rand McNally). Rev. ed. 1987.

Hammond World Atlas. 1984.

Historical Atlas of Canada: From the Beginning to 1800. [1987].

National Atlas of Canada. 5th ed. 1985.
National Geographic Atlas of the World. 5th ed. 1981.
Oxford Economic Atlas of the World. 4th ed. 1972.
Rand McNally World Atlas of Nations. 1988.
The Times (London) Atlas of the World: Comprehensive Edition. 1983.
U.S. Department of the Interior Geological Survey. *The National Atlas of the United States of America*. 1970.

Yearbooks—current events

Americana Annual. 1923–.
Annual Register. 1758–.
Britannica Book of the Year. 1938–.
Canada Year Book. 1867–.
Canadian Almanac and Directory. 1847–.
Canadian News Facts. 1967–.
Canadian World Almanac and Book of Facts. 1987–.
Facts on File. 1940–.
Information Please Almanac. 1947–.
Pears Cyclopedia. 1898–.
Quick Canadian Facts. 1945–.
Reader's Digest Almanac and Yearbook. 1966–.
Statesman's Year-Book. 1864–.
Statistical Abstract of the United States. 1878–.
World Almanac and Book of Facts. 1868–.

Biography

Canadian Who's Who. 1875–.
Contemporary Authors. 1962–.
Current Biography. 1940–.
Dictionary of American Biography. 16 vols. and index. 1927–80. Supplements.
Dictionary of Canadian Biography. 11 vols. and index (vols. 1–4). 1966–.
Dictionary of National Biography (British). 22 vols. 1882–1953. Rpt. 1981. Supplements.

Dictionary of Scientific Biography. 16 vols. 1970–80.
International Who's Who (London). 1935–.
Macmillan Dictionary of Canadian Biography. 4th ed. 1978.
McGraw-Hill Encyclopedia of World Biography. 12 vols. 1973.
Webster's Biographical Dictionary. 1976.
Who's Who in America. 1899–. [See also *Marquis Who's Who Publications: Index to All Books* (revised annually).]

Literature

Bartlett's Familiar Quotations. 15th ed. 1981.
Benét's Reader's Encyclopedia. 3rd ed. 1987.
Cambridge History of American Literature. 3 vols. in 1. 1943.
Cambridge History of English Literature. 15 vols. 1907–33.
Canadian Essay and Literature Index. 1973–.
Carpenter, Humphrey, and Mari Pritchard. *Oxford Companion to Children's Literature.* 1984.
Colombo, John Robert. *Colombo's Canadian Quotations.* 1974.
Drabble, Margaret. *Oxford Companion to English Literature.* 5th ed. 1985.
Essay and General Literature Index. 1900–.
Evans, Bergen. *Dictionary of Quotations.* 1968.
Fiction Catalog. 10th ed. 1980. Supplements.
Granger's Index to Poetry. 7th ed. 1982.
Hamilton, Robert M., and Dorothy Shields. *Dictionary of Canadian Quotations and Phrases.* 2nd ed. 1982.
Hart, James D. *Oxford Companion to American Literature.* 4th ed. 1965.
Harvey, Sir Paul. *Oxford Companion to Classical Literature.* 2nd ed. 1937. Rpt. 1980.
Hirsch, E.D., Joseph E. Kett, and James Trefil. *Dictionary of Cultural Literacy.* 1988.
Holman, C. Hugh. *Handbook to Literature.* 5th ed. 1986.
Klein, Leonard G. *Encyclopedia of World Literature in the 20th Century.* 2nd ed. 4 vols. 1981–84.
Klinck, Carl F., et al. *Literary History of Canada.* 2nd ed. 3 vols. 1965.
New Cambridge Bibliography of English Literature. 5 vols. 1969–77.

Oxford Dictionary of Quotations. 3rd ed. 1979.

Patterson, Margaret C. *Literary Research Guide.* 2nd ed. 2nd rev. ptg. 1984.

Play Index (Wilson). 5 vols. 1949–.

Seymour-Smith, Martin. *Funk and Wagnalls Guide to Modern World Literature.* 1975.

Short Story Index (Wilson). 1953. Supplements.

Smith, Horatio. *Columbia Dictionary of Modern European Literature.* 2nd ed. 1980.

Spiller, Robert E., et al. *Literary History of the United States.* 4th ed. 2 vols. 1974.

Toye, William. *Oxford Companion to Canadian Literature.* 1983.

Watters, Reginald Eyre. *A Checklist of Canadian Literature and Background Materials, 1628–1960.* 1972.

Watters, Reginald Eyre, and Inglis Freeman Bell. *On Canadian Literature, Its Authors and Language.* 1973.

(2) Prepare a working bibliography.

A working, or preliminary, bibliography contains information (titles, authors, dates, and so on) about the materials you think you might use. Write down the most promising sources you can find. Put each on a separate card (preferably 12.7 cm × 7.6 cm [3 × 5 inches]) so that you can readily drop or add a card and can arrange the list alphabetically without recopying it. Follow consistently the bibliographical form you are instructed to use. Following that style from the start will save you valuable time later, when you must compile a formal list of works cited to appear at the end of your paper.

The style illustrated by the samples on the next page follows the 1988 guidelines of the Modern Language Association (MLA). On pages 443–57 are examples of all the kinds of entries you are likely to need.

BIBLIOGRAPHY CARDS

Rodden, John. "The Politics of Literary
        Reputation: George Woodcock and
        the Anarchists' Orwell." <u>Queen's
        Quarterly</u> 95 (1988): 330–349.

Connelly, Mark. <u>The Diminished Self:
        Orwell and the Loss of Freedom.</u>
        Pittsburgh: Duquesne UP, 1987.

PR
6029
.R8
Z624
1987

■ **Exercise 2**   Select a subject (the one you chose for Exercise 1
on page 413 or a different one) and prepare a working bibliography.
Often you will find helpful bibliographies in the books that you
consult, especially in encyclopedias and other reference works.

34c
Evaluate and take notes on your sources.

As you take notes on your readings, learn how to find and
evaluate useful passages with a minimum of time and effort.
Seldom will a whole book, or even a whole article, be of
use as subject matter for any given research paper. To get
what is needed for your paper, you will find that you must

turn to many books and articles, rejecting most of them altogether and using from others only a section here and there. You cannot always take the time to read each book completely. Use the table of contents and the index of a book, and learn to skim the pages until you find the passages you need.

One important consideration always is the reliability of the source. Do others speak of the writer as an authority? As you read, do you find evidence that the author is competent, well informed, not prejudiced in any way? Is the work recent enough to provide up-to-date information? Is the edition the latest one available? The *Book Review Digest*, which contains convenient summaries of critical opinion on a book, may help you make decisions about which sources in your bibliography are most dependable.

As you take notes, be especially careful to indicate clearly on each note card what part of the information is your own idea and what came from the source; write down exactly where an idea or a quotation appears in the source and check the bibliographic information to be sure it is accurate. Scrupulous care now can prevent a multitude of problems later on—such as your having to go back to the library to check the accuracy of a quotation or to look up additional bibliographic information about a source when you are actually drafting your paper.

One of the best ways to take notes is on cards of uniform size, preferably 10 cm × 15 cm (4 × 6 inches). Each card must show the source of the note, including the exact page from which it is drawn. When information is taken from more than one page, be sure to indicate in your notes exactly where one page ends and another begins. It is a good idea to put a single note, or closely related ideas from a single source, on one card with a heading—a key word or phrase. You can then easily arrange your note cards as you make changes in organization.

BIBLIOGRAPHY CARD WITH SOURCE

> Voorhees, Richard J. _The Paradox of_
> _George Orwell_. Humanities Series.
> Lafayette: Purdue U Studies,
> 1961.

SOURCE (from page 87)

From the middle thirties until his death Orwell was a propagandist harping on the significance of totalitarianism because he knew that thousands upon thousands of people in democratic countries were only remotely aware of it, and still more thousands thought that there was a lot to be said for it in one form or another. _Nineteen Eighty-Four_ is his fiercest piece of propaganda.

NOTE CARD

> Orwell as propagandist
> (Voorhees 87)
>
> Orwell a propagandist from mid 1930s on —
> kept "harping on" totalitarianism.
>
> Why? He knew many people didn't know about
> its evils.
>
> "Nineteen Eighty-Four is his fiercest piece of
> propaganda."

For other examples of note cards, see pages 470, 472, 482.

Another way to take notes is to use photocopies of short excerpts from materials you think you may quote directly. On a photocopy you may mark quotable material and jot down your own ideas as you study the source.

PHOTOCOPIED SOURCE WITH NOTES

from Vol. IV - Orwell's Essays

Politics and the English Language   137

covering up all the details. The great enemy of clear language is insincerity. When there is a gap between one's real and one's declared aims, one turns as it were instinctively to long words and exhausted idioms, ~NEWSPEAK~ like a cuttlefish squirting out ink. In our age there is no such thing as "keeping out of politics". All issues are political issues, and politics ← 1984 itself is a mass of lies, evasions, folly, hatred and schizophrenia. When the general atmosphere is bad, language must suffer. I should expect to find—this is a guess which I have not sufficient knowledge to verify— that the German, Russian and Italian languages have all deteriorated in the last ten or fifteen years, as a result of dictatorship. → like Big Brother's

[But] if thought corrupts language, language can also corrupt thought. debatable A bad usage can spread by tradition and imitation, even among people BUT who should and do know better. The debased language that I have been quotable discussing is in some ways very convenient.

Direct quotations

Any quotations that you use in your paper should be convincing and important ones. They should be made an integral part of your text. (For examples of ways this can be done, see pages 475, 479.) When you discover a quotable passage in your reading, you should take it down verbatim—that is, copy every word, every capital letter, and every mark of punctuation exactly as in the original. Be sure to enclose the quoted passage in quotation marks. When you are quoting, quote accurately. When you are not quoting, use your own sentence structure and wording, not a slightly altered version of your source. Any quotation (except well-known or proverbial passages) of the words of another person should be placed inside quotation marks (or indented if over four lines in length), and exact sources should be cited.

```
In Nineteen Eighty-Four, Orwell defines doublethink

as "the power of holding two contradictory beliefs

in one's mind simultaneously, and accepting both of

them" (215).
```

[Quotation marks enclose copied words, and internal documentation indicates the source.]

For other examples of the use and the documentation of direct quotations, see the sample research paper on pages 462–99.

As you write your research paper, keep a few guidelines in mind when you are quoting the exact words of another. Pay close attention to form, punctuation, and spacing: see **16a**. Use ellipsis points appropriately to indicate omissions: see **17i**. But do not use ellipsis points before quotations that are only parts of sentences. To avoid ellipsis points at the beginning of a quotation (especially one that begins a paragraph), use a word like *that* or an introductory word group before the quotation.

Paraphrase

A paraphrase is a restatement of the source in about the same number of words. As you compare the source on the next page with the paraphrase that follows, notice differences in sentence structure and word choice.

SOURCE (from *Propaganda* by Jacques Ellul)

The aim of modern propaganda is no longer to modify ideas, but to provoke action. It is no longer to change adherence to a doctrine, but to make the individual cling irrationally to a process of action.

PARAPHRASE

Jacques Ellul states that modern propaganda does not try any longer to change a person's ideas or loyalties to certain principles; instead, it seeks to make individuals irrationally follow a given procedure (25).

For further examples of the use and documentation of paraphrases, see pages 468–71 and 474–77.

Summary

A summary is a concise restatement (shorter than the source). When you paraphrase or summarize, avoid not only copying the actual words but also imitating the writer's style or sentence structure. If you cannot do this and you need the material, quote it directly.

SOURCE (from *Nineteen Eighty-Four* by George Orwell)

> . . . the subtlest practitioners of *doublethink* are those who invented *doublethink* and know that it is a vast system of mental cheating. In our society, those who have the best knowledge of what is happening are also those who are furthest from seeing the world as it is. In general, the greater the understanding, the greater the delusion: the more intelligent, the less sane.

SUMMARY

As Orwell observed in <u>Nineteen Eighty-Four</u>, it is the inventors of doublethink who are best at using their brand of "mental cheating." In modern times, he contends, even the best-informed do not see realities; generally speaking, "the greater the understanding, the greater the delusion: the more

intelligent, the less sane" (216).

■ **Exercise 3**   Carefully read paragraphs 1 (pages 325–26) and 38 (pages 349–50) in Section **32**. First write a paraphrase of one of these paragraphs. Then write a summary of the same paragraph. Unless you are quoting directly, avoid using the sentence patterns of the source. To convey the ideas in the source exactly, choose your words carefully.

Plagiarism

You must acknowledge all material quoted, paraphrased, or summarized from any work. Failing to cite a source, deliberately or accidentally, is plagiarizing—presenting as your own work the words or ideas of another. As the *MLA Handbook* (New York: Modern Language Assn., 1988) states,

> The most blatant form of plagiarism is to repeat as your own someone else's sentences, more or less verbatim. . . . Other forms of plagiarism include repeating someone else's particularly apt phrase without appropriate acknowledgment, paraphrasing another person's argument as your own, and presenting another's line of thinking as though it were your own. (sec. 1.6)

After you have done a good deal of reading about a given subject, you will be able to distinguish between common knowledge in that field—facts, dates, and figures—and the distinctive ideas or interpretations of specific writers. When you use the ideas or information that these writers provide, be sure to cite the exact source of the material used.

NOT   In *Nineteen Eighty-Four*, doublethink is defined as the power of holding two contradictory beliefs in one's mind simultaneously, and accepting both of them. [undocumented copying]

BUT   In *Nineteen Eighty-Four*, Orwell defines doublethink as "the power of holding two contradictory beliefs in one's mind simultaneously, and accepting both of them" (215). [Quotation marks enclose copied words, and the page number in parentheses cites the source.]

NOT   *Nineteen Eighty-Four* is Orwell's most ferocious propaganda. [an undocumented idea from the work of another writer]

BUT   *Nineteen Eighty-Four* has been called Orwell's most ferocious propaganda (Voorhees 87).

OR   Richard J. Voorhees states, "*Nineteen Eighty-Four* is his [Orwell's] fiercest piece of propaganda" (87).

If you are in doubt about whether you need to cite a source, the best policy is to cite it.

34d
Make a working plan or outline.

After completing a working bibliography and taking notes on your subject, make a working plan for your paper. Be careful, though, not to adhere too rigidly to this plan. No plan or outline should be regarded as complete until the research paper has been finished. As you write the paper, you will probably revise your original plan frequently, adding points, changing points, and perhaps dropping points you had originally intended to cover.

It is sometimes useful, especially if your paper is long or complicated, to have a detailed outline before you actually begin to write. If you work best with a formal outline, decide whether to use a topic outline or a sentence outline. A topic outline presents information in parallel phrases or single words (see pages 385 and 461). A sentence outline presents the same ideas in declarative statements (see page 384). If your instructor has asked you to submit a formal outline of your paper before you begin to draft, prepare a topic or sentence outline as you are directed.

When you have finished drafting your paper, a good way to check your organization is to correlate the ideas in your text with those in an outline and to make any needed revisions. Also check the form of your outline; see **33f**, pages 383–84. As you study the sample research paper on pages 461–99, notice that the arrangement of paragraphs accords with that of the divisions of the topic outline.

34e

Draft and revise the research paper. Use an acceptable form for your citations and prepare a list of works cited.

After you have taken notes and organized your material, you should be ready to begin writing. Using the headings on your note cards (see page 427), arrange your notes in the order of your working plan or outline and then use them as the basis of your paper. Naturally you will need to expand some parts, cut others, and provide transitions. As you draft the paper, remember that it is *your* paper. Write it in your own words, your own style. Integrate your source material— paraphrases, summaries, quotations—with your own statements rather than making the paper a patchwork of other people's comments.

(1) Citations

Since the material in your research paper comes largely from the work of others, you will need to give proper credit by citing your sources. Traditionally, such citations took the form of notes numbered consecutively throughout the paper and placed either at the bottoms of the appropriate pages (footnotes) or all together at the end of the paper (endnotes).

For examples of the endnote (or footnote) style and the APA system for citation, see pages 502–507 and 510–11. Beginning in 1984, however, the practice recommended by the Modern Language Association is to place citations of sources directly in the text, in parentheses. Numbers in the text refer to supplementary or explanatory comments (see the notes on page 493). Parenthetical citations refer the reader to a list of works cited at the end of the paper.

The basic elements of the citation are the author's last name, a shortened but easily understood form of the title (with, if necessary, the volume number), and the page number of the material used from the source. However, only enough information to guide the reader to the appropriate source is necessary. In other words, the author's name and the title of the source can be omitted from the parenthetical citation if they are clearly identified outside the parentheses nearby in the text of the paper. Furthermore, if only one work by a given author is listed in ''Works Cited,'' the work's title can be omitted from the parenthetical citation. As you study the following examples, observe that common sense rather than hard and fast rules determines the information that must be included in a parenthetical citation.

A work by one author

The following examples from the research paper on pages 463–99 provide sufficient information to refer readers to the appropriate pages of the works listed alphabetically in the list of works cited at the end of the paper.

Nineteen Eighty-Four has been called George Orwell's most ferocious propaganda (Voorhees 87). Orwell was quick to admit that he was a propagandist. In fact, in 1940, during a BBC radio

```
broadcast, he said that "every artist is a
propagandist in the sense that he is trying,
directly or indirectly, to impose a vision of life
that seems to him desirable" (Essays 2: 41).
```

In the first citation, the author is not identified in the text, and his name therefore appears within parentheses. Because only one work by Voorhees is included in the list of works cited, there is no need to use the title in the parentheses. However, the reference to a specific passage and not to the Voorhees work as a whole requires citing the page number.

In the second citation, Orwell has been identified in the text of the paper as the source of the quotation and need not be named in the citation. However, since Orwell is the author of three works appearing in the list of works cited, the title (shortened) is necessary. Further, because this work comprises four volumes, the volume number must be given as well as the specific page of the quotation.

Both citations supply only the information the reader needs to identify the source, but suppose the opening sentence were worded differently, as in the following example. Notice the information that must change for the citations to be complete.

```
Nineteen Eighty-Four--unquestionably a work of
art--supports the argument that "every artist is a
propagandist in the sense that he is trying,
directly or indirectly, to impose a vision of life
that seems to him desirable" (Orwell, Essays 2:
41). The critic Richard Voorhees has called the
novel Orwell's most ferocious propaganda (87),
```

suggesting that Orwell believed in the forceful if
indirect imposition of his own values.

Observe that although the same sources as before are cited, Orwell must now be identified as the author of the direct quotation, and Voorhees, now named in the actual text of the second sentence, needs no further mention in the citation.

Suppose that the text of the first sentence of this example had been written differently and provided additional information about the source, as in the following version.

In the second volume of his Collected Essays,
Orwell suggests that "every artist is a
propagandist in the sense that he is trying,
directly or indirectly, to impose a vision of life
that seems to him desirable" (41).

Because author, title, and volume are clear from the context, the citation is simply a page number.

A work by two authors

By cleverly manipulating carefully selected facts,
propagandists today either ignore or play down any
evidence that might effectively refute their one-
sided arguments—the old card-stacking trick
(Cantril and Hart).

Both authors are included in the parenthetical citation. Note, incidentally, that this citation of an encyclopedia article does not require a page reference, since encyclopedias are arranged alphabetically and a reader would have no trouble locating the source.

A work by three authors

If you are citing a source by three authors, supply the names of all three.

```
Value theory attracted the interest of many

economists in the 1980s. They were particularly

interested in working out a theory of industrial

organization that explained the relationship

between monopolies and contestable markets (Baumol,

Panzar, and Willig).
```

The absence of a page number in this citation indicates that the reference is to an entire work rather than to a specific passage. (See page 444 for the corresponding bibliographic entry.)

More than three authors

If you are citing a source by more than three authors, supply the name of the first author and follow the name with *et al.*, the Latin abbreviation for ''and others.''

```
The rise of the American public school system has

been attributed, at least in part, to the lack of

other "authoritative institutions" (Bailyn et al.

513).
```

Works by different authors with the same last name

Occasionally your list of works cited will contain sources by two authors with the same last name—for example, K. Patricia Cross and Wilbur Cross. In such cases, whenever mention of an author's name is required, you must use the first name as well as the last.

Educator Wilbur Cross has suggested that the
situation of the mature student has excited
considerable interest in academic circles (8–9).
Other commentators explore the ways that academe
can serve these students (K. Patricia Cross 32,
41).

Notice also in these examples the treatment of references to
more than one page: 8–9 identifies continuous pages; 32, 41
indicates that the reference is to two separate pages.

Poetry, drama, and the Bible

When you refer to poetry, drama, and the Bible, you must
often give numbers of lines, acts, and scenes, or of chapters
and verses, rather than page numbers. This practice enables
a reader to consult an edition other than the one you are
using. Nonetheless, your list of works cited should still
identify your edition.

Act, scene, and line numbers (all Arabic) are separated
by periods with no space before or after them. Biblical
chapters and verses are treated similarly. In both cases, the
progression is from larger to smaller units.

The following example illustrates a typical citation of
lines of poetry.

Emily Dickinson concludes "I'm Nobody! Who Are
You?" with a characteristically bittersweet stanza:

> How dreary to be somebody!
>
> How public, like a frog
>
> To tell your name the livelong June
>
> To an admiring bog! (5–8)

The following citation shows that Hamlet's "To be, or not to be" soliloquy appears in Act 3, Scene 1, lines 56–89 of *Hamlet*.

```
In Hamlet Shakespeare presents the most famous

soliloquy in the history of the theatre: "To be, or

not to be . . . " (3.1.56–89).
```

The following reference to the Bible indicates that the account of creation in Genesis extends from chapter 1, verse 1, through chapter 2, verse 22.

```
The Old Testament creation story (Gen. 1.1–2.22),

told with remarkable economy, culminates in the

arrival of Eve.
```

Notice that names of books of the Bible are neither underlined (italicized) nor enclosed in quotation marks and that abbreviation is desirable.

Punctuation and mechanics

Commas are used to separate authors' names and titles (Orwell, *Essays*) and to indicate interruptions in a sequence of pages or lines (44, 47). Hyphens are used to indicate continuous sequences of pages (44–47) and lines (1–4). Colons separate volume and page numbers (*Essays* 2: 41). A space follows the colon. Periods separate acts, scenes, and lines in drama (3.1.56–89) and chapters and verses in the Bible (Gen. 1.1).

Citations should, wherever possible, appear just before punctuation in the text of the paper.

```
Wilbur Cross speaks of adult learners who "range in

age from the mid-twenties to the upper sixties, and
```

vary in background from nurses, teachers, business people and government employees to truck drivers, police officers and 'just ordinary family people'" (116), whereas K. Patricia Cross views adult learners as a class of students disproportionately young, white, and affluent (45).

Wilbur Cross's citation falls just before a comma, K. Patricia Cross's just before a period. However, in a sentence such as the following the citations cannot precede punctuation.

Wilbur Cross (116) and K. Patricia Cross (45) speak of different kinds of adult learners.

In quotations set off from the text (see Section **16a**), citations follow the final punctuation.

As Ralph A. Ranald has observed,

> Orwell's <u>1984</u> is about religion
> reversed, . . . and above all, language
> reversed: not simply corrupt, but
> reversed. . . . [Orwell converts] all the
> positives of Western civilization into
> their negatives. (544–45)

(2) List of works cited

When you are ready to make the final revision of your paper, you will know which sources from your working bibliography you have actually used and cited in your paper. Now eliminate the bibliography cards for the works that you do not cite, and arrange the remaining cards in alphabetical order by authors' last names. You are now ready to prepare the list of works cited that will conclude your paper. As you make your final revision, you will be checking your citations against this list to ensure that they are complete and correct. Other documentation styles handle this list differently and have different names for it.

In MLA style the list of works cited is arranged alphabetically by author and is double-spaced throughout. The first line of each entry is flush with the left margin; subsequent lines are indented to leave five spaces. If you use more than one work by the same author, list the works alphabetically by title. Give the author's name with the first title, but substitute three hyphens for the name in subsequent entries.

Berton, Pierre. <u>Arctic Grail: The Quest for the</u>

    <u>North West Passage and the North Pole, 1818–</u>

    <u>1909</u>. Toronto: McClelland, 1988.

———. <u>Vimy</u>. Toronto: McClelland, 1986.

Bibliographical entries often consist of only three units, which are separated by periods:

Newman, Peter C. <u>Sometimes a Great Nation</u>. Toronto:

    McClelland, 1988.

1. *Name of the author*. Give the last name first. Your final list of works cited will be arranged alphabetically by authors' last names.
2. *Title of the book*. Underline (italicize) the title, and capitalize it in accordance with **9c**. Always include the book's subtitle, and underline it as well.
3. *Publication data*. Include the place of publication, the publisher, and the latest copyright date as shown on the copyright page. Give a shortened form of the publisher's name as long as it is clear.

Some entries, however, require more than three units and must be given special treatment. As you study the following MLA-style bibliographical entries, which cover most of the special problems you are likely to encounter, observe both the punctuation and the arrangement of information. See also pages 457–60 for a list of abbreviations that are permissible in bibliographies, notes, and tables. Note that the MLA style favours Arabic numbers throughout and that such abbreviations as *vol.* and *sec.* are not capitalized.

Sample Bibliographical Entries

Books

One author

Galbraith, John. Economics in Perspective: A

     Critical History. Boston: Houghton, 1987.

Notice that a colon is used before a subtitle and before the publisher's name; note, too, that the underlining of the complete title is continuous.

Frye, Northrop. On Education. Markham, ON:

     Fitzhenry, 1988.

The publisher's name (in this instance, Fitzhenry and Whiteside) is shortened as much as possible while remaining clearly identifiable.

Two authors

McLuhan, Marshall, and Eric McLuhan. Laws of Media:

     The New Science. U of Toronto P, 1988.

Note that a comma follows the first author's name (inverted order) and that the second author's name is not inverted. Here, too, the publisher's name (in this instance, University of Toronto Press) is shortened as much as possible. Note that there is no period after the *U* for *University* or the *P* for *Press*.

Three authors

```
Baumol, William J., John C. Panzar, and Robert D.

     Willig. Contestable Markets and the Theory of

     Industry Structure. Rev. ed. New York:

     Harcourt, 1988.
```

Note that the names of the second and third authors are given in the usual order (rather than surname first) and that commas are used after both the first and second names. Note the inclusion of information to indicate a revised edition. See entries below for notation of subsequent editions.

More than three authors

```
Baumol, William J., et al. Economics: Principles

     and Policy. 2nd Can. ed. Toronto: Harcourt,

     1988.

---. Economics: Principles and Policy.

     Macroeconomics. 2nd Can. ed. Toronto:

     Harcourt, 1988.
```

A comma follows the first author's name (inverted order); "et al." is not underlined. Note the indication of an adaptation of a text for a Canadian audience. Note also the use of three hyphens and a period to indicate the second citation for the same author or authors.

Corporate author

Canadian Red Cross Society. <u>First Aid for You and</u>

   <u>Me</u>. 16th ed. Toronto: CRCS, 1984.

Edition after the first

Clark, Bruce, and John K. Wallace. <u>Canada: Land of</u>

   <u>Diversity</u>. 2nd ed. Scarborough, ON: Prentice,

   1989.

Note: Always give the city of publication to help in identifying the book. In this case, the province is also included for readers unfamiliar with the location of Scarborough or for readers who might confuse Scarborough, Ontario with Scarborough, England.

Editors

Barnet, Sylvan, Morton Berman, and William Burto,

   eds. <u>An Introduction to Literature</u>. 9th ed.

   Glenview, IL: 1988.

McLeod, Jack, ed. <u>The Oxford Book of Canadian</u>

   <u>Political Anecdotes</u>. Toronto: Oxford UP, 1988.

A translation

Roy, Gabrielle. <u>Enchantment and Sorrow: The</u>

   <u>Autobiography of Gabrielle Roy</u>. Trans.

   Patricia Claxton. Toronto: Lester, 1987.

An "edition"

Moodie, Susanna. <u>Roughing It in the Bush, or, Life</u>

<u>in Canada</u>. 1852. Ed. Carl Ballstadt. Ottawa:

Carleton UP, 1988.

The term "edition" indicates a work by one author that has been prepared for print by an editor. Historical works and literary works of authors no longer living (for example, Shakespeare, Milton, Tennyson) usually list the editor on the title page. Note, too, that the original date of publication is given, followed by a period and two spaces.

Literary work from an anthology

Ryga, George. <u>The Ecstasy of Rita Joe</u>. <u>Modern</u>

<u>Canadian Plays</u>. Ed. Jerry Wasserman.

Vancouver: Talon, 1985. 27–55.

The title of the play is underlined, as it would be if the text were printed separately. Cite the inclusive pages for the work at the end of the entry, following the date and period.

Cohen, Leonard. "As the Mist Leaves No Scar."

<u>15 Canadian Poets Plus 5</u>. Ed. Gary Geddes and

Phyllis Bruce. Toronto: Oxford, 1978. 131.

The title of the poem is put into quotation marks.

Non-literary work from an anthology

Spence, Donald. "Passive Remembering." <u>Remembering</u>

<u>Reconsidered: Ecological and Traditional</u>

<u>Approaches to the Study of Memory</u>. Ed. Ulric

Neisser and Eugene Winograd. Cambridge:

Cambridge UP, 1988. 311–25.

Donovan, Timothy R. "Seeing Students as Writers."

Composition and Teaching 1 (1978): 13–16. Rpt.

in The Writing Teacher's Sourcebook. Ed. Gary

Tate and Edward J. Corbett. New York: Oxford,

1981.

For previously published non-literary works, give both the original publication data and the publication data for the anthology.

Reprint

Gallant, Mavis. The Pegnitz Junction: A Novella and

Five Stories. New York: Random, 1973. Toronto:

Laurentian Library–Macmillan, 1982.

If the book has been reprinted by a publisher that did not print the original, give the dates of both the original edition and the reprint. In this example, the original hard-cover edition was published by Random nine years earlier than the Macmillan paperback.

Tweedsmuir Park: British Columbia, Canada, August,

1937. British Columbia, Dept. of Lands, 1938;

rpt. British Columbia, Ministry of Environment

and Parks, 1988.

In this example, the reprint information signals that this book is of historic interest. (Note that although both editions are published by the government of British Columbia, the names of the government agencies have changed.)

A non-English work

Boucher, Denise. <u>Les fées sont soif</u>. Montréal:

Intermède, 1978.

In general, treat non-English works as you would any English book, but provide a translation of the title in square brackets (*Les fées sont soif [The Fairies Are Thirsty]*) if it needs clarification. Note that capitalization practices differ from language to language. Here, only the first word of the title is capitalized, in keeping with conventional practice for French: in both titles and subtitles, only the first words and proper nouns are capitalized (for example, *La route d'Altamont* for *The Road Past Altamont*). Copy non-English titles exactly as printed. For guidance with non-English bibliographic entries, consult the *MLA Handbook*.

A work in more than one volume

Potter, G.R., et al., eds. <u>The New Cambridge Modern</u>

<u>History</u>. 14 vols. Cambridge: Cambridge UP,

1957–70.

The multivolume work above was published over a period of years.

Sandburg, Carl. <u>Abraham Lincoln: The War Years</u>. 4

vols. New York: Harcourt, 1939.

The work above consists of four volumes published in the same year.

A work in more than one volume with a separate volume title

Pelikan, Jaroslav. <u>Reformation of Church and Dogma</u>

<u>(1300–1700)</u>. Vol. 4 of <u>The Christian</u>

Tradition: A History of the Development of
Doctrine. Chicago: U of Chicago P, 1985.

A work in a series

Neatby, Hilda. Quebec: The Revolutionary Age, 1760–
1791. Canadian Centenary Series. Toronto:
McClelland, 1977.

Strong-Boag, Veronica. The Canadian Campaign for
Woman Suffrage. Canada's Visual History Series
30. Ottawa: National Museum of Man and
National Film Board, 1977.

In the entry above, the volume number is given in Arabic
numerals (*30*) and without the abbreviation *vol.*

Green, Otis Howard. The Literary Mind of Medieval
and Renaissance Spain. Introd. John E. Keller.
Studies in Romance Langs. 1. Lexington: UP of
Kentucky, 1970.

Notice that a separate author wrote the introduction.

A foreword, preface, introduction

Vidal, Gore. Foreword. Out of This Century:
Confessions of an Art Addict. By Peggy
Guggenheim. New York: Anchor-Doubleday, 1980.

Note: Publishers sometimes use different imprints to identify particular types or lines of books they publish, as for
example the Anchor imprint in the Doubleday title above.
In such cases, give the imprint, followed by a hyphen and

the publisher's name (for example, New Canadian Library–McClelland, Viking–Penguin).

Government Publications

Canada. Mackenzie Valley Pipeline Inquiry. <u>Northern Frontier, Northern Homeland: The Report of the Mackenzie Valley Pipeline Inquiry</u>. By Thomas Berger. Lorimer, 1977. Rev. ed. Vancouver: Douglas, 1988.

Canada. <u>Pornography and Prostitution in Canada: Report of the Special Committee on Pornography and Prostitution</u>. 2 vols. Ottawa: Minister of Supply and Services, 1985.

United States. Bureau of Labor Statistics. <u>Tomorrow's Manpower Needs</u>. Washington: GPO, 1973.

Notice the squence of data given for a government publication: government, agency (if given), title—each followed by a period and two spaces. An individual author is sometimes identified in a government report: in such cases, the author's name, following the word *By*, is usually given after the title (see the Mackenzie Valley Pipeline report in the example above). The publisher in the last example is the U.S. Government Printing Office.

Conference and Symposium Proceedings

Cotton, C.E., et al., eds. <u>Fifth Biennial Conference Symposium of the Canadian Society</u>

for Biomechanics: Proceedings. London, ON:

Spodym, 1988. Conference held 16-19 Aug. 1988

in Ottawa.

Enter the published proceedings of a conference as you would a book. If the title does not include pertinent details about the conference, add them.

Gavora, J.S., et al., eds. Animal Breeding: Recent

Advances and Future Prospects. Ottawa: Animal

Research Centre, Agriculture Canada. [1988].

Presented in part at the symposium "Genetics

in Agriculture" at the 1983 Annual Meetings of

the Genetics Society of Canada.

In the example above, no date of publication appears in the printed proceedings. This information, obtained from the library catalogue, should be added in square brackets.

Magazines, Journals, and Newspapers

Unsigned articles

"The Free-Trade Helter Skelter." The Economist

5 Nov. 1988: 44.

Note: As a rule, the names of months except May, June, and July are abbreviated.

Daily Newspaper

Suzuki, David. "Ignite Science Interest before High

School." Globe and Mail 17 Dec. 1988, weekend

ed.: D4.

When not part of the publisher's name, the city's name should be given in square brackets after the title: *Straits Times* [Singapore]. For nationally published newspapers (*Globe and Mail, New York Times*), the city may be omitted. Column numbers are not used. If a specific edition is named on the masthead, it is specified, preceded by a comma, after the date: `16 Mar. 1989, late ed., sec. A: 14`.

Note that *The* should not be included in citing the newspaper's name (*Winnipeg Free Press*, not *The Winnipeg Free Press*).

Weekly magazine or newspaper

```
Allen, Glen. "AIDS and Civil Rights." Maclean's
        3 Oct. 1988: 50.

Raspberry, William. "The Perils of 'Quebecking.'"
        Manchester Guardian Weekly 8 Jan. 1989: 19.
```

Volume numbers are unnecessary because specific dates are given. Notice that words in quotation marks in the title are put into single quotation marks.

Monthly magazine

```
Fraser, John. "Misha, Misha! Where Are You Going?"
        Saturday Night Dec. 1988: 35-40.
```

Note: The period is omitted after titles that end with a question mark or an exclamation point.

Journal—continuous pagination through year

```
Hahn, Frank. "On Monetary Theory." Economic Journal
        98 (1988): 957-73.
```

If the pages of a journal are numbered continuously, by volume, throughout each year, only the volume number, followed by the year in parentheses, is required; the issue number and the month may be omitted.

Journal—separate pagination

Kirby, Michael. "Structural Analysis/Structural

Theory." The Drama Review 20.4 (1976): 51–68.

If the pages of a journal are numbered separately (starting with page 1) in each issue, both the volume and issue number must be included. Note that an issue number follows a volume number, separated by a period.

Hood, Hugh. "The Elephant in the Next Room: Anatomy

of a Long Work." Canadian Literature 116

(1988): 97–108.

Some journals, such as *Canadian Literature* in the example above, use only issue numbers (rather than volume numbers). In such cases, cite the issue number (*116* in our example) as you would a volume number.

Editorials, signed and unsigned

Hodgson, Gordon W. "Who Owns the Land?" Editorial.

Arctic 41 (1988): iii.

Here, the editorial appears in the prefatory pages of the journal, which are numbered with lower-case Roman numerals.

"Debt Forgiveness Could Be Incentive." Editorial.

Financial Post 9 Jan. 1989, sec. 1: 12.

Book review

```
Fulford, Robert. "Kernel of Glass at the Heart of

     New Atwood Heroine." Rev. of Cat's Eye, by

     Margaret Atwood. Quill and Quire Oct. 1988:

     18.
```

Note on magazine pagination   Sometimes a magazine article is printed on pages that are separated by other articles; for example, the first part appears on pages 137–39, the balance on pages 188–203. In such cases, give only the first page number followed by a plus sign: 137 + .

Encyclopedias and Almanacs

Entry signed with name or initials

```
Marsh, James. "Labrador." Canadian Encyclopedia.

     1988 ed.
```

Full publication information is not required for a familiar reference work.

```
R[ichard], P. H[all]. "Protozoa." Encyclopaedia

     Britannica: Macropaedia. 1985 ed.
```

Square brackets enclose the added parts of the name. A list of contributors is ordinarily supplied in the index volume or in the front matter of an encyclopedia.

Entry Unsigned

```
"Language: New Words." Reader's Digest Almanac and

     Yearbook. 1980 ed.
```

In this almanac, main sections (like "Language") are arranged alphabetically in the text.

"Utrecht, Peace of." New Columbia Encyclopedia.

1975 ed.

The title indicates that the article is listed under *U*.

"Alfred H. Nobel Prize Winners." Canadian World

Almanac and Book of Facts. 1987 ed. 520-22.

Notice that page numbers may be supplied for ease of reference, though the front matter of this almanac does list topics alphabetically.

Pamphlets and Bulletins

CIP: The Canadian Cataloguing in Publication

Program, Publisher's Guide. Ottawa: National

Library of Canada, 1983.

Safety Data Sheet—Kitchen Machines. Pamphlet 690.

Chicago: Natl. Restaurant Assn., 1970.

Titles of pamphlets are italicized (underlined).

Unpublished Dissertation

Nicosia, Francis R.J. "Germany and the Palestine

Question, 1933-1939." Diss. McGill, 1977.

Micropublications

Document a book or periodical photographically reproduced in miniature form as though the work were in its original form. Refer to a microform as such in a list of works cited only if that is the original form.

Non-print Sources

Motion picture

The Decline of the American Empire. Dir. Denys

    Arcand. NFB—Corporation Image, 1986.

Television or radio program

Williams, Tennessee. Cat on a Hot Tin Roof. Dir.

    Jack Hofsiss. American Playhouse. PBS. KCET,

    Los Angeles. 24 June 1985.

Gzowski, Peter. Morningside. CBC, Toronto. 5 Jan.

    1989.

Stage play

Six Characters in Search of an Author. By Luigi

    Pirandello. Dir. Robert Brustein. American

    Repertory Theatre, New York. 20 July 1988.

Recording

Coin, Christophe, and Patrick Cohen. Beethoven:

Sonata and Variations. HM France, 901180, 1988.

Lecture

Dye, Kenneth. "Financial Management and the Federal Deficit." Vancouver Institute Lecture. UBC, Vancouver. 19 Mar. 1988.

Interview

Bodden, Mary Catherine. Personal interview. 14 May 1989.

Additional non-print sources

For samples of citations of other non-print sources—such as microforms, games, globes, filmstrips, microscope slides, and transparencies—consult Eugene B. Fleischer's *A Style Manual for Citing Microform and Nonprint Media* (Chicago: American Library Association, 1978).

COMMON ABBREVIATIONS

The following is a list of abbreviations commonly used in bibliographies, tables, or notes (but not the text) of research papers. For a more complete list see the *MLA Handbook for Writers of Research Papers*, 3rd ed. New York: Modern Languages Assoc., 1988.

abr.	abridged, abridgment
Acad.	Academy
adapt.	adaptation, adapted by
anon.	anonymous

app.	appendix
Apr.	April
Assn.	Association
Aug.	August
biog.	biography, biographer, biographical
bk., bks.	book, books
bull.	bulletin
c.	*circa*, "about" (for example, "c. 1966")
cf.	compare
ch., chs.	chapter, chapters
col., cols.	column, columns
Coll.	college
comp.	compiled by, compiler
cont.	contents; continued
DAB	*Dictionary of American Biography*
DCB	*Dictionary of Canadian Biography*
Dec.	December
dept.	department
dir.	directed by, director
diss.	dissertation
div.	division
DNB	*Dictionary of National Biography*
ed., eds.	edition(s) OR editor(s)
enl.	enlarged (as in "rev. and enl. ed.")
et al.	*et alii*, "and others"
Feb.	February
fig.	figure
front.	frontispiece
fwd.	foreword, foreword by
gen. ed.	general editor
govt.	government
GPO	Government Printing Office
HMSO	Her (His) Majesty's Stationery Office
i.e.	*id est*, "that is"
illus.	illustrated by, illustrator, illustration
inc.	incorporated, including
Inst.	Institute, Institution
intl.	international
introd.	[author of] introduction, introduced by

Jan.	January
jour.	journal
mag.	magazine
Mar.	March
ms., mss.	manuscript, manuscripts
n, nn	note, notes (used immediately after page number: 6n3)
natl.	national
NB	*nota bene*, "take notice," "mark well" (always in upper case)
n.d.	no date [of publication]
no., nos.	number [of issue], numbers
Nov.	November
n.p.	no place [of publication], no publisher
n. pag.	no pagination
Oct.	October
OED	*Oxford English Dictionary*
op.	*opus*, "work"
P	Press (used in documentation; see "UP")
p., pp.	page, pages (omitted before page numbers unless reference would be unclear)
pref.	preface, preface by
proc.	proceedings
prod.	produced by, producer
pseud.	pseudonym
pt., pts.	part, parts
pub.	published by, publisher, publication
rept.	reported by, report
rev.	revision, revised, revised by OR review, reviewed by
rpt.	reprinted, reprint
sec., secs.	section, sections
Sept.	September
ser.	series
sic	"thus," "so" (in square brackets)
Soc.	Society
supp.	supplement
trans.	translated by, translator, translation
U	University (used in documentation; see "UP")

| UP | University Press (used in documentation: Oxford UP) |
| vol., vols. | volume, volumes (omitted before volume numbers unless reference would be unclear) |

(3) Final revisions and proofreading

After writing and carefully documenting the first draft of your paper, make needed revisions. To make your writing as clear and effective as possible, you will probably need to rewrite some sentences, and strike out or add others. Use the Reviser's Checklist on pages 403–405. (You may wish to review pages 390–92 of Section **33**.) Refer to **8b** and especially to the sample research paper on pages 463–99 as you put your paper in final form. Even when writing final copy, you will probably continue to make changes in word choice and to correct occasional errors in spelling, mechanics, or grammar. Type or write legibly. Proofread your final revision before handing it in.

Some instructors ask their students to submit outlines, notes, and drafts along with the final paper. Other instructors require a title page and a final outline along with the text of the paper. A title page usually gives the title of the paper, the author, the name of the course and its section number, the instructor's name, and the date—all attractively centred on the page: see the example on page 501. MLA recommends using no title page and giving the identification on the first page before the title of the paper: see page 463.

When submitted with the text of a research paper, the final outline serves as a table of contents. The following sample is a topic outline. (If your instructor specifies a sentence outline, see the sample on page 384.) Some instructors ask students to make the introduction and conclusion numbered headings. Others require an outline only of the main discussion and suggest that references to introduction and conclusion be omitted from the outline.

Outline

Thesis: Big Brother disseminates the most dangerous kind of propaganda.

Introduction: Sustained interest in *Nineteen Eighty-Four*; Orwell's hatred of political propaganda
  I. The propagandized Oceanians
     A. Their loss of individuality
     B. Their reverence for Big Brother
     C. Their use of doublethink
 II. The bureaucratic propaganda machine
     A. Its housing—symbolic
     B. Its parts—interrelated
III. The media in a totalitarian world
     A. All materials supplied
     B. The Party's ideal propagated
 IV. The falsification of history
     A. Purpose of changes
     B. Methods of "rectification"
        1. Use of memory hole
        2. Use of clerical teams
     C. Effect on Winston
  V. The manipulation of thought and emotion
     A. Preventing thought—Newspeak
     B. Rousing the emotions
        1. Love for Big Brother
        2. Hatred of his enemies
Conclusion: *Nineteen Eighty-Four* as a warning

Sample Research Paper

A sample research paper follows. The left-hand pages contain passages from sources, some note cards, and comments on content and form.

■ **Exercise 4**   Prepare for a class discussion of the strengths and weaknesses of the following research paper.

COMMENTS

1. The identification, double-spaced, begins 2.5 cm (one inch) from the top of the page and flush with the left margin. A double space precedes the title of the paper. A margin of about 2.5 cm (one inch) is provided at the left, right, and bottom of the page.

2. Four spaces separate the centred title from the first line of the text. A title consisting of two or more lines is double-spaced, and each line is centred. For example:

```
Big Brother's Propaganda:

Thought Control in a Totalitarian State
```

3. All pages (including the first page) are numbered with Arabic numerals in the upper right-hand corner, about 1.25 cm (a half inch) from the top. Notice that no period follows page numbers.

4. There are four brief paragraphs of introduction. To place her discussion in the context of the sustained public interest in *Nineteen Eighty-Four* as it relates to Orwell's concerns about propaganda, the writer provides a somewhat longer introduction than would usually be required. (See pages 380, 387.)

5. The Woodcock citation credits the *source of the quoted passage*. The citations for Gray, Hopkins, and Saar and for Gray acknowledge the *sources of information* for the figures about publishing and sales. Notice that despite the similarity of surnames, these citations refer to two different books. See the list of works cited on pages 495–99. No page reference is needed for the Chilton and Aubrey citation in paragraph 2, since it refers to the entire work rather than a particular passage in the work.

1

Tracy Monahan

English 131.03

Mr. Richards

March 12, 1988

                    Big Brother's Propaganda

1   George Orwell's <u>Nineteen Eighty-Four</u>, an
extraordinary mix of fantasy, naturalism, romance,
and above all, "bitter satire on certain existing
political systems and implied satire on others"
(Woodcock 19), has enjoyed an enormous audience.
As the year 1984 approached, the public and
academics alike showed a remarkable interest in
the novel. The public's interest was reflected in
sales. In the thirty-five years following its
publication, tens of millions had read it, in
sixty-two languages (Gray, Hopkins, and Saar 42).
As the book went into its sixty-sixth printing at
the beginning of 1984, paperback sales averaged
62 000 copies per month (Gray 111).

2   The academics' interest was reflected in many
"get-ready-for-1984" activities. In 1983, books
discussing Orwell's relevance in 1984 and the
novel's history and impact (Chilton and Aubrey)
were beginning to appear, and conferences were

COMMENTS

1. All pages after the first page give a shortened form of the author's name (usually the last name preceded by an initial) and the page number. This information is placed in the upper right-hand corner, about 1.25 cm (one-half inch) from the top. A double space separates the writer's name from the first line of the text.

2. Notice that the Broderick quotation is taken from the preface to a volume of published conference proceedings, which is listed by its title in the list of works cited because no volume editors are identified in the book. (See also page 494.)

3. In paragraph 4, the Voorhees citation credits the *source of an idea*. In the *Essays* citation, which credits the source of the quoted passage, it is not necessary to include Orwell's name because it is clear from context that he is the author.

SOURCE

For Orwell quotation:

> ORWELL: "I have always maintained that every artist is a propagandist. I don't mean a political propagandist. If he has any honesty or talent at all he cannot be that. Most political propaganda is a matter of telling lies, not only about the facts but about your own feelings. But every artist is a propagandist in the sense that he is trying, directly or indirectly, to impose a vision of life that seems to him desirable. I think that we are broadly agreed about the vision of life that proletarian literature is trying to impose."

being planned. In fact, there were so many that Library of Congress researcher John C. Broderick later observed, "In some respects, it would have been more distinctive for the Library of Congress not to have an Orwell conference in 1984, since so many occurred elsewhere" (George Orwell vii). What had sustained such interest in Orwell's novel?

3   While many facets of the novel interest readers, it is Orwell's vision of the "utopia-in-reverse" of Oceania (Woodcock 19), his hard look at the political machine of Big Brother, and his own use of propaganda that continue to fascinate.

4   Nineteen Eighty-Four has been called George Orwell's most ferocious propaganda (Voorhees 87). Orwell was quick to admit that he was a propagandist. In fact, in 1940, during a BBC radio discussion, he said that "every artist is a propagandist in the sense that he is trying, directly or indirectly, to impose a vision of life that seems to him desirable" (Essays 2: 41). But Orwell hated political propaganda which deliberately falsifies reality, especially the hypocritical kind used solely for the purpose of keeping totalitarian regimes in power. During the

COMMENTS

1. In the indented quotation (over four lines in length), the interpolation in brackets supplies a subject and verb to complete the shortened sentence. See also **17g**. Notice that the citation follows the final punctuation of a quotation set off from the text, whereas it precedes the final punctuation of a quotation within the text.

2. Notice that the punctuation before the first ellipsis point is retained to ensure the integrity of the sentence: see **12d(1)**. See also **17i**.

SOURCE

For Ranald quotation:

> Orwell's *1984* is about religion reversed, law and government reversed, and above all, language reversed: not simply corrupted, but reversed. In the mad world of *1984*, the mad world which Orwell sought by his writing to lead men to *avoid*—for he was a political activist not interested in simple prediction—in this world, which I call Orwell's ''antiuniverse,'' because of his conversion of all the positives of Western civilization into their negatives, all the channels of communication are systematically being closed down, restricted to just the minimums necessary for the technical functioning of society.

3. Paragraph 5 states the thesis.

T. Monahan 3

1930s and 1940s he was repelled by the propaganda
machines of dictators like Hitler and Stalin
(Colmer 183). It is this kind of propaganda that
Orwell satirizes in <u>Nineteen Eighty-Four</u>, a novel
that presents his vision of life--in reverse. As
Ralph A. Ranald has observed,

> Orwell's <u>1984</u> is about religion
> reversed, law and government reversed,
> and above all, language reversed: not
> simply corrupted, but reversed. In the
> mad world of <u>1984</u>, the mad world which
> Orwell sought by his writing to lead men
> to <u>avoid</u>--for he was a political
> activist not interested in simple
> prediction--in this world, which I
> call Orwell's "antiuniverse," . . .
> [Orwell converts] all the positives of
> Western civilization into their
> negatives. . . . (544-45)

And in Orwell's crazy world, it is Big Brother's
political propaganda that helps to sustain and
perpetuate this reversal of values.

5   To control society, to sustain the awesome
power of the State, Big Brother uses what Oliver
Thomson calls the most dangerous kind of

COMMENTS

1. Paragraph 6 begins the discussion of point I of the outline (see page 461): The propagandized Oceanians. Paragraph 7 continues the development of point I.

2. As you read the source below, observe how Tracy Monahan combines paraphrase and direct quotation in paragraphs 7 and 8.

SOURCE

Nineteen Eighty-Four (179)

Given this background, one could infer, if one did not know it already, the general structure of Oceanic society. At the apex of the pyramid comes Big Brother. Big Brother is infallible and all-powerful. Every success, every achievement, every victory, every scientific discovery, all knowledge, all wisdom, all happiness, all virtue, are held to issue directly from his leadership and inspiration. Nobody has ever seen Big Brother. He is a face on the hoardings, a voice on the telescreen. We may be reasonably sure that he will never die, and there is already considerable uncertainty as to when he was born. Big Brother is the guise in which the Party chooses to exhibit itself to the world. His function is to act as a focusing point for love, fear, and reverence, emotions which are more easily felt toward an individual than toward an organization.

T. Monahan 4

propaganda: a "steady drip, drip" of toxic, power-oriented ideas not recognized as propaganda. These ideas pollute the environment and saturate all art forms. Such propaganda deadens the awareness of its targets (132).

6   Big Brother is always watching. Thoroughly propagandized, the inhabitants of Oceania respond mechanically to his every command, no matter how illogical it is. If anyone dares to act or even think like an independent person, Big Brother resorts to liquidation or re-education. Such an individual either becomes an "unperson," one who has never existed, or a reprogrammed android, one who again loves and serves the State.

7   Ironically enough, the Oceanians have never seen Big Brother (just big pictures of him), for he is the mythical Leader so often created by propagandists. His image is projected by the Inner Party to maintain its ruling powers. Propaganda depicts him as a deity, omnipresent, omniscient, and omnipotent. "Every success, every achievement, every victory, every scientific discovery, all knowledge, all wisdom, all happiness, all virtue, are held to issue directly from his leadership and inspiration" (Orwell, Nineteen 179).

COMMENTS

1. Paragraph 8 continues the development of point I of the outline (see page 461). Paragraph 9 begins point II of the outline: The bureaucratic propaganda machine. Tracy Monahan draws on Thomson for her discussion in paragraph 9.

BIBLIOGRAPHY CARD FOR THOMSON

Thomson, Oliver. <u>Mass Persuasion in History: An Historical Analysis of the Development of Propaganda Techniques</u>. New York: Crane, 1977.

NOTE CARD USED FOR PARAGRAPH 9

Bureaucratic propaganda
(Thomson 41)

T. thinks <u>architecture</u> is an important propagandist medium that people don't pay much attention to.

A building can be "graphic communication." Can inspire awe and power—with long-term impact.

"... the pyramids projected the massive dominance of the Pharaohs."

T. Monahan 5

8   Oceanians are programmed in the art of doublethink, which the novel defines as "the power of holding two contradictory beliefs in one's mind simultaneously, and accepting both of them" (183). The Oceanians, not aware of their loss of human rights, firmly believe that everybody is equal in their society, but they serve their king and accept the State's rigid hierarchy. The pyramidal power structure is the natural order of things in their classless society. Naturally, Big Brother sits on top of the pyramid; he represents the Inner Party, less than two percent of society. Just below him or them is the Outer Party, the bureaucratic toadies, about thirteen percent. At the base of the pyramid are the proles—"the dumb masses" (179)—about eighty-five percent.

9   Big Brother's bureaucracy consists of four ministries. These ministries are housed in huge white buildings, enormous pyramidal structures dominating London, the capital of Airstrip One, a province of Oceania. These towers contrast sharply with the run-down stores and shabby houses of the rest of the city. The very architecture of Big Brother's government buildings is an important propagandistic symbol because it is a "graphic

34e res

COMMENTS

1. The discussion of the bureaucratic propaganda machine continues.
2. In paragraph 10, Tracy Monahan uses the superscript number 1 to refer readers to an endnote that supplies additional information: see page 493.

NOTE CARD

Notice below that Tracy Monahan's own ideas are placed in brackets.

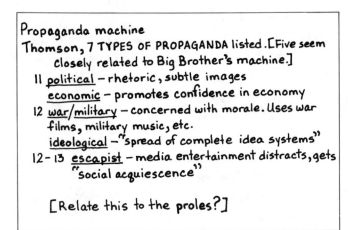

Propaganda machine
Thomson, 7 TYPES OF PROPAGANDA listed.[Five seem
   closely related to Big Brother's machine.]
  11 <u>political</u> — rhetoric, subtle images
    <u>economic</u> — promotes confidence in economy
  12 <u>war/military</u> — concerned with morale. Uses war
    films, military music, etc.
    <u>ideological</u> — "spread of complete idea systems"
  12-13 <u>escapist</u> — media entertainment distracts, gets
    "social acquiescence"

    [Relate this to the proles?]

T. Monahan 6

communication" of awesomeness. Like the great
Egyptian pyramids, they project a political image
of massive, lasting power (Thomson 41).

10   All four ministries are active, interrelated
parts of Big Brother's massive propaganda machine.
For example, they work together when grinding out
materials for Hate Week. Each cog, however, has
its particular job to do. The Ministry of Plenty
(Miniplenty) specializes in economic propaganda;
the Ministry of Peace (Minipax) in the military
type. The Ministry of Love (Miniluv) reinforces or
intensifies ideologic propaganda.[1] Perhaps the
biggest, most responsible cog in the machine,
however, is the Ministry of Truth (Minitrue).
Minitrue--with its slogans WAR IS PEACE, FREEDOM
IS SLAVERY, IGNORANCE IS STRENGTH--not only
produces political images and rhetoric in
accordance with Big Brother's input but also co-
ordinates and edits the propagandistic output of
Miniplenty and Minipax. The huge machine never
stops its propagandizing, and its perpetual,
continuous noise has a mesmerizing effect on the
whole society.

COMMENTS

1. Paragraph 11 turns to point III of the outline (on page 461): The media in a totalitarian world.

2. In paragraph 11, the use of such phrases as "According to Richard S. Lambert" and "Jacques Ellul writes" helps make direct quotations fit smoothly into the text. Notice also how the indented quotations in paragraph 11 are grammatically integrated with the sentence that introduces them. The first quotation provides an object for the preposition *with*; the second, an object for the verb *supplies*.

Read the source, and notice the way Tracy Monahan combines paraphrase with quotation.

SOURCE

Nineteen Eighty-Four (41–42)

> And the Records Department, after all, was itself only a single branch of the Ministry of Truth, whose primary job was not to reconstruct the past but to supply the citizens of Oceania with newspapers, films, textbooks, telescreen programs, plays, novels—with every conceivable kind of information, instruction, or entertainment, from a statue to a slogan, from a lyric poem to a biological treatise, and from a child's spelling book to a Newspeak dictionary. And the Ministry had not only to supply the multifarious needs of the Party, but also to repeat the whole operation at a lower level for the benefit of the proletariat. There was a whole chain of separate departments dealing with proletarian literature, music, drama, and entertainment generally. Here were produced rubbishy newspapers containing almost nothing except sport, crime, and astrology, sensational five-cent novelettes, films oozing with sex, and sentimental songs which were composed entirely by mechanical means on a special kind of kaleidoscope known as a versificator.

11   According to Richard S. Lambert, the internal propaganda of a totalitarian government "seeks to impose complete uniformity of thought, as well as of action, upon its citizens" (138).2 All-wise Big Brother knows this. "Where film production, the press, and radio transmission are not centrally controlled," Jacques Ellul writes, "no propaganda is possible" (102). Big Brother harnesses communication. The Party specialists who run the Ministry of Truth provide Oceanic society with all its

> newspapers, films, textbooks, telescreen
> programs, plays, novels—with every
> conceivable kind of information,
> instruction, or entertainment, from a
> statue to a slogan, from a lyric poem to
> a biological treatise, and from a
> child's spelling book to a Newspeak
> dictionary. (Orwell, Nineteen 41)

The proles have such limited intelligence that Big Brother has to adapt his communication to their level. For their benefit, Minitrue supplies

> rubbishy newspapers containing almost
> nothing except sport, crime, and
> astrology, sensational five-cent

COMMENTS

1. Observe Tracy Monahan's use of repetition as a transitional device in paragraph 12. The introduction to the long quotation ends with ''the Party's ideal,'' and the quotation begins with ''The ideal set up by the Party.''

2. Paragraph 12 discusses point III(B) of the outline: Big Brother's use of the media to propagate the Party's ideal.

T. Monahan 8

> novelettes, films oozing with sex, and
> sensational songs which were composed
> entirely by mechanical means on a
> special kind of kaleidoscope known as a
> versificator. (41–42)

This kind of escapist material, along with the
state lottery and numerous pubs, keeps the minds
of the proles busy with things other than the
impact of power politics on their lives.

12   Big Brother uses the media for mass hypnosis.
He disseminates misinformation that goes unrecog-
nized as propaganda. His propaganda preaches
only one gospel: the Party's ideal.

> The ideal set up by the Party was
> something huge, terrible, and glitter-
> ing—a world of steel and concrete, of
> monstrous machines and terrifying
> weapons—a nation of warriors and
> fanatics, marching forward in perfect
> unity, all thinking the same thoughts
> and shouting the same slogans, perpet-
> ually working, fighting, triumphing,
> persecuting—three hundred million
> people all with the same face. (67)

COMMENT

Paragraphs 13–17 develop point IV of the outline: The falsification of history. Observe the unified flow of Tracy Monahan's ideas as you read these paragraphs, paying special
attention to the selection and arrangement of the three quotations, the first and third from Orwell, the second from
Zwerdling.

REVISION OF AN EARLIER DRAFT—WITH A PURPOSE

The following revisions in paragraph 13 provide transitions
between ideas. Such transitions not only help the reader but
prevent the impression that quotations have been thrown in
like confetti.

In <u>Nineteen Eighty-Four</u>, the Records Department in

Minitrue controls history. A party slogan declares, "Who controls the past

controls the future: who controls the present

controls the past" (34). Always tampering with

records, Big Brother distorts, re-creates, or

destroys the past. As Zwerdling has noted:

           No matter how intolerable the present

           is, the sense of alternative possibil-

T. Monahan 9

The doublethinkers of Oceania parrot the media's
message.

13   Orwell considered "the disappearance of
objective history and the willingness of
individuals to work toward its elimination" as the
"most frightening propagandistic achievement of
the twentieth century" (Zwerdling 52). In Nineteen
Eighty-Four, the Records Department in Minitrue
controls history. A Party slogan declares, "Who
controls the past controls the future: who
controls the present controls the past" (34).
Always tampering with records, Big Brother
distorts, re-creates, or destroys the past. As
Zwerdling has noted:

> No matter how intolerable the present
> is, the sense of alternative possibili-
> ties that objective history inevitably
> presents can still liberate the imagina-
> tion and perhaps lead to significant
> change. But once the past is perpetually
> "rectified" to conform to the present,
> this escape is no longer possible. (53)

14   Thousands working in the Records Department
look upon such "rectification" as daily routine.

COMMENT

Reread paragraphs 13–17 and carefully observe interrelations, a few of which are indicated by arrows below.

<u>IV</u>. The falsification of history

¶13   a reference to propagandistic achievement◄

Orwell: Two things are frightening: ◄

(1) the disappearance of history
(2) the willingness of people
to eliminate history

Zwerdling: A "rectified" past makes escape
from present impossible.

14   a transitional paragraph echoing Zwerdling
and referring to "rectification" as routine
in the Records Department

15   One example of "rectification":

Winston makes history disappear––a
routine part of his job.

16   Another example:

Many individuals work to eliminate
history––a constant chore.

17   a reference to totalitarian propaganda◄

Winston thinks that wiping out the past is
"more terrifying than torture and death." ◄

T. Monahan 10

This department falsifies the past to make it fit
changes in present government policies.

15   False promises must be changed to suit present conditions. A clerk at the Speakwrite machine,
Winston Smith "rectifies" materials sent to him
through a pneumatic tube. Proficient in Newspeak
(the official language), he reads a message:
"times 14. 2. 84 miniplenty malquoted chocolate
rectify" (Orwell, <u>Nineteen</u> 37). Winston dials on
the telescreen for the copy of the <u>Times</u> (February
14, 1984) that carries Miniplenty's promise not to
reduce the chocolate ration in 1984. He changes
the optimistic promise to a pessimistic prediction: rationing may be necessary in April. He
returns the altered version for filing and destroys
the original by putting it into the memory hole, a
kind of incinerator for irrelevant history.

16   The history of Oceania's wars must also be
"rectified" regularly. It is the State's policy to
be in a constant state of war either with Eurasia
or with Eastasia. Yet the Party insists that the
present enemy has always been the enemy. When
roles are reversed, the former enemy has never
been an enemy but always an ally. Record clerks

COMMENT

"As might be expected" (in paragraph 18) provides the transition from point IV to point V. Paragraph 18 covers point V(A): Newspeak as a thought preventive.

NOTE CARDS FOR PARAGRAPH 18

Newspeak   ②

Steinhoff 166: "Newspeak is the principal intellectual means by which doublethink is transformed into
a conditioned reflex."

Newspeak – doublethink   ③

Zwerdling 54: from a discussion of schizophrenic
thinking in 1984: "an occupational disease of propagandists that is called 'reality control' or 'doublethink.'"

Newspeak   ①
In 1984 – 51 AND the appendix – aim, nature, etc.

Newspeak words – compounding, adding prefixes and
suffixes
    bellyfeel, prolefeed, Minitrue, Pornosec,
    facecrime, sexcrime, crimestop, thought-
    crime – ungood, doubleplusgood, goodwise,
    gooder – duckspeaking

A duckspeaker, a fast talker in love with own
voice, keeps quacking on and on.

T. Monahan 11

work frantically to make expedient changes in
mountains of references to Eurasia and Eastasia.

17   Eventually, Winston's experiences teach him
to recognize totalitarian propaganda for what it
is. Very disturbed by the systematic attack on the
past, he thinks: "If the Party could thrust its
hand into the past and say of this or that event,
it never happened—that, surely, was more
terrifying than torture and death" (34).

18   As might be expected, Big Brother manipulates
language to suit his purpose. His aim is to
destroy words—the material for expressing ideas—
and to eventually wipe out completely the
necessity for thought. "The Inner Party's greatest
achievement in Nineteen Eighty-Four is the
creation of a new language, Newspeak, designed
actually to restrict the range of meaning and
nuance" (Lewis and Moss 50). The words in Newspeak
are formed in various ways: for example, by
compounding (thought-crime, duckspeak, prolefeed,
Minipax) and by adding prefixes or suffixes
(ungood, thinkful). Doubleplusgood gets rid of
superlatives like best or finest and synonyms like
superb or excellent. According to William
Steinhoff, Newspeak is "the principal intellectual

COMMENT

Three paragraphs (19 through 21) develop one subheading of point V of the outline: rousing the emotions.

means by which doublethink is transformed into a conditioned reflex" (166). Doublethink is Big Brother's "reality control" (indeed "the occupational disease of propagandists") (Zwerdling 54). Working in the Research Department as a compiler of the Newspeak dictionary, a clerk remarks that, unlike Oldspeak, the new language has a vocabulary that grows smaller, not larger. He says, "We're destroying words—scores of them, hundreds of them every day. . . . It's a beautiful thing, the destruction of words" (Orwell, <u>Nineteen</u> 48).

19   Big Brother's propaganda not only straitjackets thought but also manipulates emotions. Doublethinking Oceanians know that unqualified hatred of the State's enemies is a social necessity in their kingdom of love—love for Big Brother. Though living in a police state and (except for proles) under constant surveillance by Thought Police and Junior Spies, <u>loyal</u> citizens have nothing to fear, for they love their Leader and hate his enemies.

20   Those who love their leader, however, must have no room in their hearts for anyone else. When affection for others rises spontaneously, that love is considered subversive, something to be

COMMENTS

1. Note the acknowledgment of sources of ideas that are expressed in paraphrases (rather than in the exact words of the author).
2. The main discussion ends with paragraph 21. The conclusion begins with paragraph 22.

SOURCES

Below are two statements by Irving Howe that are paraphrased in paragraphs 20 and 21. Note the differences between the paraphrases and the originals.

> Oceania seeks to blot out spontaneous affection because it assumes, for good reason, that whatever is uncalculated is subversive. —IRVING HOWE

> For the faithful [in Oceania], sexual energy is transformed into political hysteria. —IRVING HOWE

T. Monahan 13

eliminated (Howe 48). Love and eroticism are both
at odds with state policy whether marriage is
involved or not; in fact, the Party denies
permission to marry to anyone who indicates any
kind of physical attraction to a partner. Clearly,
"the only recognized purpose of marriage was to
beget children for the service of the Party.
Sexual intercourse was to be looked on as a
slightly disgusting minor operation, like having
an enema. . . . The sexual act, successfully
performed, was rebellion. Desire was thought-
crime" (Orwell, Nineteen 60-61). Winston's desire
for an affair with Julia is therefore a capital
offence; the state must purify his heart in
Miniluv's torture chambers.

21   Big Brother wisely turns the sex drive into
"political hysteria" (Howe 49). The fanatical
Oceanians stand ready to strike terror into the
hearts of any enemies. To stimulate hatred, Big
Brother not only sets up a mythical Adversary but
also uses such propaganda techniques as exciting
rituals, stirring military music, barbaric
rhythms, noisy rallies, slogan-chanting mobs,
rabble-rousing war films, staged hangings. The
daily Two Minute Hate and the Hate Week intensify

COMMENT

Reread the first four paragraphs of the paper, paying particular attention to paragraph 4. Notice the words and ideas that are repeated in paragraph 22. References to the title of Orwell's novel and to the nature of totalitarian propaganda are two examples of repetition. Linking the ideas in the introduction and those in the conclusion contributes to the unity of the paper.

the mood. Like many another propagandist, Big
Brother knows the unifying value of hate.

22   In <u>Nineteen Eighty-Four</u>, Orwell uses artistic
exaggeration to help make his warning clear.[3] The
reader can easily recognize Big Brother's
propaganda for what it is—an obvious mixture of
absurd lies and gross distortions of truth. But
today's political propaganda is not always so
easily recognized. Indeed, propaganda in one form
or another is now pervasive in our society.

        In recent decades, nearly every
        significant government, political party,
        special-interest group, social movement,
        and big business firm . . . has develop-
        ed its own corps of specialized research-
        ers, propagandists, or "opinion managers"
        (sometimes referred to as information
        specialists, lobbyists, legislative
        representatives, or vice-presidents in
        charge of public relations). Some have
        become members of parliaments, cabinets
        and corporate boards of directors. The
        most expert among them sometimes are
        highly skilled or trained, or both, in

COMMENTS

1. A page reference is not required for an encyclopedia article—as shown in the Smith and the Cantril and Hart citations.
2. Note the use of the source (a book review) for the first sentence of paragraph 23.

SOURCE

> Orwell was never very clear about what sort of political system might work, nor was he particularly sophisticated about the peculiarities of *any* political organization. But he knew what he didn't like, and he knew why; the two short novels that emerged from his metamorphosis—*Animal Farm* and *1984*—are probably the most widely read literary/political polemics ever written in English.   —ATLANTIC MONTHLY

history, psychiatry, politics, social
psychology, survey research, and statistical inference. (Smith)

By cleverly manipulating carefully selected facts,
propagandists either ignore or play down any
evidence that might effectively refute their one-
sided arguments--the old card-stacking trick
(Cantril and Hart). Such propaganda, like Big
Brother's, eulogizes the Leaders, hiding their
mistakes and magnifying their success (Lang 43).

23   Orwell's Animal Farm and Nineteen Eighty-Four
"are probably the most widely read literary/
political polemics ever written in English"
(Transformation 126). Of the two novels, perhaps
Nineteen Eighty-Four is more likely to be
remembered. It is a nightmare that haunts the
memory because its world looks much like our own
Orwell felt that the outlook for the twentieth
century was bleak, "and yet he felt that view did
not exonerate one from action, and writing
Nineteen Eighty-Four as a warning was for him the
one appropriate action he could take" (Woodcock
183). If we take Orwell's warning seriously,
Nineteen Eighty-Four will never become reality.

COMMENT

Three endnotes provide supplementary information that is not directly related to the thesis but that might be of interest to readers.

Notes

[1]For a description of seven types of propaganda, see Thomson (11–13).

[2]Lambert also points out that the totalitarian state is more concerned with internal propaganda than with external: "But great as have been the external propagandist efforts of the dictator-ruled countries, they are half-hearted and indirect as compared with their internal organization" (138).

[3]Orwell also warns us about "veiled censorship" in a free press. See "The Freedom of the Press."

COMMENTS

1. All (and only) works cited as sources in the paper should be included in the list of works cited.

2. Alphabetization: Initial articles (*A, An, The*) are ignored in alphabetizing. For example, Orwell's *The Collected Essays* precedes *Nineteen Eighty-Four* (*C* before *N*).

3. Punctuation: Observe the use and placement of periods and commas, especially in relation to parentheses and quotation marks. A colon separates a title from a subtitle and the place of publication from the publisher's name. A colon precedes page numbers of articles from periodicals.

4. For Cantril and Hart, an encyclopedia article, page numbers are not required.

5. Notice that a book title within an underlined (italicized) book title is *not* underlined (see, for example, the Chilton and Aubrey entry). Compare the treatment of a book title within an article or essay title enclosed in quotation marks (see, for example, the Gray entry).

6. Published conference proceedings in which no author or volume editor is identified are cited by title (see the *George Orwell and Nineteen Eighty-Four* entry). For additional information on citing conference and symposium proceedings, see the sample bibliographical entries on pages 450–51.

7. Titles with authors who have identical surnames are entered in alphabetical order according to the first names of first authors (in the two entries under Gray, for example, *Paul* comes before *W. Russel*).

T. Monahan 17

Works Cited

Cantril, Hadley, and Clyde W. Hart. "Propaganda."
World Book Encyclopedia. 1975 ed.

Chilton, Paul, and Crispin Aubrey. Nineteen Eighty-
Four in 1984: Autonomy, Control and
Communication. London: Comedia, 1983.

Colmer, John. Coleridge to Catch-22: Images of
Society. New York: St. Martin's, 1978.

Ellul, Jacques. Propaganda: The Formation of Men's
Attitudes. Trans. Konrad Kellen and Jean
Lerner. New York: Knopf, 1965.

George Orwell and Nineteen Eighty-Four: The Man and
the Book. Preface by John C. Broderick. A
Conference at the Library of Congress, 30
Apr.-1 May, 1984. Washington: Library of
Congress, 1985.

Gray, Paul, Anne Hopkins, and John Saar. "That Year
Is Almost Here." Time 28 Nov. 1983: 42-48.

Gray, W. Russel. "Nineteen Eighty-Four and the
Massaging of the Media." George Orwell. Ed.
Courtenay Wemyss and Alexej Ugrinsky.
Contributions to the Study of World Literature
23. New York: Greenwood, 1987. 111-117.

COMMENTS

1. For a non-literary work in an anthology (see the Howe entry) give the original publication data for the essay followed by ''Rpt. in'' and the publication data for the anthology.

2. Annotation: If you are asked to submit an annotated bibliography, supply a brief description of each entry, as in this example:

Bolton, W.J. <u>The Language of</u> 1984. Oxford:

    Blackwell, 1984.

    W.J. Bolton, the distinguished English

    scholar, discusses the theories Orwell

    developed about language and the practices he

    employed, based on the entire canon of his

    work (not just <u>Nineteen Eighty-Four</u>). Bolton

    also traces the changes in the English

    language that have occurred in the years since

    Orwell's death in 1950. The author's discus-

    sion of "language machines" (computers) is

    particularly interesting in light of Orwell's

    view that technology inevitably has a negative

    effect on writing.

3. Note that the entry for Orwell's *Collected Essays* provides two publishers for the same date. The editions were published simultaneously (and they employ identical pagination throughout).

T. Monahan 18

Howe, Irving. "1984: History as Nightmare."
Politics and the Novel. New York: Horizon,
1957. 235–51. Rpt. in Twentieth Century
Interpretations of 1984: A Collection of
Critical Essays. Ed. Samuel Hynes. Englewood
Cliffs: Prentice, 1971. 41–58.

Lambert, Richard S. Propaganda. Discussion Books
13. London: Nelson, 1938.

Lang, John S. "The Great American Bureaucratic
Propaganda Machine." U.S. News and World
Report 27 Aug. 1979: 43–47.

Lewis, Florence, and Peter Moss. "The Tyranny of
Language." Nineteen Eighty-Four in 1984:
Autonomy, Control and Communication. Ed. Paul
Chilton and Crispin Aubrey. London: Comedia,
1983. 45–57.

Orwell, George. The Collected Essays, Journalism
and Letters of George Orwell. Ed. Sonia Orwell
and Ian Angus. 4 vols. London: Secker and
Warburg; New York: Harcourt, 1968.

———. "The Freedom of the Press." New York Times
Magazine 8 Oct. 1972: 12.

COMMENTS

1. Tracy Monahan cites the commonly available paperback edition of *Nineteen Eighty-Four*, but also provides the original publication data since she makes reference to the book's publishing history in her introduction.

2. The citation for the article from *Encyclopaedia Britannica* by Smith indicates, through the use of square brackets, that the article is signed with initials only. Tracy Monahan has checked the index of contributors to find the name of the writer.

3. Note that the anonymous, untitled review of Stansky and Abraham's book *The Transformation* (cited in paragraph 23 of Tracy Monahan's paper) is alphabetized by the title of the work reviewed: *Transformation*. (The designation *Rev. of* and the article *The* are ignored for purposes of alphabetizing.)

T. Monahan 19

——— Nineteen Eighty—Four. London: Secker and
     Warburg, 1949. Harmondsworth, Middlesex:
     Penguin, 1984.

Ranald, Ralph A. "George Orwell and the Mad World:
     The Anti—Universe of 1984." South Atlantic
     Quarterly 66 (1967): 544—53.

S[mith], B[ruce] L[annes]. "Propaganda." Encyclo-
     paedia Britannica: Macropaedia. 1985 ed.

Steinhoff, William. George Orwell and the Origins
     of 1984. Ann Arbor: U of Michigan P, 1975.

Thomson, Oliver. Mass Persuasion in History: An
     Historical Analysis of the Development of
     Propaganda Techniques. New York: Crane, 1977.

Rev. of The Transformation, by Peter Stansky and
     William Abrahams. Atlantic Monthly Apr. 1980:
     126—27.

Voorhees, Richard J. The Paradox of George Orwell.
     Humanities Series. Lafayette: Purdue U
     Studies, 1961.

Woodcock, George. Orwell's Message: 1984 and the
     Present. Madeira Park, BC: Harbour, 1984.

Zwerdling, Alex. Orwell and the Left. New Haven:
     Yale UP, 1974.

Note: If your instructor will accept a handwritten rather than typewritten paper, you may find the following sample page helpful.

9

"Where film production, the press, and radio transmission are not centrally controlled," writes Jacques Ellul, "no propaganda is possible" (102). Knowing this, Big Brother holds tight reins on the Party specialists who run the Ministry of Truth. Minitrue provides Oceania with all its

> newspapers, films, textbooks, telescreen programs, plays, novels — with every conceivable kind of information, instruction, or entertainment, from a statue to a slogan, from a lyric poem to a biological treatise, and from a child's spelling book to a Newspeak dictionary. (Orwell, <u>Nineteen</u> 41)

Those outside the Party have such limited intelligence that Big Brother has to adapt his communication to their level. For their benefit, Minitrue supplies

> rubbishy newspapers containing al—

Note: If your instructor prefers that you include a title page, here is a model you can follow (unless a different style is specified).

```
                    Big Brother's Propaganda

                         Tracy Monahan

                        English 131.03

                         Mr. Richards

                        March 12, 1988
```

Endnote (or Footnote) Style

As you consult sources, you will notice that many of them use footnotes or endnotes rather than parenthetical citations in the text. Some instructors prefer this system. Footnotes and endnotes are identical except for their location: footnotes appear at the foot of the relevant page, while endnotes appear together at the end of the paper. Either way, reference to the notes is by consecutive superscript numbers at the appropriate points throughout the text of the paper.

The first page of Tracy Monahan's paper (see page 463) is shown on page 503 as it would appear with superscript references rather than parenthetical ones. Endnotes corresponding to all of Monahan's parenthetical citations are presented in sequence on pages 504–507. (Notice that the discursive notes on page 493 are integrated, in consecutive order, with the endnotes.) The style followed in these sample notes is one of several currently deemed acceptable—see page 508.

In research papers that use footnotes or endnotes instead of parenthetical citations, a list of works cited (more commonly referred to in such cases as a *bibliography*) is usually, but not always, required. Check with your instructor.

1

Tracy Monahan
English 131.03
Mr. Richards
March 12, 1988

Big Brother's Propaganda

1 George Orwell's <u>Nineteen Eighty-Four</u>, an
extraordinary mix of fantasy, naturalism, romance,
and above all, "bitter satire on certain existing
political systems and implied satire on others,"[1]
has enjoyed an enormous audience. As the year 1984
approached, the public and academics alike showed
a remarkable interest in the novel. The public's
interest was reflected in sales. In the thirty-
five years following its publication, tens of
millions had read it, in sixty-two languages.[2] As
the book went into its sixty-sixth printing at the
beginning of 1984, paperback sales averaged 62 000
copies per month.[3]

2 The academics' interest was reflected in many
"get-ready-for-1984" activities. In 1983, books
discussing Orwell's relevance in 1984 and the
novel's history and impact were beginning to
appear,[4] and conferences were being planned. In
fact, there were so many that Library of Congress

T. Monahan 16

Notes

[1]George Woodcock, <u>Orwell's Message:</u> 1984 <u>and the Present</u> (Madeira Park, BC: Harbour, 1984), p. 19.

[2]Paul Gray, Anne Hopkins, and John Saar, "That Year Is Almost Here," <u>Time</u> 28 Nov. 1983, p. 46.

[3]W. Russel Gray, "<u>Nineteen Eighty-Four</u> and the Massaging of the Media," in <u>George Orwell</u>, ed. Courtenay Wemyss and Alexej Ugrinsky, Contributions to the Study of World Literature 23 (New York: Greenwood, 1987), p. 111.

[4]Paul Chilton and Crispin Aubrey, Nineteen Eighty-Four <u>in 1984: Autonomy, Control and Communication</u> (London: Comedia, 1983).

[5]John C. Broderick, preface, <u>George Orwell and</u> Nineteen Eighty-Four: <u>The Man and the Book</u>, a conference at the Library of Congress, 30 Apr.- 1 May, 1984 (Washington: Library of Congress, 1985).

[6]Woodcock, p. 19.

[7]Richard J. Voorhees, <u>The Paradox of George Orwell</u>, Humanities Series (Lafayette: Purdue Univ. Studies, 1961), p. 87.

[8]Printed in <u>My Country Right or Left</u>, Vol. II of <u>The Collected Essays, Journalism and Letters of George Orwell</u>, ed. Sonia Orwell and Ian Angus (London: Secker and Warburg; New York: Harcourt, 1968), p. 41.

[9]John Colmer, <u>Coleridge to</u> Catch–22 (New York: St. Martin's, 1978), p. 183.

[10]"George Orwell and the Mad World: The Anti–Universe of <u>1984</u>," <u>South Atlantic Quarterly</u>, 66 (1967), 544–45.

[11]Oliver Thomson, <u>Mass Persuasion in History</u> (New York: Crane, 1977), p. 132.

[12]George Orwell, <u>Nineteen Eighty–Four</u> (Hammondsworth, Middlesex: Penguin, 1984), p. 179. Subsequent page references in the text are to this edition.

[13]Thomson, <u>Mass Persuasion</u>, p. 41.

[14]For a description of seven types of propaganda, see Thomson, pp. 11–13.

[15]<u>Propaganda</u>, Discussion Books, No. 13 (London: Thomas Nelson, 1938), p. 138. Lambert also points out that the totalitarian state is more concerned with internal propaganda than with

external: "But great as have been the <u>external</u>
propagandist efforts of the dictator-ruled
countries, they are half-hearted and indirect
as compared with their <u>internal</u> organization"
(p. 138).

[16]<u>Propaganda</u>, trans. Konrad Kellen and Jean
Lerner (New York: Knopf, 1965), p. 102.

[17]Alex Zwerdling, <u>Orwell and the Left</u> (New
Haven: Yale Univ. Press, 1974), p. 52.

[18]Zwerdling, p. 53.

[19]Florence Lewis and Peter Moss, "The Tyranny
of Language," in Nineteen Eighty-Four <u>in 1984:
Autonomy, Control and Communication</u>, ed. Paul
Chilton and Crispin Aubrey (London: Comedia, 1983),
p. 50.

[20]William Steinhoff, <u>George Orwell and the
Origins of</u> 1984 (Ann Arbor: Univ. of Michigan
Press, 1975), p. 166.

[21]Zwerdling, p. 54.

[22]Irving Howe, "<u>1984</u>: History as Nightmare,"
in <u>Twentieth Century Interpretations of</u> 1984, ed.
Samuel Hynes (Englewood Cliffs: Prentice-Hall,
1971), p. 48.

T. Monahan 19

[23]Howe, p. 49.

[24]Orwell also warns us about "veiled censorship" in a free press. See "The Freedom of the Press," New York Times Magazine, 8 Oct. 1972, p. 12.

[25]B[ruce] L[annes] S[mith], "Propaganda," Encyclopaedia Britannica: Macropaedia, 1985 ed.

[26]Hadley Cantril and Clyde W. Hart, "Propaganda," World Book Encyclopedia, 1975 ed., XV, 727.

[27]John S. Lang, "The Great American Bureaucratic Propaganda Machine," U.S. News and World Report, 27 Aug. 1979, p. 43.

[28]Rev. of The Transformation, by Peter Stansky and William Abrahams, Atlantic Monthly, April 1980, pp. 126–27.

[29]Woodcock, p. 183.

Varying Styles of Documentation

Each department of a college or university ordinarily suggests a particular style for bibliographies and citations. Use the style your instructor specifies. Instructors in the sciences, business, economics, and so forth may recommend a documentation form in one of the style books listed below. If you are asked to use one of these manuals, study it carefully, and make sure your bibliography and notes correspond exactly to the examples it provides. Following the list are a few examples from the style of the American Psychological Association (APA), commonly used in the social and behavioural sciences.

Style books and manuals

American Institute of Physics. Publications Board. *Style Manual for Guidance in the Preparation of Papers*. 3rd ed. New York: American Inst. of Physics, 1978.

American Chemical Society. *American Chemical Society Style Guide and Handbook*. Washington: American Chemical Soc., 1985.

American Mathematical Society. *A Manual for Authors of Mathematical Papers*. 8th ed. Providence: American Mathematical Soc., 1984.

American Psychological Association. *Publication Manual of the American Psychological Association*. 3rd ed. Washington: American Psychological Assn., 1983.

Associated Press. *The Associated Press Stylebook and Libel Manual: The Journalist's Bible*. Reading, MA: Addison, 1987.

Canada. Secretary of State. *The Canadian Style: A Guide to Writing and Editing*. Toronto: Dundurn, 1985. (Text in French and English)

The Canadian Press. *Canadian Press Stylebook: A Guide for Writers and Editors*. Toronto: CP, 1983.

The Chicago Manual of Style. 13th ed. Chicago: U of Chicago P, 1982.

Council of Biology Editors. Style Manual Committee. *CBE Style Manual: A Guide for Authors, Editors, and Publishers in the*

Biological Sciences. 5th ed. Bethesda: Council of Biology Editors, 1983.

Harvard Law Review: *A Uniform System of Citation.* 13th ed. Cambridge: Harvard Law Review Assn., 1981.

McGill Law Journal. *Canadian Guide to Uniform Legal Citation.* 2nd ed. Toronto: Carswell, 1988.

Turabian, Kate L. *A Manual for Writers of Term Papers, Theses, and Dissertations.* 5th ed. Chicago: U of Chicago P, 1987.

United States. Government Printing Office. *Style Manual.* Rev. ed. Washington: GPO, 1973.

References in APA style

In APA style, the alphabetical list of works cited is called ''References.'' The reference entries below follow the style of the 1983 edition of the APA *Publication Manual.* Observe all details of indention, spacing, punctuation, and mechanics. (Note that the first line of each entry is flush with the left margin, and subsequent lines are indented three spaces.)

Book—one author

Gazzaniga, M. (1985). The social brain: Discovering the networks of the mind. New York: Basic.

Book—two authors

Klein, D.F., & Wender, P.H. (1981). Mind, mood, and medicine: A guide to the new biological psychiatry. New York: Farrar, Straus & Giroux.

Journal—one author

Jaffe, A. (1988). Saluting in social context. Journal of Applied Behavioral Science, 24, 263–276.

Journal—multiple authors

```
Jackson, J.M., Buglione, S.A., & Glenwick, D.S.

    (1988). Major league baseball performance as a

    function of being traded. Personality and Social

    Psychology Bulletin, 14, 46–56.
```

If you use more than one work by the same author, list the works in order of publication date, earliest first. Repeat the author's name for each entry.

```
Gould, S.J. (1985). The flamingo's smile: Reflec-

    tions in natural history. New York: Norton.

Gould, S.J. (1987). Time's arrow, time's cycle:

    Myth and metaphor in the discovery of geological

    time. Cambridge: Harvard UP.
```

Citations in APA style

The basic elements of an APA citation are the author's last name, the year of publication, and the page number if the reference is to a specific passage in the source. If the author's name is mentioned in the text of the paper, the date alone or the date and the page number are given within the parentheses. In the following examples, note the details of punctuation and the treatment of the page number.

Short quotation

```
One writer has stated, "How the brain stores

information and through what kind of logical

structure it retrieves information is about as
```

exciting an intellectual question as you can get"
(Gazzaniga, 1985, p. 100), an observation with
which the leading researchers on split-brain theory
agree.

Long quotation (four lines or more)

Gazzaniga (1985) has stated the following:

>Amnesia is not only the stuff of popular
>suspense novels. It is a clinical state that
>has been carefully studied for decades by a
>host of talented neuropsychologists. How the
>brain stores information and through what kind
>of logical structure it retrieves information
>is about as exciting an intellectual question
>as you can get. (p. 100)

Paraphrase

Gazzaniga (1985) has pointed to the fascination of
neuropsychologists with the clinical state of
amnesia: they believe that amnesia patients may
provide valuable clues to the brain's system for
storing and retrieving information. (p. 100)

Notice that an APA citation never uses the title. The reader
can easily find the title, however, by checking the references
to find the entry with the same author and date.

Business Writing

35

Write effective letters and résumés, memos, and reports.

Business writing is practical writing—a clear sense of audience and purpose and careful attention to correctness and the conventions of usage are rewarded very directly and tangibly. Whether it is a letter, memo, résumé, or formal report, a piece of business writing generally combines the informative and persuasive aims (see **33a**): it gives necessary information and at the same time is designed to win a favourable response from the reader. Additionally, such documents often become important records for the company or other organization concerned—sometimes with legal implications—and for this reason, too, should be objective, clear, and concise.

35a
Write effective letters and résumés; use an acceptable format.

A knowledge of how to write business letters, application letters, and résumés can be useful to you not only in job-related situations, but in your college and personal life as well. The three main formats for business letters—full block, modified block, and indented—can be used for any kind of business letter.

(1) Use an acceptable business letter format.

Business letters are usually typed on only one side of white, unlined, 21.6 cm × 27.9 cm (8½ × 11 inch) paper. Standard business envelopes measure about 9 cm × 16.5 cm (3½ × 6½ inches) or 10.15 cm × 25.5 cm (4 × 10 inches). Letterhead stationery and envelopes vary in both size and colour.

Check to see if your company or organization has a policy about letter format. Most companies use either full block, modified block, or indented formats for regular correspondence, though an indented format is often used for personal business correspondence such as thank-you notes, congratulations, and the like.

A business letter has six parts: (1) heading, (2) inside address, (3) salutation, (4) body, (5) closing, which consists of the complimentary close and signature, and (6) added notations.

The *heading* gives the writer's full address and the date. If letterhead stationery is used, the date is typed beneath the head, flush left, flush right, or centred, depending on your format. If plain stationery is used, the address of the writer followed by the date is placed toward the top of the page— the distance from the top arranged so that the body of the letter will be attractively centred on the page—flush with the left- or right-hand margin, as in the letters on pages 519 and 524. Notice that the heading has no end punctuation.

The *inside address*, typed two to six lines below the heading, gives the name and full address of the recipient.

The *salutation* (or greeting) is written flush with the left margin, two spaces below the inside address, and is followed by a colon (a comma is used after salutations in French).

When the surname of the addressee is known, it is used in the salutation of a business letter, as in the following examples.

Dear Dr. Davis:	Dear Mayor Rodriguez:
Dear Mrs. Greissman:	Dear Ms. Joseph:
Chère Mlle Desrosiers,	Chère Mme Gagnon,
Cher M. Paré,	Cher M. Roy,

Note: Use *Miss* or *Mrs.* if the woman you are addressing has indicated a preference. Otherwise, use *Ms.*, which is always appropriate and which is preferred by many businesswomen, whatever their marital status.

In letters to organizations, or to persons whose name and sex are unknown, such salutations as the following are customary:

Dear Sir or Madam:	Dear Tilley Endurables:
Dear Subscription Manager:	Dear Registrar:

For the appropriate forms of salutations and addresses in letters to government officials, military personnel, and so on, check an etiquette book or the front or back of your college dictionary.

The *body* of the letter should follow the principles of good writing. Typewritten letters are usually single-spaced, with double spacing between paragraphs. The first sentence of each paragraph should begin flush with the left margin (in full block or modified block) or should be indented five to ten spaces (in indented format). The subject matter should be organized so that the reader can grasp immediately what is wanted, and the style should be clear and direct. Do not use stilted or abbreviated phrasing:

NOT	The aforementioned letter
BUT	Your letter
NOT	Please send it to me ASAP.
BUT	Please send it to me as soon as possible.

The *closing* is typed flush with the left-hand margin in full-block style. In modified block and indented style, it is typed to the right of the letter, in alignment with the heading. Here are the parts of the closing:

Complimentary close: This conventional ending is typed, after a double space, below the last paragraph of the body of the letter. Among the endings commonly used in business letters are the following:

FORMAL	LESS FORMAL
Very truly yours,	Sincerely,
Sincerely yours,	Cordially,

Typed name: The writer's full name is typed three or four lines below the closing. A woman may choose to indicate her marital status or preferred title in parentheses:

Sylvia Tanazaki   (Ms.) Eloise Browne

(Mrs. Hiro Tanazaki)

Title of sender: This line, following the typed name, indicates the sender's position, if he or she is acting in an official capacity.

Manager, Employee Relations
Chairperson, Search Committee

Signature: The letter is signed between the complimentary close and the typed name.

Notations are typed below the closing, flush with the left margin. They indicate, among other things, whether anything is enclosed with or attached to the letter (*enclosure* or *enc.*, *attachment* or *att.*); to whom copies of the letter have been sent (*cc: AAW, PTN*); and the initials of the sender and the typist (*DM/cll*).

MODEL BUSINESS LETTER

QUEEN CITY REGIONAL HEALTH SERVICES

1502 Regent Street   Regina, Saskatchewan S4N 1R9

March 2, 1989

Dr. Nathan Boyko
Community Health Centre   } **INSIDE ADDRESS**
433 Cheadle Street West
Swift Current, SK
S9H 0B1

Dear Dr. Boyko: **SALUTATION**

We have completed our study of the nutrition
education program being conducted by the Community
Health Centre. The findings are encouraging.
However, we believe that awareness training for
the staff, a few schedule changes, and greater
involvement of the parents could significantly   } **BODY**
improve the program.

Our final report, available by March 30, will
explain these recommendations more fully. Rachel
Walsh, our Chief Consultant, will be happy to work
with you if you would like her assistance.

We look forward to hearing from you soon.

Sincerely,   **Complimentary close**

Dorothy Muir   **Signature**   } **CLOSING**

Dorothy Muir   **Typed name**
Director   **Title**

DM/ewl   **NOTATION**

BUSINESS ENVELOPES

The address that appears on the envelope is identical to the inside address, with one exception: while the traditional abbreviations for provinces or states are still often used in the inside address, the modern two-letter postal abbreviations (*not* followed by a period) should always be used on the envelope. The traditional and the current postal abbreviations for the provinces are as follows:

Alta.	B.C.	Man.	N.B.	Nfld.	N.S.	Ont.	P.E.I.	Que.	Sask.
AB	BC	MB	NB	NF	NS	ON	PE	PQ	SK

The return address regularly gives the full name and address of the writer, including the postal code (or U.S. zip code).

MODEL ADDRESSED ENVELOPE

```
Lisa Henderson
2002 rue St Hubert
Montréal, PQ
H2L 3Z5


                    Mr. Adam Troikos
                    Personnel Manager
                    Echo Electronics
                    1726 Macdonald Street
                    Vancouver, BC
                    V6K 1M5
```

Note that the postal code should appear on a separate line for scanning.

(2) Write effective application letters and résumés.

Application letters and résumés are essential parts of applying for a job. In both, your main concern is to emphasize
your strong points, to present yourself in the best light so
that a prospective employer will grant you an interview.
Usually written to draw the reader's attention to the résumé,
the letter of application should indicate the job you want and
state your qualifications briefly. In the last paragraph you
should indicate when you are available for an interview. The
résumé (pages 521–22) that accompanies the letter of application gives more information about you than your letter
can. Ordinarily, your letter should be no longer than one
typed page, and your résumé should not exceed two pages.

A résumé is a list of a person's qualifications for a job
and is enclosed with a letter of application. It is made up of
four basic categories of information:

1. Personal data: name, mailing address, telephone
   number
2. Educational background
3. Work experience
4. References

If appropriate or requested, information concerning awards,
honours, personal achievements, or extracurricular activities
related to the position may also be included.

Make your résumé look professional. Like the letter of
application, the résumé is a form of persuasion designed to
emphasize your qualifications for a job and to get you an
interview. Since there is usually more than one applicant
for every job, your résumé should make the most of your
qualifications. Consider devising a résumé especially tailored to each job you apply for so you can present your
qualifications in the strongest light. After reading all the
letters and résumés received, a potential employer usually
decides to interview only the best-qualified candidates.

APPLICATION LETTER

2002 rue St Hubert
Montréal, PQ
H2L 3Z5
April 3, 1989

Mr. Adam Troikos
Personnel Manager
Echo Electronics
1726 Macdonald Street
Vancouver, BC
V6K 1M5

Dear Mr. Troikos:

Please consider me for the position of Assistant Director of Employee Benefits in the Personnel Division of Echo Electronics.

As you can see from my résumé, my major was Business Administration with an emphasis in personnel management. Whenever possible, I have found jobs and campus activities that would give me experience in dealing with people. As an assistant at UBC's Gage Towers Conference Services, I dealt with visitors to campus, made conference arrangements, and co-ordinated tours. The position required good organizational skills, as well as an understanding of people.

As an administrative intern with Echo last summer, I learned a great deal about the management of a company. Through first-hand experience, I was able to gain a firmer grasp of the contribution that personnel management makes to the overall objectives of the company.

I would very much like to put my interests and my training to work for Echo Electronics, and I am available for an interview at your convenience.

Sincerely,

Lisa Henderson

Lisa Henderson

enc.

Writing a résumé requires the same planning and attention to detail that writing a paper does. First, make a list of the jobs you have had, the activities and clubs you have been part of, and the offices you have held. Amplify these items by adding dates, job titles and responsibilities, and a brief statement about what you learned from each of them. Arrange these items with the most recent first. Activities that may not seem relevant to the job you want can often be explained to show that you learned important things from them. The résumé on pages 521–22 illustrates the following tips on résumé writing.

TIPS ON RÉSUMÉ WRITING

1. Don't forget to include your name, address, and telephone number; unless relevant to the job, personal data such as age and marital status are better left out.
2. Mention your degree, college or university, and pertinent areas of special training.
3. Think about career goals but generally reserve mention of them for the application letter or interview (and even then make sure they enhance your appeal as a candidate). Your interest should be to match your qualifications to the employer's goals.
4. Even if an advertisement asks you to state a salary requirement, any mention of salary should usually be deferred until the interview.
5. Whenever possible, make evident any relationship between the jobs you have had and the job you are seeking.
6. Use an acceptable format and make sure the résumé is neat, orderly, and correct to show that you are an efficient, well-organized, thoughtful person.

RÉSUMÉ

RÉSUMÉ

LISA HENDERSON
2002 rue St Hubert
Montréal, Québec
H2L 3Z5
(514) 845-8328

EDUCATION
Administration, Bachelor of Arts, Concordia University, (May 1989); major in administrative management; minor in personnel management; additional course work in corporate economy and in entrepreneurship and small business management.

Arts One Programme, University of British Columbia, 1983-84

RELATED EXPERIENCE

Summers 1988
Intern, Echo Electronics. Learned about pension plans, health-care benefits, employee associations, and work regulations as they affect employee relations and personnel management.

1987
Conference Assistant, Gage Towers, UBC. Assisted campus visitors and conference delegates. Co-ordinated local tours, travel arrangements, and shuttle service to the airport. Also served as translator for Francophone visitors.

1985-1986
Orientation Leader, Student Counselling Office, Concordia University. Met with prospective students and their parents; conducted tours of campus; answered questions; wrote reports for each orientation meeting.

1984	<u>Volunteer Worker</u>, Crane Library for the Blind, UBC. Preparation of taped materials for the Crane Library. Provided assistance and orientation for visually impaired students arriving in the summer.
HONOURS	Copely—Starr Bursary (Administrative), 1988. TELEBANK Business Writing Prize, 1987.
LANGUAGES	English, Swedish, and conversational French.
REFERENCES	Gage Towers Conference Services University of British Columbia 1875 East Mall, Vancouver, BC V6T 1W5 (604) 228-3219
	Ms. Jocelyne Lauré Student Counselling Office Concordia University 8812 Sherbrooke Street West Montréal, Québec H4B 1R6 (514) 845-4083

You may find it helpful to consult one of the following books for further information on application letters, résumés, and interviews:

Juvenal L. Angel. *The Complete Resume Book and Job-Getter's Guide*. 3rd ed. New York: Pocket Books, 1989.

Richard N. Bolles. *What Color Is Your Parachute? A Practical Manual for Job-Hunters and Career-Changers*. Rev. ed. Berkeley: Ten Speed Press, 1989.

John J. Komar. *The Job Game*. New York: New Century, 1988.

Michael H. Smith. *The Resumé Writer's Handbook*. Rev. ed. New York: Barnes and Noble, 1987.

University Career Planning Association. *The Résumé*. Rev. ed. Toronto: U of Toronto Career Counselling Service, 1982.

(3) Write effective business letters.

LETTER OF INQUIRY

Essentially a request for information, a letter of inquiry should first explain your reasons for writing—both why you are seeking the information and why you think your reader is the person to supply the information. If you need the information by a certain date, mention that fact in the introduction along with your explanation of why you are writing.

Next, state the questions you need answered. You will be more likely to get a response if your questions are specific and detailed. Finally, since you have asked someone to take time to answer your questions, express appreciation, and, if the answers will help you with some project, offer to share the results. (See the sample letter of inquiry on the following page.) It is courteous to send a stamped, self-addressed envelope with the request (if you are not a potential customer).

If you are asked to respond to an inquiry and you can provide the information, follow the order for your responses that was used for the questions. When appropriate, number your responses the same way the questions were numbered. If you cannot provide the information requested, explain why you cannot help and, if possible, offer to help with future requests.

CLAIM AND ADJUSTMENT LETTER

The more specifically and exactly the claim and adjustment letter describes what is wrong, the easier and quicker it will be to correct the situation. If an airline has lost your suitcase, describe it fully and include the flight number, date, and destination. If an appliance is faulty, identify the brand,

LETTER OF INQUIRY

March 20, 1989

High Flyers Angling Club
275 Malaspina Street
Nanaimo, BC   V6R 2R4

Mr. Mark Blodgett, Secretary
Miramichi Atlantic Salmon Society
1106 Shoreview Road
Chatham, NB   E1N 3V7

Dear Mr. Blodgett:

I understand your society can provide information about streams in northern New Brunswick and adjacent Quebec. I am chairing a committee our local anglers' club has formed to prepare—by July—a booklet listing good fly-fishing locations in your area. Also, many members have questions about the effects of acid rain on the streams and rivers in that area.

We are particularly interested in the answers to two questions:

1. Who gathers information on Atlantic salmon populations in the Restigouche and streams in the area?
2. Has the ongoing study of the Miramichi found any increased acidity?

We will very much appreciate any help you can give us in collecting this information. And, if you are interested, we will be happy to send you a copy of our booklet when it is completed.

Sincerely,

Richard James

Richard James
Chairman, Booklet Committee

RJ/lh

style, model, and serial number. A company will often do exactly what you request, if possible. The more reasonable and courteous your request, the better your chance of getting the adjustment you want.

CLAIM AND ADJUSTMENT LETTER

                                          Box 293
                                          Legal, AB
                                          T0G 1L0
                                          February 11, 1989

Mr. Norman Huckley
Huckley Electronics, Inc.
235 Central Avenue
Edmonton, AB
T0G 1M0

Dear Mr. Huckley:

A week ago today I bought a 19" Supersonic colour television set from you, model number 0300-B, serial number 0137-8112-77. All week the set has worked perfectly, but when I turned it on today, nothing happened. The trouble is not with the electrical outlet, which I checked by plugging in another appliance.

I would like to bring the set in for on-the-spot repair on Saturday, February 18th. I trust you will honour the conditions of sale and either repair it free of charge or replace it with another 19" Supersonic. My telephone number is 689-4140, and you can call me any day from noon to 5:00 p.m.

                          Sincerely,

                          Thomas McNally

                          Thomas McNally

THANK-YOU LETTER

Thank-you letters are written often in private life, and they are also used in business. If a representative of a company has been helpful or done more than you expected, a thank-you letter or note is an appropriate way of showing appreciation. A gift, recommendation, award, or prize should also be acknowledged with a letter of thanks.

Usually, thank-you letters are in the indented style. It is not necessary to include an inside address, and a comma replaces the colon after the salutation. There are some who think thank-you letters should be handwritten, but typewritten ones are equally correct.

THANK-YOU LETTER

                                12 Cardinal Knoll
                                Brantford, ON
                                N3R 6C9

Dear Dean Rutledge:

        Thank you very much for recommending me for
the Young Forester's Bursary. I'm happy to tell you
that I am the recipient of the 1989 bursary. I have
already received a letter from the Awards Office
advising me that the Foresters' Association has
released funds for my second-term fees. I am very
pleased to be so honoured.

                        Sincerely,

                        Norman R. Ahrends

                        Norman R. Ahrends

35b

Write effective memos.

Generally, memos are used for communicating a variety of information within an organization—directives on policy or procedures, requests and responses to requests for information, trip reports and monthly action summaries, and informal reports such as field reports or lab reports. While the length of the memo varies according to its purpose, the basic format is relatively standardized, though companies often have specially printed forms for the first page. Usually, memos identify the person or persons to whom the memo is addressed in the first line, the person who wrote the memo in the second line, and subject of the memo in the third line.

> To: J. Karl Meyer, Managing Editor
> From: Lee Dawson, Project Editor
> Subject: Status Report on Books in Production

If the memo is long, it sometimes begins with a *statement of the purpose*, and then gives a *summary* of the discussion. This summary helps a manager or executive, who may receive thirty or forty or more memos a day, decide which ones to read carefully and which to skim. The *discussion* is the main part of the memo. If it is more than a page long, it may benefit from the use of headings to highlight the main parts. If appropriate, the memo closes with *recommendations* for action to be taken. Clearly state in this part of the memo who is to do what and when it is to be done.

The tone of a memo can be casual, informal, or formal, depending on its purpose and audience. Naturally, a trainee would use a relatively formal tone in a memo addressed to a supervisor, but a more casual tone in one addressed to co-workers. Whatever the tone, the memo should be clear, concise, and correct. Notice the format and the tone of the sample memos. The first is from a member of a marketing group to a member of a sales group. The second was sent by an executive to the people he supervises. In the first memo, the tone is casual; in the second, it is more formal, but not stilted. Both are clear and concise.

MEMO

EASTGATE PHARMACEUTICALS, INC.   **MEMORANDUM**

A SUBSIDIARY OF HALL-CHURCH COMPANY

TO _____ Jack Hammond _____

FROM _____ Sharon Lincoln _____

DATE _____ March 26, 1989 _____

SUBJECT _____ SunSafe _____

Thanks for the comments and ideas on the SunSafe sales display.

We are out of the consumer pamphlets we used with the displays. I can, however, send the pamphlets intended for use in doctors' offices. How many do you need?

I am also exploring, with John Seto of our agency, your suggestion about designing a SunSafe reference card for pharmacists. I like the idea. The timing may be a problem for 1989, but if it is, I'll include the idea in the 1990 plans. I'll keep you posted on my progress. I appreciate your interest and suggestions.

SRL/js

cc: Neil Thomlinson
    District Managers

INTERNAL MEMO

To: All Field Personnel

From: R.W. Morgan
Vice-President, Field Operations

Date: October 7, 1989

Subject: PICCOLO 973 SOFTWARE DIRECTORY

The first issue of the PICCOLO 973 SOFTWARE
DIRECTORY is attached. It lists CP/M-compatible
software products that are on the market now for
people with Z80-based microcomputer systems such as
the Piccolo 973.

We are trying to list only those products that we
have seen demonstrated on the 973 or that a vendor,
dealer, or distributor claims will run on the 973;
but we make no guarantees.

Please note: Inclusion in the directory does not
imply that Piccolo endorses the products or
suppliers or recommends them in preference to
others not listed. Further, Piccolo does not
warrant that these products are compatible with
Piccolo systems. The buyer is solely responsible
for determining application and suitability.

Although this directory can be copied for
distribution to others, it is a temporary listing
intended primarily for your own use. In late
November it will be revised and published in
booklet form as a stock item.

Approximately 250 vendors have already been
contacted for information on software products that
might be appropriate in the directory. A Software
Vendor Listing Form is included in the back of the
directory for additional vendors to whom you may
wish to give copies.

RWM/jh

35c
Write effective reports.

Formal reports differ from informal memo reports in length and tone, and in the addition of such elements as a letter of transmittal, title page, abstract, executive summary, table of contents, glossary, and appendix (although not all reports include all of these elements). Writing a formal report often requires many of the same skills and basic techniques as writing a research paper (see Section **33**). Many organizations have a format guide for formal reports; in the absence of such a guide, you might begin by studying several successful reports from the company files.

An *abstract* is a brief summary of the material in the report, usually in language similar to that of the report (whether technical or non-technical). The abstract enables prospective readers to determine whether the report will be useful and whether they need to read all of it or only parts of it. If a report intended for technical personnel will also be read by non-technical management, it often includes an *executive summary*, in non-technical language, in addition to an abstract.

A *table of contents* provides a guide to the structure of the report and makes finding the exact section of the report needed easier for readers. If you have used effective and accurate headings in the body of your report, the simplest way to create a table of contents is to list them.

A *glossary* is an alphabetical list defining terms used in the report. Using a glossary lets you continue your discussion without having to stop to define terms. Generally, a glossary appears at the end of a report, but it may also be placed after the table of contents.

An *appendix* contains information that is relevant to the report but is too detailed or extensive to be included in the discussion. For example, an appendix might contain data tables, maps, supplementary diagrams, or a list of references. An appendix usually appears last.

You may find it helpful to consult one of the following books for further information on letters, memos, and reports.

Brusaw, C.T., G.J. Alred, and W.E. Oliu. *Handbook of Technical Writing*. 3rd ed. New York: St. Martin's, 1987.

Damerst, William A. *Clear Technical Reports*. 2nd ed. New York: HBJ Media Systems, 1982.

MacGregor, A.J. *Graphics Simplified: How to Plan and Prepare Effective Charts, Graphs, Illustrations, and Other Visual Aids*. Toronto: U of Toronto P, 1979.

Mathes, J.C., and D.W. Stevenson. *Designing Technical Reports*. Indianapolis: Bobbs, 1976.

■ **Exercise 1**

1. Prepare a résumé, and then write a letter of application for a position you are competent to fill.
2. Write to a former teacher to express appreciation for recommending you for a summer job.
3. Call the attention of your representative in city government to repairs needed on neighbourhood streets.
4. Write to a record company complaining about the technical quality of a record you ordered from them.

Grammatical Terms

This glossary presents brief explanations of frequently used grammatical terms. Consult the index for references to further discussion of most of the terms and for a number of terms not listed.

absolute phrase   A grammatically unconnected part of a sentence—generally a noun or pronoun followed by a participle (and all the words associated with it). Some absolute phrases have the meaning (but not the structure) of an adverb clause. See **24a** and **30b(4)**. See also **phrase** and **sentence modifier**.

> We will have a cookout, **weather permitting**.   [noun + present participle]
> COMPARE   We will have a cookout *if the weather permits*. [adverb clause: subordinator (*if*) + subject + predicate]

> **The national anthem sung for the last time**, the old stadium was closed.   [noun + past participle with modifier]
> COMPARE   *After the national anthem had been sung for the last time*, the old stadium was closed.   [adverb clause]

> The two of us worked on the homecoming float—**Tom in the morning and I at night**.   [Note the use of *I*, the subjective case.]
> COMPARE   *Tom worked in the morning, and I worked at night*.

abstract noun   A word referring to a quality, concept, or emotion (*sweetness, honesty, justice, ratio, hatred*) rather than to a concrete reality perceptible by one or more of the senses (*candy, trees, sleet*). See **20a(3)**.

active voice The form of a transitive verb indicating that its subject performs the action the verb denotes: "Emily *sliced* the ham." See **29d**. See also **voice** and **verb**.

adjectival A clause, phrase, or word (especially one without degrees of comparison) used to modify a noun or pronoun: *a Revenue Canada* audit, *Nancy's end-of-term* jitters, the search *for truth*, films *I like*. See **4d** and **18f(1)**. See also **comparison**.

adjective A part of speech regularly used to modify a noun or a pronoun. Limiting adjectives restrict the meaning of the words they modify; descriptive adjectives usually have degrees of comparison; proper adjectives are derived from proper nouns. See **4b**, **4c**, **12c(2)**, and **9a(3)**. See also **comparison** and **predicate adjective**.

DESCRIPTIVE	**newer** car, **green** one, **beautiful** eyes
LIMITING	**that** cheese, **a** boy, **its** roots, **both** steps
PROPER	**Christlike** figure, **Irish** humour, **Roman** candle

adjective clause A subordinate clause used as an adjective: people *who bite their fingernails*. An adjective clause is either restrictive or non-restrictive. See **12d(1)** and **25a(3)**. See also **clause**.

adverb A part of speech regularly used to modify (describe, limit, or qualify) a verb, an adjective, or another verb: *slowly* ate, *too* tall, left *very quietly*. See **4a**, **4c**, and **30b(1)**. An adverb may also modify a verbal, a phrase or clause, or the rest of the sentence.

Naturally, the villain succeeds at first by **completely** outwitting the hero. [*Naturally* modifies the rest of the sentence; *completely* modifies the gerund *outwitting*.]

adverb clause A subordinate clause used as an adverb. An adverb clause may indicate time, place, cause, condition, concession, comparison, purpose, or result. See **12b** and **30b(1)**. See also **clause** and **conditional clause**.

If parents are too demanding [condition], their children may behave like hermits or rebels.
Although he is usually quiet [concession], everyone listens to him **when he speaks** [time] **because he makes good suggestions** [cause].

adverbial A clause, phrase, or word (especially one without degrees of comparison) used as an adverb. See **12b**. See also **adverb**.

> **When the hail started**, we ran **into the library**. [adverb clause and prepositional phrase]
>
> **Wow**, I forgot to ask; **however**, I'll see him **Friday**. [interjection, conjunctive adverb, and adverbial noun]

adverbial conjunction See **conjunctive adverb**.

agreement The correspondence in form of one word with another to indicate number/person/gender. See Section **6**.

> this type, these types, that girl, those girls [number]
> I ask, a boy asks, boys ask, they ask [person and number]
> the woman herself, the man himself [gender and number]

antecedent A word or word group that a pronoun refers to. The antecedent usually precedes (but may follow) the pronoun. See **6b** and Section **28**.

> **Greg** paid his bills before he left town. [*Greg* is the antecedent of *his* and *he*.]
>
> Ask a **person** who owns an IBM, not an Apple. [*Person* is the antecedent of *who*.]
>
> Like their trainers, **pets** can be polite or rude. [The pronoun *their* precedes the antecedent *pets*.]

appositive A noun (or nominal) placed next to or very near another noun (or nominal) to identify, explain, or supplement its meaning. Appositives may be restrictive or non-restrictive. See **12d(1)**, **24a**, **30b(4)**, and **30c(3)**. See also **nominal**.

> Our guide, a **Mr. Davis**, did not see the grizzly. [The appositive refers to and identifies the noun *guide*.]
>
> A **preservative** used in many canned goods, salt is not only tasty but nutritious. [The appositive (with its modifier, a participial phrase) supplements the meaning of *salt*.]

article *The*, *a*, or *an*, used adjectivally before nouns: *the* cups, *a* cup, *an* extra cup. *The* is a definite article. *A* (used before consonant sounds) and *an* (used before vowel sounds) are indefinite articles. See **9f**.

auxiliary A form of *be*, *have*, or *do* (or a modal, such as *will*, *should*) used with a verb. An auxiliary, or helping verb, regularly indicates tense but may also indicate voice, mood, person, number. See **6a** and Section **7**.

is eating	**did** eat	**will be** eating
have eaten	**should** eat	**had been** eaten

Modal auxiliaries—*will, would, shall, should, may, might, must, can, could*—do not take such inflectional endings as *-s, -ing*.

case The form or position of a noun or pronoun that shows its use or relationship to other words in a sentence. The three cases in English are the *subjective* (or nominative), the *possessive* (or genitive), and the *objective* (sometimes called the accusative). See Section **5** and **15a**.

clause A sequence of related words within a sentence. A clause has both a subject and a predicate and functions either as an independent unit (*main clause*) or as a dependent unit (*subordinate clause*, used as an adverb, an adjective, or a noun). See Section **24**. See also **sentence**.

SENTENCES
Only a few stars came out. The moon was bright.
I know Herb. He will run for office.

MAIN CLAUSES
Only a few stars came out, for **the moon was bright**.
I know Herb; he will run for office.
[sentences connected by using the co-ordinating conjunction *for* and by using a semicolon and lower case for *he*]

SUBORDINATE CLAUSES
Only a few stars came out **because the moon was bright**.
[adverb clause]

I know Herb, **who will run for office**. [adjective clause]

I know **that Herb will run for office**. [noun clause—direct object]

[sentences converted to subordinate clauses by using the subordinating conjunctions *because* and *that* and the relative pronoun *who*, a subordinator]

Elliptical clauses have omitted elements that are clearly understood: see **elliptical construction**.

collective noun   A noun singular in form that denotes a group: *flock, jury, band, public, committee*. See **6a(7)**.

common gender   A term applied to words that can refer to either sex, feminine or masculine (*parent, instructor, salesperson, people, human beings, anyone, everyone*), rather than to only one of the sexes (*mother, father, waitress, waiter*). See also **6b(1)**.

common noun   A noun referring to any member or all members of a class or group (*woman, city, apples, holidays*) rather than to a specific member (*Kay Macpherson, Toronto, Winesap, New Year's Day*). See **9f**.

comparative   See **comparison**.

comparison   The inflection or modification of an adjective or adverb to indicate degrees in quality, quantity, or manner. There are three degrees: positive, comparative, and superlative. See **4c**.

POSITIVE	COMPARATIVE	SUPERLATIVE
good, well	better	best
high	higher	highest
quickly	more quickly	most quickly
active	less active	least active

complement   A word or words used to complete the sense of a verb. Although the term may refer to a direct or an indirect object, it usually refers to a subject complement, an object complement, or the complement of a verbal like *to be*.

The lasagna tasted **delicious**. [subject complement]

We made the ferret our **mascot**. [object complement]

To be a good **leader**, one must learn how to follow. [complement of the infinitive *to be*]

complete predicate   A simple predicate (a verb or verb phrase) along with any objects, complements, or modifiers: "We *ate the fresh homemade pie before the salad.*" See also **predicate**.

complete subject   A simple subject (a noun or nominal) along with any modifiers: "*Everyone at the picnic* liked the pie." See also **subject**.

complex sentence   A sentence containing one main clause and at least one subordinate clause. See Section **24** and **30c(1)**. See also **clause**.

Someone in the neighbourhood noticed a stranger [main clause] who looked suspicious [subordinate clause].

compound-complex sentence   A sentence containing at least two main clauses and one or more subordinate clauses. See **clause**.

When the lights went out [subordinate clause], there was no flashlight or candles around [main clause], so we sat outside and gazed at the stars [main clause].

compound predicate   Two or more predicates having the same subject: "Canada's Nursing Sisters *cared for the wounded during World War II* and *won the nickname 'the bluebirds' for their distinctive dress.*" See **2c** and **30c(2)**. See also **predicate**.

compound sentence   A sentence containing at least two main clauses and no subordinate clause. See **12a** and **14a**. See also **clause**.

The water supply was dwindling, so rationing became mandatory.   [Pattern: Main clause, *so* main clause.]

compound subject   Two or more subjects of the same verb. See **5a** and **6a**. See also **subject**.

Either **Phil** or **she** has to stay with Danny.
Women, men, and **children** call the crisis centre.

concrete noun   A non-abstract word referring to something material or to specific realities than can be perceived by one or more of the senses (*cologne, sunset, onions, thorns*) rather than to a quality or concept (*humanity, essence, truth, envy*). See **20a(3)**.

conditional clause   An adverb clause (beginning with such conjunctions as *if, unless, whether,* or *provided*) expressing a real, imagined, or non-factual condition. See **7c**. Sentences with conditional clauses often follow this pattern:

> **If** . . . [condition stated], **then** . . . [consequence/conclusion].
> **If she does a good job**, then I will promote her.
> **If everyone were a millionaire**, we would all be poor.

conjugation   A set or table of the inflected forms of a verb that indicate tense, person, number, voice, and mood. A conjugation of the irregular verb *see* follows.

PRINCIPAL PARTS: *see, saw, seen*

INDICATIVE MOOD

	Active Voice		*Passive Voice*

PRESENT TENSE

Singular	*Plural*	*Singular*	*Plural*
1. I see	we see	I am seen	we are seen
2. you see	you see	you are seen	you are seen
3. one (he/she/it) sees	they see	one (he/she/it) is seen	they are seen

PAST TENSE

1. I saw	we saw	I was seen	we were seen
2. you saw	you saw	you were seen	you were seen
3. one saw	they saw	one was seen	they were seen

FUTURE TENSE

1. I shall see	we shall see	I shall be seen	we shall be seen
2. you will see	you will see	you will be seen	you will be seen
3. one will see	they will see	one will be seen	they will be seen

PRESENT PERFECT TENSE

1. I have seen	we have seen	I have been seen	we have been seen
2. you have seen	you have seen	you have been seen	you have been seen
3. one has seen	they have seen	one has been seen	they have been seen

PAST PERFECT TENSE

1. I had seen	we had seen	I had been seen	we had been seen
2. you had seen	you had seen	you had been seen	you had been seen
3. one had seen	they had seen	one had been seen	they had been seen

FUTURE PERFECT TENSE (seldom used)

1. I shall have seen	we shall have seen	I shall have been seen	we shall have been seen
2. you will have seen	you will have seen	you will have been seen	you will have been seen
3. one will have seen	they will have seen	one will have been seen	they will have been seen

SUBJUNCTIVE MOOD

Active Voice   *Passive Voice*

PRESENT TENSE

Singular: if I, you, one see   if I, you, one be seen
Plural: if we, you, they see   if we, you, they be seen

PAST TENSE

Singular: if I, you, one saw   if I, you, one were seen
Plural: if we, you, they saw   if we, you, they were seen

PRESENT PERFECT TENSE

Singular: if I, you, one have seen   if I, you, one have been seen
Plural: if we, you, they have seen   if we, you, they have been seen

PAST PERFECT TENSE

(Same as the Indicative)

IMPERATIVE MOOD

PRESENT TENSE

see   be seen

grt

conjunction A part of speech (such as *and* or *although*) used to connect words, phrases, clauses, or sentences. There are two kinds of conjunctions: co-ordinating and subordinating.

The co-ordinating conjunctions—*and, but, or, nor, for, so, yet*—connect and relate words and word groups of equal grammatical rank. See Section **26**. See also **correlatives**.

> Dick **and** Mario sang beautifully, **for** their host had paid them well.
> Colour-blind people can usually see blue, **but** they may confuse red with green **or** with yellow.

Subordinating conjunctions (such as *although, if, when*—see the list on page 20) mark a dependent clause and connect it with a main clause. See Section **24**.

> **When** Frank sulks, he acts **as if** he were deaf.

conjunctive adverb A word (*however, therefore, nevertheless*—see the list on page 37) that serves not only as an adverb but also as a connective. See **3b**, **14a**, and **32b(4)**.

connective A word or phrase that links and relates words, phrases, clauses, or sentences, such as *and, although, otherwise, finally, on the contrary, which, not only . . . but also*. Conjunctions, conjunctive adverbs, transitional expressions, relative pronouns, and correlatives function as connectives. See also **32b(4)**.

construction A grammatical unit (a phrase, clause, or sentence) or the arrangement of related words in a grammatical unit.

co-ordinating conjunction One of seven connectives: *and, but, for, or, nor, so,* or *yet*. See **12a** and Section **26**. See also **conjunction**.

co-ordination The use of identical constructions (such as adjectives, prepositional phrases, or noun clauses): the *cool, clear, sparkling* water, *what they do* and *what they say*. See **12c, 24b**, and Section **26**.

correlatives Connectives used in pairs: *both . . . and, either . . . or, neither . . . nor, not only . . . but also,* *whether . . . or.* Correlatives link grammatically equal constructions: *both* Jane *and* Fred, *not only* in Peru *but also* in Mexico. See **26c**.

dangling modifier An adjectival or an adverbial that modifies nothing in a sentence or does not clearly refer to another word or word group in the sentence. Not a dangler, an absolute phrase modifies the rest of the sentence. See **25b**.

DANGLING   **Racing to class**, the running tap went unnoticed. [*Racing* modifies nothing in the sentence. The reader expects *racing* to modify the subject—which is *tap*.]

REVISED   **Racing** to class, **I** did not notice that running tap. [*Racing* clearly refers to the subject *I*.]

COMPARE   *The running tap going unnoticed*, I ran right past it on my way to class. [absolute phrase]

declension A set or table of inflected forms of nouns or pronouns: see the examples on page 52.

demonstratives Four words that point out: *this, that, these, those.*

Those are as good as **these**. [pronouns]
Those curtains have never been cleaned. [adjective]

dependent clause A subordinate clause: see **clause**.

determiner A word (such as *a, an, the* or *my, their*) which signals the approach of a noun: **the** newly mown *hay*.

direct address A name or descriptive term (set off by commas) designating the one (or ones) spoken to.

Falstaff enters and exclaims, "Well said, **Hal!**"
Don't forget, **backseat passengers**, to use those seatbelts.

direct object A noun (or nominal) naming *whom* or *what* after a transitive active verb: "Emily sliced the *ham*." See **object**.

grt

direct quotation A repetition of the exact spoken or written words of others. See **16a** and **34c** (pages 429–30).

DIRECT QUOTATIONS   John asked, **"Sue, where are you going?"**
"Where an opinion is general," writes Jane Austen, **"it is usually correct."**

INDIRECT QUOTATIONS   John asked **Sue where she was going.** According to Jane Austen, **a general opinion, as a rule, is correct.**

double negative A non-standard construction containing two negatives and having a negative meaning: "We can*not* do *nothing* about the weather." See **4e**.

elliptical construction A construction in which words are omitted but clearly understood.

The curtains are newer than the carpet [is].
Whenever [it is] possible, get a full night's sleep.
His hair is black; his face [is] deeply tanned.

expletive The word *there* or *it* used as a structural filler and not adding to the meaning of the sentence.

There were only a few ballet tickets left.   [Compare "Only a few ballet tickets were left."]
It is obvious that they do not like us.   [Compare "That they do not like us is obvious."]

faulty predication The use of a predicate that does not logically belong with a given subject. See **23d**.

FAULTY   One superstition is a black cat.
REVISED   One superstition **has to do with** a black cat.

finite verb A verb form that can function as the only verb in the predicate of a sentence: "They *ate* a can of pork and beans." Verb forms classified as gerunds, infinitives, or participles cannot. See **predicate**. Contrast **verbal**.

form change   See **inflection**.

function words   Words (such as prepositions, conjunctions, auxiliaries, and articles) that indicate the functions of other words
(*vocabulary words*) in a sentence and the grammatical relationships
between them. See also **vocabulary words**.

gerund   A verbal (non-finite verb) that ends in *-ing* and functions
as a noun. Gerunds may take objects, complements, or modifiers.

> He escaped by *swimming* **rapidly**.   [The gerund *swimming*
> is the object of the preposition *by* and is modified by the
> adverb *rapidly*.]
>
> *Borrowing* **money** is a mistake.   [The gerund phrase—the
> gerund *borrowing* and its object, *money*—serves as the sub-
> ject of the sentence.]

A possessive noun or pronoun before a gerund may be classified
either as an adjectival (modifying the noun element of the verbal)
or as the subject of the gerund.

> **His borrowing** money is a mistake.   [Compare *"his* action"
> and "He *borrowed* the money."]

helping verb   See **auxiliary**.

imperative   See **mood**.

indefinites   The article *a* or *an* (*a* cigar, *an* idea) as well as
pronouns (*anybody, everyone*) and adjectives (*any* book, *few*
friends, *several* pages) that do not specify distinct limits. See **6a(1)**
and **6b(1)**.

independent clause   A main clause: see **clause**.

indicative   See **mood**.

indirect object   A word (or words) naming the one (or ones)
affected—but not directly affected—by the action of the verb:
"Emily sliced *me* some ham." See also **object**.

indirect quotation   A report of the written or spoken words of
another without the use of the exact words of the speaker or writer:
"The registrar said *that my cheque for tuition was returned to
him*." See also **direct quotation**.

infinitive   A verbal (non-finite verb) used chiefly as a noun, less frequently as an adjective or an adverb. The infinitive is usually made up of the word *to* plus the present form of a verb (called the *stem* of the infinitive), but the *to* may be omitted after such verbs as *let*, *make*, and *dare*. Infinitives may have subjects, objects, complements, or modifiers.

> Hal wanted **to open** the present.   [*Present* is the object of the infinitive *to open*; the whole infinitive phrase is the object of the verb *wanted*.]
>
> The work **to be done** overwhelms me.   [The infinitive is used adjectivally to modify the noun *work*.]
>
> **To tell** the truth, our team almost lost.   [The infinitive phrase is used adverbially to modify the rest of the sentence.]

inflection   A change in the form of a vocabulary or lexical word to show a specific meaning or grammatical relationship to some other word or group of words. See **4c**, **15a**, and **18d** and Sections **5, 6**, and **7**.

VERBS	drink, drinks, drank, drunk; grasp, grasps, grasped
PRONOUNS	**I, my** life, a gift for **me**
NOUNS	dog, dogs; dog's, dogs'
ADJECTIVES	a **good** one, a **better** one, the **best** one
ADVERBS	carefully, **more** carefully, **most** carefully

intensifier   A modifier used for emphasis: *very* boring, *so* pleased, *certainly* did. See also **qualifier**.

intensive/reflexive pronoun   The *-self* pronouns (such as *myself, himself, themselves*). The intensive is used for emphasis:

> The teenagers **themselves** had the best idea.

The reflexive is used as an object of a verb, verbal, or preposition:

> He blames **himself**.   She bought a present for **herself**.

Note that an intensive or a reflexive pronoun always refers to another noun or pronoun that denotes the same individual or individuals.

interjection   A word (one of the eight parts of speech) expressing a simple exclamation: *Whew! Ouch!* When used in sentences, mild interjections are set off by commas. See **17c**.

interrogatives   Words like *which, whose,* or *why* used to ask a question.

> **Which** did he choose?   [pronoun]   **Whose** car is it?
> [adjective]
> **Why** is real estate a good investment?   [adverb]

intransitive verb   A verb (such as *appear* or *belong*) that does not take an object. See **verb**.

inversion   A change in the usual word order of a sentence: "In the middle of the lake is a small island." See **29f**.

irregular verb   A verb not inflected in the usual way—that is, by the addition of *-d* or *-ed* to the present form (or the stem of the infinitive). Below are the principal parts of five common types of irregular verbs. See **7a**.

> swim, swam, swum   [vowels changed]
> beat, beat, beaten   [*-en* added]
> feel, felt, felt   [vowel shortened, *ee* changed to *e*]
> send, sent, sent   [*-d* changed to *-t*]
> set, set, set   [no change]

lexical words   See **vocabulary words**.

linking verbs   A verb that relates the subject complement to the subject. Words commonly used as linking verbs are *become, seem, appear, feel, look, taste, smell, sound,* and forms of the verb *be*. See **4b** and **5f**.

> She **is** a pharmacist.   The music **sounds** brassy.

main clause   An independent clause: "When I explored the Black Hills, *I found many rocks to add to my collection.*" See **12a** and **14a**. See also **clause**.

misplaced modifier   An adjectival or adverbial in an awkward position—usually, far away from what it modifies. Sometimes a misplaced modifier confuses the reader because it could qualify either of two words. See **25a**.

MISPLACED I heard how to make ketchup flow out of the bottle **on the radio**.

REVISED I heard *on the radio* how to make ketchup flow out of the bottle.

MISPLACED To do one's best **sometimes** is not enough.

REVISED To do one's best is **sometimes** not enough.

OR It is not enough to do one's best **sometimes**.

modal auxiliary See **auxiliary**.

modifier A word or word group that describes, limits, or qualifies another: a *true* statement, walked *slowly*, yards *filled with rocks*, the horse *that jumped over the barrel*. See Sections **4** and **25**.

mood The way a speaker or writer regards an assertion—that is, as a declarative statement or a question (*indicative* mood), as a command or request (*imperative*), or as a supposition, hypothesis, recommendation, or condition contrary to fact (*subjunctive*). Verb forms indicate mood. See **7c** and **7d**.

INDICATIVE Joe **was** a winner.
Does he drop by?

IMPERATIVE **Be** a winner.
Do drop by!

SUBJUNCTIVE Joe talked as though he **were** a loser.
I recommend that he **do** this soon.

nominal A clause, phrase, or word (a noun but especially a pronoun or gerund) used as a noun. See **noun**.

Repairing that machine was not easy.
He contends **that selfless love is power**.

nominative See **case**.

non-finite verb A verb form used as a noun, an adjective, or an adverb. A non-finite verb cannot stand as the only verb in a sentence. See **2a**. See also **verbal**.

Listeners call **to express** their opinion. [infinitive]

Elisa delights in **facing** new challenges. [gerund]
The help **offered** at that time was refused. [participle]

non-restrictive Non-essential to the identification of the word or words referred to. A word or word group is non-restrictive (parenthetical) when it is not necessary to the meaning of the sentence and may be omitted. See **12d**.

My best friend, **Pauline**, understands me. [word]
That airplane, **now being manufactured in large numbers**, is of immense commercial value. [phrase]
That airplane, **which is now being manufactured in large numbers**, is of immense commercial value. [clause]

noun A part of speech that names a person, place, thing, idea, animal, quality, or action: *Mary, Europe, apples, justice, goose, strength, departure*. A noun usually changes form to indicate the plural and the possessive case, as in *man, men; man's, men's*.

TYPES OF NOUNS

COMMON	a **man**, the **cities**, some **trout** [general classes]
PROPER	**Mr. Park**, in **Venice**, the **Forum** [capitalized, specific names]
COLLECTIVE	a **flock**, the **jury**, my **family** [groups]
CONCRETE	an **egg**, the **bus**, his **ear**, two **trees** [tangibles]
ABSTRACT	**honour, jealousy, pity, hatred** [ideas, qualities]
COUNT	one **dime**, ten **dollars**, a **job**, many **times** [singular or plural—often preceded by adjectivals telling how many]
MASS	much **money**, more **work**, less **time** [singular in meaning—often preceded by adjectivals telling how much]

FUNCTIONS OF NOUNS

SUBJECT OF FINITE VERB **Dogs** barked.
OBJECT OF FINITE VERB OR OF PREPOSITION He gave **Marcelle** the **key** to the **house**.
SUBJECT COMPLEMENT (PREDICATE NOUN) She is a **lawyer**.

OBJECT COMPLEMENT   They named him **Jonathan**.
SUBJECT OF NON-FINITE VERB   I want **Ivan** to be here.
OBJECT OF NON-FINITE VERB   I prefer to drive a **truck**.
APPOSITIVE   Moses, a **prophet**, saw the Promised Land.
ADVERBIAL   **Yesterday** they went **home**.
ADJECTIVAL   The **magazine** article highlighted **Saskatchewan** winters.
DIRECT ADDRESS   What do you think, **Angela**?
KEY WORD OF ABSOLUTE PHRASE   The **food** being cold, no one really enjoyed the meal.

noun clause   A subordinate clause used as a noun. See **clause**.

Whoever comes will be welcome.   [subject]
I hope **that he will recover**.   [direct object]
I will give **whoever comes first** the best seat.   [indirect object]
Spend it on **whatever seems best**.   [object of a preposition]
This is **what you need**.   [subject complement]
I loved it, **whatever it was**.   [appositive]
Whoever you are, show yourself!   [direct address]

number   The inflectional form of a word that indicates singular (one) or plural (more than one): *river—rivers, this—those, he sees—they see*. See Section **6** and **18d**.

object   A noun or noun substitute governed by a transitive active verb, by a non-finite verb, or by a preposition.

A *direct object*, or the *object of a finite verb*, is any noun or noun substitute that answers the question *What?* or *Whom?* after a transitive active verb. A direct object frequently receives, or is in some way affected by, the action of the verb.

William raked **leaves**.
What did he say?
The Andersons do not know **where we live**.

As a rule, a direct object may be converted into a subject with a passive verb: see **voice**.

An *object of a non-finite verb* is any noun or its equivalent that follows and completes the meaning of a participle, a gerund, or an infinitive.

Washing a **car** takes time.
He likes to wear a **tie**.
Following the **truck**, a bus rounded the bend.

An *indirect object* is any noun or noun substitute that states *to whom* or *for whom* (or *to what* or *for what*) something is done. An indirect object ordinarily precedes a direct object.

He bought **her** a watch.
I gave the **floor** a second coat of varnish.

It is usually possible to substitute a prepositional phrase beginning with *to* or *for* for the indirect object.

He bought a watch for her.

An *object of a preposition* is any noun or noun substitute which a preposition relates to another word or word group.

Cedars grow tall in these **hills**.   [*Hills* is the object of *in*.]
What am I responsible for?   [*What* is the object of *for*.]

object complement   A word that helps to complete the meaning of such verbs as *make, paint, elect, name*. An object complement refers to or modifies the direct object. See **4b**. See also **complement**.

They painted the cellar door **blue**.
If it's a girl they will name her **Kiyo**.

objective   See **case**.

parenthetical element   Non-essential matter (such as an aside or interpolation) usually set off by commas but often by dashes or parentheses to mark pauses and intonation. A word, phrase, clause, or sentence may be parenthetical. See **12d, 17e**, and **17f**.

Granted, over eighty million people, **according to that estimate**, did watch one episode.
In fact, the parachute ride—**believe it or not**—is as safe as the ferris wheel.

participle A verb form that may function as part of a verb phrase (was *laughing*, had *finished*) or as an adjectival (a *finished* product OR the players, *laughing* at their mistakes).

The present participle ends in *-ing* (the form also used for verbal nouns: see **gerund**). The past participle of regular verbs ends in *-d* or *-ed*; for past participle forms of irregular verbs, see **7a**. See also **irregular verb**.

Functioning as adjectivals in *participial phrases*, participles may take objects, complements, and modifiers. See **25b(1)** and **30b(2)**.

> The prisoner *carrying* **the heaviest load** toppled forward.
> [The participle *carrying* takes the object *load*; the whole participial phrase modifies *prisoner*.]
> The telephone operator, **very *confused* by my request**, suggested that I place the call later. [The participle *confused* is modified by the adverb *very* and by the prepositional phrase *by my request*; the participial phrase modifies *telephone operator*.]

parts of speech The eight classes into which most grammarians group words according to their form changes and their position, meaning, and use in the sentence: *verbs, nouns, pronouns, adjectives, adverbs, prepositions, conjunctions,* and *interjections.* Each of these is discussed separately in this glossary. See also **1c**.

passive voice The form of the verb which shows that its subject does not act but is the object or the receiver of the action: ''The ham *was sliced* by Emily.'' See **29d**. See also **voice**.

person Changes in the form of pronouns and verbs denoting or indicating whether one is speaking (*I am*—first person), spoken to (*you are*—second person), or spoken about (*it is*—third person). In the present tense, a verb changes its form to agree grammatically with a third-person singular subject (*I eat, a bird eats*). See **6a** and **27b**.

personal pronoun Any one of a group of pronouns—*I, you, he, she, it,* and their inflected forms—referring to the one (or ones) speaking, spoken to, or spoken about. See Section **5**.

phrasal verb   A unit consisting of a verb plus one or two unin-
flected words like *after, in, up, off,* or *out* (particles) and having
the force of a single-word verb.

> We **ran out on** them.   [Compare "We deserted them."]
> He **cut** me **off** without a cent.   [Compare "He disinherited
> me."]

phrase   A sequence of grammatically related words without a
subject and a predicate. See **2a** and **30c(4)**.

TYPE OF PHRASE

NOUN	A **young stranger** stepped forward.
VERB	All day long they **had been worrying**.
PREPOSITIONAL	**By seven o'clock** the lines stretched **from the box office to the corner**.
GERUND	**Building a sun deck** can be fun.
INFINITIVE	Do you want **to use your time that way**?
PARTICIPIAL	My friends **travelling in Italy** felt the earthquake.
APPOSITIVE	I introduced her to Bob, **my roommate**.
ABSOLUTE	**The game over**, we shook hands.

positive   See **comparison**.

possessive   See **case**.

predicate   A basic grammatical division of a sentence. A predicate is the part of the sentence comprising what is said about the
subject. The *complete predicate* consists of the main verb along
with its auxiliaries (the *simple predicate*) and any complements
and modifiers.

> We *used* **a patriotic theme for our celebrations that year**.
> [*Used* is the simple predicate. *Used* and all the words that
> follow it make up the complete predicate.]
> *Had* the team **already** *been preparing* **themselves psycholog-
> ically**? [The simple predicate is the verb phrase *had been
> preparing*.]

predicate adjective　An adjective used as a subject complement: "The bread tastes *sweet*." See **4b**. See also **linking verb**.

predicate noun　A noun used as a subject complement: "Bromides are *sedatives*." See **4b**. See also **linking verb**.

predication　See **faulty predication**.

preposition　A part of speech that links and relates a noun or nominal to some other word in the sentence. See pages 13–14 for a list of words commonly used as prepositions.

> The paintings hung **in** the hall.　[The preposition *in* connects and relates *hall* (its object) to the verb *hung*.]

prepositional phrase　A preposition with its object and any modifiers: *in the hall, between you and me, for the new van*. See **preposition**.

principal parts　The forms of any verb from which the various tenses are derived: the present infinitive (*take, laugh*), the past (*took, laughed*), and the past participle (*taken, laughed*). See **7a**.

progressive verb　A verb phrase consisting of a present participle (ending in *-ing*) used with a form of *be* and denoting continuous action. See the synopsis on page 75.

> **I have been playing** tennis all afternoon.

pronoun　One of the eight parts of speech. Pronouns take the position of nouns and function as nouns do. See Sections **5** and **28** and **6b**. See also **noun** and the separate entries for the types of pronouns listed below.

PERSONAL	**She** and **I** will see him in Tokyo.
RELATIVE	Leslie is the one **who** likes to bowl.
INDEFINITE	**Each** of you should help **someone**.
INTENSIVE	I **myself** saw the crash.
REFLEXIVE	Roy blames **himself**.
DEMONSTRATIVE	**Those** are riper than **these**.
INTERROGATIVE	**Who** are they? **What** is right?

proper adjective　An adjective (such as *Scottish*) derived from a proper noun (*Scotland*). See **9a(3)**.

proper noun   A noun (written with a capital letter) referring to a particular or specific member of a class or group (*Wayne Gretzky, Lake Nipigon, November, God*) rather than to any member or all members (*man, lake, months, gods*). See **9a**.

qualifier   Any modifier, descriptive or limiting. Frequently, however, the term refers only to those modifiers that restrict or intensify the meaning of other words. See also **intensifier**.

> **Many** thieves lie. **Almost** all of them do.   [Compare "Thieves lie."]
> **Sometimes** children are **too** selfish to share.

quotation   See **direct quotation**.

reciprocal pronoun   One of two compound pronouns expressing an interchangeable or mutual action or relationship: *each other* or *one another*.

reflexive pronoun   See **intensive/reflexive pronoun**.

regular verb   A verb that forms its past tense and past participle by adding -*d* or -*ed* to the present form (or the stem of the infinitive): *love, loved; laugh, laughed*. See **7a**.

relative clause   An adjective clause introduced by a relative pronoun: the suits *that they wore*. See **relative pronoun**.

relative pronoun   One of a small group of noun substitutes (*who, whom, whose, that, which, what, whoever, whomever, whichever, whatever*) used to introduce subordinate clauses. See **5b, 5c**, and **6a(5)**.

> He has a son *who is a genius*.   [adjective clause introduced by the relative pronoun *who*]
> *Whoever* wins the prize must have talent.   [noun clause introduced by the relative pronoun *whoever*]

restrictive   Essential to the identification of the word or words referred to. A word, phrase, or clause is restrictive when it is necessary to the meaning of the sentence and cannot be omitted. See **12d**.

> The word *interest* is a synonym for *concern*.   [restrictive appositive]

Every drug **condemned by doctors** should be taken off the market. [restrictive phrase]

Every drug **that doctors condemn** should be taken off the market. [restrictive clause]

sentence A grammatically independent unit of expression. A simple sentence contains a subject and a predicate. See Section **1**. Sentences are classified according to structure:

SIMPLE We won. [subject—predicate]

COMPOUND They outplayed us, but we won. [two main clauses]

COMPLEX Although we did win, they outplayed us. [subordinate clause, main clause]

COMPOUND-COMPLEX I know that they outplayed us, but we did win. [two main clauses—the first of which contains a subordinate clause]

Sentences are also classified according to their purpose.

DECLARATIVE We will fly to Montreal. [statement]

IMPERATIVE Fly to Montreal. [command]

INTERROGATIVE Shall we fly to Montreal? [question]

EXCLAMATORY Would we like to fly to Montreal! [exclamation]

sentence modifier An adverbial that modifies all the rest of the sentence, not a specific word or word group in it.

Yes, the plane arrived on time.

To tell the truth, a few are takers, not givers.

All things considered, Yellowknife is a good place to live.

structure words See **function words**.

subject A basic grammatical division of a sentence. The subject is a noun or nominal about which something is asserted or asked in the predicate. It usually precedes the predicate. (Imperative sentences have subjects that are not stated but are implied.) The *complete subject* consists of the *simple subject* and the words associated with it.

The dog locked in the hot car needed air. [*Dog* is the simple subject. *The dog locked in the hot car* is the complete subject.]

subject complement   A word (or words) that completes the meaning of a linking verb and that modifies or refers to the subject. See **4b**. See also **linking verb**.

The old car looked **expensive**. [predicate adjective]
The old car was an **eyesore**. [predicate noun]

subjective   See **case**.

subjunctive   See **mood**.

subordinate clause   A dependent clause: "Her cough vanished *after she had quit smoking*." See **clause**.

subordinating conjunction   A connective such as *although, if*, or *when*: see the list on page 20. See also **conjunction**.

subordination   The use of dependent structures (phrases, subordinate clauses) lower in grammatical rank than independent ones (simple sentences, main clauses). See Section **24**.

subordinator   A connective (such as *unless, whose, that, why*) which marks the beginning of a subordinate (dependent) clause: see page 20.

suffix   An added sound, syllable, or group of syllables attached to the end of a base or root (or another suffix). Suffixes change meanings, create new words, and indicate grammatical functions. See also **inflection**.

the plays   play**er**   play**er's**   play**ing**
play**ed**   play**ful**   play**fully**   play**fulness**

superlative   See **comparison**.

syntax   Sentence structure. The grammatical arrangement of words, phrases, clauses.

tense   The form of the verb that denotes time. Inflection of single-word verbs (*pay, paid*) and the use of auxiliaries (*am paid, was paid, will pay*) indicate tense. See Section **7**.

transitive See **verb**.

verb A part of speech denoting action, occurrence, or existence (state of being). Inflections indicate tense (and sometimes person and number) and mood of a verb: see **inflection, mood, voice**, and Section **7**.

A *transitive verb* is a verb that requires an object to complete its meaning. Transitive verbs can usually be changed from the active to the passive voice: see **object** and **voice**.

> Sid **hung** a wreath on his door.   [direct object: *wreath*]

An *intransitive verb* is a verb (such as *go* or *sit*) that does not have an object to complete its meaning. Linking verbs, which take subject complements, are intransitive.

> She **has been waiting** patiently for hours.
> I **was** sick last Christmas.

The same verb may be transitive in one sentence and intransitive in another.

> TRANSITIVE   Dee **reads** novels.   [direct object: *novels*]
> INTRANSITIVE Dee **reads** well.

verbal A non-finite verb used as a noun, an adjective, or an adverb. Infinitives, participles, and gerunds are verbals. Verbals (like finite verbs) may take objects, complements, modifiers, and sometimes subjects. See also **non-finite verb** and **gerund, infinitive, participle**.

> Mr. Nelson went *to see* **his daughter**.   [*To see*, an infinitive, functions as an adverb modifying the verb *went*. The object of the infinitive is *daughter*.]
> Cars *parked* **in the loading zone** will be towed away. [*Parked*, a participle, modifies *cars*.]
> *Studying* **dialects in our area** was fun. [*Studying*, a gerund, heads the phrase that is the subject of the verb *was*.]

verb phrase See **phrase**.

vocabulary (lexical) words   Nouns, verbs, and most modifiers—those words found in vocabulary-building lists. See also **function words**.

voice   The form of a transitive verb that indicates whether or not the subject performs the action denoted by the verb. A verb with a direct object is in the *active voice*. When the direct object is converted into a subject, the verb is in the *passive voice*. A passive verb is always a verb phrase consisting of a form of the verb *be* (or sometimes *get*) followed by a past participle. See also **29d**.

ACTIVE	Priscilla **chose** John. [The subject (*Priscilla*) acts.]
PASSIVE	John **was chosen** by Priscilla. [The subject (*John*) does not act.]

Speakers and writers often omit the *by*-phrase after a passive verb, especially when the performer of the action is not known or is not the focus of attention.

Those flowers **were picked** yesterday.
The guilty ones **should be punished** severely.
We just heard that a new secretary **was hired**.

word order   The arrangement of words in sentences. Because of lost inflections, modern English depends heavily on word order to convey meaning.

Nancy gave Henry $14 000.
Henry gave Nancy $14 000.

Tony had built a barbecue pit.
Tony had a barbecue pit built.

Index

Boldface numbers refer to rules; other numbers refer to pages.

Index

Index

Index

Index

Index

Index

Acknowledgments

The authors and publisher wish to thank the following for permission to reprint the material listed below:

RANDOM HOUSE, INC.   For the dictionary entries *empty* and *empty-handed*. Reprinted by permission from the *Random House College Dictionary*, Revised Edition, copyright © 1988 by Random House, Inc. For the thesaurus entry *empty*. Reprinted by permission from the *Random House Thesaurus*, College Edition, copyright © 1984 by Random House, Inc.

RICHARD M. PRESTON   For his essay "Ice."

PATENT TRADER   For the essay "Heat on the Hoof" by Roxanna Barry. Reprinted by permission of the publisher.

THE H.W. WILSON COMPANY   For entries from *The Readers' Guide to Periodical Literature*, Volume 44, 1984/85. All material reproduced by permission of the publisher.

THE ESTATE OF THE LATE SONIA BROWNELL ORWELL AND MARTIN SECKER & WARBURG   For the photocopied excerpt from "Politics and the English Language" by George Orwell, copyright 1946 by Sonia Brownell Orwell; renewed 1974 by Sonia Orwell. Reprinted from *Shooting an Elephant and Other Essays* by George Orwell.

BUCK STROBECK   For his essay "The Purple Martin—Birds of Our Feather?"

TRACY MONAHAN   For her research paper "Big Brother's Propaganda."

Every reasonable effort has been made to acquire permission for copyright material used in this book, and to acknowledge all such indebtedness accurately. Any errors and omissions called to our attention will be corrected in future printings.

NOTES

NOTES

LISTS FREQUENTLY CONSULTED	OTHER CORRECTION SYMBOLS